# Handbook of Social Cognition
## *Volume 1*

# HANDBOOK OF
# SOCIAL COGNITION

## Volume 1

**Edited by**
**ROBERT S. WYER, JR.**
**THOMAS K. SRULL**
*University of Illinois*

LAWRENCE ERLBAUM ASSOCIATES, PUBLISHERS
1984  Hillsdale, New Jersey                              London

Lawrence Erlbaum Associates, Inc., Publishers
365 Broadway
Hillsdale, New Jersey 07642

**Library of Congress Cataloging in Publication Data**

Main entry under title:

Handbook of social cognition.

Includes bibliographical references and indexes.
1. Social perception—Addresses, essays, lectures.
2. Cognition.  I. Wyer, Robert S.  II. Srull, Thomas K.
[DNLM:  1. Cognition—Handbooks.  2. Social perception—
Handbooks.  BF 311 H2367]
HM132.H333  1984        302'.12        84-6021
ISBN 0-89859-338-7 (v. 1)
ISBN 0-89859-339-5 (v. 2)
ISBN 0-89859-340-9 (v. 3)
ISBN 0-89859-337-9 (set)

Printed in the United States of America
10  9  8  7  6  5  4  3

# Contents

# Preface

Social cognition is currently the most active and dynamic area in psychology. New and important theoretical developments are occurring on a regular basis. Moreover, the flurry of research activity in this area has reached proportions one could never have anticipated as little as 10 years ago. It was a rare event in the mid-1970s to meet someone who was specifically interested in social cognition. In contrast, it is now difficult to meet anyone at all who does not profess to be working on some problem related to this general domain of inquiry.

The emergence of social cognition as a major area of psychology reflects, at its core, a convergence of two hitherto distinct disciplines in pursuit of a common set of problems. This convergence was not instigated by any single individual, nor was it stimulated by any specific set of empirical findings. Rather, it occurred spontaneously as a result of the independent recognition by researchers in each discipline that continued advancement in their own area required at least a partial understanding of phenomena being investigated in the other. For example, social psychologists had long been concerned with the effects of situational and individual difference variables on judgments and behavioral decisions. However, they began to realize that their past efforts had largely been restricted to a description of simple input-output relations. That is, experimental investigations were examining the relations among certain classes of stimulus variables and certain classes of overt responses. Evidence bearing on these relations often provided very little insight into the fundamental psychological processes that underlie their existence. Thus, many social psychologists began turning to cognitive theory and methodology for guidance in conceptualizing the underlying processes that mediate such judgments and decisions.

Simultaneously, researchers in cognitive psychology began to realize that continued advancement in their work would require a far more serious consideration of the role of real-world knowledge in the interpretation and cognitive organization of new information. Accordingly, they literally began to move from the "word" to the "sentence," and then to the type of complex stimulus materials that are very similar to those of traditional interest to social psychologists. At the conceptual level, researchers interested in the processing of prose material began talking about things like empathy, the role of attributions in comprehension, and the subjective identification of the reader (an inherently social being) with one or more characters in a story. Moreover, a concern with the role of prior knowledge in interpreting and organizing new information led mainstream cognitive psychologists to consider the effects of self-referential knowledge, and of transitory cognitive and emotional states, on the processing of information. Consequently, questions related to the role of the "self-concept" in responses to information, and the influence of emotional and affective states on information processing, which had long been of interest to social psychologists, suddenly became the focus of attention of many cognitive psychologists as well.

Even these brief historical descriptions convey the fact that investigators with quite different perspectives and backgrounds appeared to spontaneously converge on a common set of problems to which both sets of knowledge and skills were necessary. Consequently, the institutional boundaries that have historically existed between many areas of cognitive and social psychology have become more and more artificial, and the "cognitive" and "social" labels attached to researchers in these areas are often more a reflection of their past history than of their current theoretical and empirical interests.

The present set of volumes reflects this convergence. In combination, the volumes provide a comprehensive treatment by both cognitive and social psychologists, often in collaboration, of issues that are central to social information processing. The volumes are intended to be a resource for researchers trained in both traditional disciplines, permitting them to review the most important conceptual and empirical advances in each area. In doing so, the volumes are intended to increase further the cross-disciplinary communication and cross-fertilization of ideas that we believe is required for continued progress, and that anticipates what we believe will ultimately be an even more formal integration of these two historically distinct disciplines.

The handbook is divided into three volumes. Volume 1 provides an overview of central issues in the field. Two chapters (Ostrom; Holyoak & Gordon) focus on how traditional concerns in social and cognitive psychology have blended into the new discipline of social cognition. Other chapters provide a review and analysis of three basic phenomena that cut across theory and research in the area: social categorization (Lingle, Altom, & Medin), the nature and functions of schemata (Brewer & Nakamura; Rumelhart[1]), and cognitive heuristics (Sherman & Corty).

The focus of Volume 2 is on various aspects of memory, including methodological issues associated with the study of social memory (Srull), theoretical and empirical issues surrounding the cognitive representation of social information (Wyer & Gordon), and reviews of recent theory and research in the areas of social memory (Hastie, Park, & Weber), semantic and episodic memory (Shoben), and visual memory (Klatzky).

Volume 3 addresses a variety of topics of interest to both cognitive and social psychologists concerned with various aspects of social information processing, including the role of automatic and controlled processing of social information (Bargh), implications of theory and research on story comprehension for the interpretation of social events (Black, Galambos, & Read), the dynamics of social communication (Kraut & Higgins), the role of the self in information processing (Greenwald & Pratkanis), and output processes in social judgment (Upshaw).

A project such as this simply could not be completed without the help of many people. Most important, we want to thank the large number of investigators who, as a result of their day-to-day research activities, have made this one of the most enjoyable and exciting areas in which to work. We also owe a large debt to each of the authors. Their enthusiasm and commitment to the project is reflected in the universally outstanding chapters of the handbook. We have found our interactions with them during the course of the project to be professionally stimulating and personally rewarding.

The contributions of others are less obvious. We owe a special note of thanks to Professor Jon Hartwick of McGill University. He has been an important source of intellectual stimulation to us for many years, and our early discussions with him were instrumental in the decision to embark on the project.

Finally, we want to express our gratitude to Larry Erlbaum for his confidence and encouragement throughout the project, as well as for giving us an absolutely free hand in trying to accomplish our objectives. Without his advice, encouragement, and gentle prodding, the project would not have been nearly as successful or rewarding.

Robert S. Wyer
Thomas K. Srull

---

[1]The chapter by Rumelhart, unlike the others in this handbook, is an adaptation of an earlier theoretical analysis of cognitive schemata. It is included in the present handbook because the conceptualization is extremely important and the earlier version was targeted to a very small audience. The original version appeared in *Theoretical issues in reading comprehension: Perspectives from cognitive psychology, linguistics, artificial intelligence, and education*, a volume edited by R. J. Spiro, B. C. Bruce, and W. F. Brewer (Lawrence Erlbaum Associates, 1980).

# Contents

# Handbook of Social Cognition
## *Volume 1*

# 1

# The Sovereignty of Social Cognition

Thomas M. Ostrom
*Ohio State University*

**Contents**

Most would agree that the area of social cognition is a very recent addition to the field of psychology. As of the beginning of the 1980s few graduate level seminars and probably no undergraduate lecture courses were offered under the "social cognition" title. No textbook provided a comprehensive treatment of the subject; in fact the term "social cognition" was only rarely found in the introductory texts of general psychology, social psychology, or cognitive psychology. The term had not yet even come into common usage in the titles and abstracts of empirical investigations. As a separate area, social cognition had yet to achieve these visible signs of professional legitimacy.

Beneath this calm surface was an incredible amount of intellectual agitation surrounding the emergence of social cognition as a legitimate field of inquiry. Beginning in the mid 1970s a number of social psychologists with interests in person perception came to recognize the relevance of new developments in

1

cognitive psychology to understanding social processes. This new awakening could be found in all regions of the United States and Canada. Unlike many "fad" topics that arise periodically in psychology, this one could not be traced back to a single influential paper, to the insights of one dominant scholar, or even to one center of graduate training. This intellectual spore was cast across the entire continent.

This created an intellectual climate that may be unique in the history of social psychology (and perhaps even for psychology as a whole). In complete disregard of the usual conventions governing academic haughtiness, researchers began avidly reading one another's work and initiating enduring informal bonds with other workers all across the country. Even more unusual is the fact that academic seniority was irrelevant to these relationships. Because the field was without clear definition, and because no one had any more expertise than anyone else, all were on an equal footing. The new Ph.D., in fact, had the advantage of more thorough and organized exposure to recent concepts in cognitive psychology through enrollment in graduate seminars on the subject.

Traditionally, the first signs of a newly developing field can be found in papers and symposia at conventions. Parallel traces can be found in university-sponsored colloquia and in the subsequent appearance of edited volumes. Social cognition was one of the dominant convention topics throughout the last half of the 1970s for social psychology. In the first 3 years of the 1980s, it was clearly the most popular subject of edited volumes in social psychology. Both of these consequences illustrate the heterogeneity in background of those researchers attracted to the field of social cognition. Young and old, trained in all parts of the country, these contributors gathered to learn as well as to instruct one another in their latest insights. This studied ingeniousness, this eagerness to absorb others' ideas allowed the field to progress toward maturity in a surprisingly short period of time.

By 1980, the American Psychological Association had officially recognized social cognition as being more than a "fad" topic by designating a subsection of the *Journal of Personality and Social Psychology* as specializing in "Attitudes and Social Cognition." By 1982, the first issue of the newly created journal titled *Social Cognition* had appeared. A comprehensive textbook titled "Social Cognition" (by Fiske & Taylor, in press) was written in 1982. In addition, the present *Handbook* amply documents the substantial accumulation of data and the development of theoretical perspectives on social cognition. It appears that social cognition is here to stay.

One of the most interesting consequences of this ferment surrounding the development of social cognition is the struggle to understand the interdependence between cognition and social behavior. Social psychology has been absorbed with this issue from its very beginnings, but the social cognition "movement" invited a reappraisal of this interdependence.

It is this general issue to which the present chapter is devoted. Many writers have been struggling with the best way to define social cognition, with the distinction between social and nonsocial cognition, with the relation between action and cognition, and with the meaning of the concept of "process." These issues are fundamental to understanding the role of social cognition in both social psychology and cognitive psychology. They provide a basis for placing past work in perspective and setting priorities for future research. The views I express on these issues are clearly personal, but they reflect the insights of a large number of others whose works I have drawn upon.

## PREVIEW

A number of issues will be addressed in this chapter, some familiar to the reader and others unfamiliar. Some of my conclusions may be unexpected and possibly disputable in the minds of some readers. As a guide through the following sections, I begin by offering a glimpse of my major conclusions.

Social cognition is sovereign in ways that, I believe, have implications both for social and cognitive psychologists. Social psychology has been vitally concerned with the study of cognition since 1900. However, the field of social cognition has adopted a very different level of analysis in its approach to the problem than has characterized previous work by social psychologists on cognitive processes. Past theoretical constructs (such as those recorded in the cognitive theory chapters of the 1954 and 1968 *Handbook of Social Psychology* volumes) will need to be either abandoned, revised, or subordinated to the conceptual approaches now being developed in social cognition.

All knowledge is social knowledge, and all social knowledge derives from action on the environment. The classic vocabulary of "stimulus" and "response" has carried cognitive and social psychology a long way, but now it is time to recognize the limitations inherent in this terminology for the study of human cognition. It is misleading to view persons as responding to elements in the stimulus field; it is misleading to view objects in the proximal environment as having an existence independent of the perceiver and as capable of being cognitively represented as discrete (and isolatable) stimulus entities. The "meaning" of stimulus objects (and hence their cognitive representation) derives from patterns of action-reaction that emerge as the perceiver encounters the object over time. This viewpoint, related in part to the "ecological approach" advocated by Gibson (1979), applies as much to knowledge of the physical world as to the social world. Such a view has implications for how to conceptualize knowledge structures and for concerns over what constitutes the most informative avenues of research.

The remainder of this chapter is divided into four sections. The first section establishes that there is a grievous lack of consensus regarding the use of the term "social cognition." These differences have led some researchers to unnecessarily deprecate the work of others. Other researchers have been unnecessarily narrow in their methods, ignoring the complexities of social cognition. The next two sections grapple with these definitional differences. The sections offer an analysis of these differences, moving toward a resolution that should allow disparate researchers to benefit from one another's efforts. One section deals with the concept of *social knowledge* and the other section examines the concept of *cognitive processes* as it is employed by social cognition researchers. The final section of this chapter addresses the question of sovereignty; what is it about the field of social cognition that makes it sovereign?

## A CLUTTER OF DEFINITIONS

It is to be expected that early in the evolution of a field, many of its contributors will struggle to articulate suitable definitions. This exercise is of use both to the investigator and to the audience, enabling each to differentiate this new body of research from that which preceded it. Many of the papers, chapters, and books on social cognition include a brief discussion of the domain of social cognition. No doubt this tendency will abate as the field matures. But for now, these presentations display the heterogeneity of usages to which the term is subjected.

### A Sampler

In reading the papers in this area, it is impossible to find two definitions that match. Each person includes nuances of special importance to his or her interests. I have not come across one instance in which an author is content to cite another's definition, and proceed from there without further comment. To provide the reader with a feeling for this diversity, I will offer a variety of definitions that can be found in the literature. I defer analysis and commentary until later in the chapter.

Hamilton (1981) views the field of social cognition as including a "consideration of all factors influencing the acquisition, representation, and retrieval of person information, as well as the relationship of these processes to judgments made by the perceiver" (p. 136). Isen and Hastorf (1982) prefer the phrase "cognitive social psychology" to social cognition, and define it as "an approach that stresses understanding of cognitive processes as a key to understanding complex, purposive, social behavior" (p. 2). Forgas (1981a) sees social cognition "as not merely the information-processing analysis of social domains, but as a field genuinely devoted to the study of everyday knowledge and understanding" (p. 259). Damon (1981) focuses on two interconnected meanings of social cognition. The "organizational aspect" refers to "the basic categories and principles that structure a person's social knowledge and that shape his or her understanding of social reality" (p. 157). The "processing aspect" of social cognition refers to "communication and change through social interaction" (p. 157), and later "all the ways in which the child exchanges, receives and processes information from others. These ways include some general cognitive processes, such

as attention and memory as well as some that are strictly social, such as communication and perspective taking" (p. 162). Kosslyn and Kagan (1981) observe
that the term "usually refers to two kinds of cognition—that about people,
groups, and social events and that colored by feelings, motives, attitudes, and
emotional states" (p. 82). Hoffman (1981), contrasting social cognition with
cognition in the physical domain, regards it as operating "in the context of a
complex, mutually facilitative give and take between affective and cognitive
processes" (p. 78). Wegner and Vallacher (1977) regard social cognition as the
study of "how people think about people" (p. *viii*). Roloff and Berger (1982)
state that "Social cognition represents the organized thoughts people have about
human interaction" (p. 21). Nelson (1981) views social cognition as "the process of representing knowledge about people and their relationships" (p. 97).
Sherrod and Lamb (1981) define social cognition as referring to "the way
individuals perceive and understand other people" (p. 1). Shantz (1982) observes that "The term refers usually to conceptions and reasoning about people,
the self, relations between people, social groups, roles and rules, and the relation
of such conceptions to social behavior" (p. 376).

## Definition by Priority

Academic custom often grants the earliest user of a term greatest influence in
determining its definition. "Social cognition" first came into wide verbal use in
the late 1970s. Taylor in 1981 assumed it was only 5 years old. The very first
published use of the term by a social psychologist is found in the 1954 *Handbook
of Social Psychology*. Bruner and Tagiuri's chapter on "the perception of people" defines social cognition as "placing the 'knowing of people' in the wider
theoretical context of how we know the environment generally" (p. 634). This
was a bit vague, but from the context it was intended to include both the question
of how people perceive and judge other people and the question of how social
factors affect perception, memory, and thinking. That is, social cognition is
involved when either the dependent variables or the independent variables in
cognitive research pertain to persons. This distinction was retained by Tagiuri in
his 1969 *Handbook of Social Psychology* chapter on person perception. The two
sides of this coin could be described, respectively, as the study of "Cognition in
Social Psychology" and the "Social Psychology of Cognition" (Higgins, 1982;
Simon, 1976).

The earliest use of the term in the title of an empirical paper (at least by a
social psychologist) was by Gollob (1974). His paper was titled, "The *S*ub-
ject-*V*erb-*O*bject approach to social cognition." However, the term here was
used more as a euphemism for "person perception" than to represent a new
domain of inquiry.

The first usage of the term in a book title appeared in 1979. Wyer and
Carlston titled their book, *Social Cognition, Inference, and Attribution*. Despite
the prominence of the term in the title, the term appears only infrequently in the

text of the book. No formal definition is offered. The book's contents, however, make clear what research areas were included under the social cognition label. The book focuses on the role of memory processes (encoding, storage, and retrieval) in mediating inferences and attributions. The term "person memory" appears to be regarded as synonymous to social cognition. The book is notable in that it is the first comprehensive attempt to employ cognitive psychology models of the mind to understand the dynamics of social inference and attribution.

## Definition Through Reflection

It often occurs that following an initial definitional tempest, one or more persons will take on the task of providing an historical overview of the field, offer commentary on its current role in the discipline, and in the process provide a reasoned basis for accepting one particular definitional approach. This has already occurred in the field of social cognition, but not in a manner that has yet yielded consensus. Employing what I considered to be fairly narrow criteria of categorization, I identified 22 papers and chapters that offered a historical and/or boundary-setting analysis of the field of social cognition. The largest number were written by social psychologists (Baron, 1980; Farr, 1981; Forgas, 1981b; Isen & Hastorf, 1982; Higgins, Kuiper, & Olson, 1981; Taylor, 1976, 1981; Weary, Swanson, Harvey & Yarkin, 1980; Zajonc, 1980) and by developmental psychologists (Chandler, 1977; Damon, 1981; Flavell, 1974; Gelman & Spelke, 1981; Glick, 1978; Hoffman, 1981; Shantz, 1975; Sherrod & Lamb, 1981). The remainder were by a personality psychologist (Mischel, 1979, 1981), by cognitive psychologists (Neisser, 1980, Simon, 1976), and by authors in the field of communications (Roloff & Berger, 1982). While all are enlightening in a variety of ways, they should not be read in hopes of uncovering a consensual definition of social cognition. These sources are more concerned with advancing their personal interpretations than with analyzing and reconciling the many differences that exist.

## Toward a Resolution

Two sets of issues have been muddled throughout most of the discussions on the definition of social cognition. One set has to do with the *nature of social knowledge*. A more careful analysis of what and how the person extracts information from his or her social environment is needed. One frequently addressed question is whether social knowledge differs in any significant way from knowledge about nonsocial objects. The second general issue pertains to the *nature of cognitive processes*. A great deal of unnecessary fractiousness has been produced by differential usage of the term "process." Of special concern here is the question of whether different processes are involved for social versus nonsocial knowledge.

# THE NATURE OF SOCIAL KNOWLEDGE

For social psychologists, the immediate precursor to social cognition was the field of person perception. Research in person perception traces its origins to a 1946 paper by Solomon Asch on impression formation. The major topics of interest addressed in the subsequent years were informational determinants of liking ratings, the effects of implicit personality theories on trait inferences, and in more recent years, the study of attributions and hueristics. Throughout these three decades of research, little formal consideration was given to the nature of the stimulus information on which subjects based their reactions. The stimulus information consisted primarily of traits and attitudes, and was conveyed to subjects in the form of sentences and paragraphs (Ostrom, 1975).

Beginning in the late 1960s, some reservations were being expressed about the use of this narrow array of stimulus materials. Such items of social information were viewed as only pale images of the kinds of information one obtains in ongoing interaction. For most commentators, the issue of external validity was at the heart of this concern. That is, would the principles that emerge when people react to trait and attitude information generalize to the more complex stimulus field found in naturalistic social settings? The recommended solution to this problem was to alter research practices by adopting more naturalistic forms of stimulus information. Some chose to abandon trait words in favor of sentences or paragraphs describing behavioral acts, others used photographs of the person or of an event. The "ideal" stimulus display, it was argued, was one in which the subject could observe a video tape, movie, or otherwise staged version of an ongoing behavioral display.

The field of social cognition, like that of person perception, should properly be concerned over the nature of the stimuli commonly used by its researchers. However, I disagree with those who believe the issue is one of external validity (e.g., Taylor, 1981). The differences between any two "naturalistic" settings are so vast, that it is no easier to generalize from naturalistic stimuli than from trait stimuli. What is required, rather, is a clearer understanding of the fundamental nature of social knowledge. It is far more practical to know the conceptual features that differentiate one kind of stimulus event from another than it is to know whether one is more naturalistic than the other.

## Contrasting Social and Nonsocial Knowledge

Cognitively oriented social psychologists have persistently been concerned with the differences between social and nonsocial knowledge. The first comprehensive integration of research on the cognitive basis of social behavior (Kretch & Crutchfield, 1948) devoted several pages to the issue. Most of the current papers and chapters that deal with the definition of "social cognition" contain a section contrasting social with "nonsocial" cognition.

Earlier writings that dealt with this distinction did so using the terminology of person (or social) perception versus object (or nonsocial) perception. (Heider, 1958, preferred "thing" perception over "object" perception, since both things and persons could be the "objects" of perception.) The term "cognition" has replaced the earlier "perception." This is probably because the types of processes most salient to the researchers have shifted over the last 30 years. Kretch and Crutchfield (1948) and Heider (1958) were drawing more on Gestaltist principles of perceptual organization (e.g., constancy, good figure, imbededness) when contrasting the two domains. In recent years, the focus has shifted more to the information processing orientation with its focus on mediating cognitive activities. These two conceptual orientations roughly correspond to the two extremes of Baron's (1980) continuum of social knowing. One can come to know the social world through direct perception or through reflective cognitive activity.

I have preferred to cast the distinction between person perception and object perception in somewhat different terminology, namely as the difference between social and nonsocial *knowledge*. The concerns being addressed in this section of the chapter are descriptive rather than process oriented. That is, they deal with an analysis of the characteristics of the stimulus event that the person apprehends through sensory experience and action, and whether these properties differ from social to nonsocial objects. These issues can be separated (at least provisionally) from concerns over the psychological mechanisms involved in the perception and cognitive rendering of this stimulus event.

There appears to be no satisfactory way to abstractly characterize the two categories of objects (social versus nonsocial). All would agree that social objects are animate and sentient, and that the prototype instance is a person or a group of persons. The prototype instance of a nonsocial object is an inert object like a vase or rock. But how do we classify a person who was raised in an inanimate world? Is this person capable of either providing or receiving social knowledge? Problems also emerge when trying to classify tadpoles and puppy dogs, thunderstorms and streams, volcanos and fire, and roses and dew. All display some form of animation, and their capacity for sentience has been a matter of dispute from the ancient Greeks to the modern eastern mystics. It is sufficient for our purpose to use the two above mentioned prototypes as the basis for the following discussion. This seems to have been the path taken by most of those who have written on the issue.

A fairly large number of differences between social and nonsocial knowledge have been proposed over the years. Unfortunately, no fully cogent classification system has gained acceptance, so most discussions of the issue take the form of lists. For example, Hoffman (1981) reviewed some eight differences mentioned by Glick (1978) and Gelman and Spelke (1981), and then added three more of his own. Bretherton, McNew, and Beeghly-Smith (1981) summarize a list of twelve differences provided by Shields (1978) and add two more of their own.

The present analysis of social versus nonsocial knowledge differs from previous discussions in two ways. First, it focuses solely on describing the differences between the two kinds of stimulus events, and avoids for the present the question of whether different cognitive and perceptual mechanisms are involved. This distinction between description and process has rarely been addressed in the past discussions of social knowledge. Second, the concept of action is integral to the analysis provided here. To the perceiving organism, the stimulus field has a unity over time. Events do not pop out at us like pieces of bread from a toaster, but rather fit into a coherent pattern. Later events take their meaning from earlier events; present reactions are shaped by the effects of past actions. This unity in the stream of experience is automatically violated by any attempt to categorize the nature of objects and events occurring in that stream. It therefore follows that any decomposition of the stimulus field (including the analysis offered here) is in part arbitrary and in part misleading.

The stimulus field is not a series of snapshots, but rather a continuously changing configuration of information. The concept of action applies both to the capacity of the perceiver and the objects of perception to change over time. It is important to highlight this capacity in any analysis of the differences between social and nonsocial knowledge. The two forms of knowledge differ in four ways: properties of the object, properties of the perceiver, properties of contingencies in human action, and properties of the perceiver as a participant in interactions.

*Properties of the Object.*    This classification system invites the separation of self and object. Therefore, in identifying the properties of the object, it is necessary to omit from this category descriptions that involve perceiver interpretations. The properties mentioned in this section are those which would be registered on mechanical recording devices. That is, it offers a description of objects from the perspective of nonsocial objects. Two major differences between social and nonsocial knowledge are described.

The first difference pertains to the prominence of static versus labile properties. Nonsocial objects show very little change in appearance over time. Vases and rocks retain their basic physical appearance and composition for years and years. A person, in contrast, is in a constant state of flux. The shape, color, sounds, and smell of a person may (and usually do) change from moment to moment. This means that any physical record of a person will be dominated by change rather than stability. "Knowledge" of that record must therefore focus on the regularities evident in change rather than the regularities inherent in static features.

This difference underlies the argument that social knowledge involves the perception of *behavior* (e.g., Heider, 1958; Hastie & Carlston, 1980). Behavior or action refers to changes in the person over time. Knowledge of another person is derived from a stream of observations extended in time rather than from a single glimpse.

The second difference between social and nonsocial objects has to do with the forces that produce change. A vase may appear different in the sunlight versus the shadows, its color might fade if scrubbed with a strong detergent, it might break if pushed off the table. All these forces are external to the object. Most of the changes observed in nonsocial objects can be attributed to such external forces. On the other hand, most of the changes recorded in social objects cannot be attributed to such external forces. Thus our mechanical (but sentient) recorder would be forced to conclude that the behavior of social objects is either random or is guided by unobserved internal forces. (Apparently the human observer is faced with the same dilemma, as is indicated by the prominence of research on internal versus external locus of control.)

Heider (1958), as well as many others, have emphasized this difference. People, unlike nonsocial objects, act as causal agents. Behavior is often self initiated. Certain other features sometimes accompany descriptions of the "agency" property (e.g., that behavior is purposive), but those other features involve interpretations regarding the nature of the internal forces. Therefore, they are best left to the following section on the nature of the interpreting object.

Other summaries of the differences between social and nonsocial objects have been offered that overlap extensively with the two features highlighted in this section. Some have argued that the primary difference is one of stimulus complexity (e.g., Hoffman, 1981; Glick, 1978; Kretch & Crutchfield, 1948). For example, Kretch and Crutchfield (1948) posit a continuum of objects ranging from simple (static and immobile) to complex (mobile, powerful, capricious, causal), with most social objects at the complex end and most nonsocial objects at the simple end. This view led them to conclude that there was no intrinsic difference between the two classes of objects, only that they distributed themselves differently over the continuum. Another somewhat related summary concept has been one of "unpredictability" (e.g., Gelman & Spelke, 1981; Glick, 1978; Hoffman, 1981; Wilder & Cooper, 1981). The two characteristics presented previously in this section (dynamic properties and internal forces) appear to underlie both the complexity and unpredictability concepts.

*Properties of the Perceiver.* The human perceiver is not merely a camera or a tape recorder. Information about the stimulus world is not simply recorded in a passive fashion, but rather the perceiver's sensory capacities, past experiences, and motivational states can all affect just what information gets stored. Of special concern in this section is the question of whether these properties of the perceiver have different implications for social versus nonsocial objects. A number of people have argued that such differences do exist (e.g., Bretherton et al., 1981; Flavel, 1974; Gelman & Spelke, 1981; Hastie & Carlston, 1980; Heider, 1958; Hoffman, 1981; Schneider, Hastorf, & Ellsworth, 1979; Shields, 1978; Tagiuri, 1958; Zajonc, 1980). The many proposed differences can be sorted into four subcategories: intersubjectivity, causal attribution, egocentric appraisal, and multiple sensory systems.

*Intersubjectivity* is a term found most often in the writings of developmental psychologists (e.g., Bretherton et al., 1981). It refers in its broadest sense to the point that when persons are the objects of perception, a high degree of similarity exists between perceiver and object. The perceiver recognizes that social objects are more similar to himself or herself than are nonsocial objects. This similarity leads the perceiver to assume that the object, when social, has the same properties as does the self. By having observed oneself all one's life, a larger number of human characteristics become known to the perceiver. These features, then, become part of the explanatory apparatus available to us when trying to understand the behavior of another person.

At least ten of these "implicit" characteristics have been discussed in the literature: (1) We assume that others have a sensory capacity, enabling them to see, hear, smell, taste and feel as we do. (2) We assume that others have cognitive capacities, that they learn, think, make inferences and judgments, and that they remember. (3) We assume that people have motives, emotions, drives, goals, and a wide variety of dispositional characteristics. (4) We assume that cognitive and affective internal states are more important in understanding behavior than are external factors (i.e., that people can initiate action, or have "agency" [Bretherton et al., 1981] or are "causal agents" [Heider, 1958]). Assumptions about these internal states can be further elaborated. For example, they are viewed as being quite variable, often unknowable, by even the self, yet capable of description to others and capable of deliberate misrepresentation.

The next assumed characteristic is that (5) overt behavior can be misleading in what it tells about the person's internal state. (6) We assume that the meaning of an act is context-dependent. (7) We assume that people differ in their capacity (or potential) to engage in specific acts, that is, education and physical capacities enable some people to do things others can't. (8) We assume that people can duplicate a previous act at a later point in time and in different contexts. (9) We assume that people identify one another, that others are discriminable and significant elements in the stimulus field. (10) Finally, we assume that persons have a unity over time, that despite changes in outward appearance the holistic essence of each person remains unchanged.

We acquire a great volume of world knowledge as we accumulate experiences. Basically, the "intersubjectivity" argument is that this knowledge differs considerably from social to nonsocial objects. For social objects, we are not just an observer of external forces operating in the stimulus field, but we can also draw upon our own personal experiences in trying to understand the array of factors contributing to the behavior of others. This entire set of implicit assumptions about others is invoked to bring stability and consistency to our social environment. Not only do they help us understand others' behavior toward ourselves, but we use them as well to understand patterns of behavior we observe occurring between two or more other persons.

*Causal attributions* constitute the second subcategory of perceiver properties. While it is doubtlessly true that people are, in general "explanation seekers," this tendency takes on special emphasis when the objects of perception are people. Social objects, because of their extreme lability and the role of internal forces in producing behavior, are especially intriguing phenomena to delve into. More important, social objects exert far more control over the perceiver's personal outcomes than do nonsocial objects. Life would indeed be miserable if we were unable to acquire a causal understanding of social behavior in interdependent relationships. It is in the formation of causal attributions that we make use of all the assumptions listed in the preceding subcategory on intersubjectivity.

*Egocentric appraisal* refers to the many features of the self that become engaged when encountering and responding to objects in our world. The ego can become involved in a wide variety of tasks, both social and nonsocial (for an early review, see Sherif & Cantril, 1945, 1946). Social objects are special in several ways. Since they are so instrumental to our future outcomes, their presence is likely to activate concerns over personal goals, future action possibilities, and expectancies regarding potential outcomes. Second, other persons have an extraordinary capacity to arouse the extremes of affect, both positive and negative. These occur in both long term relationships as well as in fleeting encounters. Third, other persons activate social comparison processes for attitudes, abilities, and probably a myriad of other internal states (e.g., Festinger, 1954). Nonsocial objects rarely provide the basis for self comparison. Usually only the poets compare a man's power to that of a thunderstorm and his passion to that of Mount Vesuvius.

The *multiple sensory systems* possessed by the human perceiver create a very different recording device than is found in a tape recorder or a camera. A single event can be simultaneously experienced through sight, sound, smell, touch, and taste. And the human as a recording device has the capacity to integrate these qualitatively disparate sensations into a single impression.

Few objects in our environment actually present us with all forms of sensation simultaneously, but social objects typically arouse more than nonsocial objects. More important, these different sensory channels typically provide important, nonredundant information to the perceiver. An attractive, attentive person with unpleasant body odor will be responded to quite differently if the olfactory information is not available.

*Contingencies in Human Action.*   Observe a man handling his "pet rock." The rock is completely passive. It responds to the person in a variety of ways, but those responses are always the consequence of predictable external forces. Stand it on end and it will roll over, toss it in the air and it will return to the ground.

People are not pet rocks. As mentioned in the two preceding subsections, their behavior is not simply the result of forces external to themselves. As the terms "agency" and "action center" imply, much of people's behavior is caused by internal forces. This fact brings us to one of the most widely emphasized sources of difference between social and nonsocial objects. Social objects don't just act or react to the perceiver, but they *interact* in a manner contingent on the perceiver's own previous behavior. When two people are interacting, each is an initiator (i.e., a stimulus for the other) as well as a responder. A given action almost always contains both stimulus and response information.

The field of social psychology has long defined itself as the discipline most concerned with the study of interpersonal contingencies. The concept of interaction is at the heart of most textbook definitions of the field. Concepts such as power, conflict, and cooperation are usually defined in terms of contingencies (e.g., Thibaut & Kelley, 1959). Certainly, the concept of response contingency is central to understanding any pattern of human communication (Clark, in press).

The perceiver who observes two people interacting is aware of the importance of these behavioral contingencies when trying to make sense of each person's behavior patterns. The perceiver assumes that each participant is observing, interpreting, and remembering the others' actions, and that the resulting cognitive representation directly influences the participant's future acts. This Lewinian perspective has been termed reciprocal sensitivity (Kretch, 1951) and reciprocal perception (Schneider et al., 1979).

Despite the universal importance accorded the perception of contingencies, surprisingly little empirical work has been done in the area. This is not to say that social psychologists have ignored the importance of prior context in interpreting social behavior. Past behavior affects the frame of reference people use in interpreting present acts (e.g., Ostrom & Upshaw, 1968). Kelley's (1967) work on attributional processes highlighted the importance of distinctiveness, consistency, and consensus information when interpreting specific actions. Higgins' (1981) "communication game" research has shown that social context and goals can affect memory for past events and the accuracy of future communication about those events.

None of this research, however, dealt with specific sequential contingencies that emerge when two persons are interacting in a face-to-face situation. Perhaps one lesson to be learned from the research on case history versus base rate information (e.g., Nisbett & Borgida, 1975) is that perceivers find individuating contingency information (as was present in the case histories) far more informative than base rate (or consensus) information.

One promising line of research on the problem of contingencies has been initiated by Davis and her associates (Davis, 1982; Davis & Holtgraves, 1982; Davis & Perkowitz, 1979). Her concept of "responsiveness" is defined in terms of the sequential contingencies that exist in social behavior. The antecedents of responsiveness include such factors as attention to one's partner and possession of a relevant response repertoire. Variations in responsiveness can affect such things as the maintenance of the interaction, communication accuracy, and the kinds of attributions each makes about the other.

*The Perceiver as an Interaction Participant.*   We have now reached the fourth category of differences between social and nonsocial knowledge. This is a category for which I found no precedent in the empirical literature. It was one which was forced on me by the logic of the preceding three. The first and second categories (characteristics of the object and characteristics of the perceiver, respectively) contrast social and nonsocial objects as they exist in isolation. The object characteristics were ones that could be determined when the objects are in social isolation. The perceiver characteristics are ones that are present when the perceiver views objects in social isolation. The two differ, of course, in that the first refers to characteristics of the object and the second to characteristics of the perceiver.

The first and third categories (characteristics of the object and contingencies in human interaction) differ in terms of whether more than one object is present in the stimulus field. The object is alone in the first, but at least two persons are required for contingencies to become relevant. What is more important is to point out the common feature of these two categories. They both focus on the object of perception; the perceiver is left in the passive role of an observer, a mere recording device.

The two dimensions that differentiate categories one versus two and one versus three are orthogonal to one another. I have labeled them entity and sociality, respectively. The resulting four-fold classification is portrayed in Table 1.1.

The fourth category that emerges from this classification system pertains to the characteristics of the ''on line'' behavior of the perceiver while in direct, face-to-face interaction with the object. It is clear that all the differences between social and nonsoical knowledge from the first three categories come together in this category. The complexities inherent in social knowledge that result from combining the other three categories are doubtlessly more than just the simple

TABLE 1.1
A Classification System for Identifying the Differences Between
Social and Nonsocial Knowledge

|  |  | Entity | |
|  |  | Object | Perceiver |
| --- | --- | --- | --- |
| SOCIALITY | *Alone* | *Category 1*<br>Characteristics of the object | *Category 2*<br>Characteristics of the perceiver (as an observer) |
|  | *With others* | *Category 3*<br>Contingencies in human action | *Category 4*<br>The perceiver as an interaction participant |

summation of the separate effects. Such a compounding of differences would be sufficient to highlight this fourth category. However, a bit of reflection reveals that new considerations arise which are unique to this category, considerations that have not been independently addressed by previous writers examining the question of social versus nonsocial knowledge.

When the perceiver is in direct interaction with a social object, a number of concurrent tasks must be performed. As a passive observer, the perceiver need only attend to, record, and interpret the behavior of the object, and deal with whatever attributional and egocentric appraisal consequences that may result. On the other hand, consider the following list of concurrent tasks usually accomplished by the interaction participant, tasks the perceiver may be faced with during the brief interval of time sandwiched between two sequential acts initiated by the perceiver's interaction companion:

1. The perceiver must observe the instigating action. This involves selective attention to the stimulus field and to sensory modalities.
2. Observations are entered into the cognitive system.
3. Past observations of the same stimulus person are retrieved to provide a context for interpreting the instigating act.
4. Inferences, judgments, and attributions are implicitly made, evaluated, and revised.
5. Since the perceiver must respond to the other person's instigating act, a review of possible response alternatives is made.
6. Short- and long-term consequences of each alternative must be evaluated.
7. The perspective of the other toward each alternative is reviewed. Will the other veridically interpret it and make the desired response?
8. One response alternative is selected and enacted.
9. The partner's response is observed and interpreted in light of the behavior enacted by the self.
10. Based on feedback from the partner, the adequacy of the self-enacted behavior is evaluated according to whether it produced the intended consequences. It is compared in effectiveness to alternative responses that could have been selected for enactment.
11. Affective processes that may have been aroused are dealt with.
12. The significant observations and thoughts that resulted from this brief interaction segment are recorded in memory for future use.

This list of twelve is only illustrative. For some interpersonal events, even more tasks may be performed; for other events, fewer might be performed. We are not in a position as yet to exhaustively enumerate all possibilities or to identify the circumstances under which each will be actively involved. Higgins' (1981) list of general "rules" that implicitly underlay social communication incorporates several of the above concurrent tasks.

It is staggering, indeed, to realize that these myriad concurrent tasks are compressed into the time it takes to nod understandingly, raise an eyebrow, or fleet a smile. The motivational, cognitive, and affective mechanisms that allow us to perform them are at present bafflingly complex and poorly understood. Of course, this quest for understanding has always been, and will continue to be, the primary objective of psychology. It is in the field of social cognition that the full complexity of the task becomes apparent. When the person is not engaged in contingent (or "on line") behavior, as is often the case in research with nonsocial objects, this array of concurrent tasks is far simpler.

The complexities of understanding social cognition and social behavior are most evident in this fourth category of social knowledge. It is knowledge in this category that the field knows the least about. Very little research has been done on the effects of different mixtures of concurrent tasks. Communication game research (e.g., Higgins, 1981), cognitive tuning research (e.g., Zajonc, 1960), and work on impression versus memory sets (e.g., Hamilton, Katz, & Leirer, 1980) has looked at the effects of different processing goals on memory and the structure of impressions, but there is no systematic empirical work on the effects of multiple, concurrent goals.

The field of social cognition has been criticized for ignoring the cognitive consequences of social interaction. Indeed, it has been argued that the entire cognitive orientation interferes with understanding group and societal social phenomena (Pepitone, 1981; Sampson, 1981). Research on concurrent social responsibilities (especially in those arising in the context of social interaction) will move us a long way toward addressing the issues raised by these critics.

*Perceiver and Object as Integral Constituents of Social Knowledge.* The four-category classification system in Table 1.1 presumes that both the perceiver and the object are necessary components to analyzing the nature of social knowledge. This perspective is fundamentally different than one that attempts to describe the stimulus world independently of the perceiver. Divorcing the object from the perceiver would lead us to address only those few differences described in categories one and three in Table 1.1. The present perspective argues, on the other hand, that knowledge of stimulus objects cannot be disentangled from knowledge of the self.

The present orientation varies substantially from the traditional "stimulus-response" analysis that has guided psychology throughout most of its history (and continues to guide a great deal of contemporary work in social cognition). The four categories of social knowledge are not simply a way of classifying different forms of stimuli in the external world. Social knowledge does not refer merely to the "contents" of cognition, to qualitative features of cognitions that the perceiver encodes, stores and retrieves. Rather, it refers to the kinds of interdependencies that exist between the perceiver and the stimulus field in knowledge acquisition and action. The stimulus in social cognition is an "event" rather than a static entity present in the physical world.

The present perspective is not deviant in any way from the history of thought in social psychology. These two constituents, the perceiver and the object, are integral to one another and are linked through the concept of action. It is to this linkage that I turn next.

## Action Is the Root of Social Knowledge

It is instructive to read the early history of social psychology. An impressively comprehensive survey was published in 1932 by Fay Karpf (1932/1971). Up through the 1920s, papers published in social psychology were far more conceptual than empirical. American social psychologists shared the view that human action was the basis of social knowledge. This can be seen, for example, in the writings of Baldwin (1906), Mead (1934), and Thomas and Znaniecki (1918). The interest these early theorists showed in the nature of social information was definitely not due to concerns over the external validity of research operations (as has been the case in recent years). Rather, they were grappling with the fundamental nature of social knowledge.

It was obvious to these social psychologists that humans were "doers" rather than "watchers." From the time of birth (and even before) a person learns about the world through acting on it and experiencing the consequences of that action. Baby's rattle feels smooth to the touch of finger, cheek and tongue, and makes noise when shaken. The college sophomore discovers that a compliment to a friend brings a smile, but a compliment to a professor produces the suspicion of ingratiation. Integral to both social and nonsocial knowledge is the actions of the self.

This is a very different concern than the one over external validity of trait information. It argues that all social knowledge is reflexive in character. That is, knowledge of others always reflects back on the self. Knowledge of others intrinsically incorporates knowledge of self-initiated actions (along with their probable consequences) that are relevant to interactions with the other persons. Self knowledge and other knowledge are inextricably bound together through the concept of action.

The work of Thomas and Znaniecki (1918) offers one illustration of this orientation. They are best known for their work on the effects of cultural change on values and attitudes. Their empirical work was based on an analysis of diaries and letters written by Polish peasants who had immigrated to the United States. Societal values, they argue (e.g., see page 361), have no meaning in the absence of behavior. The "meaning of these values becomes explicit when we take them in connection with human action" (page 361). Later on the same page we find, "By attitude we understand a process of individual consciousness which determines real or possible activity of the individual in the social world,'' and ''Attitude is the individual counterpart to social values, activity is the bond between them.''

It is interesting to note that throughout the 1970s attitude theorists have been concerned with the question of whether attitudes are related to behavior. Yet one of the earliest conceptual analyses of attitude assumed that behavior was integral to the very definition of attitude. Thomas and Znaniecki would no doubt be mystified by conceptualizations and measurement procedures for attitudes that exclude action.

This original concern over action nearly disappeared during the heyday of person perception research (the decades of the 1950s, 1960s, and 1970s). The few that spoke of it (e.g., Heider, 1958; Ittelson & Slack, 1958) did not study it at an empirical level. Attention was focused almost exclusively on the determinants of overall impression, the interrelations among elements of the impression, and inferences based on the impression. Issues regarding the contents of the impression (i.e., social knowledge) and the manner in which those contents are abstracted from the environment were set aside as being of lesser interest. Consequently, researchers selected their stimulus items on the basis of convenience. The concepts being tested were indifferent to the issue of whether action was or was not a component of the stimulus domain. In a sense, they were following the practices of experimental psychologists who routinely subordinated ecological fidelity to the methodological conveniences of theory testing. (I might add, this continues to be true of most research in cognitive psychology and of a great deal of contemporay research in social cognition.)

A resurgence of interest has emerged within social psychology over the role of action in knowledge. These general issues have been directly addressed in papers by Baron (1980), McArthur (1980), Forgas (1981a, 1981b), Vallacher and Wegner (in press), and Zajonc (1980). Empirical work is now emerging from the ''situated action'' perspective (Brenner, 1980; Ginsburg, 1980; Harré & Secord, 1972). Most psychological research in the Soviet Union explicitly acknowledges the central role played by social action (e.g., Wertsch, 1981). Researchers in cognition (Neisser, 1976, 1980) and perception (Gibson, 1979) are also turning to these issues.

Although concerns over the role of action in knowledge are fairly recent within cognitive, perception, and social psychology, this is not the case for developmental psychology. The work of Piaget has long been anchored to the premise that knowledge about the world derives from action on it (e.g., Piaget, 1952, 1954). Although widely ignored by social and cognitive psychologists, a great amount of excellent empirical work has been completed on the development of social knowledge (e.g., Glick & Clarke-Stewart, 1978; Lamb & Sherrod, 1981; Lock, 1978; Flavell & Ross, 1981; Mischel, 1974; Overton & Gallagher, 1977). The concept of action is explicitly addressed in most of this work.

*The Role of Action in Cognitive Theory.*   Cognitive theory addresses a wide variety of phenomena, including recognition of letters, comprehension of prose, and the structure of free recall. It clearly is not necessary for every theorist to explicitly incorporate the concept of action when modeling subsystems of cognitive activity. However, the modeling of human interaction is a different matter. Whether interpersonal exchanges be primarily verbal or nonverbal in nature, the behavior of each participant is a continuous source of information to the other. Posture, gestures, facial expressions, back-channel responses, and expressions of agreement or disagreement all provide the background for the manifest content of a conversation. Since people are simultaneously giving and receiving social information, it is reasonable to assume that units of social knowledge contain both forms of information. A priority task for the field of social cognition is to identify the nature of those units.

As with general cognitive theory, theories of social cognition should properly address a wide variety of phenomena. Not all such theories need to directly account for all forms of social knowledge. It is entirely appropriate (and clearly useful) to develop theory pertaining to such problems as the use of information about traits, race, gender, or nationality in the formation of impressions and inferences. However, it needs to be explicitly recognized that these theoretical effects apply primarily to passive settings stripped of all but the most minimal action requirements. Because the models that have emerged in these areas of research (e.g., Schneider et al., 1979) ignore the concept of action, there is no reason to assume that they reflect the psychological processes that are actually occurring during ongoing interaction episodes.

I am not prepared to argue that theory which explicitly incorporates the concept of action is superior to theory of more socially isolated and passive processes. On the other hand, it is true that social psychology has made very little progress in understanding the processes involved in interpersonal interaction. Despite a traditional reliance on cognitive theory as the basis for empirical research, that theory has not in recent years incorporated the concept of action. This historical fact is vividly displayed in the cognitive theory chapters that were written for the 1954 and 1968 editions of the *Handbook of Social Psychology* (Scheerer, 1954; Zajonc, 1968). A priority concern, then, for the field of social cognition is to tackle the theoretical and empirical implications of action as the basis of social knowledge.

*The Role of Action in Research Methodology.*   It is important to reiterate that this emphasis on action as the basis of social knowledge is a conceptual argument, and not a methodological one. It is very different than the oft heralded plea for external validity in the study of person perception (e.g., Forgas, 1981b; Taylor, 1976, 1981). It is not true that this view requires the abandonment of trait information as stimulus material in favor of behavioral statements or scenes of ongoing behavior. It is not true that laboratory settings should be abandoned in favor of naturalistic observations. It is not true that dependent variables such as button pushing and recognition memory tests should be abandoned in favor of content analyses of interaction sequences.

The field of social cognition should be open to all methodologies. The choice of stimulus materials, research setting, and response records should be based on the conceptual issues at stake, rather than on some vague, atheoretical concern over external validity. For example, there is (at least for some purposes) far more "action-potential" information in the trait "honest" than there is in the behavioral observation, "did not cheat on his Ph.D. Qualifying Exam." When people use the trait "honest," they usually are conveying much more about the person than is contained in a single static behavioral observation. That is, the trait conveys action-relevant, contextually contingent information. It implies honesty over a variety of situations, honesty in the face of repeated temptation, and honesty when interacting with a variety of other persons (including the recipient of the information). One form of social information is no more or no less "valid" than another. It depends on the theoretical aims of the research.

*"Knowing" Social Knowledge.*    One of the most important contributions made by those urging an "ecological" orientation toward social knowledge is their emphasis on describing the significant features of a stimulus event. In both visual and social perception, there are many features that can only be known through actions of the perceiver over time. It is not possible to construct an adequate theory of social cognition until we obtain a full description of the stimulus event. It is vital to determine exactly what properties are significant to the perceiver's cognitive representation because these properties not only emerge through action, but are simultaneously involved in the initiation of action.

Many of the advocates of this perspective erroneously wed their advocacy to specific methodologies (e.g., Damon, 1981; Forgas, 1981b; Harré, 1977; Baron, 1980). Since the aim is to provide a better description of the stimulus event and how the perceiver derives knowledge from it, the adovcated methodology has been direct observation of ongoing interactions (including both the verbal and nonverbal components). Also recommended are procedures that invite the participants to overtly express their thoughts about self and others through interviews and questionnaires. They reject data from the laboratory as being irrelevant to the descriptive enterprise.

It is shortsighted to dismiss any methodology on such a priori grounds. The test is whether the methodology yields information that advances understanding of the stimulus event engaged by the social knower. It is quite possible to be a "cognitive naturalist" without leaving the experimental laboratory. For example, it is important to know the conditions under which a person will respond to the other members of a group on an individual, person-by-person basis opposed to dealing with them as an undifferentiated entity (e.g., Ostrom, Pryor, & Simpson, 1981; Wilder & Cooper, 1981). This descriptive problem can (and should) be approached either by direct observation of interpersonal behaviors in small groups, or by systematic analysis of the "group" stimulus field in a laboratory setting using such indices as response time and recall for past observations. Both methodologies allow for an investigation of the role of action in social knowledge. Each has different strengths and limitations. Neither should be discarded out of hand.

## THE NATURE OF COGNITIVE PROCESSES

It is important to distinguish between social knowledge and cognitive processes in the field of social cognition. A great many of the differences found among the several definitions of social cognition result from inattention to this distinction. To a large extent, the differences derive from divergent interpretations of the term "process."

The term "process" is used widely in the social and behavioral sciences. We see references to "societal processes," "normative processes," and "group processes." Rather than possessing a single technical meaning, or even different (but specific) technical meanings for each field, it has come to refer generally to the entire set of empirical and theoretical relationships that typify that field. "Group processes," for example, denotes the diverse forces (both known and unknown) that influence the group as a whole as well as the responses of each individual within the group. However, this use of the term is silent on a number of issues. It does not refer to any specific set of causal models, the unit of analysis can be at either the group or individual level, and it encompasses both theoretical principles and empirical observations.

The situation is very different in the field of cognitive psychology. The use of "cognitive processes" is far more circumscribed. The study of cognitive processes involves an analysis of the stages, structures, and dynamic mechanisms involved in mental activity, including both the receipt of information from the environment and the initiation of responses. It is concerned with processing stages such as encoding, storage, and retrieval; it includes memory structures such as schema and prototypes; it evaluates the credibility of alternative theoretical mechanisms such as associative networks and computer models of mental activity.

In reviewing the several definitions of social cognition presented earlier in this chapter, it can be seen that the term "process" appears fairly frequently. For most of the remaining definitions, the term appears in the surrounding text where the author elaborates on the term. For some of the authors (e.g., Hamilton, 1981; Isen & Hastorf, 1982), the term coincides with the definition used in cognitive psychology. Others were willing to use the term in this way (as in "general" cognitive processes), but also felt free to use it in the more diffuse nonspecific sense. For most of these writers, the term "social cognition processes" was not limited to the cognitive psychology referents. Rather, it was intended to encompass a wide range of empirical and theoretical domains. We find references to "attributional processes," "communication processes," "developmental processes," "heuristics processes," and "affective processes."

If the field of social cognition is to ever represent a genuine blending of social psychology (including it's allied areas) with cognitive psychology, some consensus is needed regarding the use of the term "process." It is difficult enough for each to learn the unique terms in the others' scientific lexicon, without having to also cope with noncommon definitions of identical terms. More important, however, is the need for social psychologists to reach consensus on their own use of the term. The lack of consensus can be seen most vividly in discussions over whether "different processes" are involved in social versus nonsocial cognition. This question would be approached in very different ways by a cognitive psychologist than by a person who assumes the question also includes attributional processes and communication processes. My recommendation is that social psychologists working in the field of social cognition agree to reserve the term "process" for research and theory on mental activity, thereby sharing the term with cognitive psychologists. This certainly should be the case when used explicitly in the context of issues relating to cognition or social cognition. The reader will note that this convention has been adopted by most writers in the present *Handbook*.

## Contrasting Social and Nonsocial Cognitive Processes

No comprehensive review is yet available of research on the differences between social and nonsocial cognitive processes. A modest number of studies have compared peoples responses to social and nonsocial stimuli, but even at the empirical level, this work has not been brought together in a single source. The diversity of past work on this issue is illustrated in the following examples.

Several authors have argued that the number and variety of categories available to classify or encode stimuli differs for social and nonsocial objects (Hastorf, Schneider, & Polefka, 1970; Cantor & Mischel, 1979). Persons may be the most frequent object that people encounter in their environment. Pairing that with the obvious fact that no two social encounters are identical (even with the same person in the same setting), it is reasonable to assume that people develop a much wider array of categories for social objects than for nonsocial objects. At present, it is unclear how such differences in the number and variety of categories would affect processing mechanisms.

Research by Abelson and Kanouse (1966) and Gilson and Abelson (1965) has shown that there is greater acceptance of generalizations from person categories (e.g., tribes and foreigners) than from object categories (e.g., bees and cities).

Subsequent work by Wyer and Podeschi (1978) indicated that this finding might be due to two factors. People appear to define person categories more disjunctively and object categories more conjunctively. Second, people appear to assign more universal implicit quantifiers (e.g., all *versus* some) to categories of persons than they do to categories of objects.

Differences in the determinants of concept formation have been found between physical concepts and social concepts (Cottrell, 1975). Concept learning takes increasingly more trials as the number of relevant dimensions increases when dealing with physical stimuli that vary on such dimensions as shape, color and size. A reversal of this effect was found for social stimuli involving affective bonds (e.g., like and in favor of). Certain three-dimensional concepts (e.g., balanced social structures) were easier to learn than were two- and one-dimensional social concepts.

Some research has been done on the question of whether speech perception (i.e., the perception of sounds generated by social objects) is different than the perception of other environmental sounds. Repp (1982) concluded that differences do emerge when the perceiver integrates an acoustic signal. The signal is converted into meaningful linguistic units (phonemes) when integrated in the context of human speech.

Quite a bit of research has been conducted on infants and children to see if they respond differently to social and nonsocial events. Reviews of the literature (e.g., Gelman & Spelke, 1981; Hoffman, 1981; Sherrod, 1981) suggest there are differences in visual attention, in the assumptions made about object permanence, and in attributions of causality.

It can be seen from the above illustrations that the question of social versus nonsocial cognition has implications for many different research areas. Not enough data is yet available to determine whether different processes are involved in the two, but it is possible to identify some ground rules governing how such a quest should be conducted.

On the empirical side, the most useful studies are those that look for interactions rather than main effects. While it is of some interest to know that infants attend more to social than nonsocial stimuli, it would be more informative to determine whether there are factors that differentially affect attention to social versus nonsocial objects. That is, are the obtained relationship involving social objects functionally comparable (Ostrom, 1973) to those obtained with nonsocial objects? Only if the functions are clearly noncomparable is there reason to suppose that different theoretical processes are involved for social and nonsocial knowledge.

If such research is to establish that different cognitive processes are involved, the interpretation of functional differences must involve theoretical constructs from cognitive psychology. Is it possible that different encoding and retrieval mechanisms are involved? May it be that persons are best represented by schemas and nonsocial objects by prototypes? Such possibilities strike me as being implausible, but this may change as our conceptual understanding of cognitive processes improves.

Some guidance can be provided in the search for different processes by the four-fold analysis of social knowledge described in the first part of this chapter (see Table 1.1). If processing differences do exist between social and nonsocial events, those differences should be coordinated with the different properties of social knowledge. Most of the research reviewed in the preceding paragraphs dealt only with the kinds of differences represented in categories one and two of Table 1.1. The more interesting (and difficult to study) differences derive from the remaining two categories.

*Three Points of View.*    Although no comprehensive empirical analysis has been made of the possible differences in the processes involved in social versus nonsocial cognition, many social psychologists have speculated about the differences. Three points of view have been espoused.

Social psychology historically has accepted the premise that individual social behavior derives from underlying psychological processes, including cognitive, perceptual, motivational, and physiological. This assumption can be seen in explicit treatments of "theory" in social psychology. The very beginning of both the 1954 and 1968 editions of the *Handbook of Social Psychology* is devoted to chapters on theory. With the exception of chapters on Role Theory (which is highly cognitive in nature), all the other theoretical chapters dealt with underlying psychological processes. This same emphasis on individual psychological processes is present in textbooks on social psychological theory (Shaw & Costanzo, 1982; West & Wicklund, 1980).

Out of this intellectual milieu emerged a *building-block* view of the relation between the processes involved in social and nonsocial cognition. This argument is that the processes involved in dealing cognitively with nonsocial events are simpler and conceptually more fundamental than the processes involved with social events. The study of cognitive processing in the context of nonsocial stimuli provides a foundation on which the more complex social cognition principles can be built. This position is inherent in the writings of Heider (1958), Higgins et al. (1981), MacLeod (1951), Sherif and Cantril (1945, 1946), Simon (1976), and Tagiuri (1958, 1969). The kinds of variables that are viewed as supplementing nonsocial cognition principles are individual differences, affect, personal experience, and self-relevance.

A second viewpoint, the *fundamentalist* position, argues that there are no intrinsic differences in the cognitive processes involved in social versus nonsocial cognition. Each person develops a wide variety of cognitive capacities and processing mechanisms to cope with the stimulus world, and these are available regardless of whether the stimulus events involve social or nonsocial objects.

This position is present in the writings of Eiser and Stroebe (1972), Hastie, Ostrom, Ebbesen, Wyer, Hamilton, and Carlston (1980), Isen and Hastorf (1982), Kretch and Crutchfield (1948), McArthur (1980), and Peak (1958).

The fundamentalists accept the null hypothesis that there are no differences in processing mechanisms for social and nonsocial knowledge. Should data suggest that differences exist, (due, for example, to affect or self-relevance), they prefer to search for underlying properties that, when held constant, eliminate the obtained effects. For example, Kretch and Crutchfield (1948) and Isen and Hastorf (1982) suggest that many of the obtained differences may be due to the fact that social objects tend to be more familiar and more complex than nonsocial objects.

A third point of view is now gaining ascendence among social psychologists. The *realist* position is in many ways the opposite of the building block position. It derives from a pragmatic analysis of the response demands placed on people by their social and nonsocial environment. Realists argue that the foundation of all cognitive processes derives from episodes involving social objects (as opposed to nonsocial objects).

In recent years, developmental psychologists have noted that immediately upon birth (and even before) the infant is immersed in a social environment. It is an environment in which other persons are perceptually salient, an environment that places social demands on the infant, and one that responds to the infant's actions in predictable ways. From the very start, then, life is a Category Four (from Table 1.1) environment.

It follows from the above that the stimulus episodes that should have the greatest impact on the initial development of cognitive mechanisms are episodes involving social rather than nonsocial objects. Strategies of encoding and retrieval, schematic and categorical representations, information integration styles, and response capacities all evolve primarily in response to processing social knowledge. It is only later that the infant must begin mastering its nonsocial world to obtain desired outcomes. This position has been advocated by Chandler (1977), Damon (1981), DeCharms (1968), Forgus (1981a), Gelman and Spelke (1981), Hoffman (1981), Piaget (1952, 1954), and Zajonc (1980). For some (but not all) of its advocates, this position shares with the fundamentalist viewpoint a belief in the continuity of processes between social and nonsocial cognition.

Several lines of research suggest that social knowledge takes developmental precedence over nonsocial knowledge. Adults know that persons can move about at will, but that ordinary chairs cannot. However, young children must learn this difference. Golinkoff and Harding (1980, reported in Gelman & Spelke, 1981) offer data suggesting that infants (at 16 months) assume that all objects are like social objects, namely that all objects have the capacity for independent action. They show no surprise when either persons or chairs move in the absence of external forces. However, by the age of 24 months, infants begin to show surprise when chairs move about at will. Such developmental differences appear to occur in other areas as well. In research reviewed by Hoffman (1981), it is argued that children understand causality for social events at an earlier age than they do for physical events. Hoffman (1981) also described research suggesting that person permanence (i.e., having an internal representation of a person that persists in the person's absence) developmentally precedes object permanence.

From the realist point of view, all the ingredients of social knowledge represented in Table 1.1 are inherent in the social episodes experienced by infants. Factors that become of interest to the building-block advocates only after a foundation has been constructed, factors such as affect, goals, and self-relevance, are viewed by the realists as integral to the original development of cognitive processes in humans. As noted by Zajonc (1980), it is social cognition that is the "general case" in the study of cognitive processes; research with nonsocial objects represents a limited "special case" in which the parameters on most important social dimensions are set to zero.

## Action is Integral to Cognitive Processes

Category Four in Table 1.1 highlights the "on line" properties of social knowledge, properties that emerge in the context of interpersonal interaction. The individual is at once absorbed with bringing meaning to the actions of the other as well as enacting his or her own responses. Theories of cognitive processes are obligated to account for both sides of this duality.

Most analyses of cognitive processes conducted by social psychologists have dealt exclusively with the issues of representing and processing passively received information about other persons (e.g., Hastie et al., 1980). They have ignored the companion obligation to work toward an understanding of how action goals are formulated, behavioral plans are structured, and muscle movement instructions are initiated. An understanding of these mechanisms is necessary if we are to account for the complexities resulting from the many concurrent tasks involved in interaction episodes. Lack of attention to these issues has led some commentators (e.g., Forgas, 1981a; Taylor, 1981) to speculate that theories of cognitive processes are fundamentally unable to provide a theoretical account for patterns of interpersonal behavior.

Cognitive systems must have the capacity to represent and indicate action. Such actions may be either molar (as in plans) or molecular (as in muscle movement). The actions may derive from protracted deliberative rumination or they may be an automatic reflex to a stimulus event. All (except for spinal reflexes) are centrally mediated and therefore must be represented and processed cognitively.

Cognitive theorists have not overlooked the need to incorporate action into cognitive theory. Such authors as Anderson (1976), Miller, Galanter, and Pribram (1960), Newell (1973), Norman and Rummelhart (1975), Shank and Abelson (1977), and Winograd (1975) have all offered an analysis of the cognitive processes involved in behavioral enactments. Other relevant research on this problem is conducted by workers in physical education and kinesiology (e.g., Kelso, 1981; Schmidt, 1975, 1982) and by workers in the neurosciences (e.g., Evarts, 1979).

The role of action in cognitive processing, however, has been neglected by social cognition researchers (for recent felicitous exceptions, see Carver & Scheier, 1982, and Vallacher & Wegner, in press). This is unfortunate, for it is with just these "Category Four" issues that social cognition theorists have the most to contribute. Norman (1981) has persuasively argued in his "Twelve issues for cognitive science" that a full understanding of cognitive processes will ultimately encompass such domains as emotion, interaction, language, development, skill, and performance.

The "knowledge derives from action" orientation advanced in the first part of this chapter implies that this most poorly understood feature of cognitive processes is in fact the most important. It is especially important for scholars in the field of social cognition. If man is a behaving organism, then the cognitive system must be dominated by impulses to initiate behavior. In interaction settings, people are continuously moving their faces, limbs, and trunk. In addition to overt, directed communication, they fidgit, shift weight from foot to foot, look off into the distance, as well as a multitude of other acts. As communication theorists have shown, many of these serve to regulate the interaction pattern. And even when alone, people find it impossible to simply sit still.

Action at the level of muscles is nearly continuous, and in social settings, feedback from these actions is similarly continuous. This implies that cognitive systems are continuously involved with the production of action and assessing it's consequences. Such an analysis invites reconceptualization of such social psychological concepts as attitude and the self.

Attitude theory that incorporates action as a fundamental unit of knowledge should produce constructs quite congenial with those proposed in the early part of this century by Thomas and Znaniecki (1918). Attitude is not a point on a continuum, but a bundle of molar and molecular response dispositions that help us to interpret and regulate interactions with the social and physical world.

In a similar vein, social psychology can no longer be content to conceptualize the self cognitively as a set (or hierarchy) of self-descriptive traits. Rather, the self is viewed as an initiator of actions that yield favorable or unfavorable consequences for the self. Self knowledge is not a trait label plus its schematic implications. Instead, self knowledge that is drawn upon in the midst of social interactions derives from the store of actions previously engaged in with the same (or similar) partners under comparable circumstances. Just as stimuli cannot be described independently of the perceiver, the self has no existance independent of the world in which it acts.

## THE SOVEREIGNTY OF SOCIAL COGNITION

The field of social cognition has captured the attention of a number of the social and behavioral sciences. A variety of different interpretations of what constitutes theory and research in social cognition were espoused as each attempted to define the field. It has been my intent in preparing this chapter to synthesize the many different points of view that have been expressed. It has not been my intent to disfranchise any subfields of research, casting them away as being irrelevant to understanding in social cognition. Nor was it my intent to rank order the different types of contribution in terms of their importance or relevance to advancing understanding in social cognition. I believe that all the different contributions referred to in this chapter play vital roles in our scientific advance.

The many different definitions of social cognition listed earlier in the chapter were useful in helping to identify the major characteristics of the domain. As is now evident to the reader, I was not content with any one of the offered definitions. In fact, I do not believe that it will ever be possible to arrive at a totally satisfactory definition of the term. Terms get defined by their use and by the kinds of research issues that they summarize. Since those issues naturally shift from time to time and from field to field, it seems unlikely that a universally acceptable definition of social cognition will ever be adopted.

My definition is this entire chapter. No single sentence can adequately convey all the considerations relevant to specifying the domain of social cognition. My views evolved as I was immersed in the background readings and in the actual writing of the chapter. Shortly before beginning this background reading, I had proposed a definition of social cognition for the *Wiley Encyclopedia of Psychology* (Ostrom, in press). At that time, I was primarily concerned with the field's need to develop improved models of cognitive processes. Consequently, my definition focused on the role of cognitive processes in mediating social behavior.

While not abandoning the focus on cognitive processes, my readings in the history of social psychology (especially in regard to attitudes and person perception) and my readings in social cognition by researchers outside of the information processing tradition convinced me that the field could not advance without a realistic appraisal of social episodes. A large number of writers were explicitly discontented with an exclusive focus on cognitive processes; their reasons were varied and diverse. By grouping these reasons together under the heading of "social knowledge" they coalesced into a second foci that complemented my initial focus on cognitive process.

The field of social cognition is concerned with determining the nature of social knowledge and with specifying the cognitive processes that mediate social behavior. Research on the nature of social knowledge strives to describe events and relationships among events that influence cognitive processes and structures. It is a descriptive enterprise in which we attempt to identify the complexities inherent in the phenomena. Most of the past research in person perception (including impression formation, implicit personality theory, and attribution theory) contributes to this social knowledge foci. Research and theory on mental activity, of course,constitutes the second foci. As has been argued earlier, neither can prosper without the other.

## Why Sovereign?

The cognitive approach to understanding social behavior has always ruled over social psychology. Research practices have always favored subjective verbal responses over behavioral observations. In fact, the field might better be characterized as the study of rating scale behavior than the study of social interaction. A glance at any text book or handbook on theory in social psychology shows that cognitive theory dominates. Cognitive concepts even play central roles in other theoretical positions such as stimulus-response theory and Freudian theory. A strong case for this historical commitment by social psychologists to the cognitive approach can be found in a paper by Zajonc (1980) and so need not be developed further here.

The field of social cognition reigns sovereign for at least six reasons. It's throne is even more secure than was true for the previous cognitive orientations in social psychology.

1. Contemporary research on memory and cognition has yielded empirical findings regarding mental activity that is much more relevant to understanding social behavior than was true for previous research. In the 1940s and 1950s, social psychologists were most influenced by gestalt principles of visual perception. This can be seen in the influential textbook by Kretch and Crutchfield (1948) and in the cognitive theory chapter of the 1954 *Handbook of Social Psychology* (Scheerer, 1954). These authors borrowed liberally from research in experimental psychology and applied it to social phenomena. By 1968, however, the cognitive theory chapter focused narrowly (as did the entire field) on principles of cognitive balance and the dimensions of cognitive structure (Zajonc, 1968). It contained only a negligible amount of material from basic research in experimental psychology.

The picture now is very different for social cognition. Principles of interest to cognitive psychologists are directly pertinent to understanding the phenomena of social psychology. The cognitive theory chapter for the third edition of the *Handbook of Social Psychology* (Markus & Zajonc, in press) draws heavily on basic research in memory and cognition.

2. Cognitive processing models (e.g., Anderson, 1976; Kintsch, 1974; Wyer & Srull, 1980) offer a conceptual vocabulary that enables a wider array of social phenomena to be understood in their terms. Ostrom (1981) has identified four

characteristics that distinguish the utility of these new models from the previous cognitive approaches used by social psychologists.

In most previous social perception research, the experimenter placed severe constraints on the response modalities available to subjects. Most often, bounded rating scales were used. Current theory encourages us to look at relatively unconstrained descriptions, attributions, accounts, and other comparatively spontaneous behaviors.

Most previous theory was univariate in nature. A single response was measured by the experimenter, and it proved sufficient to test existing theory. But cognitive activity is extended in time and it is reflected in a variety of responses. The use of converging operations, then, is a direct byproduct of the social cognition orientation. Associative network theories make predictions about response time, accuracy level, item sequence in free recall, and differential error rates in forgetting. An even more important set of multiple responses should emerge when applying such models to the analysis of ongoing social behavior.

Most previous cognitive theory in social psychology has been quantitative rather than qualitative in its predictions. This derives largely from the fact that most predictions were tested on undimensional scales. Most theories adopted a "dimensional," as opposed to a "categorical," conception of psychological structure. Constructs in the areas of attitude theory, information integration theory, implicit personality theory, Baysian theory, social judgment theory, and value-expectancy theory were defined as a "point on a continuum." All these approaches overlooked the qualitative reality of social interaction and cognitive activity. Any sequential analysis of thought patterns shows a noticeable absence of undimensionality. Thoughts hop from one topic to another, with little reverence for logical consistency or thematic coherence. Often interpersonal interactions show the same apparent unpredictability. Current models of cognition allow for this qualitative variability and offer conceptual avenues to make the unpredictable understandable.

Earlier approaches to person perception ignored the role of memory in judgment. Research practices encouraged this disregard through seldom requiring subjects to rely on memory when performing person perception tasks. Most studies relied on stimulus-based rather than memory-based judgments (Lingle & Ostrom, 1979). Because of its concern with the encoding and retrieval of information, contemporary cognitive research explicitly invites a comprehensive analysis of the role of memory in judgments and other social behaviors.

The above four characteristics have not only opened up new and important problem areas within the traditional field of social perception, but they have also encouraged cognitive analyses of other problem areas in social psychology. We can expect cognitive process models to be applied in the near future to categories of social phenomena that are at present poorly understood from the cognitive point of view. The area of conformity is a prime example; other areas that can benefit are aggression, negotiation, leadership, and helping behavior.

3. It has been a long time since any research area has been so eagerly adopted by so many different fields, both within psychology and across the other social and behavioral sciences. Social cognition research is not a remote province neglected by all but social and cognitive psychologists. Research on social cognition is being conducted in most areas of psychology, including developmental, personality, clinical, industrial-organizational, educational, and community psychology. Outside of psychology, work is being conducted in communications, marketing, linguistics, and (of course) computer sciences departments. Such rapid and enthusiastic acceptance of a research area hasn't been seen since the introduction of information theory (Shannon, 1948) and control theory (Wiener, 1948). Few aspiring sovereigns in the field of psychology have enjoyed such conquests.

4. As described earlier in this chapter, it appears that social cognition is developmentally prior to nonsocial cognition. Because of the prevalence and importance of the social milieu from birth onwards, it is reasonable to assume that cognitive processes develop initially to deal with the intricate complexities of social knowledge (especially those represented in Category Four). It is these processes, these assumptions about the nature of the world, that must be later modified to accomodate nonsocial events in one's world. While principles of social cognition may apply to nonsocial knowledge, the opposite is probably not true (at least for most people). When the subjects in Heider and Simmel's (1944) study were asked to describe a moving array of geometric figures, they avoided their "object" vocabulary of shapes and motions, preferring instead the "social" vocabulary of persons, intentions, and goals.

5. Affect (and its allied concepts such as emotion, mood, and motivation) is an integral constituent of human social behavior. Yet it had been relatively ignored in past years by researchers in social and cognitive psychology. Some of the more prominent efforts did not lead to much of an advance in the understanding of affect, either as a unique system or as a system related to cognitive processes. Work on cognitive balance regarded "affective" bonds as possessing the same cognitive features as did "unit formation" bonds. Thus, affect was treated as just another form of cognition. The tripartite approach toward attitudes viewed affect as an attitude component, and examined the correlation between it and the cognitive and conative (or behavioral) components. But again, no attempt was made to identify the unique conceptual features that characterized affect.

The social cognition perspective has changed all this. A number of different researchers have recently attacked the affect-cognition problem in a programatic manner. Investigators have gone beyond simply looking at the correlation between affect and cognition. The real problem is one of understanding the interdependencies that exist between the two. How does affective arousal influence cognitive processing and how do cognitive mechanisms influence affective reactions? Real advances (along with new controversies) have been made on this problem, as can be seen in such sources as Bower (1981), Cacioppo and Petty (1981), Clark and Fiske (1982), and Lazarus (1982). The chapter by Isen in Volume 3 of this *Handbook* reviews the work in this area.

6. In 1948 MacCorqudale and Meehl offered a distinction between two categories of theory. An *intervening variable* is a theoretical variable that need have no potential basis in physical reality. It can be simply a verbal or mathematical summary that facilitates the specification of predictable relationships. Most past theorizing in social perception (including integration theory, implicit personality theory, and attribution theories) would be categorized as intervening variables.

MacCorqudale and Meehl's (1948) other category of theory was the *hypothetical construct*. The theoretical terms and processes in this cateogry of theory potentially are grounded in physical reality. For example, Hebb (1949) was interested in coordinating the conceptual nature of mental structures with existing knowledge about the neural characteristics of the brain.

One advantage of associative network theories, with their nodes and pathways, is that these primative constructs are potentially amenable to being linked to the physiological structure of the central nervous system (e.g., Arnold, in press; Donchin, in press; Hinton & Anderson, 1981; Weingartner & Parker, in press). Work is being done on integrating models of learning and motor control with research on biomechanics and neural control (e.g., Schmidt, 1982) and also relating them to biological constraints on learning (Johnston, 1981). I have no doubt that a grand integration of the psychological with the physiological is in the far distant future, but like a true sovereign, the field of social cognition has boundless aspirations.

## ACKNOWLEDGMENTS

The preparation of this chapter was facilitated by a contract from the Organizational Effectiveness Research Program, Office of Naval Research, United States Navy (Code 452) under control number N00014-81-K-0112, NR 170-927. I am grateful to Trish Devine, Reid Hastie, and Doug McCann for their helpful comments on an earlier draft of this chapter and to Jerry Ginsburg for the many spirited discussions we have had on the issues covered in this chapter.

## REFERENCES

Abelson, R. P., & Kanouse, D. E. The subjective acceptance of verbal generalizations. In S. Feldman (Ed.), *Cognitive consistency: Motivational antecedents and behavioral consequences.* New York: Academic Press, 1966.

Anderson, J. R. *Language, memory, and thought.* Hillsdale, N.J.: Lawrence Erlbaum Associates, 1976.

Arnold, M. B. *Memory and the brain.* Hillsdale, N.J.: Lawrence Erlbaum Associates, in press.

Asch, S. E. Forming impressions of personality. *Journal of Abnormal and Social Psychology,* 1946, *41,* 258–290.

Baldwin, J. M. *Thought and things.* London: Swann Sonnenschein, 1906.

Baron, R. M. Contrasting approaches to social knowing: An ecological perspective. *Personality and Social Psychology Bulletin,* 1980, *6,* 591–600.

Bower, G. H. Mood and memory. *American Psychologist,* 1981, *36,* 129–148.

Brenner, M. (Ed.). *The structure of action.* New York: St. Martin's Press, 1980.

Bretherton, I., McNew, S., & Beeghly-Smith, M. Early person knowledge as expressed in gestural and verbal communications: When do infants acquire a "Theory of Mind"? In M. Lamb & L. Sherrod (Eds.), *Infant social cognition: Empirical and theoretical considerations.* Hillsdale, N.J.: Lawrence Erlbaum Associates, 1981.

Bruner, J. S., & Tagiuri, R. The perception of people. In G. Lindzey (Ed.), *Handbook of Social Psychology,* (Vol. 2). Cambridge, Mass.: Addison-Wesley, 1954.

Cacioppo, J. T., & Petty, R. E. Electromyograms as measures of extent and affectivity of information processing. *American Psychologist,* 1981, *36,* 441–456.

Cantor, N., & Mischel, W. Prototypes in person perception. In L. Berkowitz (Ed.), *Advances in experimental social psychology* (Vol. 12). New York: Academic Press, 1979.

Carver, C. S., & Scheier, M. F. Control theory: A useful conceptual framework for personality-social, clinical, and health psychology. *Psychological Bulletin,* 1982, *92,* 111–135.

Chandler, M. J. Social cognition: A selective review of current research. In W. Overton & J. Gallagher (Eds.), *Knowledge and development.* New York: Plenum Press, 1977.

Clark, H. H. Language use and language users. In G. Lindzey & E. Aronson (Eds.), *Handbook of social psychology* (3rd Ed.). Reading, Mass.: Addison-Wesley, in press.

Clark, M. S., & Fiske, S. T. (Eds.). *Affect and cognition.* Hillsdale, N.J.: Lawrence Erlbaum Associates, 1982.

Cottrell, N. B. Heider's structural balance principle as a conceptual rule. *Journal of Personality and Social Psychology,* 1975, *31,* 713–720.

Damon, W. Exploring children's social cognition on two fronts. In J. Flavell & L. Ross (Eds.), *Social cognitive development: Frontiers and possible futures.* Cambridge: Cambridge University Press, 1981.

Davis, D. Determinants of responsiveness in dyadic interactions. In W. Ickes & E. Knowles (Eds.), *Personality, roles, and social behavior.* New York: Springer-Verlag, 1982.

Davis, D., & Holtgraves, T. *Perception of unresponsive others: Attributions, attraction, understandability, and memory for their utterances.* Unpublished manuscript, University of Nevada, Reno, 1982.

Davis, D., & Perkowitz, W. T. Consequences of responsiveness in dyadic interaction: Effects of probability of response and proportion of content-related responses on interpersonal attraction. *Journal of Personality and Social Psychology,* 1979, *37,* 534–551.

DeCharms, R. *Personal causation: The internal affective determinants of behavior.* New York: Academic Press, 1968.

Donchin, E. (Ed.). *Cognitive psychophysiology.* Hillsdale, N.J.: Lawrence Erlbaum Associates, in press.

Eiser, J. R., & Stroebe, W. *Categorization and social judgment.* London: Academic Press, 1972.

Evarts, E. V. Brain mechanisms of movement. *Scientific American,* 1979, *241,* 164–179.

Farr, R. The social origins of the human mind: A historical note. In J. Forgas (Ed.), *Social cognition: Perspectives on everyday understanding.* London: Academic Press, 1981.

Festinger, L. A. A theory of social comparison processes. *Human Relations,* 1954, *7,* 117–140.

Fiske, S. T., & Taylor, S. E. *Social cognition.* Reading, MA: Addison-Wesley, in press.

Flavell, J. H. The developmental inferences about others. In T. Mischel (Ed.), *Understanding other persons.* Totowa, N.J.: Rowman and Littlefield, 1974.

Flavell, J. H., & Ross, L. (Eds.). *Social cognitive development: Frontiers and possible futures.* Cambridge: Cambridge University Press, 1981.

Forgas, J. P. Epilogue: Everyday understanding and social cognition. In J. Forgas (Ed.), *Social cognition: Perspectives on everyday understanding.* New York: Academic Press, 1981a.

Forgas, J. P. What is social about social cognition. In J. Forgas (Ed.), *Social cognition: Perspectives on everyday understanding.* London: Academic Press, 1981b.

Gelman, R., & Spelke, E. The development of thoughts about animate and inanimate objects: Implications for research on social cognition. In J. Flavell & L. Ross (Eds.), *Social cognitive development: Frontiers and possible futures.* Cambridge: Cambridge University Press, 1981.

Gibson, J. J. *The ecological approach to visual perception.* Boston: Houghton Mifflin, 1979.

Gilson, C., & Abelson, R. P. The subjective use of inductive evidence. *Journal of Personality and Social Psychology,* 1965, *2,* 301–310.

Ginsburg, G. P. Situated action: An emerging paradigm. In L. Wheeler (Ed.), *Review of personality and social psychology,* Vol. 1. Beverly Hills, CA: Sage, 1980.

Glick, J. Cognition and social cognition: An introduction. In J. Glick & K. Clarke-Stewart (Eds.), *The development of social understanding.* New York: Gardner Press, 1978.

Glick, J., & Clarke-Stewart, K. A. (Eds.). *The development of social understanding.* New York: Gardner Press, 1978.

Golinkoff, R. M., & Harding, C. G. *The development of causality: The distinction between animates and inanimates.* Paper presented at the International Conference on Infant Studies, New Haven, April 1980.

Gollob, H. F. The subject-object-verb approach to social cognition. *Psychological Review,* 1974, *81,* 286–321.

Hamilton, D. L. Cognitive representations of persons. In E. Higgins, C. Herman, & M. Zanna (Eds.), *Social cognition: The Ontario symposium,* Vol. 1. Hillsdale, N.J.: Lawrence Erlbaum Associates, 1981.

Hamilton, D. L., Katz, L., & Leirer, V. Organizational processes in impression formation. In R. Hastie, T. Ostrom, D. Hamilton, E. Ebbesen, R. Wyer & D. Carlton (Eds.), *Person memory: The cognitive basis of social perception.* Hillsdale, N.J.: Lawrence Erlbaum Associates, 1980.

Harré, R. The ethogenic approach: Theory and practice. In L. Berkowitz (Ed.), *Advances in experimental social psychology,* Vol. 10. New York: Academic Press, 1977.

Harré, R., & Secord, P. F. *The explanation of social behavior.* Oxford: Blackwell, 1972.

Hastie, R., & Carlston, D. Theoretical issues in person memory. In R. Hastie, T. Ostrom, E. Ebbesen, R. Wyer, D. Hamilton, & D. Carlston (Eds.), *Person memory: The cognitive basis of social perception.* Hillsdale, N.J.: Lawrence Erlbaum Associates, 1980.

Hastie, R., Ostrom, T., Ebbesen, E., Wyer, R., Hamilton, D., & Carlston, D. (Eds.), *Person memory: The cognitive basis of social perception.* Hillsdale, N.J.: Lawrence Erlbaum Associates, 1980.

Hastorf, A. H., Schneider, D. J., & Polefka, J. *Person perception.* Reading, MA: Addison-Wesley, 1970.

Hebb, D. O. *Organization of behavior.* New York, Wiley, 1949.

Heider, F. *The psychology of interpersonal relations.* New York: Wiley, 1958.

Heider, F., & Simmel, M. An experimental study of apparent behavior. *Americal Journal of Psychology,* 1944, *57,* 243–259.

Higgins, E. T. The "communication game": Its implications for social cognition and persuasion. In E. Higgins, C. Herman, & M. Zanna (Eds.), *Social cognition: The Ontario symposium,* Vol. 1. Hillsdale, N.J.: Lawrence Erlbaum Associates, 1981.

Higgins, E. T. Social cognition and communication. Seventh Annual Interdisciplinary Conference, Jackson Hole, WY, January, 1982.

Higgins, E. T., Kuiper, N. A., & Olson, J. M. Social cognition: A need to get personal. In E. Higgins, C. Herman, & M. Zanna (Eds.). *Social cognition: The Ontario symposium,* Vol. 1. Hillsdale, N.J.: Lawrence Erlbaum Associates, 1981.

Hinton, G. E., & Anderson, J. A. (Eds.). *Parallel models of associative memory.* Hillsdale, N.J.: Lawrence Erlbaum Associates, 1981.

Hoffman, M. L. Perspectives on the difference between understanding people and understanding things: The role of affect. In J. Flavell & L. Ross (Eds.), *Social cognitive development: Frontiers and possible futures.* Cambridge: Cambridge University Press, 1981.

Isen, A. M., & Hastorf, A. H. Some perspectives on cognitive social psychology. In A. Hastorf & A. Isen (Eds.), *Cognitive social psychology.* New York: Elsevier/North-Holland, 1982.

Ittelson, W. H., & Slack, C. W. The perception of persons as visual objects. In R. Taguiri & L. Petrullo (Eds.), *Person perception and interpersonal behavior.* Stanford, CA: Stanford University Press, 1958.

Johnston, T. D. Contrasting approaches to a theory of learning. *Behavioral and Brain Sciences,* 1981, *4,* 125–173.

Karpf, F. B. *American social psychology: Its origins, development, and European background.* (First published 1932, New York: McGraw-Hill) Dubuque, Iowa: Brown Reprints, 1971.

Kelley, H. H. Attribution theory in social psychology. In D. Levine (Ed.), *Nebraska symposium on motivation.* Lincoln: University of Nebraska Press, 1967.

Kelso, J. A. S. Contrasting perspectives on order and regulation in movement. In J. Long & A. Baddelay (Eds.), *Attention and performance IX.* Hillsdale, N.J.: Lawrence Erlbaum Associates, 1981.

Kintsch, W. *The representation of meaning in memory.* Hillsdale, N.J.: Lawrence Erlbaum Associates, 1974.

Kosslyn, S. M., & Kagan, J. "Concrete thinking" and the development of social cognition. In J. Flavell & L. Ross (Eds.), *Social cognitive development: Frontiers and possible futures.* Cambridge: Cambridge University Press, 1981.

Kretch, D. Psychological theory and social psychology. In H. Helson (Ed.), *Theoretical foundations in psychology.* New York: Van Nostrand, 1951.

Kretch, D., & Crutchfield, R. S. *Theory and problem of social psychology.* New York: McGraw-Hill, 1948.

Lamb, M. E., & Sherrod, L. R. (Eds.). *Infant social cognition: Empirical and theoretical considerations.* Hillsdale, N.J.: Lawrence Erlbaum Associates, 1981.

Lazarus, R. S. Thoughts on the relations between emotion and cognition. *American Psychologist,* 1982, *37,* 1019–1024.

Lingle, J. H., & Ostrom, T. M. Retrieval selectivity in memory-based impression judgments. *Journal of Personality and Social Psychology,* 1979, *37,* 180–194.

Lock, A. *Action, gesture and symbol: The emergence of language.* New York: Academic Press, 1978.

MacCorqudale, K., & Meehl, P. E. One distinction between hypothetical constructs and intervening variables. *Psychological Review,* 1948, *55,* 95–107.

MacLeod, R. B. The place of phenomenological analysis in social psychological theory. In J. H. Rohrer & M. Sherif (Eds.), *Social psychology at the cross-roads.* New York: Harper, 1951.

Markus, H., & Zajonc, R. B. The cognitive perspective in social psychology. In G. Lindzey & E. Aronson (Eds.), *Handbook of social psychology,* 3rd ed. Reading, MA: Addison-Wesley, in press.

McArthur, L. Z. Illusory causation and illusory correlation: Two epistemological accounts. *Personality and Social Psychology Bulletin,* 1980, *6,* 507–519.

Mead, G. H. *Mind, self, and society.* Chicago: University of Chicago Press, 1934.

Miller, G. A., Galanter, E., & Pribram, K. *Plans and the structure of behavior.* New York: Holt, Rinehart, & Winston, 1960.

Mischel, T. (Ed.). *Understanding other persons.* Totowa, N.J.: Rowman and Littlefield, 1974.

Mischel, W. On the interface of cognition and personality: Beyond the person-situation debate. *American Psychologist,* 1979, *34,* 740–754.

Mischel, W. Personality and cognition: Something borrowed, something new? In N. Cantor & J. Kihlstrom (Eds.), *Personality, cognition, and social interaction.* Hillsdale, N.J.: Lawrence Erlbaum Associates, 1981.

Neisser, U. *Cognition and reality.* San Francisco: W. H. Freeman, 1976.

Neisser, U. On "Social Knowing." *Personality and Social Psychology Bulletin,* 1980, *6,* 601–605.

Nelson, K. Social cognition in a script framework. In J. Flavell & L. Ross (Eds.), *Social cognitive development: Frontiers and possible futures.* Cambridge: Cambridge University Press, 1981.

Newell, A. Production systems: Models of control structures. In W. G. Chase (Ed.), *Visual information processing.* New York: Academic Press, 1973.

Nisbett, R. E., & Borgida, E. Attribution and the psychology of prediction. *Journal of Personality and Social Psychology,* 1975, *32,* 932–943.

Norman, D. A. Twelve issues for cognitive science. In D. Norman (Ed.), *Perspectives on cognitive science.* Norwood, N.J.: Ablex, 1981.

Norman, D. A., & Rumelhart, D. E. Memory and knowledge. In D. Norman & D. Rumelhart (Eds.), *Explorations in cognition.* San Francisco: Freeman, 1975.

Ostrom, T. M. The bogus pipeline: A new *Ignis Fatuus? Psychological Bulletin,* 1973, *79,* 252–259.

Ostrom, T. M. *Cognitive representation of impressions.* Paper presented at the meeting of the American Psychological Association, Chicago, September, 1975.

Ostrom, T. M. Theoretical perspectives in the analysis of cognitive responses. In R. Petty, T. Ostrom, & T. Brock (Eds.), *Cognitive responses in persuasion.* Hillsdale, N.J.: Lawrence Erlbaum Associates, 1981.

Ostrom, T. M. Social cognition. In R. J. Corsini (Ed.), *Wiley encyclopedia of psychology.* New York: Wiley, in press.

Ostrom, T. M., Pryor, J. B., & Simpson, D. D. The organization of social information. In E. Higgins, C. Herman, & M. Zanna (Eds.), *Social cognition: The Ontario symposium,* Vol. I. Hillsdale, N.J.: Lawrence Erlbaum Associates, 1981.

Ostrom, T. M., & Upshaw, H. S. Psychological perspective and attitude change. In A. Greenwald, T. Brock, & T. Ostrom (Eds.), *Psychological foundations of attitudes.* New York: Academic Press, 1968.

Overton, W., & Gallagher, J. (Eds.), *Knowledge and development.* New York: Plenum Press, 1977.

Peak, H. Psychological structure and person perception. In R. Tagiuri & L. Petrullo (Eds.), *Person perception and interpersonal behavior.* Stanford, CA: Stanford University Press, 1958.

Pepitone, A. Lessons from the history of social psychology. *American Psychologist,* 1981, *36,* 972–985.

Piaget, J. *The origins of intelligence in children.* New York: Norton, 1952.

Piaget, J. *The construction of reality in the child.* New York: Basic Books, 1954.

Repp, B. H. Phonetic trading relations and context effects: New experimental evidence for a speech mode of perception. *Psychological Bulletin,* 1982, *92,* 81–110.

Roloff, M. E., & Berger, C. R. Social cognition and communication: An introduction. In M. Roloff & C. Berger (Eds.), *Social cognition and communication.* Beverly Hills, CA: Sage, 1982.

Sampson, E. E. Cognitive psychology as ideology. *American Psychologist,* 1981, *36,* 730–743.

Scheerer, M. Cognitive theory. In G. Lindzey (Ed.), *Handbook of social psychology* (Vol. 1). Reading, MA: Addison-Wesley, 1954.

Schmidt, R. A. A schema theory of discrete motor skill learning. *Psychological Review,* 1975, *82,* 225–260.

Schmidt, R. A. *Motor control and learning: A behavioral emphasis.* Champaign, IL: Human Kinetics, 1982.

Schneider, D., Hastorf, A., & Ellsworth, P. *Person perception,* 2nd ed. Reading, MA: Addison-Wesley, 1979.

Shank, R. C., & Abelson, R. P. *Scripts, plans, goals, and understanding: An inquiry into human knowledge structures.* Hillsdale, N.J.: Lawrence Erlbaum Associates, 1977.

Shannon, C. E.  A mathematical theory of communication. *Bell Systems Technical Journal*, 1948, *27*, 379–423, 623–656.

Shantz, C. U.  The development of social cognition. In M. E. Hetherington (Ed.), *Review of child development research* (Vol. 5). Chicago: University of Chicago Press, 1975.

Shantz, C. U.  Thinking about people thinking about people. *Contemporary Psychology*, 1982, *27*, 376–377.

Shaw, M. E., & Costanzo, P. R.  *Theories of social psychology*, 2nd ed. New York: McGraw-Hill, 1982.

Sherif, M., & Cantril, H.  The psychology of attitudes: I. *Psychological Review*, 1945, *52*, 295–319.

Sherif, M., & Cantril, H.  The psychology of attitudes: II. *Psychological Review*, 1946, *53*, 1–24.

Sherrod, L. R.  Issues in cognitive-perceptual development: The special case of social stimuli. In M. Lamb & L. Sherrod (Eds.), *Infant social cognition: Empirical and theoretical considerations*. Hillsdale, N.J.: Lawrence Erlbaum Associates, 1981.

Sherrod, L. R., & Lamb, M. E.  Infant social cognition: An introduction. In M. Lamb & L. Sherrod (Eds.), *Infant social cognition: Empricial and theoretical considerations*. Hillsdale, N.J.: Lawrence Erlbaum Associates, 1981.

Shields, M. M.  The child as psychologist: Construing the social world. In A. Lock (Ed.), *Action, gesture and symbol*. New York: Academic Press, 1978.

Simon, H. A.  Discussion: Cognition and social behavior. In J. Carroll & J. Payne (Eds.), *Cognition and social behavior*. Hillsdale, N.J.: Lawrence Erlbaum Associates, 1976.

Tagiuri, R.  Introduction. In R. Tagiuri & L. Petrullo (Eds.), *Person perception and interpersonal behavior*. Stanford, CA: Stanford University Press, 1958.

Tagiuri, R.  Person perception. In G. Lindzey & E. Aronson (Eds.), *Handbook of social psychology*, 2nd ed. (Vol. 3). Reading, MA: Addison-Wesley, 1969.

Taylor, S. E.  Developing a cognitive social psychology. In J. Carroll & J. Payne (Eds.), *Cognition and social behavior*. Hillsdale, N.J.: Lawrence Erlbaum Associates, 1976.

Taylor, S. E.  The interface of cognitive and social psychology. In J. Harvey (Ed.), *Cognition, social behavior, and the environment*. Hillsdale, N.J.: Lawrence Erlbaum Associates, 1981.

Thibaut, J. W., & Kelley, H. H.  *The social psychology of groups*. New York: Wiley, 1959.

Thomas, W. I., & Znaniecki, F.  *The Polish peasant in Europe and America*, Vol. 1. Boston: Badger, 1918.

Vallacher, R. R., & Wegnar, D. M.  *A theory of action identification*. Hillsdale, N.J.: Lawrence Erlbaum Associates, in press.

Weary, G., Swanson, H., Harvey, J. H., & Yarkin, K. L.  A molar approach to social knowing. *Personality and Social Psychology Bulletin*, 1980, *6*, 574–581.

Wegner, D. M., & Vallacher, R. R.  *Implicit psychology: An introduction to social cognition*. New York: Oxford University Press, 1977.

Weingartner, H., & Parker, E. S. (Eds.), *Memory consolidation: Psychobiology of cognition*. Hillsdale, N.J.: Lawrence Erlbaum Associates, in press.

Wertsch, J. V. (Ed.).  *The concept of activity in Soviet psychology*. Armonk, N.Y.: Sharpe, 1981.

West, S. C., & Wicklund, R. A.  *A primer of social psychological theory*. Monterey, CA: Brooks/Cole, 1980.

Wiener, N.  *Cybernetics: Control and communication in the animal and machine*. Cambridge, MA: MIT Press, 1948.

Wilder, D. A., & Cooper, W. E.  Categorization into groups: Consequences for social perception and attribution. In J. Harvey, W. Ickes, & R. Kidd (Eds.), *New directions in attribution theory research*, (Vol. III). Hillsdale, N.J.: Lawrence Erlbaum Associates, 1981.

Winograd, T.  Frame representations and the declarative-procedural controversy. In D. Bobrow & A. Collins (Eds.), *Representation and understanding*. New York: Academic Press, 1975.

Wyer, R. S., & Carlston, D. E.  *Social cognition, inference, and attribution*. Hillsdale, N.J.: Lawrence Erlbaum Associates, 1979.

Wyer, R. S., & Podeschi, D. M. The acceptance of generalizations about persons, objects, and events. In R. Revlin & R. Mayer (Eds.), *Human reasoning*. Washington, D.C.: V. H. Winston, 1978.

Wyer, R. S., & Srull, T. K. The processing of social stimulus information: A conceptual integration. In R. Hastie, T. Ostrom, E. Ebbesen, R. Wyer, D. Hamilton, & D. Carlston (Eds.), *Person memory: The cognitive basis of social perception*. Hillsdale, N.J.: Lawrence Erlbaum Associates, 1980.

Zajonc, R. B. The process of cognitive tuning in communication. *Journal of Abnormal and Social Psychology*, 1960, *61*, 159–167.

Zajonc, R. B. Cognitive theories in social psychology. In G. Lindzey & E. Aronson (Eds.), *The handbook of social psychology* (2nd Ed.). Reading, MA: Addison-Wesley, 1968.

Zajonc, R. B. Cognition and social cognition: A historical perspective. In L. Festinger (Ed.), *Retrospectives on social psychology*. New York: Oxford University Press, 1980.

# 2 Information Processing and Social Cognition

Keith J. Holyoak
Peter C. Gordon
*University of Michigan*

**Contents**

## INTRODUCTION

### How Does Social Cognition Relate to Cognitive Psychology?

The mutual influence of social psychology and the information-processing paradigm of cognitive psychology has intensified dramatically over the past decade. The resulting new subdiscipline—social cognition—now has its own distinct

39

identity. The present *Handbook* testifies to the continuing promise of this interdisciplinary interaction, which nonetheless is not without critics (Zajonc, 1980a). Intellectual exchanges between scientific disciplines are cultural phenomena; like any meeting between two cultures, that between social and cognitive psychology provides both opportunities and challenges. When one culture influences another, its beliefs and customs are typically not so much borrowed as reconstructed in the context of the adopting culture. But in some cases the reconstruction may be incomplete, leaving an awkward graft rather than a natural extension. In addition, the most salient elements of each culture may be especially beguiling to the other, while other elements, less obvious but perhaps of greater potential value, may remain unnoticed. Often the commerce has an asymmetric impact, as one culture increasingly adopts the customs of the other. In such cases the adopting culture may neglect important aspects of its own heritage, while the other may miss out on valuable insights it could have received.

What is the proper relationship between social and cognitive psychology? It is tempting, especially for a cognitive psychologist, to view social cognition as a derivative area in which general principles of cognition are applied to a specific domain. This view has a degree of validity, since social cognition is in part defined by a particular subject matter, the psychological mechanisms involved in human social interaction. Furthermore, as its name implies, the mechanisms of central concern are cognitive processes. In this context it would be a parsimonious outcome to find that cognitive principles that apply in other domains can account for social phenomena as well. Without strong supporting evidence, a cognitive psychologist is likely to be skeptical of claims that social stimuli or behaviors deserve some special theoretical status. Social stimuli may well tend to be particularly complex, interesting, and memorable; however, the cognitive psychologist will favor explanations of such properties in terms of broader models of perception, attention, and memory.

But at the same time, social cognition is clearly more than a subarea of cognitive psychology. As its name equally implies, social cognition is also a part of social psychology, from which it inherits several distinctive features. First, social cognition is concerned with the *interactions* between persons, with the mutual adaptation of each individual to others. In contrast, present-day cognitive psychology is heavily biased toward the study of single individuals performing cognitive tasks in social isolation. This is not a principled limitation of cognitive psychology (group problem-solving and decision-making remain worthwhile if neglected areas of investigation), but a pragmatic one. Most cognitive psychologists feel they face formidable complexity in studying individual processing, and for the time being wish to leave aside the extra difficulties posed by interpersonal interactions. However, from the social perspective this suggests that current cognitive models will not provide an adequate account of the interactive aspects of social cognition.

A second feature which social cognition derives from social psychology is a direct concern with *behavior*—with the actions people take in real-world social contexts. This feature leads to several important consequences. It follows that social cognition has especially strong natural ties to the allied disciplines of cultural anthropology and sociology. In addition, research on social cognition (to the extent it is in fact directed at social behavior that occurs outside the laboratory as well as in it) has more transparent ecological validity than does most cognitive research. Cognitive psychologists are concerned with mental processes that actually (or even potentially) underlie human performance. The theoretical emphasis is typically on the mental processes themselves, rather than on any particular behavior that may result from them. This emphasis on general cognitive processes, coupled with a high regard for experimental rigor, often leads to experiments in which the actual observed behavior (e.g., button pressing) is quite incidental to the basic theoretical questions. The dangers inherent in cognitive paradigms are well-known. A great deal of research may be devoted to explorations of particular mental processes or structures, with relatively little investigation of their behavioral functions. Work on iconic memory, for example, seems open to such a criticism. In some cases the emphasis on general mental processes may degenerate into compulsively detailed modeling of particular laboratory tasks. Social cognition, by focusing on naturally occurring behaviors, should more readily avoid such problems.

Finally, its relationship with social psychology implies that social cognition should be concerned with the relative roles of cognitive and non-cognitive factors that govern social behavior, where non-cognitive factors would include emotional reactions, unconscious motivations, and so on. We do not mean to imply that the boundary between cognitive and non-cognitive factors is clearcut; in fact, it is likely that cognitive processes are intertwined with emotions and motivations (Beck, 1976; Bower, 1981). However, in one way or another a complete theory of social cognition will need to take account of a wider range of mental mechanisms than have been emphasized by mainstream cognitive psychology.

In addition to its input from social psychology, social cognition has been heavily influenced by personality psychology, which emphasizes the study of individual differences. While cognitive psychology has not ignored individual differences in cognitive processing (e.g., Hunt, Frost, & Lunneborg, 1973), they have typically been downplayed. In contrast, individual differences in social cognition have begun to receive careful attention (e.g., Markus & Smith, 1982; Snyder, 1979).

These individuating aspects of social cognition—concern with interpersonal interaction, naturally occurring behaviors, interactions between cognitive and non-cognitive processes, and the study of individual differences—must be kept in mind when evaluating the interchange with cognitive psychology. There is a real danger that the influence of cognitive psychology will lead social psychologists away from these central research issues. Indeed, a cursory survey of current research in social cognition suggests that the modal experiment involves socially-isolated subjects performing standard laboratory tasks from which non-cognitive factors and individual differences are excluded as much as possible—in other words, the modal cognitive experiment with social stimuli. To the extent this picture is accurate (and there are certainly notable exceptions), it suggests that social psychologists need to attempt a more radical restructuring of information-processing psychology in the context of social research. This is not to say that the above "modal experiment" is not valuable; it may be entirely justified to study individual social cognition as an essential step toward eventual understanding of social interactions. But it is important for research in social cognition to keep sight of its heritage from social and personality psychology. Not only are concepts such as mutual adaptation and interactions with non-cognitive mechanisms central to theories of social cognition, in more general forms they must eventually be incorporated into theories in other cognitive domains. There is good reason to hope that the intellectual commerce between social and cognitive psychology will benefit both. By reconstructing cognitive principles within a social context, social cognition has the potential to be not just an application of cognitive psychology, but part of its leading theoretical edge.

## What Does Cognitive Psychology Have to Offer?

For the remainder of this chapter we will leave the above caveats aside, and discuss the potential contributions of current cognitive psychology to social cognition. Why should social psychologists be interested in the models and paradigms of cognitive psychology? The basic answer is straightforward—there is widespread conviction that social behavior is heavily influenced by cognitive processes. People seem to behave as they do toward one another because of their beliefs, because of the ways in which they categorize their world and the people in it, and because of the strategies that guide their decisions. As Zajonc (1980a) has emphasized, social psychology has long been a cognitive psychology, and was in fact a refuge for cognitive ideas during the decades in which such concepts were eclipsed in experimental psychology under the behaviorist pall. It is therefore only natural that the emergence of the cognitive information-processing paradigm as the dominant force within human experimental psychology should attract the attention of social psychologists.

However, cognitive psychology has not remained static over its two decades of existence, and it is probably more than coincidental that the rise of social cognition over the past decade as an identifiable subdiscipline parallels important developments within cognitive psychology. It may be useful to sketch in broad strokes the cognitive psychology of circa 1970, and to compare it with the discipline as it appears in the early 1980s. (For a discussion of the intellectual roots of cognitive psychology, see Lachman, Lachman & Butterfield, 1979).

In 1970 the dominant area of cognitive psychology was memory, and more specifically, memory for "episodes" or events that the person had experienced

(Tulving, 1972). In 1968 Atkinson and Shiffrin had presented a conceptual integration of encoding, storage and retrieval processes, which stressed distinctions among various structural components of the memory system, particularly the short-term and long-term memory stores. The Atkinson and Shiffrin model emphasized serial processing, and hence was complemented by Sternberg's (1966) development of the additive-factors method for analyzing reaction-time data within a serial-stage framework, and his strikingly successful applications of the method to experiments on short-term item recognition. The serial-stage view of cognition was coupled with what in retrospect seem to be a rather restricted set of major research paradigms. Short-term memory was primarily investigated in the context of Sternberg's "memory scanning" procedures, while studies of long-term memory typically used various rote-learning tasks (e.g., paired-associate learning) adapted from the earlier verbal-learning tradition in experimental psychology.

The more recent developments in cognitive psychology are best characterized as scientific evolution rather than revolution. (For a recent overview of the field see Glass, Holyoak, & Santa, 1979.) Two types of intellectual forces effected the changes. First, there were serious direct attacks on the core theoretical models of the times. Craik and Lockhart (1972; Craik & Tulving, 1975) criticized the stage conception of memory, and began to develop a "levels of processing" framework that stressed the importance of qualitative distinctions among memory codes. Strictly serial models of information processing came to be viewed as unduly restrictive even in apparently elementary tasks, and more flexible parallel-processing models were proposed (McClelland, 1979). Second, and perhaps more importantly, the domain of mainstream cognitive psychology was greatly extended, so that many of the central issues of the previous decade faded toward the periphery. The levels of processing framework was both revised (Jacoby & Craik, 1979) and criticized (Baddeley, 1978; Nelson, 1977), and most current theorists accept some type of distinction between working memory and long-term memory. However, issues related to memory stores no longer seem as basic as they once did. Cognitive research has fanned out into areas such as semantic memory, text processing, scene perception, spatial representation, and motor performance. Traditional areas such as attention and perception have been explored vigorously, and previously tangential areas such as problem solving and decision-making have been drawn into the mainstream of the field.

The past decade has been a time of ferment within cognitive psychology, during which researchers have tried to open up new directions for investigation, rather than to pursue a small number of specific paradigms. While some experimental procedures (such as the lexical decision task introduced by Meyer & Schvaneveldt, 1971, 1976) are used extensively, they are more often used as tools to address a wider range of theoretical questions (e.g., Fischler, 1977). These developments have for several reasons fostered closer ties with social psychology. A growing wariness of task-bound modeling has motivated researchers interested in basic cognitive theory to closely examine real-world cognitive tasks, such as reading, typing, route-finding, and expert problem solving. In this context the issues of social cognition offer the twin attractions of ecological importance and realistic complexity. In addition, as will be elaborated in the rest of this chapter (and indeed this *Handbook*), many of the major themes of current cognitive psychology appear to be directly related to aspects of social cognition. Such themes include network-model approaches to long-term memory, schema models, natural categorization, analog representation, the acquisition of knowledge structures, unconscious and automatic cognitive processes, and intuitive reasoning.

## Overview

In the remainder of this chapter we will explore a number of such themes in more detail. Our choice of themes is not meant to be exhaustive, and is doubtless rather eclectic. We will touch relatively lightly on some areas that will receive more detailed discussion in subsequent chapters, and emphasize some areas that will not. Some of the themes to be discussed are already focal points of interaction between social and cognitive psychology, but have yet to be fully exploited; others have received less attention in the context of social cognition, but strike us as promising candidates for future exploration.

The remainder of this chapter is divided into four major sections. The first section sets the stage for those that follow by providing an overview of current conceptions of mental representation. The structure of categories is discussed in some detail, emphasizing similarities and differences between object and social categories. Since models of categorization developed in cognitive psychology have already had considerable impact within social cognition, this topic permits an illustrative critique of a social-psychological application of theoretical concepts taken from cognitive psychology.

The subsequent sections pursue a variety of themes related to the mental representation of social knowledge. The second section deals with mechanisms by which complex knowledge structures may be learned. The final two sections then deal with specific types of representation. The third section is concerned with the potential roles of spatial representations and reference points in social cognition. The fourth section, which examines the nature and functions of affective and motoric knowledge, includes a critique of recent discussions of the relationship between affect and cognition.

## THE STRUCTURE OF SOCIAL KNOWLEDGE

### Issues Concerning Mental Representation

One consequence of the broadening of the mainstream of cognitive psychology is that the field seems less unified. Indeed, the immediate prospects for an overarching theory may even have receded over the past decade. But if there is any current theme that serves as an integrative framework, it is the concept of knowledge structures or *schemas*. Schemas are integrated "packets" of information that can be used to construct *mental models* of particular objects or situations. A mental model can be viewed as an organized internal representaion of aspects of a world, including (perhaps) a representation of the individual cognizer. A model serves as a representation by virtue of some systematic mapping between elements of the model and of a world. We say *a* world rather than *the* world because people can readily conceive of worlds which do not and perhaps never will exist (the cognitive ability that underlies counterfactual reasoning).

The concept of mental representations, which underlies such notions as "schema" and "mental model," raises a variety of thorny issues. An important distinction can be drawn between the *content* of a representation and its *code,* or *format* (Kosslyn, 1981; see Glass et al., 1979, Chapter 1 for an introductory exposition). The distinction is close to that between the semantics and syntax of a language: the content of a representation is its meaning, while its format is defined by the rules of formation that determine the set of possible representations. Different representational formats can be viewed as alternative "languages of thought" (Fodor, 1975), which can be used to store information and construct mental models. The nature, number, and identifiability of mental formats has been the focus of a long debate in cognitive psychology (Anderson, 1978; Kosslyn, 1981; Kosslyn & Pomerantz, 1977; Pylyshyn, 1973; Pylyshyn, 1981), which has generated fairly constant warmth and occasional flickers of light. Anderson (1978) has advanced the extreme view that models of mental representation are inherently indeterminate. Since Anderson's arguments depend upon the rejection of such standard heuristics of science as broadening the relevant data base and attending to constraints of parsimony, there is in fact no reason to suppose that the identification of representational formats is impossible in principle (Hayes-Roth, 1979; Pylyshyn, 1979). This is not to deny, however, that the task may be extremely difficult in practice.

A major source of the apparent difficulty is the need to conceptually clarify the criteria for distinguishing representational formats. Palmer (1978) has distinguished between *extrinsic* representations, in which relations between entities in the represented world correspond to explicit elements of the representation, and *intrinsic* representations, in which relations are implicit. For example, if a scene in which an umbrella is above a man is described by the sentence "The umbrella is above the man," the relation of aboveness is represented by an explicit symbol (the word "above"). If the same scene is represented by a picture of an umbrella above a man, then the relation of aboveness is left implicit, to be inferred by a comparison of the relative locations of the two pictured objects. The sentence is thus an extrinsic representation, whereas the pictorial representation is intrinsic.

Since one could imagine representations in which some relations are explicit and some implicit, the extrinsic/intrinsic distinction seems best viewed as a continuum rather than a dichotomy. Furthermore, it is correlated with two other important representational dimensions, referential arbitrariness and independence of feature encoding. Extrinsic representations tend to be arbitrary in the sense that there is no necessary connection between a symbol and its referent. Thus the word "above" refers to aboveness simply by virtue of the tacit agreement of English speakers. In contrast, intrinsic representations are less arbitrary; for example, there is likely considerable overlap between the mental procedures by which a person "sees" aboveness in a scene or in a corresponding pictorial representation. Likewise, extrinsic representations allow a greater degree of independence in the encoding of features of the world than do intrinsic representations. Because intrinsic representations represent some relations and properties implicitly, a well-formed representation must sometimes of necessity encode certain types of information (Kosslyn, 1981). Thus our picture may show a red umbrella above a tall man, but the sentence "The umbrella is above the man" represents relative location while avoiding any commitments regarding color or size.

The contrast between extrinsic and intrinsic representations bears a rough correspondence to the currently popular distinction between "propositional" and "analog" codes, which are often described as quasi-linguistic and quasi-pictorial, respectively. While the debate has probably yet to close, some type of distinction between an abstract propositional code and a spatial code seems by now to be well supported (Kosslyn, 1981). Moreover, the present view of representational formats as falling along a set of (probably imperfectly) correlated continua leaves open the possibility that current dual-code theories (e.g., Paivio, 1975) will eventually have to be elaborated as multi-code theories. The case could be made that distinctions need to be drawn among an abstract propositional code, a spatial code, imagery codes corresponding to different sense modalities, a motoric code, and perhaps others.

As these representational issues are still unsettled within cognitive psychology, their import for social cognition remains unclear. Progress in identifying representational formats may well have important implications for social-psychological models. Nonetheless, in many cases it seems that social psychologists can afford to treat the issues regarding format distinctions with a degree of benign neglect. Many of the central theoretical problems in social cognition hinge more on the content of social cognition than on its representational format. Since the same content may often be potentially represented in various alternative formats, theorists need to be careful not to confuse issues of content with those of format. For example, social psychologists occasionally speak of the "image" of a person playing a role in social cognition. In such cases all that may be meant by "image" is perceptual information about the person (a particular content). But in such a context the term "image" strikes the cognitive psychologist as needlessly contentious, since such perceptual information might be represented by an abstract description rather than (or as well as) by visual imagery. When questions of content are paramount, it will often be wise to set questions of format aside.

## Knowledge Structures and the Social World

The organization and content of knowledge structures (whatever the formats in which they are represented) raise especially important issues for social cognition. The concepts of schemas and mental models have been tied to a rather bewildering array of interrelated theoretical terms, which in addition to "model" and "schema" include "frame," "script," "scenario," "plan," "semantic network" and "prototype," all of which need to be sorted out. As a concrete example, consider a businessman about to enter a meeting with various associates and a prospective client. He will presumably construct a mental model of the situation he expects to be in, and update it as the meeting unfolds. In constructing this model he will likely draw on a wealth of information stored in long-term memory. Much of this information will consist of abstract representations of various classes of entities, such as "person," "prospective client," "my boss," "business meeting," etc. We may use "schema" as the general term for any of these various representations of categories, individuals or event sequences. A schema can be viewed as an abstract description which includes a set of "slots" to be filled or parameters to be set in order to represent a particular instance of the class (see Rumelhart, 1980). Schemas for object concepts can vary from the very general ("person") to the very specific ("my boss"); but since even an individual varies over time along dimensions related to appearance and behavior, both individuals and categories must correspond to mental representations with variable parameters. On a particular occasion a schema can be instantiated by fixing its variable parameters ("my boss as he appears now sitting at this table"). The schema may include prior probabilities associated with the values of its variable parameters, thus creating (fallible) expectations ("my boss will wear his usual ridiculous tie"). In this sense a schema may be partially instantiated prior to encountering the specific instance. The term "prototype" has various uses, of which a major one corresponds to the subjectively most probable or "typical" instantiation of a category schema ("a typical prospective buyer"). The term "frame" is variously used as a synonym for schema, or for a schema partially or fully instantiated. A schema establishes retrieval pathways among its elements (e.g., the schema for "business meeting" may call to mind various roles for its participants, characteristic features of the meeting room, etc.), which can be represented by links between nodes in an associative network (e.g., Anderson & Bower, 1973).

A mental model will often include actual or imagined event sequences (e.g., the initial round of introductions that begins the meeting), which are termed "scenarios." A schema for a class of stereotyped event sequences (e.g., business meetings) is called a "script." In our example the businessman's mental model can be viewed as an integrated representation of numerous hierarchically organized schemas, instantiated in whole or in part, which will be used to make decisions and guide his behavior. The model will likely include representations of his goals for the occasion, such as making a sale and impressing his boss, and plans for accomplishing them. A major function of the internal model is to allow "mental simulations" of the outcomes of alternative possible scenarios. ("How is this client likely to react to an aggressive presentation? To feigned reluctance to make a committment?") This type of counterfactual reasoning plays a major role in decisions about social and other situations (Kahneman & Tversky, 1982).

The concept of schemas integrated into mental models provides a framework for a variety of current work in social cognition. The nature of the internal model will depend on the schemas used to construct it, the selection of which will depend on numerous factors, including those referred to as availability and representativeness (Tversky & Kahneman, 1973) and salience (Taylor & Fiske, 1978). Individual differences may influence both schema selection and the planning process (e.g., Markus & Smith, 1982). Decisions relevant to social behavior will also reflect the heuristic strategies that guide the process of "mental simulation," thus determining the relative ease of imagining alternative hypothetical outcomes (Kahneman & Tversky, 1982). In addition, the general concept of a schema emphasizes that mental representations of qualitatively different types of content, such as persons and situations, may adhere to similar organizational principles. A schema may well encode information about types of people within particular situations, such as judges as they behave in courtrooms (Cantor, 1982). Indeed, there is good reason to expect that a great deal of knowledge about people will be contextually bound, particularly since a wealth of evidence from memory studies indicates that objects are encoded in relation to the context in which they are embedded (see Glass et al., 1979, Chapters 3 and 4). Thus the colleague we have only known at work may seem vaguely unfamiliar when unexpectedly encountered at a wedding party. Schematic structures may therefore reflect varying degrees of contextual dependency.

## Structure of Social Categories

Our overview of schemas and mental models made brief mention of the structure of social categories; however, the topic deserves closer scrutiny. Over the past decade some of the most influential work in cognitive psychology has dealt with the structure of object categories and the basis for evaluating similarity between concepts (most notably, Rosch, 1973, 1975; Rosch & Mervis, 1975; Rosch, Mervis, Gray, Johnson, & Boyes-Braem, 1976; Tversky, 1977). The Roschian view of object categories has already had a direct influence on conceptions of social categories, particularly through the work of Cantor and Mischel (1979; Cantor, 1982). It may be instructive to assess the benefits and shortcomings associated with this particular interaction between the two fields.

To place current models in perspective, it may be useful to present a broad view of the structure and function of social categories. *Role concepts* seem to have a great deal of influence on the structure of social knowledge. A tremendous amount of "who we are" can be attributed to the roles we play in relation to others—friends, husbands, lovers, parents, children, employers, colleagues, members of a profession, and so on. These roles are in large part ultimately defined by their functions within the socioeconomic context of our culture. In a complex modern society few "lay sociologists" are likely to have a deep understanding of the overall structure in which their social roles are embedded; nonetheless, all must learn a great deal about the roles they play and interact with in order to function effectively.

The relations among social roles provide prime examples of the mutual adaptation of social behavior, alluded to earlier. When the introverted novice professor steps up on the lecture podium, the students expect him or her to talk to them, usually in something approximating a monologue. The professor knows the students have this expectation and shares it with them. This simple framework of mutual expectations has been known to elicit forceful deliveries and moments of eloquence from the most unlikely speakers. As the example suggests, role-based behavior serves to partially insulate the fulfillment of role functions from the vagaries of the persons who fill them. While people typically have more freedom than do actors speaking lines written by another, social roles limit the range of acceptable improvisations. Thus in the normal course of events a shopper and a check-out clerk can perform their joint ritual of economic exchange without either being forced to concern themselves unduly with the idiosyncracies of the other's personality. Of course, roles vary widely in the latitude of behavior they allow their actors. In addition, we each take on "microroles" that can be "personalized"; exactly what it means for Susan to be a friend of Bob depends in part on how the two participants mold their relationship.

We can thus attempt an approximate characterization of the role knowledge that people must acquire in order to function effectively within their culture. They must learn the essential behavioral requirements of social roles, including both roles they will play and roles they may have to deal with. They must also learn something about the kind and degree of variability that each role normatively permits, which implies the ability to distinguish deviance from normalcy. Such substantive knowledge will constitute the central content of role schemas. In addition, social skill requires procedural knowledge regarding how roles can be created and differentiated to meet individual needs.

The present emphasis on the centrality of role knowledge seems to provide a somewhat different perspective on social categories than do current models of categories of "persons" and "situations" (Cantor & Mischel, 1979; Cantor, 1982), which continue to be influenced by the earlier trait psychologies (Mischel, 1982). We would expect to find that most psychologically salient social categories are defined in terms of roles. Schemas for social situations can be viewed as descriptions of a set of interconnected roles. In addition, many "traits" of persons can be viewed as propensities to take on particular types of roles. An "extravert," for example, seems to be a person who is "type-cast" as playing roles requiring the initiation of social interactions. Other everyday trait attributions (e.g., aggressiveness, conscientiousness) seem to be made on the basis of the actor's apparent selection of roles and the nuances of his or her performances in them. Most such trait terms are used as adjectival descriptors ("honest person") rather than as nouns, in contrast to the many nominal role terms. This linguistic difference tends to support the hypothesized psychological primacy of role categories. The "person taxonomies" studies by Cantor and Mischel (1979) consisted primarily of terms defined by roles (e.g., "campaign manager"), with the exception of a few terms based on psychiatric categories.

Assuming that role categories are central in social cognition, we can now contrast their structure with that of object categories. Both similarities and differences are apparent. Role categories, like object categories, typically seem to be represented psychologically by a bundle of correlated features probabilistically related to category membership. Role terms such as "lawyer" tend to be defined by some core function plus a loose set of subjectively correlated attributes. Some social categories lack any clear defining features. It follows that social categories, like natural object categories, admit of degrees of "typicality" among their members (Cantor & Mischel, 1979). But at the same time a variety of important differences are apparent, which can be related to the nature of role concepts. As compared with object categories, roles are more "fluid": people move from one role to the next, combine roles, and create new ones. For roles to overlap in various ways is more the rule than the exception. Accordingly, social categories are seldom disjoint, as Cantor and Mischel (1979) have pointed out; a person can easily be both a father and a fisherman, and the truly adventurous can aspire to be both a liberal and a Republican. Accordingly, role concepts are likely linked by "family resemblance" structures (i.e., successive overlap among feature sets; Rosch & Mervis, 1975) to an even greater extent than are object concepts.

As Cantor and Mischel (1979) noted, the high degree of overlap among role categories makes it difficult to represent them in terms of set-inclusion relations or a clear semantic hierarchy (Collins & Quillian, 1969). Thus the hierarchy of person categories derived by Cantor and Mischel (1979) contains some violations of set-inclusion relations. Role concepts can certainly vary from the specific (e.g., "circus clown") to the general (e.g., "extravert") in accordance with the number of attributes characteristically associated with the concept, but often the more specific categories are not strictly included in more general ones.

There are other reasons to suppose that hierarchical relations are less important for social than for object categories. Rosch et al. (1976) introduced the concept of a "basic level" of categorization for objects. They defined the basic-level term in a hierarchy by several converging measures (e.g., the most rapid categorization response, the term learned at the earliest age), and found that it typically was the middle term in a hierarchy of abstraction (e.g., of the terms *furniture, chair* and *kitchen chair, chair* is basic). While Cantor and Mischel (1979) argued that the intermediate terms in their person taxonomies also constitute a Roschian basic level, their evidence is not compelling. For hierarchies such as *extraverted person, comic joker,* and *circus clown,* they demonstrated that the more specific categories elicit more total attributes, more attributes that are shared with alternative categories at the same level of the taxonomy, and more concrete, imageable attributes. These results would be predicted by virtually any model of categorization, since more specific categories necessarily have at least as many attributes as more general ones, and also must divide the world up more finely. However, Cantor and Mischel's findings do not establish the entire set of Roschian criteria for a basic level. The basic level of a hierarchy can be viewed as a compromise between the greater certainty of general categorizations and the greater informativeness of specific ones. Rosch et al. (1976) placed considerable emphasis on their demonstrations of greater knowledge differences between the superordinate and basic levels than between basic and subordinate levels; e.g., while people know much more about chairs than about furniture, they seem to know little more about kitchen chairs than about chairs in general, except perhaps that the former belong in kitchens. The data of Cantor and Mischel do not consistently reveal such patterns. As the "chair" example also illustrates, basic-level terms in the object domain are virtually always monolexemic, while subordinate terms tend to be multilexemic. In contrast, seven of the eight middle-level terms studied by Cantor and Mischel are multilexemic (e.g., *social activist*), and the single exception, *phobic,* seems rather marginal as a noun.

It is by no means apparent, then, that the Roschian concept of a basic level will have much utility in the domain of social categories. We will discuss some further similarities and differences between object and social categories when we examine issues related to their acquisition.


## ACQUISITION OF KNOWLEDGE STRUCTURES

### Toward a Theory of Social Learning

A topic of rising importance within current cognitive psychology is learning (Greeno, 1980). Not long ago this topic bore the stigma of its central status within the abandoned behaviorist framework; a cognitive psychologist was one concerned with the mentalist concepts of memory, free from the S-R shackles of learning. But as the postulated mental structures grew increasingly complex, the need to explain their acquisition became apparent. How are schemas and prototypes learned? How does the course of semantic development lead to the adult organization of semantic knowledge? How are natural languages learned? How does a novice problem solver become an expert? Such questions have spurred a wide range of efforts to develop models of cognitive learning within the information-processing framework.

Our earlier sketch of social schemas and mental models suggests that research on the acquisition of complex skills and knowledge structures should be a central component of the field of social cognition. Social knowledge appears to include such complex mental structures as schemas and prototypes for classes of people and situations, information about social roles and their behavioral consequences, social scripts and routines. How are these structures learned? Models of acquisition are not only important in their own right, but they could potentially clarify the nature of the postulated knowledge structures. Schema theorists, for example, are commonly caught between their apparent need to capture the diversity and flexibility of human cognitive categories, and their embarrassment at the lack of theoretical constraints that they are able to place on the schema construct. It seems possible that a model of schema acquisition could serve in part to provide such constraints, by affording predictions about the knowledge structures that will result from specified learning conditions.

Yet despite its apparent importance, research on learning mechanisms does not figure prominently in current work on social cognition. The main framework within social psychology in which acquisition is discussed is Bandura's (1977) "social learning theory"; however, this model is seldom related to work on social schemas and categories. In part this apparent gap may reflect the fact that social learning theory has its intellectual roots in behaviorism, and has yet to be fully integrated into the information-processing paradigm (but see Bower, 1978). In this section we will explore several themes in current cognitive research that may point the way toward a social learning theory in its broader sense.

## Reasoning About Causation

One of the most basic mechanisms of learning hinges on the ability to analyze a situation and reason about the causal factors responsible for the observed outcome. Such causal reasoning is clearly a central concern of social cognition, and has received considerable attention in research on attribution (for an overview see Ross, 1981). But as Schustack and Sternberg (1981) have pointed out, attribution research has focused on the *types* of causes to which people attribute outcomes (e.g., the self versus others, situations versus dispositions). In contrast, some recent work has begun to develop more process-oriented models of causal reasoning. One such model of everyday causal reasoning is that provided by Kahneman and Tversky (1982), who have built on earlier philosophical treatments (Hart & Honore, 1959; Mackie, 1974). To a first approximation, a causal attribution is akin to a counterfactual conditional: "If such and such had not been the case, this outcome would not have occurred." More specifically, people search for causes and effects among the *differences* they observe within the context of a constant background state, which often remains implicit. These background conditions have been collectively termed the "causal field"; while necessary for the observed outcome, they are not seen as psychological causes.

Thus if one is asked why a couple were divorced, the fact that they lived together will not suffice as an answer, despite its obvious relevance to the break-up. Rather, the facts that the couple were once married and lived together form part of the causal field. The search for potential causes will be restricted to the differences that present themselves as the "figure" against the "ground" of the causal field. Thus one might point to differences between this failed marriage and other successful ones, or to changes in the relationship over its duration. As Kahneman and Tversky (1982) emphasize, people will typically view departures from normalcy as potential causes.

The above analysis suggests that in order for a state or event to be potentially viewed as a cause, it must be identified as a difference against its causal field. We would therefore expect any manipulation that served to highlight some aspect of the situation, causing the observer to focus attention on it, to increase its perceived causal importance. Recent social psychological research supports this contention. For example, simply focusing the lighting on a particular person can increase their perceived impact on a group discussion (McArthur & Post, 1977). Some findings of attribution research can potentially be analyzed in terms of variations in salience that can alter the causal field. For example, it seems that actors are likely to ascribe their own behavior to situational contingencies, whereas observers will ascribe the same behavior to dispositional tendencies of the person (Jones & Nisbett, 1972). It seems possible that in seeking explanations actors will tend to treat their selves as part of the causal field, and look to the situation for relevant differences. In contrast, observers may view people not as background elements, but as salient aspects of the situation to be contrasted with other potential actors, and hence potentially to be classed as causes.

Notwithstanding their biases and limitations, there is little doubt that the mechanisms of causal reasoning serve as powerful learning devices. There is a firm core of rationality behind such simple heuristics as treating an initial change occurring in a previously steady state as the probable cause of a subsequent change. If a child at dinner spills the milk and observes a parent's smile change to a frown, the causal attribution will be transparent, and a valuable lesson in normative social behavior may be learned. As this example illustrates, a model of causal reasoning is likely to play a central role in a cognitive interpretation of reinforcement principles. Attributions of causality may serve to mediate assignments of credit or blame for obtained outcomes to specific factors observed in the prior situation.

## Analogical Reasoning

Heuristics for causal reasoning are powerful learning devices because they potentially make it possible to acquire information about causal relations from the observation of a single situation and its outcome (although cross-situational comparisons are often essential to test causal hypotheses). Furthermore, the causal attributions of everyday thought are readily transferred from an initial situation to subjectively similar ones; for example, if we conclude that career conflict led to divorce for a particular couple, we will likely view a similar conflict in a different marriage as an ominous sign.

The latter pattern of reasoning is illustrative of the use of *analogy,* which has been the focus of some recent work in both cognitive psychology (Gick & Holyoak, 1980, 1983; Holyoak, 1984) and artificial intelligence (Winston, 1980). Analogical reasoning is a mechanism by which information can be transferred from a known situation to a novel one, in accord with a general two-step procedure. First, certain aspects of the known situation are "mapped" (placed in one-to-one correspondence) with aspects of the unknown situation, in order to derive a representation of the relations between the two situations. Second, this initial partial mapping is used to construct additional information about the unknown situation, by appropriately transforming knowledge about the known case. The nature of the derived information can vary enormously, and may include predictions about future events, potential problem solutions, and decisions about appropriate attitudes and behavior—all clear candidates for relevance to social cognition. Analogical reasoning can be viewed as a flexible mechanism for schema selection, and as a basis for mental simulations of outcomes.

Analogical reasoning should not be viewed as an alternative to reasoning about causation; rather, the latter is an important component of the former. The basis of an appropriate analogy is not a mapping between any or all features of the two situations, but rather between features perceived as causally relevant to the outcome of the known situation. For example, in drawing an analogy between a failed marriage and one under evaluation, the fact that both exhibited career conflicts is presumably more pertinent than the observation that in each case the husband's eyes were green and the wife's were blue. Because the heuristics for causal attribution are fallible, in situations of realistic complexity analogical reasoning can only yield plausible conjectures, not irrefutable certitudes. Despite the apparent systematic resemblances between two situations, the analogist may have failed to take account of some critical discrepancy that alters the outcome of the novel case. For example, the second couple faced with a career conflict may exhibit greater flexibility in their approach to the problem, and hence confound the pessimistic prediction that had been derived by analogy to the earlier failed marriage.

It seems that a wide range of social-learning phenomena can be analyzed in terms of analogical processes. The divorce example is illustrative of many comparable decisions about the expected outcomes of interpersonal interactions, which can in turn guide behavior. In addition, some of the basic concepts of classical social learning theory can be viewed as types of analogical transfer. For example, vicarious reinforcement involves the modification of one person's behavior by observation of the reward or punishment received by another. Thus a boy who observes another student being punished for insulting the teacher may note the similarities between himself and the offender along such relevant dimensions as status in the classroom structure, and on that basis anticipate that similar behavior on his own part would elicit a comparable negative response. In the absence of countervailing motives (such as a desire to show solidarity with his fellow student), this belief derived by analogy is likely to reduce the probability of the observer displaying verbal aggression. Elementary analogical reasoning may also underlie the modification of social behavior by the process of "modeling." Wishing to be like the parent, a child may exploit salient initial correspondences (e.g., the ability to speak and walk) in order to construct additional more subtle resemblances (e.g., similar speech mannerisms or style of gait). In addition, analogical thinking may be involved in learning about social roles. For example, on her first day of school a girl may not have a clear conception of what a "teacher" is or of how to behave toward one; but by viewing her teacher as analogous to her mother on dimensions such as age and power, she may develop an initial approximation to appropriate guidelines for behavior in the classroom.

So far we have discussed examples of reasoning directly from one specific situation to another. However, similar mapping processes are very likely involved in the induction of more abstract category schemas from comparisons between specific examples (Gick & Holyoak, 1983; Winston, 1980). By comparing several teachers a child may develop a general conception of what teachers are like; by comparing such concepts as "teacher," "parent," and "policeman" she may derive the yet more general category of "authority figure." Reasoning by analogy may therefore play a central role in the development of social categories at different levels of abstraction, to which topic we now turn.

## Acquisition of Social Categories

Our earlier role-centered analysis of social categories suggests that the acquisition of social categories will require the development of a set of interwoven role schemas. (See Nelson, 1981, for a discussion of the acquisition of script concepts.) Several current themes in cognitive learning models seem potentially relevant to the process of learning such schemas. A great deal of role knowledge is intrinsically relational; accordingly, it might be worthwhile to consider whether any of the mechanisms embodied in current models of syntax acquisition (Maratsos & Chalkley, 1980; Pinker, 1981) can be related to social learning. Another potentially relevant theme derives from work on the development of expertise in specific problem domains, such as chess playing (Chase & Simon, 1973) and physics (Larkin, McDermott, Simon, & Simon, 1980). The general framework suggested by such research is that the development of domain-specific expertise is based on the induction of more finely articulated schemas that specify solution procedures for subclasses of problems. Much of social knowledge can be viewed as a set of skills, which people may perform with different degrees of expertise. Indeed, one commonly speaks of people being socially skillful or inept, sometimes with respect to particular roles. The cognitive work on expertise has already begun to be related to social cognition. For example, Fiske and Kinder (1982) provide some evidence that domain-specific social expertise leads to greater flexibility in the application of schemas. Some individual differences in social cognition may also be interpretable within this framework, in that social "styles" may depend on specific varieties of social expertise.

Other important questions center on the acquisition process itself. While some aspects of social knowledge are certainly explicitly taught, it seems that a great deal is learned incidentally in the course of social interactions. Indeed, perhaps the most salutary contribution of social learning theory has been its emphasis on the importance of learning by observation of examples (Bandura, 1971). Several lines of work in cognitive psychology deal with the effects of different learning strategies and feedback conditions on the acquisition of category knowledge. An important contribution of the levels of processing framework for memory research has been its emphasis on learning that takes place simply as a byproduct of performing various cognitive tasks (Craik & Tulving, 1975). Fried and Holyoak (in press) have demonstrated that people can learn to distinguish degrees of prototypicality among exemplars of complex visual categories without information about the category membership of individual instances in the training set, knowledge of the number of categories represented, or even knowledge that their task is to learn categories. Perhaps people can sometimes acquire conceptions of social categories under similar conditions of minimal external guidance.

The work of Reber and his associates (Reber, 1967; Reber & Allen, 1978; Reber, Kassin, Lewis, & Cantor, 1980) is also relevant in this context. They have demonstrated that people sometimes learn the structure of complex categories (letter sequences defined by a finite-state grammar) more readily when they simply observe or memorize examples, than when they consciously search for rules that define legal sequences. This advantage of implicit over explicit learning strategies is typically observed when the underlying grammar is complex and the examples are presented in an unsystematic sequence—conditions that may often be faced during the acquisition of social categories. When the underlying rules governing category membership are difficult to discover, an explicit learning strategy may not only fail to discover them, but it may also distract the person from attending to probabilistic features that predict category membership with reasonable accuracy. In contrast, an implicit learning strategy may lead people to store examples in memory (Brooks, 1978; Medin & Schaffer, 1978), so that novel instances can later be classified by an analogical strategy. Another implicit-learning mechanism may be to learn schematic representations of the central tendency and permissible degree of variability associated with exemplars of each category (Fried & Holyoak, in press). Such representations would capture some of the major aspects of category structure that seem to form the basis for social cognition.

Recent evidence, in fact, suggests that implicit learning mechanisms may underlie some types of affective responses. Gordon and Holyoak (1983) studied the "mere exposure" effect—the phenomenon that increased familiarity enhances liking of a stimulus—in the context of an implicit learning paradigm. Their experiments demonstrated that positive affect, due to stimulus exposure, generalized to novel stimuli that were related along certain abstract dimensions to the exposed stimuli. Furthermore, the pattern of generalization matched the pattern obtained when subjects made categorization judgments. These findings suggest that in some situations the same mechanisms underlie affective responding and categorization.

While there are likely many commonalities between the acquisition of social and object categories, there are also likely to be differences. Some of these differences may underlie the contrast between prototypes and stereotypes. Studies of the acqustion of object categories have demonstrated that people typically acquire some conception of the prototype or central tendency of a category, which may correspond to a kind of "average" of the presented exemplars (Posner & Keele, 1968; Reed, 1972). But while prototypes connote veridical representations of "typical" category members, social psychology's classical concept of stereotypes connotes error and bias, usually toward a negative view of category members. The prevalence of stereotypes for social categories may well be related to the nature of the acquisition process. In studies of how object categories are learned, subjects generally view several exemplars of the category, presented for a reasonable duration under clear exposure conditions. The distinguishing features of the category are concrete (usually visual). Subjects have no need to use the knowledge they acquire outside the experimental setting, and no motives that might foster biased encodings.

In contrast, social categories will often be acquired under strikingly different conditions. Knowledge of a person or class of people is typically derived on the basis of restricted and often biased opportunities for observation (Cantor & Mischel, 1979). Since observers may often have to make decisions about how to behave on the basis of fallible initial impressions of people, they may construct person schemas based on minimal information, which will in turn bias the subsequent encoding of additional evidence (Hamilton, 1979). This problem is compounded by the highly inferential nature of the connection between observed behaviors and putative personality characteristics. Furthermore, concepts of persons may often be derived more from hearsay than from any direct observations. For example, people may acquire a stereotype of Turks as cruel without ever having met one. In addition, the most pernicious social stereotypes, directed at racial, ethnic and national "out-groups," are presumably often fostered by biasing motives, such as the need to rationalize economic and political inequalities. People often have reasons why they would like to believe the worst about others. At the same time, many people may be sufficiently self-aware as to have less than perfect confidence in their own stereotype concepts; this may contribute to the ease with which stereotypical beliefs are sometimes overridden by individuating evidence about a member of the stereotyped class (Borgida, Locksley, & Brekke, 1982). It is likely that the acquisition of social categories is an aspect of social cognition in which non-cognitive factors are especially important.

## SPATIAL REPRESENTATIONS AND REFERENCE POINTS

Perhaps the most compelling evidence that analog mental representations constitute a distinctive format is based on studies of the processing of spatial information. A central feature of analog representation of space is its implicit encoding of relational information, such as distance and orientation. Thus when first asked to decide whether the bottom of a horse's tail is above or below its knees, most people report consulting a spatial image. Kosslyn (1980) reviews a wide range of experimental studies that confirm such introspective support for the use of analog representations in various cognitive tasks. In this section we will examine the possible role of spatial representations in social reasoning.

Because spatial representations are amenable to perception-like processing strategies (e.g., mental "scanning"), there seem to be cognitive advantages in recoding various abstract concepts into spatial terms. Lakoff and Johnson (1980) cite numerous examples of the spatial metaphors that pervade the English language, such as "I'm looking *forward* to it," "I'm feeling *up* today," "It's been a *long* project," and "That was a *low* trick." They suggest that the metaphorical structure of language may shape the way we think about the world and the way we act. However, given the processing advantages that may sometimes be associated with spatial representation, it is at least as plausible to suppose that the nature of mental processes strongly influences language. Another advocate of the importance of spatial metaphors is Jaynes (1976), who argues that our conception of consciousness is in fact the product of such metaphors. He suggests that we invent consciousness in ourselves and others as a "mental space," which is an analog of the physical world. In this metaphorical space abstract concepts can be "examined" and "manipulated" by analogy to physical operations. Time, for example, is treated as a spatial concept (as a line directed from left to right).

### Processing of Linear Orderings

As the latter example suggests, a major form of internal spatial representation seems to be equivalent to a unidimensional ordering. While people can apparently create mental representations of three-dimensional space (Pinker, 1980), they nonetheless exhibit a predilection for linear representations, particularly when representing subjective magnitudes of stimuli. Some of the earliest work on the cognitive processes underlying spatial reasoning was done in the context of social psychology, by DeSoto and his colleagues (DeSoto, 1961; DeSoto, London, & Handel, 1965). Judgments such as "I'm smarter than he is," "Sue is prettier than Kate," and "My political beliefs are closer to Francois Mitterand's than to Ronald Reagan's," are all based on ordering and comparison processes: "the very stuff of social reasoning," in the words of DeSoto et al. (1965). DeSoto (1961) argued that people have a schema for ordering stimuli along single dimensions, a schema which they tend to use even if the stimuli are inherently multidimensional. He proposed that such a prediliction for single orderings may account for the well-known "halo effect" obtained when people are asked to evaluate others along multiple dimensions. The obtained judgments tend to correlate too highly across dimensions; for example, rated voice quality is likely to correlate with rated intelligence, even though the two attributes are actually independent. DeSoto suggested that the halo effect may in part be a consequence of the difficulty people have in learning more than one ordering of the same set of stimuli, a phenomenon he demonstrated experimentally. De-Soto's account of the halo effect is an early example of an explanation of suboptimal social judgments in terms of cognitive limitations and strategies (rather than affective or motivational factors), foreshadowing the theoretical bent of current work in social cognition (Hamilton, 1979; Nisbett & Ross, 1980; Tversky & Kahneman, 1973).

DeSoto et al. (1965) provided more explicit links between the processing of order information and spatial representation. They pointed out a variety of linguistic clues that highlight the perceptual nature and psychological prominence of linear orderings: phrases such as "a *line* of argument," and the fact that the term *order* shares a specific meaning of "linear ordering" and a general meaning of "harmonious arrangement." DeSoto et al. also demonstrated that subjects express a preferred spatial direction for certain dimensional relationships (e.g., *better-worse* is viewed as a vertical dimension with the term "better" located at the top).

More recent work using reaction-time tasks has generated additional evidence trying order information to spatial representation. For example, suppose a person is taught a series of relations between adjacent pairs of stimuli, such as "Tom is taller than Harry, Harry is taller than Bill, Bill is taller than Peter. . ."). Subsequent decisions about which member of a pair is the taller will be made more quickly the further apart the items are in the ordering (Potts, 1974). This "symbolic distance effect" implies that subjects are faster to compare items never previously paired (widely separated pairs) than to compare items that were explicitly learned together (adjacent pairs). In addition, items near the ends of the ordering are compared more rapidly than those located near the center. Both of these effects are also observed when comparisons are based on an actual visual array (Holyoak & Patterson, 1981). Symbolic orderings thus appear to be represented in an internal array amenable to processing mechanisms analogous to those used in perceptual comparisons. As a result, response times depend on the emergent properties of the internal array, rather than on the particular item pairs used to teach the ordering.

Symbolic distance effects are also obtained when stimulus magnitudes are learned in the course of everyday life, rather than being taught as an explicit ordering by the experimenter. For example, subjects can decide that a car is larger than a shoe more quickly than that a car is larger than a horse (Moyer, 1973). Similar results are obtained for stimuli coded on abstract dimensions such as quality (Holyoak & Walker, 1976), as well as for social comparisons (Rogers, Kuiper, & Rogers, 1979).

## Reference Points in Social Cognition

Another important set of phenomena observed in symbolic comparison tasks involves the influence of "reference points." The effects of reference points are typically observed when subjects are asked to judge which of two stimuli is more similar to a third (the reference point). In general, the closer the two comparison stimuli are to the reference point, the more quickly the decision can be made. For example, Holyoak (1978) had subjects decide which of two digits was numerically closer to a third digit. He found that holding the comparison pair constant, reaction time increased with distance to the reference point (e.g., subjects could select the closer member of the pair 3-4 more quickly when the reference digit was 6 rather than 7). Holyoak interpreted these and similar results as evidence that discriminability is increased in the vicinity of a reference point because the subjective space near the reference point is stretched relative to regions far from it.

Holyoak and Mah (1982) obtained support for the above hypothesis using non-speeded rating tasks involving estimates of distances among American cities. When subjects were asked to judge how close cities were to the Pacific coast, distances among western cities appeared to be stretched relative to distances among eastern cities, while the reverse was true when subjects judged how close cities were to the Atlantic. In addition, Holyoak and Mah found some evidence that the geographical area where their subjects lived served as a kind of habitual reference point, since distances in that region were relatively overestimated regardless of the manner in which the question was phrased.

The latter result is reminiscent of earlier work in social psychology. For example, Hovland and Sherif (1952) suggested that people may make relatively fine distinctions among attitudes similar to their own. More recently, Rogers et al. (1979) have proposed that the system of attitudes and beliefs constituting the "self" is likely to serve as a reference point in many judgment tasks. They recorded subjects' latencies to decide which of two descriptions was either more like or less like the subjects' self concepts. A symbolic distance effect was obtained, as decisions were made more quickly when the two descriptions were relatively unequal in their similarity to the self (as determined in a prior rating task). Furthermore, the latency pattern did not differ across the two forms of the question ("more similar" versus "less similar"). The latter result parallels Holyoak's (1978) finding that time to compare two digits to a reference digit is sometimes independent of whether the task is to choose the "closer" or the "further" digit, suggesting that the self may function much like other reference points (even arbitrary ones) that are explicitly specified by the instructions.

The Rogers et al. (1979) study does not, in fact, provide any evidence that the self is *habitually* used as a reference point (contrary to the authors' own interpretation). For example, they did not find any effect of distance from the self to the two descriptors, whereas previous work indicated that a reference point will increase discriminability, (and hence reduce choice reaction-time) for stimuli in its vicinity. However, the failure of Rogers et al. to demonstrate increased discriminability in the region of the self may simply reflect deficiencies in their method of scaling the descriptions relative to subjects' self concepts. Holyoak and Mah's (1982) results suggest that an habitual reference point will influence non-speeded ratings as well as speeded comparisons. Accordingly, any expansion of subjects' similarity space in the region of the self would likely be reflected in the similarity ratings obtained by Rogers et al. (1979), which were then used to predict decision latencies. Thus the ratings collected by Rogers et al. probably did not yield "unbiased" estimates of the similarities among the descriptions used in their study.

We have recently used a rather different approach to investigate the status of the self and other social concepts as reference points (Holyoak & Gordon, 1983). Rosch (1975) demonstrated that habitual reference points create asymmetries in similarity judgments: ordinary stimuli are judged as more similar to reference points than vice versa. Such asymmetries can be explained by Tversky's (1977) model of similarity judgments. Accordingly, we used asymmetries in similarity judgments as indices of the degree to which various social concepts serve as reference points. In one experiment we asked subjects to rate how similar they were to a particular friend on various dimensions, or vice versa (e.g., "How similar are you to your friend in shyness?", versus "How similar is your friend to you in shyness?"). As would be expected if the self is a reference point, our subjects judged the friend to be more similar to themselves than they were similar to the friend.

However, a second experiment demonstrated that the self is by no means unrivaled as a social reference point. In our next experiment subjects compared themselves with typical examples of various college stereotypes (e.g., "How similar are you to the typical preppie?", or vice versa). The same subjects also listed attributes of each of the stereotypes, and the mean number of attributes they generated was used as a measure of our subjects' degree of knowledge of the stereotypes. For stereotypes about which relatively little was known (e.g., "co-op member") the self again appeared to serve as a reference point (i.e., the stereotype was rated as more similar to the self than vice versa). However, stereotypes about which a great deal was known (e.g., "preppie") were at least as prominent as reference points as was the self, as evidenced by reductions or reversals of the asymmetry effect.

Intuitively, this seems to be a reasonable pattern of results. The self is surely an important concept for organizing one's social knowledge. But at the same time, one may in part define one's self in relation to prominent social categories or role models. Accordingly, a variety of social concepts may serve as reference points, depending on the judgment context. Asymmetries in similarity judgments may serve as a useful methodological tool for exploring factors (perhaps including systematic individual differences) that influence the status of social concepts as reference points.

## AFFECTIVE AND MOTORIC CODES

Affective and motoric codes may at first seem like odd bedfellows, but in fact the notion that motor processes play an important role in emotion has a venerable ancestry as well as current advocates (James, 1890; Schacter & Singer, 1962; Zajonc & Markus, in press). The relationship between affect and/or motoric knowledge and social cognition is both intriguing and troublesome, and we can do no more here than highlight some salient theoretical issues. We will first discuss the relationship between affect and cognition, focusing on the position taken by Zajonc (1980b), who has addressed the issue very directly. We will then explore the implications of research on motor behavior and action for social cognition.

### Affect and Cogntiion

The task of formulating a theoretical account of the relationship between affect and cognition is immediately beset by definitional problems. Without a clear definition of either affect or cognition, neither of which appears to be forthcoming, it is obviously difficult to describe their relationship. Furthermore, it seems unlikely that either concept can be strictly defined, even if our understanding of each increases. Both affect and cognition are likely to remain fuzzy natural categories, each associated with mental processes that intuitively strike us as good examples of the concept, as well as other processes that seem to straddle the nebulous border between the two.

The above view contrasts with that of Zajonc (1980b), who argues that affect and cognition are separate and dissimilar processes. He distinguishes the two on the basis of a characterization of cognition as relatively slow, effortful, conscious and rational; as opposed to affect, which is viewed as fast, effortless, unconscious and nonrational. However, these contrasting properties do not in fact suffice to draw a sharp distinction between affective and cognitive processes.

First consider speed of operation. It has been suggested that during emergencies people and animals act on the basis of emotional rather than cognitive responses, because their emotional responses are faster. However, research in cognitive psychology provides ample evidence that some cognitive processes, such as search of active memory (Sternberg, 1966) and retrieval of lexical information from long-term memory (Meyer & Schvaneveldt, 1976) are performed extremely rapidly. It therefore seems unlikely that speed of operation clearly differentiates affective and cognitive processes.

Zajonc (1980b) has similarly argued that affective responses are not generally willed, but rather tend to occur automatically; indeed, they can sometimes only be suppressed with great effort. These same properties, however, have also been used to characterize automatic cognitive processes (Fischler, 1977; Posner & Synder, 1975; Shiffrin & Schneider, 1977). It is also the case that affective processes seem very immediate, and often do not seem to be preceded by any conscious processing. But again, many processes that are clearly cognitive are also unconscious. For example, in fluent reading we are typically aware of the meanings of words and sentences, but not of the physical components of the letters on the page. Yet some of the physical features of letters must be processed at an unconscious level in order to initiate retrieval of lexical information from long-term memory.

Both philosophers and psychologists have often attempted to distinguish between affect and cognition in terms of degree of rationality. More than a few have portrayed the mind as a scene of struggle between reason and passion; that a great deal of human behavior seems irrational has been taken as testimony to the greater strength of passion. However, the criterion of rationality as a defining feature of cognition has been soundly rejected in current information-processing psychology. Cognition is viewed as involving the coding, categorization and manipulation of information; however, cognitive processes may fail to follow consistent internal goals or to meet normative standards of rationality (Tversky & Kahneman, 1973). Thus cognitive processes may well contribute to irrational or nonrational behavior.

An additional feature that might distinguish affect from cognition, mentioned at the outset, is that the former may crucially depend on motoric responses. Motor processes are being actively investigated by cognitive psychologists (Rosenbaum, 1980; Schmidt, 1975; Sternberg, Monsell, Knoll, & Wright, 1978). The consensus of the theoretical views emerging from this research is that motor control depends on complex cognitive mechanisms akin to those invoked in models proposed for other cognitive processes. Such cognitive mechanisms include schemas (Lashley, 1951; Norman, 1981; Schmidt, 1975) and "motor programs" (detailed plans for the production of movements; Keele, 1968; Sternberg et al., 1978). Given the apparent cognitive bases of motor processes, their involvement in emotion would serve to integrate rather than separate affect and cognition.

Even if affect and cognition are in fact separable, it would seem that both must involve information-processing systems. An independent affective system would have to be able to extract featural information from stimuli, have mnemonic capabilities, and be able to generate decisions and behavioral responses. The issue of how affect and cognition are related can thus be recast in terms of the format versus content distinction we drew in our earlier discusssion of mental representation. Theorists such as Zajonc (1980b) argue that affect and cognition are distinct systems, which attend to different features of the environment and use different types of mental representations. An alternative view is that affect and cognition are based on a single information-processing system, and differ in content rather than format. Proponents of the latter view might attempt to distinguish affective processes by their experiential correlates, rather than by unique information-processing characteristics. For the time being a satisfactory characterization of the relationship between affect and cognition must await both conceptual clarification and empirical advances.

## Cognitive Analysis of Action

Until recently cognitive psychology primarily concerned itself with what might be termed input and storage questions, at the expense of what might be termed output questions. Attention was focused on processes such as perception, comprehension, memory and reasoning, rather than on the processes controlling the production of behavior. As noted in the preceding section, however, cognitive psychologists have recently begun to pay considerable attention to motor processes. Such output processes are clearly relevant to social psychology, which is concerned not only with what people think about one another, but with how they behave toward each other.

Most cognitive studies of motor processes have dealt with relatively low-level issues concerning movement control; however, some attempts have been made to describe the molar level of action most appropriate for models of social behavior. Norman (1981) presents a synthesis of ideas about the nature of action and movement control, which bears a striking resemblance to the schema theories now current as descriptions of social knowledge. He proposes that the planning and control of action is guided by a hierarchy of schemas operating at different levels of specificity. The highest level consists of consciously formulated plans that guide large action sequences (e.g., going home from work). Higher level schemas pass parameter values that specify some of the operations of lower level schemas. The lower level schemas frequently operate outside of awareness; they are automatically triggered by higher order schemas, although they can accomodate to variable environmental input.

The automaticity of lower level schemas can sometimes allow them to be triggered inappropriately, resulting in "action slips." For example, a person might start on the familiar route home from work with the intention of turning off to go to a friend's house; instead, without thinking about it the person may end up at home. In terms of Norman's schema analysis, such a slip could result if the schema for going home becomes highly activated by the environmental input obtained on route. Norman argues that action slips can result from erroneous classification of the situation, faulty activation of schemas (as in the above example), and errors in the actual execution of the actions triggered by schemas. It seems likely that many of the social gaffes that occasionally embarrass most of us can be interpreted within such a framework (such as Norman's example of a person who absentmindedly picked up a companion's piece of bread and began to eat it).

While Norman's analysis of action slips stresses cognitive rather than motivational factors, he acknowledges that some slips may be triggered by unconscious motivations. The analysis of slips was, of course, one of Freud's preferred techniques for investigating unconscious processes. Research on action slips in the social realm might therefore serve to focus attention to the interface between cognitive and motivational determinants of behavior.

## CONCLUSION

We opened this chapter with a note of caution, emphasizing that the information-processing approach to social cognition should not detract from social psychology's traditional concerns with naturally occurring behavior, mutual adaptation, non-cognitive factors, and individual differences. We hope, however, that our overview has conveyed the sense of optimism we feel about the field of social cognition. Cognitive psychology can contribute to the understanding of social behavior on many fronts. In this chapter we have surveyed some major themes in current cognitive psychology with relevance to social cognition, such as conceptions of mental representation, categorization processes, and cognitive learning mechanisms. We have touched on a few of the many points of potential contact between models of cognition and approaches to individual differences, motivation, affect, and action. As long as the information-processing approach is treated as a flexible framework for social cognition, rather than as a rigid straitjacket, the interaction between cognitive and social psychology should benefit both. What will finally emerge from this interchange remains to be seen. At best it may lead toward a richer psychology of complete human beings.

## ACKNOWLEDGMENTS

This chapter was prepared while K. J. Holyoak held an NIMH Research Scientist Development Award, 1-K02-MH00342-02, and P. C. Gordon held an NIMH Traineeship, 1-T32-MH16892-01. We thank Nancy Cantor, John Kihlstrom, Laura McCloskey, Richard Nisbett and Robert Wyer, Jr., for their helpful comments on an earlier draft.

# REFERENCES

Anderson, J. R. Arguments concerning representations for mental imagery. *Psychological Review*, 1978, *85*, 249–277.

Anderson, J. R., & Bower, G. H. *Human associative memory*. New York: Winston, 1973.

Atkinson, R. C., & Shiffrin, R. M. Human memory: A proposed system and its control processes. In K. N. Spence & J. T. Spence (Eds.), *The psychology of learning and motivation*, Vol. 2. New York: Academic Press, 1968.

Baddeley, A. D. The trouble with levels: A reexamination of Craik and Lockhart's framework for memory research. *Psychological Review*, 1978, *85*, 139–152.

Bandura, A. *Psychological modelling: Conflicting theories*. New York: Aldine-Atherton, 1971.

Bandura, A. *Social learning theory*. Englewood Cliffs, N.J.: Prentice-Hall, 1977.

Beck, A. T. *Cognitive therapy and the emotional disorders*. New York: New American Library, 1976.

Borgida, E., Locksley, A., & Brekke, N. Social stereotypes and social judgment. In N. Cantor & J. F. Kihlstrom (Eds.), *Personality, cognition, and social interaction*. Hillsdale, N.J.: Lawrence Erlbaum Associates, 1982.

Bower, G. H. Contacts of cognitive psychology with social learning theory. *Cognitive Therapy and Research*, 1978, *2*, 123–146.

Bower, G. H. Mood and memory. *American Psychologist*, 1981, *36*, 129–148.

Brooks, L. Nonanalytic concept formation and memory for instances. In E. Rosch & B. B. Lloyd (Eds.), *Cognition and categorization*. Hillsdale, N.J.: Lawrence Erlbaum Associates, 1978.

Cantor, N. A cognitive-social approach to personality. In N. Cantor & J. F. Kihlstrom (Eds.), *Personality, cognition, and social interaction*. Hillsdale, N.J.: Lawrence Erlbaum Associates, 1982.

Cantor, N., & Mischel, W. Categorization processes in the perception of people. In L. Berkowitz (Ed.), *Advances in experimental social psychology*, Vol. 10. New York: Academic Press, 1979.

Chase, W. G., & Simon, H. A. The mind's eye in chess. In W. G. Chase (Ed.), *Visual information processing*. New York: Academic Press, 1973.

Collins, A. M., & Quillian, M. R. Retrieval time from semantic memory. *Journal of Verbal Learning and Verbal Behavior*, 1969, *8*, 240–247.

Craik, F. I. M., & Lockhart, R. S. Levels of processing: A framework for memory research. *Journal of Verbal Learning and Verbal Behavior*, 1972, *11*, 671–684.

Craik, F. I. M., & Tulving, E. Depth of processing and the retention of words in episodic memory. *Journal of Experimental Psychology: General*, 1975, *104*, 268–294.

DeSoto, C. B. The predilection for single orderings. *Journal of Abnormal and Social Psychology*, 1961, *62*, 16–23.

DeSoto, C. B., London, M., & Handel, S. Social reasoning and spatial paralogic. *Journal of Personality and Social Psychology*, 1965, *2*, 513–521.

Fischler, I. Associative facilitation without expectancy in a lexical decision task. *Journal of Experimental Psychology: Human Perception and Performance*, 1977, *3*, 391–394.

Fiske, S. T., & Kinder, D. R. Involvement, expertise and schema use: Evidence from political cognition. In N. Cantor & J. F. Kihlstrom (Eds.), *Personality, cognition, and social interaction*. Hillsdale, N.J.: Lawrence Erlbaum Associates, 1982.

Fried, L. S., & Holyoak, K. J. Induction of category distributions: A framework for classification learning. *Journal of Experimental Psychology: Learning, Memory and Cognition*, in press.

Fodor, J. A. *The language of thought*. New York: Thomas Crowell, 1975.

Glass, A. L., Holyoak, K. J., & Santa, J. L. *Cognition*. Reading; Mass.: Addison-Wesley, 1979.

Gick, M. L., & Holyoak, K. J. Analogical problem solving. *Cognitive Psychology*, 1980, *12*, 306–355.

Gick, M. L., & Holyoak, K. J. Schema induction and analogical transfer. *Cognitive Psychology*, 1983, *15*, 1–38.

Gordon, P. C., & Holyoak, K. J. Implicit learning and generalization of the ''mere exposure'' effect. *Journal of Personality and Social Psychology*, 1983, *45*, 492–500.

Greeno, J. G. Psychology of learning, 1960–1980: One participant's observations. *American Psychologist*, 1980, *35*, 713–728.

Hamilton, D. L. A cognitive-attributional analysis of stereotyping. In D. Berkowitz (Ed.), *Advances in experimental social psychology*, Vol. 10. New York: Academic Press, 1979.

Hart, H. L. A., & Honore, A. M. *Causation in the law*. Oxford: Oxford University Press, 1959.

Hayes-Roth, F. Distinguishing theories of representation: A critique of Anderson's ''Arguments concerning mental imagery''. *Psychological Review*, 1979, *86*, 376–382.

Holyoak, K. J. Comparative judgments with numerical reference points. *Cognitive Psychology*, 1978, *10*, 203–243.

Holyoak, K. J. Analogical thinking and human intelligence. In R. J. Sternberg (Ed.), *Advances in the psychology of human intelligence*, Vol. 2. Hillsdale, N.J.: Lawrence Erlbaum Associates, 1984.

Holyoak, K. J., & Gordon, P. C. Social reference points. *Journal of Personality and Social Psychology*, 1983, *44*, 881–887.

Holyoak, K. J., & Mah, W. A. Cognitive reference points in judgments of symbolic magnitude. *Cognitive Psychology*, 1981, *14*, 328–352.

Holyoak, K. J., & Patterson, K. K. A positional discriminability model of linear-order judgments. *Journal of Experimental Psychology: Human Perception and Performance*, 1981, *7*, 1283–1302.

Holyoak, K. J., & Walker, J. H. Subjective magnitude information in semantic orderings. *Journal of Verbal Learning and Verbal Behavior*, 1976, *15*, 287–299.

Hovland, C. I., & Sherif, M. Judgmental phenomena and scales of attitude measurement: Item displacement in Thurstone scales. *Journal of Abnormal and Social Psychology*, 1952, *47*, 822–832.

Hunt, E., Frost, N., & Lunneborg, C. L. Individual differences in cognition. In G. H. Bower (Ed.), *Advances in learning and motivation*, Vol. 7. New York: Academic Press, 1973.

Jacoby, L. L., & Craik, F. I. M. Effects of elaboration of processing at encoding and retrieval: Trace distinctiveness and recovery of initial context. In L. S. Cermak & F. I. M. Craik (Eds.), *Levels of processing and human memory*. Hillsdale, N.J.: Lawrence Erlbaum Associates, 1979.

James, W. *Principles of psychology*. New York: Holt, 1890.

Jaynes, J. *The origin of consciousness in the breakdown of the bicameral mind*. Boston: Houghton Mifflin, 1976.

Jones, E. E., & Nisbett, R. E. The actor and the observer: Divergent perceptions of the causes of behavior. In E. E. Jones, D. E. Kanouse, H. H. Kelley, R. E. Nisbett, S. Vallins, & B. Weiner (Eds.), *Attribution: perceiving the causes of behavior*. Morristown, N.J.: General Learning Press, 1972.

Kahneman, D., & Tversky, A. The simulation heuristic. In D. Kahneman, P. Slovic, & A. Tversky (Eds.), *Judgment under uncertainty: Heuristics and biases*. New York: Cambridge University Press, 1982.

Keele, S. W. Movement control in skilled motor performance. *Psychological Bulletin*, 1968, *70*, 387–403.

Kosslyn, S. M. *Image and mind*. Cambridge, Mass.: Harvard University Press, 1980.

Kosslyn, S. M. The medium and the message in mental imagery: A theory. *Psychological Review*, 1981, *88*, 46–66.

Kosslyn, S. M., & Pomerantz, J. R. Imagery, propositions, and the form of internal representations. *Cognitive Psychology*, 1977, *9*, 52–76.

Lachman, R., Lachman, J. L., & Butterfield, E. C. *Cognitive psychology and information processing: An introduction*. Hillsdale: N.J.: Lawrence Erlbaum Associates, 1979.

Lakoff, G., & Johnson, M. *Metaphors we live by*. Chicago: University of Chicago Press, 1980.

Larkin, J. H., McDermott, J., Simon, D., & Simon, H. A. Expert and novice performance in solving physics problems. *Science*, 1980, *208*, 1335–1342.

Lashley, K. S. The problem of serial order in behavior. In L. A. Jeffress (Ed.), *Cerebral mechanisms in behavior: The Hixon Symposium*. New York: Wiley, 1951.

Mackie, J. L. *The cement of the universe*. Oxford: Oxford University Press, 1974.

Maratsos, M. P., & Chalkley, M. A. The internal language of children's syntax: The ontogenesis and representation of syntactic categories. In K. Nelson (Ed.), *Children's language*, Vol. II. New York: Gardner, 1980.

Markus, H., & Smith, J. The influence of self-schemas on the perception of others. In N. Cantor & J. F. Kihlstrom (Eds.), *Personality, cognition, and social interaction*. Hillsdale, N.J.: Lawrence Erlbaum Associates, 1982.

McArthur, L. Z., & Post, D. L. Figural emphasis and person perception. *Journal of Experimental Social Psychology*, 1977, *13*, 520–535.

McClelland, J. L. On the time relations of mental processes: An examination of systems of processes in cascade. *Psychological Review*, 1979, *86*, 287–330.

Medin, D. C., & Schaffer, M. M. Context theory of classification learning. *Psychological Review*, 1978, *85*, 207–238.

Meyer, D. E., & Schvaneveldt, R. W. Facilitation in recognizing pairs of words: Evidence of a dependence between retrieval operations. *Journal of Experimental Psychology*, 1971, *90*, 227–234.

Meyer, D. E., & Schvaneveldt, R. W. Meaning, memory structure and mental processes. *Science*, 1976, *192*, 27–33.

Mischel, W. Personality and cognition: Something borrowed, something new? In N. Cantor & J. F. Kihlstrom (Eds.), *Personality, cognition, and social interaction*. Hillsdale, N.J.: Lawrence Erlbaum Associates, 1982.

Moyer, R. S. Comparing objects in memory: Evidence suggesting an internal psychophysics. *Perception & Psychophysics*, 1973, *13*, 180–184.

Nelson, J. O. Repetition and depth of processing. *Journal of Verbal Learning and Verbal Behavior*, 1977, *16*, 151–172.

Nelson, K. Social cognition in a script framework. In J. H. Flavell & L. Ross (Eds.), *Social cognitive development: Frontiers and possible futures*. New York: Cambridge University Press, 1981.

Nisbett, R. E., & Ross, L. D. *Human inference: Strategies and shortcomings of social judgment*. Englewood Cliffs, N.J.: Prentice-Hall, 1980.

Norman, D. Categorization of action slips. *Psychological Review*, 1981, *88*, 1–15.

Paivio, A. Neomentalism. *Canadian Journal of Psychology*, 1975, *29*, 263–291.

Palmer, S. F. Fundamental aspects of cognitive representation. In E. Rosch & B. B. Lloyd (Eds.), *Cognition and categorization*. Hillsdale, N.J.: Lawrence Erlbaum Associates, 1978.

Pinker, S. Mental imagery and the third dimension. *Journal of Experimental Psychology: General*, 1980, *109*, 354–371.

Pinker, S. A theory of the acquisition of lexical-interpretive grammars. In J. Bresnan (Ed.), *The mental representation of grammatical relations*. Cambridge, Mass.: MIT Press, 1981.

Posner, M. I., & Keele, S. W. On the genesis of abstract ideas. *Journal of Experimental Psychology*, 1968, *77*, 353–363.

Posner, M. I., & Snyder, C. R. R. Attention and cognitive control. In R. L. Solso (Ed.), *Information processing and cognition: The Loyola Symposium*. Hillsdale, N.J.: Erlbaum, 1975.

Potts, G. R. Storing and retrieving information about ordered relationships. *Journal of Experimental Psychology*, 1974, *103*, 431–439.

Pylyshyn, Z. W. What the mind's eye tells the mind's brain: A critique of mental imagery. *Psychological Bulletin*, 1973, *80*, 1–24.

Pylyshyn, Z. W. Validating computational models: A critique of Anderson's indeterminacy of representation claim. *Psychological Review,* 1979, *56,* 383–394.

Pylyshyn, Z. W. The imagery debate: Analogue media versus tacit knowledge. *Psychological Review,* 1981, *88,* 16–45.

Reber, A. S. Implicit learning of artificial grammars. *Journal of Verbal Learning and Verbal Behavior,* 1967, *5,* 855–863.

Reber, A. S., & Allen, R. Analogy and abstraction strategies in synthetic grammar learning: A functional interpretation. *Cognition,* 1978, *6,* 189–221.

Reber, A. S., Kassin, S. M., Lewis, S., & Cantor, G. On the relationship between implicit and explicit modes in the learning of a complex rule structure. *Journal of Experimental Psychology: Human Learning and Memory,* 1980, *6,* 492–502.

Reed, S. K. Pattern recognition and categorization. *Cognitive Psychology,* 1972, *3,* 383–407.

Rogers, T. B., Kuiper, N. A., & Rogers, P. J. Symbolic distance and congruity effects for paired-comparisons judgments of degree of self-reference. *Journal of Research in Personality,* 1979, *13,* 433–449.

Rosch, E. On the internal structure of perceptual and semantic categories. In T. E. Moore (Ed.), *Cognitive development and the acquisition of language.* New York: Academic Press, 1973.

Rosch, E. Cognitive reference points. *Cognitive Psychology,* 1975, *7,* 532–547.

Rosch, E., & Mervis, C. B. Family resemblances: Studies in the internal structure of categories. *Cognitive Psychology,* 1975, *7,* 573–605.

Rosch, E., Mervis, C. B., Gray, W. D., Johnson, D. M., & Boyes-Braem, P. Basic objects in natural categories. *Cognitive Psychology,* 1976, *8,* 382–439.

Rosenbaum, D. A. Human movement initiation: Specification of arm, direction, and extent. *Journal of Experimental Psychology: General,* 1980, *109,* 444–474.

Ross, L. The "intuitive scientist" formulation and its developmental implications. In J. H. Flavell & L. Ross (Eds.), *Social cognitive development: Frontiers and possible futures.* New York: Cambridge University Press, 1981.

Rumelhart, D. E. Schemata: The building blocks of cognition. In R. Spiro, B. Bruce, & W. Brewer (Eds.), *Theoretical issues in reading comprehension.* Hillsdale, N.J.: Lawrence Erlbaum Associates, 1980.

Schacter, S., & Singer, J. Cognitive, social and physiological determinants of emotional state. *Psychological Review,* 1962, *69,* 379–399.

Schmidt, R. A. A schema theory of discrete motor skill learning. *Psychological Review,* 1975, *82,* 225–260.

Schustack, M. W., & Sternberg, R. J. Evaluation of evidence in causal inference. *Journal of Experimental Psychology: General,* 1981, *110,* 101–120.

Shiffrin, R. M., & Schneider, W. Controlled and automatic human information processing: II. Perceptual learning, automatic attending, and a general theory. *Psychological Review,* 1977, *84,* 127–190.

Snyder, M. Self-monitoring processes. In L. Berkowitz (Ed.), *Advances in Experimental Social Psychology,* Vol. 12. New York: Academic Press, 1979.

Sternberg, S. High-speed scanning in human memory. *Science,* 1966, *153,* 652–654.

Sternberg, S., Monsell, S., Knoll, R. L., & Wright, C. E. The latency and duration of rapid movement sequences: Comparisons of speech and typewriting. In G. E. Stelmach (Ed.), *Information processing in motor control and learning.* New York: Academic Press, 1978.

Taylor, R. E., & Fiske, S. J. Salience, attention, and attribution: Top of the head phenomena. In L. Berkowitz (Ed.), *Advances in experimental social psychology,* Vol. 11. New York: Academic Press, 1978.

Tulving, E. Episodic and semantic memory. In E. Tulving & W. Donaldson (Eds.), *Organization of memory.* New York: Academic Press, 1972.

Tversky, A. Features of similarity. *Psychological Review,* 1977, *84,* 327–352.

Tversky, A., & Kahneman, D. Availability: A heuristic for judging frequency and probability. *Cognitive Psychology,* 1973, *5,* 207–232.

Winston, P. H. Learning and reasoning by analogy. *Communications of the ACM,* 1980, *23,* 689–703.

Zajonc, R. B. Cognition and social cognition: A historical perspective. In L. Festinger (Ed.), *Four decades of social psychology.* Oxford: Oxford University Press, 1980. (a)

Zajonc, R. B. Feeling and thinking: Preferences need no inferences. *American Psychologist,* 1980, *35,* 151–175. (b)

Zajonc, R. B., & Markus, H. Affect and cognition: The hard interface. In C. Izard, J. Kagan, & R. B. Zajonc (Eds.), *Emotion, cognition and behavior.* New York: Cambridge University Press, in press.

# 3

# Of Cabbages and Kings: Assessing the Extendibility of Natural Object Concept Models to Social Things

John H. Lingle
Mark W. Altom
*Rutgers University*

Douglas L. Medin
*University of Illinois*

## Contents

"The time has come," the Walrus said,
"to talk of many things:
Of shoes—and ships—and sealing-wax—
Of cabbages—and kings—
And why the sea is boiling hot—
and whether pigs have wings."
—Carroll (1871, p. 162)


## INTRODUCTION

Consider the following description: The trains to Long Island were running behind schedule and when Robert arrived at his cousin's house the party was well under way. He went first to the wine and cheese table, noting with some amusement the inevitable Brie and Camembert, and poured himself a glass of burgundy. Then he turned his attention to the other guests. The gentleman on his left seemed vaguely familiar, but it was not until he listened to him talk for several seconds that Robert realized the man was a former neighbor. To Robert's right, another man was loudly telling a series of jokes. The jokes were very funny, and Robert wished for a moment that he could be more of an extrovert. At the other end of the table a woman was helping herself to some potato chips. She had long straight hair and wore a black leotard top with a batik print skirt. "Probably a social worker," he thought. He moved close enough to read the button she was wearing (it said, "Have you hugged your kid today?") and edged away. Then an unlikely event captured his attention. One of the guests had rolled up a shirt-sleeve and was reaching into the fish tank. Robert's first speculation was that the fish in the aquarium were piranhas and that the man was trying to impress people with his courage. But a second look revealed both that the fish were guppies and the reason for the bizzare behavior. The man was reaching for his car keys which he must have accidently dropped into the tank. "Undoubtedly drunk," Robert mused.

This chapter is concerned with categorization. The above sketch is replete with examples of categorization ranging from *Brie* to *extrovert* and from *guppy* to *drunk*. In the chapter we focus on some of the similarities and differences between two types of categories: (a) natural object categories (e.g., Brie, guppy, and cabbages) that refer to concrete, perceptual objects in the environment, and (b) social categories (e.g., extrovert, drunk, and kings) that encompass classifications of other people and socially relevant stimuli and events. Our motivation in making such a comparison stems from the large amount of research that has been conducted over the past decade by cognitive psychologists on how people classify and categorize natural objects (see Mervis & Rosch, 1981; Smith & Medin, 1981, for reviews). This work has produced a number of new cognitive processing models and concepts that have begun to be applied to social categorization (cf., Cantor & Mischel, 1979; Hastie, Ostrom, Ebbesen, Wyer, Hamilton, & Carlston, 1980). Such applications may extend the discoveries and insights of one area to another, but at the same time may be misleading if they are applied indiscriminately without considering differences among stimulus domains.

Our goal in the chapter is to identify factors that lead to beneficial as well as misleading applications of models of natural object categorization to the social domain. In doing so we hope to provide some insights into social categorization processes, while at the same time to identify some serious gaps in existing cognitive models. To anticipate the tenor of the chapter, we are more interested in examining the impact of different factors on category representation and functioning than in cataloguing all of the ways natural object and social categories might differ. Nonetheless, our analysis reveals several ways in which the two classes of categories differ in both their structure and processing, suggesting that care must be exercised in applying models from one domain to the other.

Our plan of attack is as follows: We first consider the role of categorization in cognitive functioning and describe the recent major shift in theoretical perspectives on categorization. As part of this discussion we note the relatively limited domain upon which current cognitive theories of categorization are based. We also identify some of the ways in which natural object and social categories differ both between each other and among themselves. In the heart of the chapter, we then examine how characteristic properties of classification systems such as attribute identification, category structure, and processing modes interrelate with models of category representation and functioning.

## PERSPECTIVES ON COGNITION AND CATEGORIZATION

### Category Functions

We understand new experiences by relating them to what we already know. Such relationships or concepts give our world stability, for if each entity were perceived as totally unique, we would be overwhelmed by the diversity of our experience and unable to communicate it to anyone else. By grouping objects and events together that are alike in some important respect we are able to think about and respond to them in ways we have already mastered. In this regard, "To categorize is to render discriminably different things equivalent, to group the objects and events and people around us into classes, and to respond to them in terms of their class membership rather than their uniqueness" (Bruner, Goodnow, & Austin, 1956; p. 3).

A formal definition of categorization does little to convey its ubiquitousness in cognitive functioning. From elementary perception to complex reasoning tasks, categories and categorization processes pervade our mental functioning. They allow us to identify objects, infer unobservable attributes, make predictions about the future, and understand the causes of events. Thus, in our introductory scenario Robert was able to make inferences about objects and events by grouping them with his past experiences. That is, he could infer the general taste characteristics of the Brie and Burgundy as a consequence of their category membership and decide whether or not he wished to sample them. By classifying the woman across the table as a social worker, he knew that he did not want to talk with her. And by categorizing the man by the fish tank as drunk, Robert felt he understood why the guest was putting his hand in the water.

As suggested by these examples, our mental representations of categories include various forms of information that allow them to serve several different functions. Robert, for example, identified one of the guests as a former neighbor on the basis of perceptual attributes, so presumably that information was part of his concept of the person. But Robert's concept is also likely to include a general impression of what his neighbor is like behaviorally and socially, as well as memory for particular events associated with his neighbor (e.g., going on a fishing trip with him, his neighbor's New Years Eve party, and so on). Robert's impression of this particular neighbor might also be influenced by his ideas about what neighbors in general are like. Thus, much of the power of categories derives not only from their represented or associated attributes, but also from their relationships to other concepts.

A function of categorization that seems particularly salient for social categories is understanding. Robert was concerned with why the man was reaching into the fish tank and then with why he had dropped the car keys. The latter behavior was "explained" by reference to the category, drunk. Note that Robert's reasoning was circular, but it seemed to satisfy him. It is unclear what produces such feelings of understanding. Partly, it may result from increased confidence as to what may happen next. That is, one may have few ideas as to what someone who drops their keys into a fish tank is likely to do next. However, once the person is categorized as drunk, a host of likely behaviors drawn from past experience becomes available.

The fish-tank example raises an additional point worth noting. "Drops—keys—into—tank" would probably not be directly represented in Robert's concept of a drunk. Rather, actions must often themselves be classified (e.g., in this case, as silly or uncoordinated) in order to serve as the basis for further categorization. Thus, an additional characteristic of categories that increases their utility is that they may be used as the basis for further category groupings. We will have more to say about this property in a later section.

Finally, we should emphasize at this early point that inferences and interpretations that result from categorization are not necessarily foolproof. One may classify an animal as a mammal and infer that it bears live young, but this inference would be incorrect for egg-laying mammals such as the spiny anteater.

Similarly, a particular social worker may or may not be like one's general impression of social workers as a group. Whenever nonidentical entities are categorized together, one takes advantage of similarities but one also disregards differences. Consequently, there will always be a trade off between maximizing inferences and avoiding erroneous conclusions. The ubiquitousness of people's attempts to understand the world around them suggests that the trade-off is resolved more toward maximizing inferences than toward avoiding errors.

These observations about the nature and functions of categories serve to emphasize the omnipresence of categorization in people's mental life. They also raise a host of issues that we discuss in this chapter. We begin by describing recent revisions in cognitive psychologists' views of how people mentally represent categories.

## The Emerging Picture from Cognitive Psychology

Traditionally, theories of category representation in philosophy (Aristotle, 1963; Sommers, 1965), linguistics (Katz & Fodor, 1963), as well as psychology (Bruner, Goodnow, & Austin, 1956; Bourne, 1966) have viewed categories as having defining attributes that are singly necessary and jointly sufficient for determining category membership. That is, any entity having these attributes is a member of the category, while any entity lacking even one of the attributes is not a member. In light of its dominance in theories of categorization, this position has been dubbed the "classical view" (Smith & Medin, 1981). It implies that all members of a category should be equally good or representative, and that learning a category consists of discovering its defining attributes. Any attribute not present in all members of the category would not be a defining attribute. As an example of this last point, if Robert's concept of a social worker were to include as a defining attribute "is boring to talk with" and he should ever meet a single social worker with something of interest to say, the classical position requires his concept to change since "boring to talk with" would no longer be true of all category members.

One of the major developments in cognitive psychology over the last decade has been an increasing disenchantment with the classical view's approach to category representation. When considering instances from natural object categories, not all members of a category appear to be equally good examples of the category as one might expect if membership were simply determined by whether the instance included the defining attributes. Subjects' ratings of category typicality differ systematically across category members, as do their speed and accuracy of classification (Rips, Shoben, & Smith, 1973; Rosch, 1973). Moreover, to the extent that attribute listings reflect category representation, category attributes include ones that are neither necessary nor sufficient, but are merely characteristic of category members. Furthermore, the number of characteristic attributes associated with different category members is not constant, but rather, varies with judgments of typicality and classification latency (Rosch & Mervis, 1975; Hampton, 1979). As a consequence of such findings, the current consensus among cognitive psychologists is that the classical view is unable to account for people's representation of natural object categories.

Rejection of the classical view has not been unique to psychology, but is also reflected in current research and thinking in anthropology (Berlin, 1978) and biology (Sokal, 1974). Taxonomists have distinguished between *monothetic* and *polythetic* category systems (Sneath & Sokal, 1973; Sokal, 1974). "Monothetic classifications are those in which the classes established differ by at least one property which is uniform among the members of each class. . . In polythetic classifications, taxa are groups of individuals or objects that share a large proportion of their properties but do not necessarily agree in any one property" (Sokal, 1974, p. 1117). The monothetic view corresponds to the classical view, while the polythetic approach corresponds to more recent trends in cognitive psychology. Just as the classical view has come into increasing disfavor in psychology, there is a growing tendency by taxonomists in other areas to describe category systems polythetically rather than monothetically.

In the polythetic view of classification, instances are neither arbitrarily associated with categories nor strictly linked by defining attributes. Instead, categories may reflect a "family resemblance" structure (Rosch & Mervis, 1975) in which typicality of category membership is based on the proportion of attributes or properties shared with other category members relative to the proportion of attributes shared with nonmembers of the category. Thus, many categories may not be well-defined, but may instead be based on relationships that are only true on the average. Since no single set of attributes can be used to determine category membership, categories have "fuzzy" boundaries and category members vary in the degree to which they are typical members of the category. For example, cows are rated to be better examples of the concept mammal than are whales (McCloskey & Glucksberg, 1978), and we might expect people to think guppies are more representative of fish than manta rays.

Up to this point, we have proceeded as if all categories have the same type of underlying structure. However, category structure may differ across conceptual domains. Although rejection of the classical position in cognitive psychology has been empirically based, the domain of application to which alternative polythetic models have been applied has been limited. Consequently, before considering characteristic features of category systems, we first identify some of the different types of categories within the natural object and social domains.

## Category Typologies

At a conceptual level, social categories are those that relate to people. In practice, however, the distinction between "natural object" and "social" categories is not always clear-cut. The category "human being," for example, can be thought of as either a social or natural object category, depending on whether one focuses on generalizations concerning behavior (what people are like) or relationships to other living things (i.e., plant, animal, mammal, and primate). Rather than pit one class of categories against the other, our goal throughout the chapter is to analyze the characteristic properties that distinguish among category systems and identify the conditions under which different principles of category structure and process are likely to hold. We begin, therefore, by making some rough distinctions among various types of categories that serve as the focus for the chapter.

Although not always clearly distinguishable from social categories, natural object categories can be operationally defined in terms of the extensive body of experimental research in cognitive psychology that has been conducted over the last decade. This research has concentrated on concepts that are reflected in our natural language and tend to have one-word names. More specifically, the focus has been on object concepts such as animals, plants, and human artifacts (e.g., furniture or vehicles). While some recent work in cognitive psychology has employed artificially constructed stimulus sets, they are generally designed to mimic suspected properties of natural object categories.

To date, relatively little work has been done to apply the more recent models of category representation to other classes of non-social categories. Abstract categories like *truth* and *justice* or more analytical and technical categories like *rhombus* and *trapezoid* can be seen to differ from the studied natural object categories in a number of ways, including their familiarity, accessibility, and organizational properties. At this point, it is unclear to what extent the newer cognitive models are extendable to these other concept domains (cf., Hampton, 1981).

Social categories might also be identified operationally as those studied by social psychologists. In contrast to the natural object categories studied by cognitive psychologists, social categories are heterogeneous, with a wide range of underlying structures and processes. Some taxonomies of social categories are provided by Ostrom (1975), Fiske and Cox (1979), and Wiggins (1979). Among those social categories that have been most extensively studied are traits (e.g., Rosenberg, Nelson, & Vivekananthan, 1968; Rosenberg & Sedlak, 1972; Schneider, 1973; Wiggins, 1979), groups (e.g., Rothbart, Evans, & Fulero, 1979; Rothbart, Fulero, Jensen, Howard, & Birrell, 1978; Wilder, 1981), persons, including the self and others (e.g., Gara & Rosenberg, 1979; Greenwald, 1980; Jones & Nisbett, 1972; Kelley, 1972; Ross & Sicoly, 1979; Wegner & Vallacher, 1980), and social situations (e.g., Barker, 1968; Cantor, Mischel, & Schwartz, 1982; Fredrickson, 1972; Pervin, 1976).

As we will emphasize in later sections, social concepts differ along myriad dimensions, and principles that hold for one type may not hold for another. As one example, the distinction is sometimes drawn between *proper constructs* and *categories* (see Higgins & King [1981] for a discussion of this point relevant to social concepts). Category is used to refer to information about a class or grouping of objects, events, or properties whereas proper construct refers to a body of information about a single individual or event. One difference between the two is that proper constructs are generally mutually exclusive (if one is Robert Jones, one is not usually Harry Smith). Categories, on the other hand, often form multiple overlapping classes (e.g., one's categories of golfers, tennis players, communists, and women may include some of the same individuals as members).

Even when considering only categories with multiple members, the categories may differ in their organization and structure. Thus, social groups can often be described in terms of a hierarchy of classes, whereas traits, persons, and social situations many times can not. In order to analyze relations and interactions among categories, it is convenient, if not necessary, to consider characteristics of attributes of categories. Even here, we will need to make numerous distinctions in order to discuss how attributes enter into and influence category processing.

## ATTRIBUTES: THE BUILDING BLOCKS OF CATEGORIES

### The Category-Attribute Distinction

Most people's intuitions are that robins are more similar to canaries than to squirrels, more similar to squirrels than to fish, and more similar to fish than to trees. In the same vein, people might judge a banker to be more similar to a lawyer than to a social worker. What is the basis for this intuition? The consensus view in cognitive psychology is that concepts can be analyzed into component parts or attributes and that similarities between categories and among category members derive from their shared attributes. Thus, robins are more similar to canaries than to squirrels because they share more attributes with the former than with the latter (e.g., feathers, number of legs, beak). In such an analysis, attributes form the elementary building blocks that mediate judgments of similarity among categories and category members.

The relationship between categories and attributes may at first seem straightforward. This, however, is not the case. One complexity concerns the fact that category membership itself may serve as an attribute. That is, we can describe a person in terms of particular attributes such as tall, white, and female. Yet, on other occasions these same attributes may function as socially significant categories. Category membership itself can serve as an attribute for other higher-order categories, as is illustrated in Figure 3.1. In this example, a person has been classified as falling into the categories *strong, agile,* and *competitive.* These three categories themselves then serve as attributes for classifying the person as

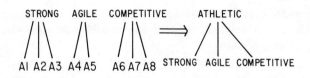

FIG. 3.1.    Illustrative example of categories functioning as attributes.

*athletic.* The chain could, of course, continue with athletic serving as an abstract attribute for further classifications (e.g., well-rounded).

The overlapping relationship between categories and attributes has led some theorists (cf., Wyer, 1974) to conclude that the distinction between them is one of convenience rather than substance. We are not so sure. Categories and attributes seem to differ in both their representations and their functions. In the remainder of this section, we discuss the basis for this claim together with some distinguishing examples.

In the following discussions, we use the terms *category* and *concept* interchangeably to refer to a grouping of entities (events, objects, situations, or whatever) based on one or more characteristics. We use the term *attribute* to refer to some characteristic of an entity that could potentially serve as the basis for a grouping. Thus, in our use of the two terms all categories or group memberships can also function as attributes, although not all attributes function as categories.

Although exceptions may exist, in general we conjecture that properties represented only as attributes are less rich in their cognitive representation than categorical representations. That is to say, people's categorical representations are likely to include associated characteristics of category members, while a simple attribute representation is less likely to do so. To illustrate this distinction between category and attribute representations consider the two groups, male persons and persons who wear wire-rimmed glasses. We would argue that while most people represent male as a social category, they represent "wears wire-rimmed glasses" as an attribute. One consequence of this difference in representation is the ease with which people can list properties associated with maleness as opposed to"wears wire-rimmed glasses."

One response to this example is that "wears wire-rimmed glasses" is also represented categorically, but that the category is impoverished because few other attributes correlate with the classification attribute. However, consider how an optician might represent "wears wire-rimmed glasses." Because of experience and occupational demands, the optician might well have represented in memory that wearers of wire-rimmed glasses are generally older, wealthier, more vain, and less athletic than wearers of plastic or horned frames. If such were the case, we would argue that the optician has a categorical representation of wire-rimmed glasses wearers as opposed to most people's attribute representation. A manifestation of this representational difference would be the speed (and perhaps accuracy) with which the optician could identify properties associated with category membership.

While disagreements are certain to remain as to the exact nature of category-attribute differences, the distinction has proved useful in investigating and understanding two phenomena: (a) memory-based decision processes and (b) category structure. We consider each of these in turn.

## Attributes versus Categories as the Basis for Decisions

While people may encode a variety of attributes about an object or event, they often form category impressions based only on a subset of properties. The set of categories that are formed, and whether or not categories or attributes are retrieved from memory, can strongly influence the decisions a person makes. As a concrete example, suppose for the moment that Robert meets Jim at the party and learns in the course of the conversation four attributes about Jim: (a) that he avoids black cats, (b) that he carries a rabbit's foot, (c) that he works as a fireman, and (d) that he lives in Philadelphia. Knowing all of this information, Robert might also categorize Jim as "superstitious" based on the first two attributes. If Robert is later asked to make an inference or decision about Jim, the decision process may be quite different depending on whether he bases his judgment on remembered attributes or his categorization of Jim as superstitious. One consequence concerns the different inferences Robert is likely to make about Jim (cf., Carlston, 1980a; Higgins, Rholes, & Jones, 1977; Lingle, Geva, Ostrom, Leippe, & Baumgardner, 1979). Thus, if asked whether his new acquaintance is likely to walk under ladders, Robert will most likely answer "No" if he uses as the basis for his response his representation of Jim as a member of the category superstitious. However, Robert may well respond in just the opposite way if he bases his judgment on remembered attributes and recalls that Jim is a fireman.

The speed with which different judgments are made can also distinguish the type of representation underlying a decision (cf., Allen & Ebbesen, 1981; Ford & Weldon, 1981; Lingle, Dukerich, & Ostrom, 1983; Lingle & Ostrom, 1979; Markus, 1977). Thus, for example, if Robert has categorized Jim as superstitious and uses this representation as the basis for decisions, he should make judgments relevant to superstitious-typical behavior at a speed unrelated to the number of attributes he has encoded about Jim. If, however, no such categorization has been made and Robert makes judgments by recalling individual attributes, his decision time should vary with the number of attributes he knows and considers in reaching a decision.

A final consequence of whether decisions are based on a categorical or attribute representation is the consistency with which they are made (cf., Altom & Lingle, 1980, 1982; Lingle & Altom, 1979). There is evidence that people better remember their categorizations than the set of attributes upon which the categorizations are based (e.g., Lingle et al., 1979; Slamecka & Graf, 1978). If people base decisions on salient categorizations, their decisions over time should be relatively stable. Judgments based on less-well-remembered attributes, on the other hand, are likely to fluctuate depending on which particular attributes come to mind at the moment of decision. Thus, if Robert has Jim categorized as superstitious and is asked on several occasions about Jim's behavior around ladders, Robert is likely to repeatedly recall "superstitious" and consistently respond that Jim is not likely to walk under them. However, in the absence of this categorical representation, Robert's responses may well fluctuate depending on whether he remembers Jim's attribute of being a fireman or his attribute of avoiding black cats.

One caveat concerning the category-attribute distinction needs mentioning before considering how attribute characteristics influence category structure. In some instances, properties may mimic categorical representations even though they are encoded and function only as attributes. For example, the tendency for members within the same group to appear more confusable than members of different groups and for better discriminations to be made within smaller groups has sometimes been taken as evidence for person categorization (cf., Taylor, Fiske, Etcoff, & Ruderman, 1978). Similar results might occur, however, even in the case group membership were encoded only as a simple attribute of different persons. The situation can be compared to a paired-associate learning task. Suppose in such a case separate responses were being learned to the stimuli of a red circle, a red square, and a blue triangle. Both during learning and after some forgetting one would expect to find, simply based on stimulus generalization, greatest accuracy in responding to the blue triangle with response errors for the red stimuli being confused with one another. This analogue may carry over to groups. Specifically, one would expect the persons (like the geometric objects) sharing an attribute of group membership (like the objects sharing the color red) to be responded to similarly relative to individuals not sharing the attribute of group membership. Likewise, attributes of minority group members (like the blue object) could be better discriminated than those of majority group members (red objects), even when people's representations of others are not organized in terms of person categories.

## Attribute Characteristics

Within a category system, attributes play many distinct roles. They form the basis for dividing objects into groups and assigning instances to particular categories. They can also serve as the basis for making inferences about unobserved qualities or for making predictions about the future. In short, attributes and relationships among them underlie the structure of the category and determine how categories and members of categories are organized and processed. In this section we are interested not so much in documenting every role that attributes play, as we are in considering how properties of attributes influence category structure and process. We will also give some consideration to problems involved in discovering which particular attributes actually form the basis of a concept.

*Dimensional versus Featural Attributes.*    The component attributes of categories can be described in terms of either dimensions or features. Cognitive, as well as social, psychologists have often treated them, at least implicitly, as though they were equivalent. Recent work by Garner (1978) and Tversky (1977), however, demonstrates that choice of dimensional or featural attributes can have important implications for assumptions of category structure and processing. Consequently, determining the type of attribute people employ in representing categories is critical to developing an adequate theory of categorization.

Dimensions are typically used to refer to quantitative components, such as size or weight, and features are used to refer to qualitative components, like "can fly" or "wears glasses" (cf., Garner, 1978). Dimensions contain mutually exclusive values, and zero typically indicates a particular level along a dimension rather than the complete absence of the dimension. Featural attributes, on the other hand, are all-or-none components in that they either exist or are absent for an object. In this case, zero is taken to represent the absence of a feature rather than some value.

All-or-none qualitative components can be represented by binary-valued dimensions and quantitative components can be represented by nested sets of features. The distinction between featural and dimensional category representations, however, extends beyond simply the number of classification units to questions of how categories are processed. Garner (1978), for example, notes that with dimensions a meaningful distinction can be made between selectively attending to a dimension (e.g., attending to the size of an object) and selectively attending to particular values on the dimension (e.g., searching for large objects). This distinction does not make sense for features, where selective attention to a feature implies attending to its value (i.e., its presence or absence). This difference between dimensional and featural attraibutes implies a difference in the types of processes needed to discriminate among categories and category members. Thus, for example, if a group of individuals are represented along a dimension of "athletic ability," fine discrimination among them is inherent in the way they are categorically represented. However, if people are represented as having (or not having) the feature "is athletic," finer levels of discrimination require the processing of additional attributes or categorizations.

Whether a category is described in terms of dimensional or featural attributes also constrains how similarity relations are represented. With dimensional descriptions, a spatial metaphor is generally used to represent category similarity, such that the closer two categories are in a multidimensional space, the greater

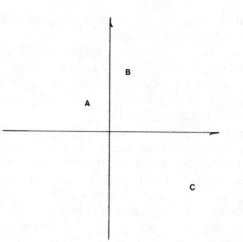

FIG. 3.2.   Two-dimensional representation of three hypothetical categories. Similarity between categories is represented by distance between points in the metric space.

their similarity (cf., Reed, 1972; Rosenberg & Sedlak, 1972). For example, in Figure 3.2 a set of hypothetical categories are represented within a two-dimensional space. Since the distance between category A and category B is less than the distance between categories A and C, category A is predicted to be judged more similar to category B than to category C.

With featural descriptions, similarity relations are represented in terms of common and distinctive features between the two categories (cf., Tversky, 1977). Figure 3.3 depicts a hypothetical example of three categories in which each is represented by a list of features. Since category A has more features in common with (and fewer features different from) category B than category C, category A is predicted to be judged more similar to B than to C.

| Category A | Category B | Category C |
|---|---|---|
| F1 | F1 | F1 |
| F2 | F2 | F2 |
| F3 | F3 | F9 |
| F4 | F4 | F10 |
| F5 | F5 | F12 |
| F6 | F10 | F13 |
| F7 | F11 | F14 |
| F8 | | |
| F9 | | |

FIG. 3.3.   Featural representation of three hypothetical categories. Similarity between categories is represented in terms of proportions of shared and distinctive features.

Dimensional and featural models of category representation imply differences in patterns of category-similarity judgments. To give a single example, spatial metaphors resting on assumptions of a metric, multidimensional space imply symmetry in the psychological distance between two categories. Some featural models, on the other hand, do not make this prediction (e.g., Tversky, 1977). We will return to the implications of dimensional and featural representations in the section on between-category structure.

For the natural object categories studied by cognitive psychologists, featural representations have received the most support. Thus, when subjects are asked to define concepts such as bird and chair or to list their properties, they typically list features such as "can fly" or "can be sat on" rather than dimensional attributes. Evidence that these features are instrumental in category representation is found in the fact that the greater the number of category features an instance has, the higher its rated typicality (Rosch & Mervis, 1975) and the faster it can be categorized (Hampton, 1979).

Some social categories also seem better represented by features. Social groups, for example, are typically described by subjects with features (cf., Cantor & Mischel, 1979; Cohen, 1981). However, other social categories, such as traits, have been viewed as being represented both featurally (Kelly, 1955; Wiggins, 1979) and dimensionally (Osgood, Suci, & Tanenbaum, 1957; Rosenberg & Sedlak, 1972). Because the two kinds of representations imply different category structures and processes, both cognitive and social psychologists need to pay strict attention to whether dimensional or featural attributes seem more consistent with how people operate on the particular class of categories being studied.

*Abstract Representational versus Concrete Identification Attributes.*   Some theories of categorization attempt to represent categories with a limited set of abstracted features (cf., Wiggins, 1979). Such attempts raise the distinction between abstracted attributes that are viewed as the core attributes of a category and more concrete attributes that are typically utilized to identify category membership of an instance (Miller & Johnson-Laird, 1976; Smith & Medin, 1981). For example, the abstract attributes of "girl" might include such features as human, female, and young, while those typically used in identification would be perceptual features like height, weight, hair length, and other physical characteristics that instantiate the concept girl.

The distinction between abstract representational attributes and identification attributes highlights the fact that there is not always a direct, one-to-one correspondence between perceptual properties of stimuli and attributes of their internal categorical representations. Consequently, the attributes that are used to represent a category can vary in the extent to which perceptual features directly support their presence as opposed to their having to be inferred. The more abstract the attributes, the greater the possibility of interpretative variability. High variability, in turn, can influence category stability and concept overlap both within and between individuals.

To the extent abstracted attributes that represent a category differ from the category's identification attributes, different views of category representation and processing may emerge when different experimental tasks are employed. Abstract representational attributes can be directly employed in tasks focusing on relations between concepts (e.g., as between boy–girl and girl–woman) or in sentence verification tasks (e.g., is the sentence, "A canary is a bird," true or false). Identification attributes, on the other hand, should play a predominant role in tasks requiring assignment of instances to categories based on their perceptual properties. To the extent that a category's abstract representational attributes and identification attributes differ, alternate sets of attributes may appear criterial across tasks.

For the types of natural object categories typically studied, analyses reveal little difference between the core representational attributes and the attributes used to identify category members. For example, experiments using pictures of objects as stimuli (which presumably require use of identification attributes) and experiments using words to represent the objects (which presumably require use of abstract representational attributes) have yielded consistent results (Smith & Medin, 1981). This suggests that perceptual properties used in the identification procedure parallel the representational attributes of the categories.

The distinction between representational and identification attributes may play a more important role for social categories. For example, one can be uncertain whether a particular person is fat, while nonetheless having a clear, core concept of fatness. For many other social categories, the representational attributes appear to be abstract (cf., our example of "drunk"). Therefore, deciding whether a representational attribute is present in a given instance may require considerable abstraction and interpretation. This can lead to wide variability in the categorization process. An example would be trait categories that are generally extrapolated from behaviors. A given behavior such as "passing notes in class" may be viewed as helpful by one person but as dishonest by another (cf., Higgins, Rholes, & Jones, 1977).

It is worth noting that abstract representational attributes are not unique to social or behavior-trait categories. Rather, the distinction often appears when categories can be thought of as comparative adjectives. The same painting, for example, can be beautiful for one person and ugly for another. Similarly, the categorized attractiveness of different kinds of natural objects like toads, spiders, and slugs is likely to differ for a 10-year old and his mother. Attribute abstractness in category representation is an important dimension that may more closely reflect differences between noun and adjective categories than between natural object and social categories per se.

*Membership versus Inference Attributes.*    One of the most salient functions of categories is their use in drawing inferences. By knowing the category membership of an instance, we are able to draw inferences about unobservable attributes. However, the attributes that are inferred from category membership are not always the attributes used to decide category membership in the first place. For example, one might infer that a truck driver is likely to drink beer, but not rely on the fact that a person is a beer drinker to classify him or her as a truck driver.

Membership attributes refer to attributes (both abstract and perceptual) that are used to assign instances to categories. Inference attributes refer to attributes that are implied as a result of assigning an instance to a category. Such a distinction is similar to the one that has been made by Ashmore and Del Boca (1979) between "identifying" and "ascribed" attributes in discussing sex stereotypes. Ashmore and Del Boca argue that the identifying (i.e., membership) attributes that enable recognition of a person's sex are physical cues such as stature, clothing, and manner of movement. The ascribed attributes that are inferred on the basis of category membership tend to be the associated traits, typical behaviors, affective components, and images that make up the individual's sex stereotype.

For the natural object categories typically studied, attributes used to assign instances to categories and the attributes inferred from category membership tend to be the same. For example, one might classify an object as a fruit and infer that it has seeds or use the fact that an object has seeds to identify it as a fruit. Based on this close correspondence, Smith and Medin (1981) go so far as to suggest that inference processes can be conceptualized as the categorization process run in reverse.

Whether or not running the categorization process in reverse proves to be adequate to account for inferences drawn from natural object categories, it clearly does not hold for inferences drawn from many social categories. For example, one may infer a fat person is good natured without referencing "good naturedness" to determine if someone is fat. Running the categorization process in reverse will not work in drawing inferences whenever a category's inference attributes differ from its membership attributes. In general, membership attributes tend to be those for which there is a high conditional probability of category membership given presence of the attribute (i.e., prob (category membership | attribute) is high). In contrast, inference attributes tend to be those for which there is a high conditional probability for presence of the attribute given category membership (i.e., prob(attribute | category membership) is high). For many social categories, these conditional probabilities are not equally high for the same attributes.

The distinction between membership and inference attributes can be seen as relevant to considering the viability of the classical view of categorization. One can imagine categories for which membership attributes are well defined, as expected by the classical view, but for which inference attributes are based only on consensual relationships. For example, membership in an occupational category such as "truck driver" may depend on a small number of defining attributes (e.g., employed for the purpose of driving a truck). Nevertheless, the attributes that are typically inferred about someone who is a truck driver (e.g., drinks beer or listens to country music) may only be characteristic and neither necessary nor sufficient for category membership. It would be a mistake, therefore, to assume that people's representations of such categories conform to the classical view based on membership attributes when their most psychologically meaningful actions typically rest on inference attributes.

*Independent versus Related Attributes.* Another important distinction with implications for how categories are represented concerns how different attributes are related to each other. Most attempts at semantic decomposition of categories, such as analysis of kin terms, have assumed that attributes (e.g., sex and age) are independent of each other. Similarly, Wiggins (1979) attempted to analyze trait concepts such as gregarious, ambitious, arrogant, warm, and unassuming in terms of different combinations of four underlying attributes (love self, love others, status of self, status of others). For example, warm was defined as +love self, +love others, +status others, and −status self, while arrogant was viewed as +love self, −love others, −status others, and +status self. Defining concepts in terms of values on independent dimensions, however, does not fit with other domains where attributes are clearly related. The attribute "lays eggs," for example, implies the attribute "animate." Similarly, a contrast relevant for comparing two animals, such as simple versus compound eyes, may be irrelevant for an organism with no eyes. That is to say, it may not make sense to assume that all living organisms can be represented by different combinations of a basic set of orthogonal attributes.

Mervis and Rosch (1981) have recently emphasized that attributes of natural objects form correlated clusters, such that all combinations of attribute values are not equally likely. For example, having fur, having a mouth, and moving about primarily on foot tend to co-occur (mammals) as do having feathers, having a beak, and flying (birds). However, the attributes having fur, having a beak, and flying do not occur together. Many social categories also appear to be based on correlated attribute structures. For example, the attributes drinks beer, carries a lunch pail, and wears jeans may co-occur (construction worker) as well as the attributes drinks martinis, carries a brief case, and wears three-piece suits (banker). The attributes drinks beer, carries a lunch pail, and wears three-piece suits, on the other hand, are not often seen together. The degree to which correlations among attributes are directly or indirectly represented as part of a category's structure is an important distinguishing characteristic of category models.

*Prestored versus Computed Attributes.*    A final distinction among attributes that we will make is that between prestored and computed attributes (cf., Smith, 1978). Prestored attributes are assumed to be directly associated with a category as part of its representation. Computed attributes, on the other hand, are deduced on the basis of other stored information. For example, one may directly store with the concept bird, an attribute like "has wings," but one might answer a question about whether small birds are more likely to sing than large birds by thinking of particular small and large birds. The correlation between size and probability of singing would not be directly stored, but would instead be computed from memory for the particular instances. Computed attributes need not be complex. For example, the attribute "has blood" might well not be directly associated with the concept bird nor "has ten toes" directly associated with one's concept of another person, even though one could readily compute such facts.

Whether an attribute is considered to be computed or prestored is clearly model dependent and will vary with representation and processing assumptions. Nonetheless, there are at least two general properties that seem likely to differentiate between prestored and computed attributes. One is the amount of time needed to generate the attribute. Other things being equal, it should take longer to respond or report a computed attribute as compared to a stored one. A second potential distinguishing characteristic is response variability. Generally, computational procedures provide greater opportunity for errors or response inconsistency. The important point is that assumptions concerning whether attributes are computed or stored will have implications for one's representational model of the categorization process.

We have identified some of the ways in which attributes can differ together with some of the consequences of these differences for category representation and processing. We conclude this section by considering some of the difficulties inherent in identifying which attributes are criterial for a given category.

## Determining Attributes

For many concepts, multiple properties can be identified that correlate with category membership. However, simply because an attribute distinguishes between concepts does not mean it necessarily is a part of a category representation. To illustrate, suppose subjects are engaged in a task of categorizing dot patterns. One could compute for each pattern the fifth and sixth moments of distribution of the inter-point distances of the dots and compare the resulting values for different patterns. Even should these computations clearly differentiate between subjects' similarity judgments of the patterns, it would be unlikely that the moments form part of their categorical representations. An important constraint, then, in identifying concept attributes is that the attributes actually be used by subjects for grouping objects, assigning instances to categories, or making comparisons between categories.

The constraint that the identified attributes actually be ones that are used makes it clear that structure and process cannot be treated as independent issues. To understand structure one must have an idea of what a category's component attributes are and, in turn, we require that the set of identified attributes be used in processing. This interrelatedness between structure and process is one reason why cognitive psychologists frequently rely on artificially constructed stimuli. By constraining possible attributes, analysis of category structure and processing becomes more tractable.

Several different techniques have been used to identify the attributes of real-world categories. One method, semantic decomposition (e.g., Clark & Clark, 1977; Miller & Johnson-Laird, 1976) focuses on identifying attributes that can account for the relationships between concepts. Another, multidimensional scaling (e.g., Rosenberg & Sedlak, 1972; Shepard, 1980) looks for a limited set of dimensions that can represent similarities in subjects' groupings of instances. Yet a third method is simply to have subjects list category attributes (e.g., Cantor & Mischel, 1979; Cohen, 1981; Rosch & Mervis, 1975).

Each of these techniques for identifying category attributes reveals different aspects of category structure. However, as a group these techniques typically fail to specify the relation between the underlying attributes they uncover and the task subjects have to perform. For example, with the attribute listing task there exists no theory concerning how subjects come up with the lists. In the absence of a specified processing model, it is difficult to anticipate how the generated list might be biased. If, for example, a particular attribute is not mentioned it may be because it is not part of the category representation, or it may simply be the result of the context imposed by the set of items being evaluated (cf., Coltheart & Evans, 1981). If subjects are asked to list attributes of only birds, they may never mention "two legs" even though this characteristic represents an important component of their categorical representation.

A similar problem exists for the multidimensional scaling approaches that make the implicit assumption that concepts differ only in their values on a set of shared underlying dimensions. The particular dimensions used to compare objects, however, are likely to be specific to a particular context or set of stimuli. Thus, for example, if subjects were asked to compare or sort the occupations of secretary, engineer, and doctor, an important identifying attribute might be "expected income." If, however, dental technician were added to the group, worker gender might become salient as the basis for classification. Again, it is inappropriate to identify category attributes without considering processing models that may underlie subjects' generated responses in a task.

Identification of attributes, then, is not model free, but instead must be embedded within assumptions about both structure and process. Attributes are criterial only to the extent they can be shown to be generic to some categorization process. Since different attributes may be used for different processes, the particular function must be specified. With this in mind, we turn to consider some current models of category representation.

## MODELS OF WITHIN-CATEGORY STRUCTURE

Neither natural object nor social categories form a continuum of all possible combinations of attributes. Instead, certain attributes tend to co-occur and people's category representations reflect this correlational structure (cf., Mervis & Rosch, 1981). Thus, for example, our social categories often reflect correlations such as drives a truck, listens to country music, and drinks beer as opposed to teaches class, listens to classical music, and drinks wine. In this section, we consider some of the different possible ways such relationships might be represented. Again, our purpose is not so much to argue for one type of structure for natural objects as opposed to social categories as it is to identify some of the consequences of assuming one type of representation over another. At this point we will focus on the internal structure of single categories; in a subsequent section we consider different structural models of relationships between categories.

### Probabilistic versus Exemplar Views of Category Structure

We have noted that the monothetic or classical view of concepts appears inadequate to account for category representation. Instead, polythetic category systems appear more promising for the representation of natural object as well as social categories. Recently, two general classes of models of category representation that fall within the polythetic framework have been explored by theorists investigating natural object categories. We will refer to these two approaches as the *probabilistic* and *exemplar* views (cf., Smith & Medin, 1981), and in light of their increasing influence, will examine some of their major assumptions and implications.

The probabilistic view of category representation can be seen as a liberalization of the classical view. Like the classical view, it assumes that the representation of a category is an abstraction from specific exemplars and that this summary representation is used to determine category membership. Unlike the classical view, however, the probabilistic view does not assume that the abstracted attributes have to be defining. Instead, the attributes may simply be salient and substantially correlated with category membership. New instances are categorized by determining their similarity to the abstracted summary representation or *prototype* of the category. An instance will be identified as a category member if it exhibits a criterial level of similarity to the prototype of the category and is more similar to that category's prototype than to the prototypes of alternative categories.

The exemplar view accepts the idea that many categories do not have defining features, but differs from the probabilistic view in assuming that category judgments are based on retrieval of specific item information rather than category-level, summary information. A new item will be identified as a category member if it cues the retrieval of a criterial number of exemplar representations from the category and does so before cuing the retrieval of a criterial number of exemplar representations from some contrasting category. The probability of retrieving a particular exemplar representation is a function of the similarity of the encoded representation of the item to the representation of the exemplar. Thus, an animal might be categorized as a rodent not on the basis of its comparison to a rodent prototype, but because it has similar attributes to a muskrat and a chinchilla, which are known to be rodents. In the same vein, one might predict a student would be a success in graduate school because he or she brought to mind someone who was successful in the past rather than because of the person's similarity to a set of prototypical attributes abstracted from past experience with graduate students.

## Assumptions and Implications of the Two Views

While the probabilistic and exemplar views might at first appear quite distinct, both are capable of accounting for most of the empirical findings in the categorization literature. When subjects learn to sort a set of instances into two or more categories and then are given transfer classification tests that include both old and new stimuli, three findings typically emerge: (a) subjects classify new, prototypic patterns as accurately and fast as they classify old training patterns, (b) on recognition tests, subjects are often more confident that they have seen a new prototype pattern than an old training pattern, and (c) when delays on the order of several days are inserted between learning and transfer tests, significantly greater forgetting is observed for old training stimuli than for a prototype of the observed stimuli. These results are highly replicable for object categories (e.g., Franks & Bransford, 1971; Homa & Chambliss, 1975; Homa & Vosburgh, 1976; Posner & Keele, 1968, 1970; Strange, Keeney, Kessel, & Jenkins, 1970) and aspects of them have been shown to hold for social categories as well (e.g., Tsujimoto, 1978; Tsujimoto, Wilde, & Robertson, 1978).

When first discovered, these phenomena were interpreted as evidence that subjects abstract out and use prototypical representations in deciding whether they have previously encountered an item. However, more recent work has shown that exemplar models can account for all three empirical relationships without assuming that any prototype has been abstracted out during learning (e.g., Hintzman & Ludlum, 1980; Medin & Schaffer, 1978). Since a prototype pattern will tend to be highly similar to several exemplars in its category (and be dissimilar to exemplars from contrasting categories), exemplar models predict excellent performance on prototype patterns. In addition, with forgetting over time, exemplar representations may actually increase in their similarity to the prototype pattern relative to their similarity to exemplar patterns. Consequently, transfer performance on old exemplars may appear to have decreased more after a delay than transfer performance on the prototype patterns. Thus, the probabilistic and exemplar models are not distinguishable by simple classification and memory recognition tests as has sometimes been assumed. The models do appear distinguishable on the basis of other predictions.

*Effects of Exemplar Memorability.*    According to the exemplar view, memorability for specific exemplars should influence classification judgments. In contrast, the probabilistic view suggests that exemplar memorability should influence classification judgments only to the extent that it influences the prototypicality or average attribute values of category members. At least three types of results implicate the importance of exemplar retrieval in classification judgments: (a) biasing effects of memorable instances, (b) density effects of category members, and (c) context effects.

A clear prediction of exemplar models is that classification of an unknown instance should be sensitive to its similarity to stored exemplars. For example, suppose an animal with fins is observed swimming through the water. Certainly, this object would be more similar to the prototypical fish than to the prototypical mammal. Nevertheless, the object might be classified as a mammal if it retrieved from memory the representation of a porpoise, which is known to be a mammal. In other words, people might base their classification judgments on similarity to readily available exemplars (cf., Tversky & Kahneman, 1973).

Closely related to the biasing effect of memorable instances are exemplar density effects. The retrieval assumptions of the exemplar view imply that classification will be based on the number of stored exemplars that are similar to the test item. Consequently, classification of a new item should be sensitive to the density of similar category members rather than to average within-category similarity. Predictions of probabilistic models are insensitive to such density effects. Substantial support has been found for the importance of exemplar density in categorization, across stimulus material (Medin & Schaffer, 1978), learning strategies (Medin & Smith, 1981), and category size (Medin & Schwanenflugel, 1981).

According to the exemplar view, any factor that affects retrieval should also influence classification. One such factor is the context present at the time of classification. Abundant evidence from the memory literature indicates that access to stored information is limited by the available retrieval cues provided by the context (cf., Tulving & Thomson, 1973). In the categorization literature, there is also evidence that classification is influenced by the retrieval cues that the context provides. With natural object categories, Roth (1980) has shown that typicality of category members is influenced by sentential contexts. In the social domain, Cantor, Mischel, and Schwartz (1982) have found judgments of personality types depend on the situational contexts in which behavior occurs. Such context effects are readily handled by the retrieval assumptions of exemplar models. In contrast, probabilistic models need to assume that people have different categories for each potential context or that they somehow differentially weight component attributes in different contexts.

*Ease of Category Learning.* The manner in which categories are represented and structured has implications for how easily different types of categories should be learned. The probabilistic view assumes that category assignment rests on a summing of evidence (i.e., the presence of characteristic features) that reflects the similarity or distance of an instance to a prototype. Such a decision process produces categories whose members are separable by a *linear discriminant function.* An example of such categories based on two dimensions is illustrated in panel *a* of Figure 3.4. Members of category A are generally high on dimension Y while low on dimension X; members of category B show an opposite pattern. As indicated by the dotted line in Figure 3.4, a straight line can be drawn separating members of category A from members of category B. The fact that a straight line divides the two categories (or, for more than two dimensions, the fact that a hyperplane divides the categories) implies that weighted evidence from each dimension can be summed to provide a perfectly valid decision rule for determining category membership. In this example, such a decision rule might be to categorize the item as a member of category A if the value on dimension Y is greater than the value on dimension X ($y - x > 0$).

An example of two categories that are not linearly discriminable is presented in panel *b* of Figure 3.4. Here, a straight line cannot be drawn that separates all

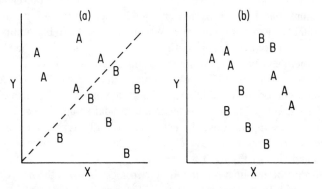

FIG. 3.4.   Two-dimensional example of two categories that are linearly separable (panel a) and are not linearly separable (panel b). In each graph, category members in categories A and B are denoted by the letters A and B, respectively.

members of category A from members of category B. Correspondingly, a linear decision rule cannot be formulated that correctly categorizes instances from the two-dimensional space.

The probabilistic view of category structure suggests categories structured similar to those of panel *a* should be more easily learned than those of panel *b*. Exemplar models of category structure, on the other hand, need not require that linearly separable categories be the most easily learned. The context model of Medin (1975; Medin & Schaffer, 1978), for example, assumes that groups of instances are most clearly distinguishable when members of one category are highly similar to more members of their own category than members in some other category. This is because higher frequencies of within-group, close matches increase the probability that one of them will be recalled as being similar to a newly encountered category member. Such a model could predict that the categories of panel *b* might be as easily learned as those of panel *a*.

What little evidence exists concerning the importance of linear separability in category learning is negative. Across a series of experiments that varied stimuli and learning procedures, Medin and Schwanenflugel (1981) found no evidence that linearly separable categories were more readily learned than categories that were not linearly separable. Since linear separability is unnecessary for category learning, by implication categorization can occur without a summing of evidence that reflects similarity of the instance to a prototype.

*Category Modification.*   Different views of category representation offer distinct perspectives on how concepts are modified. The classical view explicitly assumes that concepts are fixed once the necessary and sufficient attributes have been correctly identified, whereas both the probabilistic and exemplar views allow for concepts to be constantly updated. The nature of updating for these latter two models, however, is different. To see why, consider the hypothetical situation shown in Figure 3.5. Five examples of a category are presented at the top of the figure that differ from one another in their combined attributes. To make the example even more concrete, A1 might refer to flying ability with 1 representing the ability and 0 representing its absence. There is no attribute that all category members have in common so the classical view does not apply. According to the probabilistic view, experience with exemplars would lead to the category representation in the middle right-hand side of Figure 3.5, namely some abstract representation of the central tendency (modal value) for each attribute. According to the exemplar view, the category would be represented simply by the encoded representations of the exemplars themselves as indicated in the middle left-hand side of Figure 3.5.

Now consider the implications for these two models when the new exemplar depicted in the middle of the figure is added. If the representation of a concept is in terms of lower level exemplars, a representation of the new exemplar is simply

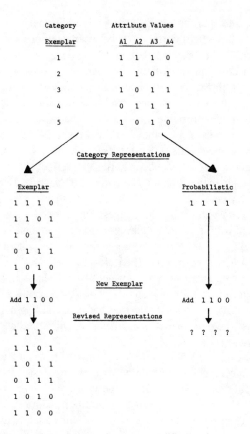

FIG. 3.5.  Hypothetical examples of category modification for an exemplar representation (left) and probabilistic representation (right).

added to the others, as indicated at the bottom left of Figure 3.5. If the representation is an abstract summary, it is less clear how the concept should be updated, especially if the exemplars from which the summary was originally abstracted have themselves been forgotten. The problem is how much weight to give the new instance in comparison to the abstracted summary. Specific predicted differences between the two models will obviously depend on the processing assumptions incorporated into the probabilistic model.

*Representation of Relational Information.*    Models within the probabilistic view assume that the same category level information is employed whenever an item is classified and that summary information is accumulated in an additive, independent manner. Such processes may be adequate for representing average attribute values. However, people generally have more information available to them about the concepts they hold. One such additional type of information is relational information about correlations between category attributes. Thus, people generally know that as birds become larger the probability that they sing decreases. As a consequence of this knowledge, people are likely to judge a large, non-singing bird as more typical of the bird category than a large, singing bird even though the latter instance exhibits more independent, bird-like features. Exemplar models provide a mechanism via instance sampling for representing correlations between attributes. Probabilistic models, on the other hand, provide no simple mechanisms for representing such relationships other than hypothesizing a complex set of subcategories that reflect different attributes (i.e., positing that people have distinct categories for large and small birds whose prototypes encompass separate constellations of attributes).

The preponderance of evidence suggests that correlations among attributes play an important role in people's classification judgments. Natural object categories appear to be formed to take advantage of correlated attribute clusters (Medin, 1983; Mervis & Rosch, 1981; Rosch, 1975, 1978), while in social categorization people seem so ready to identify correlations that they even perceive them when they are not objectively present (Chapman & Chapman, 1967; Hamilton & Gifford, 1976). People may be especially sensitive to correlated attributes because the presence of one attribute enables prediction of the presence of other attributes.

A recent series of studies by Medin, Altom, Edelson, and Freko (1982) illustrates the importance of attribute correlations in classification judgments. A simulated medical diagnosis task was employed in which presence or absence of some of the symptoms were correlated. In addition, some symptoms were characteristic of the disease, while others were only infrequently associated with the disease. In a test phase, subjects were required to choose between pairs of alternatives the case more likely to have the disease. Subjects tended to choose cases that maintained the correlation between symptom values over cases that had more characteristic symptoms but did not maintain the correlation.

Another type of information that people have available about concepts is the relative variability among category members (Walker, 1975). For example, people will generally expect more variability in living styles among artists than among business executives. Exemplar models again provide a ready mechanism for representing member variability. With probabilistic models, appropriate mechanisms for representing such information are less clear.

## The Case for Mixed Representations

In the preceding section we heavily emphasized problems for probabilistic models of category representation. The main reason for this is our belief that researchers (both social and cognitive) have often been overly quick to cite as evidence for a prototype representation data easily accounted for by an exemplar model. We hasten to add at this point that exemplar models present their own set of problems. For one, people are often exposed to category level information, and it does not make sense to assume that they are unable to encode it into their categorical representation even though it is not associated with a particular exemplar. Moreover, our concepts have more intra-category structure than that of a simple list of exemplars and their properties (cf., Smith & Medin, 1981). Ultimately, exemplar models place too few constraints on what sets of instances can form a category and how these instances might be organized.

Given the problems of both the probabilistic and exemplar views in isolation, an attractive alternative is that concepts contain both probabilistic and exemplar components (cf., Elio & Anderson, 1981; Smith & Medin, 1981). For example, people may initially represent categories in terms of exemplars and then later apply abstraction processes to yield summary representations (cf., Homa, Sterling, & Trepel, 1981). Such a mixed model would provide a means for representing configural information and instance variability as well as a guiding mechanism for updating summary representations. Thus, for example, the extent to which one were able to retrieve many stored exemplars could serve as an indicator of how much some prototypical characteristic should be altered as a result of a single discrepant experience. Evidence for such a process has been reported by Altom and Lingle (1980) who found subjects more willing to alter person categorizations under conditions in which they should have been best able to remember both consistent and inconsistent category exemplars.

While most concepts may encompass both probabilistic and exemplar information, social categories may differ from typically studied natural object categories in their proportion of each type of structure. Intuitive support for this notion comes from the fact that the two classes of concepts appear to vary in the ease with which particular exemplars come to mind. Thus, most people can rapidly list several exemplars of the category *mammal* while being less able to generate multiple instances of the concept *hostile person*. It is unclear at this point whether such differences reflect (a) differences in category versus attribute representations, (b) differences in representations of natural object as opposed to social categories, or (c) differences between noun and adjective categories.

In this section we have discussed some of the consequences of assuming different types of internal category structures, and have concluded by suggesting that a mixture of exemplars and summary characteristics appears most promising for the representation of both natural object and social categories. However, if our concepts typically include both summary attributes and exemplars, new questions are raised as to what determines which of the two types of representations is most accessible and likely to serve as the basis for classification. We anticipate that these questions will direct the next round of investigation on within-category structure. We now turn to consider some models of between-category structure and their implications.

# MODELS OF BETWEEN-CATEGORY STRUCTURE

Thus far we have focused on within-category structure, the relationship between attribute constellations and category membership. We have said little concerning how categories are related one to the other, yet the manner in which categories are organized and interrelated influences how they are processed and modified. In this section, we consider some fundamental distinctions among different models of between-category structure. Much of the research and theory on between-category structure developed within the classical view of concept representation. A primary focus of our discussion, therefore, concerns the problems of extending these models to the more recent, polythetic views of concept representation.

Two kinds of inter-category relationships have traditionally been of most interest to psychologists: (a) the degree to which categories form hierarchies with nested subset relations and (b) the similarity between categories. We will consider each of these types of relationships separately.

## Hierarchical Representations of Between-Category Structure

*Properties of Hierarchical Structures.*    Most natural object categories appear hierarchically organized with different levels of abstraction. For example, one's pet might be categorized as a poodle, a dog, a carnivore, a mammal, a vertebrate, an animal, and so on. At any one level of abstraction, the categories are mutually exclusive (being a dog rules out being a cat) and membership at one level rules out membership in contrasting categories at other levels (dogs are not reptiles). Furthermore, the hierarchical organization implies that experience with the pet could potentially modify one's impression of the categories associated with each level in the hierarchy.

The power and utility of using a hierarchical structure to represent a category system depend on the extent to which the properties of hierarchies are realized by relationships among the categories. One such property concerns transitivity among members of nested subsets. That is, in a hierarchical structure, if category C is a subset of category B and B is a subset of A, members of category C must be members of catagory A. In our example of a pet poodle, since all poodles are dogs and all dogs are carnivores, a poodle must be a carnivore.

Secondly, a single ancestory relationship is implied by a hierarchical structure. If A is the category of highest rank in the hierarchy, members of all other categories in the hierarchy must be members of A. For example, if *animal* is the highest ranking category in our hierarchical system, then members of all other categories (vertebrate, invertebrate, mammal, reptile, carnivore, herbivore, dog, cat, poodle, collie) must also be animals.

Finally, since categories of higher rank summarize and include lower rank categories, members of higher, as compared to lower, ranking categories can be described by relatively fewer attributes. Moreover, members of higher ranking categories are more variable in their characteristics than members of lower ranking categories. Thus, members of the category poodle share more characteristics than do members of the category animal.

*The Problem of Multiple Overlapping Categories.*   For the natural object categories that have been studied, hierarchical structures generally seem appropriate. While some overlap among categories may occur (e.g., pet and farm animal), it is relatively rare. With social categories, category overlap seems much more common. For example, in Figure 3.6 we reproduce a taxonomy used by Cantor and Mischel (1979) in their study of person categories. Although Cantor and Mischel arrange the categories hierarchically, one might question whether the concepts conform to the constraints of such a system. That is, a world traveler might be both a "patron of the arts" as well as a "man of the world sophisticate." On the other hand, we know soldiers of fortune and sailors are world travelers, but are we likely to infer that they belong to the highest ranking category "cultured person?" And if a soldier of fortune were a world sophisticate, and members of this latter category are assumed to be cultured persons, does transitivity hold such that the soldier is certain to be a cultured person? The problems encountered in imposing a hierarchical structure on the categories in Figure 3.6 are due to the large amounts of category overlap that are apparent among the different classes.

In cases with only moderate amounts of overlap, it may be possible to translate the properties of hierarchical structures into a probabilistic form. Thus, one might expect that the conditional probability that a person is a man of the world sophisticate, given that he is a world traveler, should be greater than the probability that the person is a patron of the arts. With large amounts of overlap, however, even probabilistic relationships may not hold, so that a hierarchical

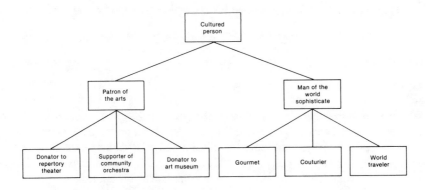

FIG. 3.6.   A hierarchical arrangement of a set of overlapping categories (from Cantor & Mischel, 1979).

representation loses all of its predictive power as a model of between-category structure.

We do not mean to imply that social categories are never hierarchically organized. Persons and groups can be seen to represent at least a simple hierarchy as can behaviors and traits. However, even here there is a somewhat different structure than seems characteristic of natural object categories. Any one person can be thought of as belonging to a large number of groups, and any one behavior may be associated with several different traits. Consequently, there is constant competition among groups and among traits as to how the same person or behavior might best be categorized.

*The Basic Level.*    With hierarchical category structures, a given instance will belong to a category at each of the different levels. However, research with natural object categories has suggested that one of these levels, referred to as the *basic level,* may be more fundamental than its associated superordinate or subordinate levels (e.g., Berlin, 1972; Rosch, Mervis, Gray, Johnson, & Boyes-Braem, 1976). Rosch et al. (1976) defined the basic level of a hierarchical structure as the one at which the categories are maximally differentiated, that is, the level at which within-category similarity is high while between-category similarity is low. They argue that for categories above the basic level, within-category similarity will be low, whereas for categories below the basic level, between-category similarity will be high. A common example would be chair as a basic-level category, while furniture and rocking chair would be higher- and lower-level categories, respectively.

Rosch et al. (1976) suggested that the basic level could be viewed as the one that maximizes category cue validity. Here, the cue validity for attribute or cue i for category j is simply the conditional probability that an instance is in category j given that it possesses cue i, that is

$$\text{cue validity} = \text{prob(category } j | \text{cue } i)$$

$$= \frac{\text{prob(category } j \text{ and cue } i)}{\Sigma_k \text{ prob(category } k \text{ and cue } i)}$$

where the summation in the denominator is over all categories at the same level in the hierarchy as category j. The category cue validity is then the sum of the cue validities for all of the attributes associated with the category.

Support for the concept of basic levels has come from research indicating that: (a) instances are categorized more quickly into basic level categories than into other level categories (Rosch et al., 1976), (b) basic levels are learned by children before other levels (Mervis & Pani, 1980), and (c) adults prefer to sort stimuli into basic level rather than non-basic level categories (Rosch et al., 1976).

Cantor and Mischel (1979) suggest that categories associated with person perception are also organized around basic levels. Thus, the categories "patron of the arts" and "man of the world sophisticate" in Figure 3.6 would be considered basic level categories relative to the superordinate category of cultured person and subordinate category world traveler. However, there are two problems with such an analysis. First, as noted, the high degree of category overlap raises the question of whether a hierarchical representation is an appropriate model for the concepts in Figure 3.6. Second, even for natural object categories that conform to a well-structured hierarchy, the idea of basic levels has recently been questioned on both empirical and logical grounds. Murphy and Smith (1982), for example, argue that categories previously identified as "basic" may be more fundamental not because of their level per se, but because they are associated with more distinctive *perceptual* attributes. Using artificially constructed categories, they found that classification latencies for superordinate and subordinate categories were faster than those for middle level categories when the former, as compared to the latter, were associated with a higher number of distinct perceptual attributes. The findings by Murphy and Smith emphasize the point that many other factors apart from category level appear to determine category accessibility.

Recently, Medin (1983) and Murphy (1982) have questioned the very logic behind the definition of basic level being the one that maximizes category cue validity. They point out that cue validity increases monotonically with increasing levels in a hierarchy. Consequently, basic level categories would have to be predicted as those that are most abstract (Rosch et al., 1976, also noted this problem with considering category cue validity as a true probability). Since the most abstract categories are not those most commonly used, factors other than cue validity must determine which particular categories are employed to encode information in different situations. We will return to discuss some of these factors in a subsequent section on category accessibility.

## Similarity Between Categories

*Dimensional Representations of Similarity.*    To a large extent, the model one adopts to represent people's perceived similarity among concepts depends on the nature of the attributes assumed to underlie the concepts. When concepts are seen to rest on dimensions, inter-category similarities are typically represented by the distance between their members in a multidimensional metric space, as is depicted in Figure 3.2. Generally, such models make several strong assumptions including those of minimality, symmetry, and triangular inequality (however, see Krumhansl, 1978, for a discussion of a metric model augmented with assumptions about category density that does not make these assumptions about category similarity). The *minimality* assumption holds that the distance (or similarity, in this case) between any entity and itself in a space should be minimal and equal to the distance between any other entity and itself. *Symmetry* implies that the distance between any two entities, A — B, should be equal to their reversed distance, B — A, such that the similarity of category A to category B in Figure 3.2 should be the same as the similarity of B compared to A. The assumption of *triangular inequality* implies that the distance between any two entities in the space should not be greater than the combined distances between each and a third entity. Thus, in Figure 3.2, the distance between categories A and C must be less than or equal to the sum of the distances between categories A and B and categories B and C.

A central criterion for evaluating the applicability of a model is the extent to which the psychological phenomenon being modeled reflects the constraints and relationships implied by the model. In the case of dimensional models of similarity, principal assumptions of the model have frequently not been tested fully. Where they have been tested, doubts have arisen as to the adequacy of the model for representing people's naturally formed concepts. Thus, Tversky and Gati (1978) found violations of the symmetry assumption when they asked subjects to judge the similarity between countries. When asked to compare large and small countries, subjects' similarity judgments differed depending on the order in which the countries were presented (e.g., whether they were asked to compare Russia to Poland or Poland to Russia). Thus, for at least some categories, the central assumptions of a dimensional similarity model are not well-supported.

For the sake of interpretability, dimensional models generally represent categories on a relatively small set of dimensions. We have already noted the problem of assuming that concepts differ only on a single set of shared dimensions. An even more perplexing problem is the fact that such an assumption appears irreconcilable with the notion of a hierarchical structure. In hierarchies, subcategories are combined into larger, more inclusive superordinate categories, and the attributes that differentiate among instances at one level form a distinct set from those that differentiate among instances at a different level. Although both hierarchical and dimensional models have sometimes been used to represent the same set of categories (e.g., Rips et al., 1973), the two models appear incompatible in that they adopt different, empirically testable assumptions about the nature of inter-category relationships.

We have noted some of the difficulties encountered by hierarchical models when confronted by category overlap. Overlap also presents problems for dimensional models of similarity. One of these is that category membership can no longer be determined by a simple relative distance measure. Even if the problem of determining category membership is resolved, problems of representing inter-category structure remain. As an example, consider categories A, B, and C in Figure 3.7. Close to a third of category B's members overlap with category A while none of category C's members overlap with A. By a simple centroid distance measure, however, category C should be judged more similar to B than A, since it is closer to the former than to the latter. Although it is an empirical

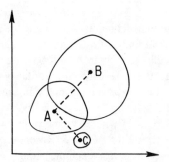

FIG. 3.7.  Illustrative example of the problem of using distance to measure similarity when category members overlap in a multidimensional space.

question, we would be surprised if distance should outweigh member overlap in people's judgments of category similarity.

*Featural Representations of Similarity.*   To account for some of the problems that have been raised for dimensional models of similarity, Tversky (1977) has proposed a featural model of inter-category similarity. Within this model, similarity between two categories is viewed as an increasing function of the number of shared features and a decreasing function of the number of distinct features. More specifically, the similarity of object or category a to b is given by

$$s(a, b) = \theta f(A \cap B) - \alpha f(A - B) - \beta f(B - A)$$

where A ∩ B are the features that a and b share in common
A — B are the features distinct to category a
B — A are the features distinct to category b
f is a nonnegative scaling function defined over the feature space
θ, α, and β are nonnegative weighting parameters.

Asymmetries in judged category similarity are accounted for by the assumption that the number of distinct features for each category is weighted differentially according to the category's relative salience: the greater a category's salience, the more its distinct features will be weighted.

As an example in applying Tversky's model, consider categories A and B in Figure 3.3. Their shared features are F1, F2, F3, F4, and F5. As distinctive features, category A contains F6, F7, F8, and F9, whereas category B contains only F10 and F11. Now suppose a subject were asked to judge the degree to which A is similar to B. Phrased in this manner, B is the referent category, while A is the variant category to be compared with it. Since the variant is the subject of the comparison, it is assumed to be more salient than the referent. By differentially weighting the contributions of the two distinct feature sets according to which category is the referent, Tversky's model can readily account for asymmetries in similarity judgments. Thus, if the distinct features of the variant are weighted more heavily than those of the referent (i.e., $\alpha > \beta$ in Equation 2), B will be judged more similar to A than A will be judged as being similar to B.

To date, a great deal of the research on similarity of social categories has relied on a multidimensional approach. In many instances, there has been little concern as to the applicability of the minimality, symmetry, and triangular inequality assumptions. In cases where symmetry has been directly tested it has not been empirically supported (cf., Gara & Rosenberg, 1979; Warr and Knapper, 1968). Gara & Rosenberg, for example, found evidence suggesting that people employ their concepts of significant others as supersets to organize their impressions of other less-significant acquaintances. Such findings indicate that featural models, such as Tversky's, may provide a more adequate representation of similarity among social categories than the commonly adopted dimensional models.

## CATEGORY PROCESSING

Category processing is multifaceted and might easily serve as a topic for its own chapter. Here we focus on three aspects: (a) processes involved in assigning instances to category membership, (b) some of the consequences of making category assignments, and (c) stability of categories both within and across individuals.

### Category Assignment

In a sense, the process of assigning an entity to its appropriate category is one of pattern recognition, in which a set or pattern of attributes is identified as suggesting membership in a particular category. In some cases, the identification process is relatively straightforward, such as when classifying a person as a "baby" based on visual appearance. In other cases, identification can be much less obvious, such as in classifying good candidates for graduate school. In either case, category assignment depends not only on how the entity is compared to category representations, but also on the particular set of categories that become available for comparison. We will consider each of these topics in turn.

*Attribute Matching.* The process by which instance and category attributes are compared one to another is an issue that divides probabilistic and exemplar models. Probabilistic models (cf., Reed, 1972) have generally posited an additive process in which attributes are compared independently, and their similarity coefficients summed to provide an overall index of similarity. For exemplar models, similarity may also be viewed as an additive function of attribute matches, weighted by their salience and criteriality. However, Medin (1975, 1983) has argued that a more fruitful approach is to assume a configural or relational attribute-comparison procedure, whereby similarity coefficients are multiplied, rather than added, together. The advantage of this approach is that it provides a mechanism that is sensitive to category density and relationships among attributes. Furthermore, it has the potential for establishing defining attributes, since a single missing attribute may drive the overall measure of similarity to zero. In contrast, with a purely additive model, a single missing attribute can be compensated for by the presence of other, highly weighted attributes.

The additive-configural controversy for natural object categorization has its counterpart in the social categorization literature, where proponents of both additive (e.g., Anderson, 1981) as well as configural (e.g., Fiske, 1982; Ostrom, 1977) attribute matching processes can be found. It would be convenient if a single attribute-comparison rule could describe all of our categorization judgments. Unfortunately, there is some evidence that this is not the case, which may be one of the causes of the existing controversies. Wallsten and Budescu (1981), for example, had both graduate students and experienced clinicians categorize people according to their scores on subsections of the MMPI. Data from the study suggested that clinicians based their classifications on configurations of scores on the various subscales, while graduate students favored a simple additive rule. Thus, the process by which people compare attributes when categorizing instances may vary as a function of their experience with and knowledge of a concept.

With natural object categories, stimulus attributes used in category identification tend to be directly perceptible. In contrast, many of the attributes involved in the categorization of social entities are ambiguous and require substantial interpretation before entering a comparison process (e.g., our earlier example of the key-dropper being drunk). The multiplicity of interpretations for the attributes of many social categories suggests much greater variability in classification as compared to natural objects and brings into focus the question of what determines the set of comparison categories likely to be used when categorization occurs.

*Category Accessibility.* An entity can often be viewed as belonging to several categories. Both the probabilistic and exemplar models of category structure most clearly predict which of two or more contrasting categories an instance is most likely to be assigned to. Consequently, an important question concerns which categories are likely to be accessed and considered when information is encoded. In experiments where categories are artificially constructed and carefully controlled, the set of potential categories to which an instance might belong is clear cut. Outside of the friendly confines of artificially constructed stimuli, how do people know which categories to test for membership of the instance?

Most recent work on natural object categories has focused on category level as a prime determinant of category use. However, we have already noted some of the problems associated with the "levels" interpretation. When categories overlap and are not hierarchical, as is the case for many social categories, factors other than "level" must determine category access. A number of these factors have been considered by investigators of social categories (see Higgins & King, 1981, for a review).

Two factors that have been shown to strongly influence the probability that a category will be used to encode stimulus information are the frequency and recency with which the category has been activated (cf., Higgins & King, 1981; Srull & Wyer, 1979, 1980). In a variety of paradigms it has been shown that the probability that a subject will use a particular category to encode information is enhanced by "priming" or activating the category in a context separate from the one in which a target stimulus is presented. Typically, models of natural object categories have not been extended to account for these types of effects. Several social categorization formulations, however, have been developed with an aim towards predicting them (cf., Wyer & Srull, 1980, 1981).

In a series of imaginative studies, McGuire and his associates (McGuire, McGuire, Child, & Fujioka, 1978; McGuire, McGuire, & Winton, 1979; McGuire & Padawer-Singer, 1976) have shown that attribute distinctiveness influences category accessibility. McGuire et al. (1979), for example, found that children were more likely to include gender in their spontaneous self-descriptions, if they were from families in which their gender was in the minority. Similarly, McGuire and Padawer-Singer (1976) found that elementary school children were more likely to mention in their self-descriptions a personal characteristic (e.g., race) if it had minority status relative to other members of their class. Thus, a complete model of category functioning must account not only for frequency and recency effects, but also mechanisms by which contextual attribute distinctiveness influences category accessibility.

A third set of factors that influence category accessibility are motivational factors such as personal goals, needs, and affective states. Research by Levine, Chein, and Murphy (1942), for example, indicates that moderate increases in hunger increase the probability that people will assign food-related labels to ambiguous stimuli. Similarly, Postman and Brown (1952) found that recent success or failure experiences increase the ease with which subjects can identify success- and failure-related words, respectively. Thus far, neither probabilistic or exemplar models of natural object categories have dealt with the ways in which motivational states might influence category assignment, although such factors seem certain to influence natural object categorizations as well.

Finally, it should be noted that category accessibility has important implications not only for classification of new instances, but also for category modification. Which category representation is modified by new experiences can be seen to depend on which categories are employed at the time of encoding. Suppose, for example, that based on some limited set of experiences a person forms an impression of a group of New Zealanders. Now suppose that the person is placed in a situation where he or she has frequent interactions with one particular New Zealander. What affect will this have on the person's impression of New Zealanders? According to the availability heuristic, this impression should be strongly influenced by interactions with this single New Zealander (cf., Rothbart et al., 1978). But suppose that the New Zealander becomes so familiar that he is thought of only as a friend, not as a New Zealander. In such a case frequent experiences with the friend might have little influence on the overall impression of New Zealanders. We know of no evidence bearing directly on this point.

## Consequences of Category Assignment

Research with natural object categories has focused on understanding category structure and the rules used for determining category membership. An equally important set of issues that has received attention from social psychologists concerns the consequences of category assignment per se or how categorizations structure memories, thoughts, and behaviors. The impact of a simple categorization is surprisingly pervasive. Evidence exists, for example, that even clearly arbitrary assignment of group memberships subsequently affects how a person perceives, judges, makes attributions about, and rewards others (e.g., Billig & Tajfel, 1973; Howard & Rothbart, 1980; Tajfel & Billig, 1974; Tajfel, Sheikh, & Gardner, 1964; Wilder, 1981). People's categorizations of another have also been shown to influence both the behavior they unconsciously elicit from the person (cf., Snyder, 1981) as well as how they themselves behave towards the person (cf., von Baeyer, Sherk, & Zanna, 1981). It has even been shown that people's abilities to solve the most elementary problems rest on their categorizations of the relationships among problem features (cf., Higgins & Chaires, 1980).

The pervasive role that categorization plays in shaping people's behavior rests to a large degree on the influence of categorization on (a) memory for events and (b) inference processes. In considering these processes, however, we are forced to alter slightly our approach used in earlier sections. Thus far, we have focused on the implications of different formal categorization models developed in natural object research to category functioning. Unfortunately, the models we have discussed have for the most part not yet been developed sufficiently to account for the multitude of ways in which categorization affects memory retrieval and inference processes. In some instances new models are beginning to be developed that do treat these phenomenon, although their link to existing natural object categorization models is not always clear. Therefore, we merely briefly note some of the more salient processing phenomenon that need to be accounted for in extending models to wider domains of category functioning.

*Memory Retrieval.*    Earlier we emphasized that both probabilistic and exemplar models can account for the finding that subjects tend to recall having seen previously unpresented prototypical exemplars. This is only one of several memory retrieval effects that have been associated with categorization. For objects, the early work of Carmichael, Hogan, & Walter (1932) demonstrated the importance of category labeling on subsequent memory for features of an object (see Riley, 1963, for a critical review of the literature on labeling effects in form memory). More recently, a number of studies have used social stimuli to further investigate the relation between categorization and memory for attributes. Research on occupation-suitability judgments, for example, has found that people tend to remember attributes that are relevant to categorizing a person better than irrelevant ones both immediately after categorization and following a delay (cf., Lingle et al., 1979; Ostrom, Lingle, Pryor, & Geva, 1980). The picture becomes less clear, however, relevant to subjects' memory for attributes that are congruent and incongruent with those typically associated with a category into which a person has been placed. In some studies, category assignment has been associated with better recall for consistent attributes (cf., Carlston, 1980a; Cohen, 1981), while in other studies categorization has been found to produce improved recall for category-inconsistent characteristics (cf., Hastie & Kumar, 1979). Carlston (1980b) reports preliminary evidence that the stage in the categorization process at which attributes are observed may be critical to determining whether category-consistent or -inconsistent attributes will be better remembered.

Hastie (1981) has recently proposed a curvilinear relationship between category-congruency and feature memorability with separate cognitive processing mechanisms being responsible for improved memory for category-congruent and incongruent attributes. Improved memory for incongruent characteristics is seen to rest on their richer encoding while that for congruent features is seen to result from category-directed memory retrieval processes. Models of classification capable of accounting for the complex relationships between membership assignment and attribute recall and recognition have only recently begun to be developed (see also Srull, 1981; Wyer & Srull, 1981).

*Inferential Processes.*    Inferences involve going beyond the information given in making predictions or in developing expectations about the presence of unobserved attributes. A primary function of categories is to allow inferences to be drawn based on incomplete information. When an attribute inference about an instance is made there are three alternative sources of information upon which it can be based: (a) memory for other attributes of the instance, (b) memory for typical attributes of a category to which the instance has been assigned (i.e., probabilistic attributes), or (c) memory for some other similar instance (i.e., exemplar comparison).

A number of social cognition studies have investigated subjects' tendencies to base inferences on remembered instance attributes as opposed to category-level information. The best assessment of these studies seems to be that subjects can use both kinds of cognitions as the basis for inferences and that it is unclear at this point what factors determine which will be used. Thus, some studies have found that subjects rely heavily on category-level information as the basis for inferences even when they are capable of recalling instance attributes that might contradict their conclusions (e.g., Lingle et al., 1979). Other studies have found a heavier reliance in inference making on memory for specific attributes (e.g., Reyes, Thompson, & Bower, 1980). Yet a third group of studies has produced evidence that subjects rely on a mixture of remembered instance attributes and category-level information when making inferences (e.g., Allen & Ebbesen, 1981; Altom & Lingle, 1980; Lingle, 1983; Lingle, Dukerich, & Ostrom, 1983). At this point a number of variables have been identified that appear to influence people's reliance on observed attributes as opposed to category membership as the basis for the inferences they make. In some instances (cf., Allen & Ebbesen, 1981; Wyer & Hartwick, 1980) more formal models have been developed treating these issues. For the most part, however, the probabilistic and exemplar models described in this chapter have not been developed to make unambiguous predictions about memory-based inference processes.

As such models are extended, an important distinction may be that proposed by Higgins & King (1981) between "identification as" and "identification with" a category. The distinction refered to is the difference between identifying someone as a member of a category (e.g., he is a member of my fraternity) as opposed to identifying something or someone as similar to a category member (e.g., he is like a fraternity brother). The similarities and differences in memory retrieval and inference processes that result from the two types of identification is an empirical issue that remains to be investigated.

## Category Stability

A great deal of research on categorization appears to presuppose that concepts are stable mental representations both within and across individuals. Concepts are stable within individuals to the extent that once a person has acquired a concept, its criterion attributes remain the same across items and contexts; concepts are stable across individuals to the extent that different people have identical (or at least similar) representations of the concept.

*Within-individual Category Stability.* Social categories often appear impervious to experience with counter-examples. For example, when someone categorized as a friendly person acts in an unfriendly manner, we modify our impression of the person, not the concept, friendly. People seem more willing to reassign an anomalous instance to a new category, than to alter the category's representation.

When compared with natural object categories, social categories (a) seem to rely more on inferred attributes, (b) prove more susceptible to factors influencing category accessibility, and (c) seem typified more by overlapping category structures. Each of these properties appears to contribute to category stability by facilitating recategorization. Thus, while experience with a penguin or ostrich may alter one's concept of a bird, an encounter with a non-stereotypic member of an ethnic group is likely to have little impact on one's social stereotypes.

*Between-Individual Category Stability.*    The fact that social categories may show relative stability within-individuals does not require that they also exhibit between-individual stability. In fact, several of the factors that allow facile reassignment of anomalous exemplars, thereby favoring within-individual category stability, work in just the opposite manner relevant to between-individual concept stability. Thus, for example, the fact that the same behavior may be interpreted as either friendly or unfriendly, depending on the context imposed on it, favors within-individual concept stability. However, at the same time it increases the probability that two people familiar with the same population will have different impressions as to who is friendly and who is unfriendly. There is a need to extend current models of category structure to help understand issues of both within- and between-individual concept variability.

## CONCLUSIONS

Over the last decade cognitive psychologists have changed how they think about people's concepts of natural objects. This reorientation has spawned several new formal models of the way people represent and process categorical information. Recently, these models have begun to be applied to social categorization. The question we have addressed is how to evaluate the extension of these models to this new domain.

Basically, we believe that applications of natural object classification models to social categories can be fruitful. However, we feel such applications are most beneficial when researchers clearly recognize and articulate the assumptions that are made when a particular model is adopted. In discussing this point we have identified several critical issues that shape the assumptions of categorization models. These are: (a) the nature of the attributes that define category membership, (b) the degree to which categories are hierarchical or mutually exclusive in their organization as opposed to multiply overlapping, (c) whether a summary representation of category attributes exists independent of individual exemplars, (d) whether feature comparison is carried out in an additive or multiplicative fashion, and (e) how a set of comparison categories is chosen during instance assignment. Each of these issues can be seen to influence directly how a category system functions and to determine the type of model that is likely to best capture its operation.

Our review has also uncovered several apparent differences between social categories and the natural object categories that have typically been studied by cognitive psychologists. As compared to the latter, social categories (a) appear highly variable in their structure, (b) are often multiply overlapping rather than hierarchical in nature, (c) frequently rest on inferred abstract attributes rather than perceptual attributes, and (d) many times encompass a rich set of inference attributes apart from basic membership attributes. As a consequence of these properties social categories frequently seem to (a) not be adequately represented by simple hierarchical or dimensional models, (b) exhibit relatively high within-individual stability, but low between-individual stability, and (c) depend on numerous factors other than basic levels as determinants of category accessibility. As a result of these differences social categories many times do not seem to be adequately represented by straight translations of existing natural object category models.

If social psychologists stand to benefit from careful and measured applications of natural object category models, so can cognitive psychologists expect to benefit from the extension of their theories to new areas. The models we have discussed have thus far been developed within a relatively narrow domain. Typically, the categories to which they have been applied comprise objects that can be labeled by nouns and represented within a single hierarchy. Traits, groups, persons, and social situations often do not fit this single category structure. Some of the principles that hold for natural object categories, such as the importance of correlated attributes, polythetic category structures, and limitations of category accessibility seem likely to hold across the wide domain of social concepts. Others we have mentioned, such as hierarchical structure, basic levels, and mutually exclusive category structure, do not. By rigorously testing categorization models and their concepts over a spectrum of category types, social psychologists present the opportunity to discover which principles are general in their applicability. The diversity of category structures that encompass social concepts are certain to both extend existing models and lead to the development of new models better able to account for phenomena in richer conceptual domains.

## ACKNOWLEDGMENTS

Preparation of this chapter was fully collaborative and order of authorship is not meant to be interpreted. We would like to thank Richard Ashmore, Tory Higgins, Edward Smith, Thomas Srull, and Robert Wyer for their comments on an earlier draft of this paper. The work was supported by National Institute of Mental Health Grants MH34979 and

MH32370 awarded to the first two and third author, respectively, as well as a National Science Foundation grant (BNS 80-23564) and a Rutgers University Research Council grant awarded JHL and MWA.

## REFERENCES

Allen, R. B., & Ebbesen, E. B. Cognitive processes in person perception: Retrieval of personality trait and behavioral information. *Journal of Experimental Social Psychology*, 1981, *17*, 119–141.

Altom, M. W., & Lingle, J. H. Episodic and categorical processes in impression change. In L. Ross (chair), *Problems in reconceptualization: Integrating new facts with old concepts.* Symposium presented at the meeting of the American Psychological Association, Montreal, 1980.

Altom, M. W., & Lingle, J. H. Memory representations and impression constancy: A dual-representational model of memory-based impression judgments. Manuscript submitted for publication, 1982.

Anderson, N. H. Integration theory applied to cognitive responses and attitudes. In R. M. Petty, T. M. Ostrom, & T. C. Brock (Eds.), *Cognitive responses in persuasion.* Hillsdale, N. J.: Lawrence Erlbaum Associates, 1981.

Aristotle. *Categories,* translated with notes by J. L. Ackrill. London: Oxford University Press, 1963.

Ashmore, R. D., & Del Boca, F. K. Sex stereotypes and implicit personality theory: Toward a cognitive-social psychological conceptualization. *Sex Roles,* 1979, *5*, 219–248.

Barker, R. G. *Ecological psychology.* Stanford: Stanford University Press, 1968.

Berlin, B. Speculations on the growth of ethnobiological nomenclature. *Journal of Language and Society,* 1972, *1*, 63–98.

Berlin, B. Ethnobiological classification. In E. Rosch & B. B. Lloyd (Eds.), *Cognition and categorization.* Hillsdale, N. J.: Lawrence Erlbaum Associates, 1978.

Billig, M., & Tajfel, H. Social categorization and similarity in intergroup behavior. *European Journal of Social Psychology,* 1973, *3*, 27–52.

Bourne, L. E. *Human conceptual behavior.* Boston: Allyn and Bacon, 1966.

Bruner, J. S., Goodnow, J. J., & Austin, G. A. *A study of thinking.* New York: Wiley, 1956.

Cantor, N., & Mischel, W. Prototypes in person perception. In L. Berkowitz (Ed.), *Advances in experimental social psychology. Volume 12.* New York: Academic Press, 1979.

Cantor, N., Mischel, W., & Schwartz, J. C. A prototype analysis of psychological situations. *Cognitive Psychology,* 1982, *14*, 45–77.

Carlston, D. E. The recall and use of traits and events in social inference processes. *Journal of Experimental Social Psychology,* 1980, *16*, 303–328. (a)

Carlston, D. E. Events, inferences, and impression formation. In R. Hastie, T. M. Ostrom, E. B. Ebbesen, R. S. Wyer, D. L. Hamilton, & D. E. Carlston (Eds.), *Person memory: The cognitive basis of social perception.* Hillsdale, N. J.: Lawrence Erlbaum Associates, 1980. (b)

Carmichael, L., Hogan, H. P., & Walter, A. An experimental study of the effect of language on the reproduction of visually perceived form. *Journal of Experimental Psychology,* 1932, *15*, 73–86.

Carroll, L. *Alice's adventures in wonderland & through the looking glass.* New York: New American Library, 1960 (*Through the looking glass* originally published 1871).

Chapman, L. J., & Chapman, J. P. Genesis of popular but erroneous psychodiagnostic observations. *Journal of Abnormal Psychology,* 1967, *72*, 193–204.

Clark, H. H., & Clark, E. V. *Psychology and language.* New York: Harcourt Brace Jovanovich, 1977.

Cohen, C. E. Person categories and social perception: Testing some boundaries of the processing effects of prior knowledge. *Journal of Personality and Social Psychology,* 1981, *40,* 441–452.

Coltheart, V., & Evans, J. St. B. T. An investigation of semantic memory in individuals. *Memory & Cognition,* 1981, *9,* 524–532.

Elio, R., & Anderson, J. R. The effects of category generalizations and instance similarity on schema abstraction. *Journal of Experimental Psychology: Human Learning and Memory,* 1981, *7,* 397–417.

Franks, J. J., & Bransford, J. D. Abstraction of visual patterns. *Journal of Experimental Psychology,* 1971, *90,* 65–74.

Fiske, S. T. Schema-triggered affect: Applications to social perception. In M. S. Clark & S. T. Fiske (Eds.), *Affect and Cognition: The 17th Annual Carnegie Symposium on Cognition.* Hillsdale, N. J.: Lawrence Erlbaum Associates, 1982.

Fiske, S. T., & Cox, M. G. Person concepts: The effect of target familiarity and descriptive purpose on the process of describing others. *Journal of Personality,* 1979, *47,* 136–161.

Ford, J. K., & Weldon, E. Forewarning and accountability: Effects on memory-based interpersonal judgments. *Personality and Social Psychology Bulletin,* 1981, *7,* 264–268.

Fredrickson, N. Toward a taxonomy of situations. *American Psychologist,* 1972, *27,* 114–123.

Gara, M. A., & Rosenberg, S. The identification of persons as supersets and subsets in free-response personality descriptions. *Journal of Personality and Social Psychology,* 1979, *37,* 2161–2170.

Garner, W. R. Aspects of a stimulus: Features, dimensions, and configurations. In E. Rosch & B. B. Lloyd (Eds.), *Cognition and categorization.* Hillsdale, N. J.: Lawrence Erlbaum Associates, 1978.

Greenwald, A. G. The totalitarian ego: Fabrication and revision of personal history. *American Psychologist,* 1980, *35,* 603–618.

Hamilton, D. L., & Gifford, R. K. Illusory correlation in interpersonal perception: A cognitive basis of stereotypic judgments. *Journal of Experimental Social Psychology,* 1976, *12,* 392–407.

Hampton, J. A. Polymorphous concepts in semantic memory. *Journal of Verbal Learning and Verbal Behavior,* 1979, *18,* 441–461.

Hampton, J. A. An investigation of the nature of abstract concepts. *Memory & Cognition,* 1981, *9,* 149–156.

Hastie, R. Schematic principles in human memory. In E. T. Higgins, C. P. Herman, & M. P. Zanna (Eds.), *Social cognition: The Ontario Symposium* (Vol. 1). Hillsdale, N.J.: Lawrence Erlbaum Associates, 1981.

Hastie, R., & Kumar, A. P. Person memory: Personality traits as organizing principles in memory for behaviors. *Journal of Personality and Social Psychology,* 1979, *37,* 25–38.

Hastie, R., Ostrom, T. M., Ebbesen, E. B., Wyer, R. S., Hamilton, D. L., & Carlston, D. E. (Eds.). *Person memory: The cognitive basis of social perception.* Hillsdale, N. J.: Lawrence Erlbaum Associates, 1980.

Higgins, E. T., & Chaires, W. M. Accessibility of interrelational constructs: Implications for stimulus encoding and creativity. *Journal of Experimental Social Psychology,* 1980, *16,* 348–361.

Higgins, E. T., & King, G. Accessibility of social constructs: Information processing consequences of individual and contextual variability. In N. Cantor & J. F. Kihlstrom (Eds.), *Personality, cognition, and social interaction.* Hillsdale, N. J.: Lawrence Erlbaum Associates, 1981.

Higgins, E. T., Rholes, C. R., & Jones, C. R. Category accessibility and impression formation. *Journal of Experimental Social Psychology,* 1977, *13,* 141–154.

Hintzman, D. L., & Ludlum, G. Differential forgetting of prototypes and old instances: Simulation by an exemplar-based classification model. *Memory & Cognition,* 1980, *8,* 378–382.

Homa, D., & Chambliss, D. The relative contributions of common and distinctive information on the abstraction from ill-defined categories. *Journal of Experimental Psychology: Human Learning and Memory*, 1975, *1*, 351–359.

Homa, D., Sterling, S., & Trepel, L. Limitations of exemplar-based generalization and the abstraction of categorical information. *Journal of Experimental Psychology: Human Learning and Memory*, 1981, *7*, 418–439.

Homa, D., & Vosburgh, R. Category breadth and the abstraction of prototypical information. *Journal of Experimental Psychology: Human Learning and Memory*, 1976, *2*, 322–330.

Howard, J., & Rothbart, M. Social categorization and memory for ingroup and outgroup behavior. *Journal of Personality and Social Psychology*, 1980, *38*, 301–310.

Jones, E. E., & Nisbett, R. E. The actor and the observer: Divergent perceptions of the causes of behavior. In E. E. Jones, N. E. Kanouse, H. H. Kelley, R. E. Nisbett, S. Valins, & B. Weiner (Eds.), *Attribution: Perceiving the causes of behavior*. Morristown, N. J.: General Learning, 1972.

Katz, J. J., & Fodor, J. A. The structure of a semantic theory. *Language*, 1963, *39*, 170–210.

Kelley, H. H. Causal schemata and the attribution process. In E. E. Jones, D. E. Kanouse, H. H. Kelley, R. E. Nisbett, S. Valins, & B. Weiner (Eds.), *Attribution: Perceiving the causes of behavior*. Morristown, N. J.: General Learning, 1972.

Kelly, G. A. *The psychology of personal constructs. Volume 1*. New York: Norton, 1955.

Krumhansl, C. L. Concerning the applicability of geometric models to similarity data: The interrelationship between similarity and spatial density. *Psychological Review*, 1978, *85*, 445–463.

Levine, R., Chein, I., & Murphy, B. The relation of the intensity of a need to the amount of labeling bias. *Journal of Consulting and Clinical Psychology*, 1942, *13*, 283–293.

Lingle, J. H. Tracing memory structure activation in impression judgments. *Journal of Experimental Social Psychology*, 1983, *19*, 480–496.

Lingle, J. H., & Altom, M. W. Processes of recategorization: When is a likeable person unlikeable? In R. Hastie (Chair), *Categorical processing and representation of person information*. Symposium presented at the meeting of the American Psychological Association, New York, 1979.

Lingle, J. H., Dukerich, J. M., & Ostrom, T. M. Accessing information in memory-based impression judgments: Incongruity vs negativity in retrieval selectivity. *Journal of Personality and Social Psychology*, 1983, *44*, 262–272.

Lingle, J. H., Geva, N., Ostrom, T. M., Leippe, M. R., & Baumgardner, M. H. Thematic effects of person judgments on impression organization. *Journal of Personality and Social Psychology*, 1979, *37*, 674–687.

Lingle, J. H., & Ostrom, T. M. Retrieval selectivity in memory-based impression judgments. *Journal of Personality and Social Psychology*, 1979, *37*, 180–194.

Markus, H. Self-schemata and processing information about the self. *Journal of Personality and Social Psychology*, 1977, *35*, 63–78.

McCloskey, M., & Glucksberg, S. Natural categories: Well-defined or fuzzy sets? *Memory & Cognition*, 1978, *6*, 462–472.

McGuire, W. J., McGuire, C. V., Child, P., & Fujioka, T. Salience of ethnicity in the spontaneous self-concept as a function of one's ethnic distinctiveness in the social environment. *Journal of Personality and Social Psychology*, 1978, *36*, 511–520.

McGuire, W. J., McGuire, C. V., & Winton, W. Effects of household sex composition on the salience of one's gender in the spontaneous self-concept. *Journal of Experimental Social Psychology*, 1979, *15*, 77–90.

McGuire, W. J., & Padawer-Singer, A. Trait salience in the spontaneous self-concept. *Journal of Personality and Social Psychology*, 1976, *33*, 743–754.

Medin, D. L. A theory of context in discrimination learning. In G. H. Bower (Ed.), *The psychology of learning and motivation. Volume 9*. New York: Academic Press, 1975.

Medin, D. L. Structural principles in categorization. In T. Tighe, B. Shepp, & H. Pick (Eds.),

*Interactions: Perception, cognition, and development.* Hillsdale, N. J.: Lawrence Erlbaum Associates, 1983.

Medin, D. L., Altom, M. W., Edelson, S. M., & Freko, D. Correlated symptoms and simulated medical classification. *Journal of Experimental Psychology: Learning, Memory, and Cognition,* 1982, *8,* 37–50.

Medin, D. L., & Schaffer, M. M. Context theory of classification learning. *Psychological Review,* 1978, *85,* 207–238.

Medin, D. L., & Schwanenflugel, P. J. Linear separability in classification learning. *Journal of Experimental Psychology: Human Learning and Memory,* 1981, *7,* 355–368.

Medin, D. L., & Smith, E. E. Strategies and classification learning. *Journal of Experimental Psychology: Human Learning and Memory,* 1981, *7,* 241–253.

Mervis, C. B., & Pani, J. R. Acquisition of basic object categories. *Cognitive Psychology,* 1980, *12,* 496–522.

Mervis, C. B., & Rosch, E. Categorization of natural objects. In M. R. Rosenzweig & L. W. Porter (Eds.), *Annual Review of Psychology,* 1981, *32,* 89–115.

Miller, G. A., & Johnson-Laird, P. N. *Language and perception.* Cambridge, Mass.: Harvard University Press, 1976.

Murphy, G. L. Cue validity and levels of categorization, *Psychological Bulletin,* 1982, *91,* 174–177.

Murphy, G. L., & Smith, E. E. Basic-level superiority in picture categorization. *Journal of Verbal Learning and Verbal Behavior,* 1982, *21,* 1–20.

Osgood, C., Suci, G. J., & Tannenbaum, P. H. *The measurement of meaning.* Urbana, Ill.: University of Illinois Press, 1957.

Ostrom, T. M. Cognitive representations of impression. Paper presented at the American Psychological Convention, Chicago, 1975.

Ostrom, T. M. Within-theory and between-theory conflict in explaining context effects in impression formation. *Journal of Experimental Social Psychology,* 1977, *13,* 492–503.

Ostrom, T. M., Lingle, J. H., Pryor, J. B., & Geva, N. Cognitive organization of person impressions. In R. Hastie, T. Ostrom, E. Ebbesen, R. Wyer, Jr., D. Hamilton, & D. Carlston (Eds.), *Person memory: The cognitive basis of social perception.* Hillsdale, N. J.: Lawrence Erlbaum Associates, 1980.

Pervin, L. A. A free-response description approach to the analysis of person-situation interaction. *Journal of Personality and Social Psychology,* 1976, *34,* 465–474.

Posner, M. I., & Keele, S. W. On the genesis of abstract ideas. *Journal of Experimental Psychology,* 1968, *77,* 353–363.

Posner, M. I., & Keele, S. W. Retention of abstract ideas. *Journal of Experimental Psychology,* 1970, *83,* 304–308.

Postman, L., & Brown, D. R. The perceptual consequences of success and failure. *Journal of Abnormal and Social Psychology,* 1952, *47,* 213–221.

Reed, S. K. Pattern recognition and categorization. *Cognitive Psychology,* 1972, *3,* 382–407.

Reyes, R. M., Thompson, W. C., & Bower, G. H. Judgmental biases resulting from differing availabilities of arguments. *Journal of Personality and Social Psychology,* 1980, *39,* 2–12.

Riley, D. A. Memory for form. In L. Postman (Ed.), *Psychology in the making: Histories of selected research problems.* New York: Knopf, 1963.

Rips, L. J., Shoben, E. J., & Smith, E. E. Semantic distance and the verification of semantic relations. *Journal of Verbal Learning and Verbal Behavior,* 1973, *12,* 1–20.

Rosch, E. On the internal structure of perceptual and semantic categories. In T. E. Moore (Ed.), *Cognitive development and the acquisition of language.* New York: Academic Press, 1973.

Rosch, E. Cognitive representations of semantic categories. *Journal of Experimental Psychology: General,* 1975, *104,* 192–233.

Rosch, E. Principles of categorization. In E. Rosch & B. B. Lloyd (Eds.), *Cognition and categorization.* Hillsdale, N. J.: Lawrence Erlbaum Associates, 1978.

Rosch, E., & Mervis, C. B. Family resemblances: Studies in the internal structure of categories. *Cognitive Psychology,* 1975, *7,* 573–605.

Rosch, E., Mervis, C. B., Gray, W. D., Johnson, D. M., & Boyes-Braem, P. Basic objects in natural categories. *Cognitive Psychology,* 1976, *8,* 382–439.

Rosenberg, S., Nelson, C., & Vivekananthan, P. S. A multidimensional approach to the structure of personality impressions. *Journal of Personality and Social Psychology,* 1968, *9,* 283–294.

Rosenberg, S., & Sedlak, A. Structural representations of implicit personality theory. In L. Berkowitz (Ed.), *Advances in experimental social psychology. Volume 6.* New York: Academic Press, 1972.

Ross, M., & Sicoly, F. Egocentric biases in availability and attribution. *Journal of Personality and Social Psychology,* 1979, *37,* 322–336.

Roth, E. Context effects on the representation of meaning. Unpublished doctoral dissertation. University of Illinois, 1980.

Rothbart, M., Evans, M., & Fulero, S. Recall for confirming events: Memory processes and the maintenance of social stereotypes. *Journal of Experimental Social Psychology,* 1979, *15,* 343–355.

Rothbart, M., Fulero, S., Jensen, C., Howard, J., & Birrell, P. From individual to group impressions: Availability heuristics in stereotype formation. *Journal of Experimental Social Psychology,* 1978, *14,* 237–255.

Schneider, D. J. Implicit personality theory: A review. *Psychological Bulletin,* 1973, *79,* 294–309.

Shepard, R. N. Multidimensional scaling, tree-fitting, and clustering. *Science,* 1980, *210,* 390–398.

Slamecka, N. J., & Graf, P. The generation effect: Delineation of a phenomenon. *Journal of Experimental Psychology: Human Learning and Memory,* 1978, *4,* 592–604.

Smith, E. E. Theories of semantic memory. In W. K. Estes (Ed.), *Handbook of learning and cognitive processes. Vol. 6: Linguistic functions in cognitive theory.* Hillsdale, N.J.: Lawrence Erlbaum Associates, 1978.

Smith, E. E., & Medin, D. L. *Categories and concepts.* Cambridge, Mass.: Harvard University Press, 1981.

Sneath, H. A., & Sokal, R. R. *Numerical taxonomy: The principles and practice of numerical classification.* San Francisco: W. H. Freeman & Co., 1973.

Snyder, M. On the self-perpetuating nature of social stereotypes. In D. Hamilton (Ed.), *Cognitive processes in stereotyping and intergroup behavior.* Hillsdale, N.J.: Lawrence Erlbaum Associates, 1981.

Sokal, R. R. Classification: Purposes, principles, progress, prospects. *Science,* 1974, *185,* 1115–1123.

Sommers, F. Predicability. In M. Black (Ed.), *Philosophy in America.* Ithaca, N. Y.: Cornell University Press, 1965.

Strange, W., Keeney, T., Kessel, F. S., & Jenkins, J. J. Abstraction over time of prototypes from distortions of random dot patterns: A replication. *Journal of Experimental Psychology,* 1970, *83,* 508–510.

Srull, T. K. Person memory: Some tests of associative storage and retrieval models. *Journal of Experimental Psychology: Human Learning and Memory,* 1981, *7,* 440–463.

Srull, T. K., & Wyer, R. S. The role of category accessibility in the interpretation of information about persons: Some determinants and implications. *Journal of Personality and Social Psychology,* 1979, *37,* 1660–1672.

Srull, T. K., & Wyer, R. S. Category accessibility and social perception: Some implications for the study of person memory and interpersonal judgments. *Journal of Personality and Social Psychology,* 1980, *38,* 841–856.

Tajfel, H., & Billig, M. Familiarity and categorization in intergroup behavior. *Journal of Experimental Social Psychology*, 1974, *10*, 159–170.

Tajfel, H., Sheikh, A. A., & Gardner, R. C. Content of stereotypes and the inferences of similarity between members of stereotyped groups. *Acta Psychologica*, 1964, *22*, 191–201.

Taylor, S. E., Fiske, S. T., Etcoff, N. L., & Ruderman, A. J. Categorical and contextual bases of person memory and stereotyping. *Journal of Personality and Social Psychology*, 1978, *36*, 778–793.

Tsujimoto, R. N. Memory bias toward normative and novel trait prototypes. *Journal of Personality and Social Psychology*, 1978, *36*, 1391–1401.

Tsujimoto, R. N., Wilde, J., & Robertson, D. R. Distorted memory for exemplars of social structure: Evidence for schematic memory processes. *Journal of Personality and Social Psychology*, 1978, *36*, 1402–1414.

Tulving, E., & Thomson, D. M. Encoding specificity and retrieval processes in episodic memory. *Psychological Review*, 1973, *80*, 352–373.

Tversky, A. Features of similarity. *Psychological Review*, 1977, *84*, 327–352.

Tversky, A., & Gati, I. Studies of similarity. In E. Rosch & B. B. Lloyd (Eds.), *Cognition and categorization*. Hillsdale, N. J.: Lawrence Erlbaum Associates, 1978.

Tversky, A., & Kahneman, D. Availability: A heuristic for judging frequency and probability. *Cognitive Psychology*, 1973, *5*, 207–232.

von Baeyer, C. L., Sherk, D. L., & Zanna, M. P. Impression management in the job interview: When the female applicant meets the male (chauvinist) interviewer. *Personality and Social Psychology Bulletin*, 1981, *7*, 45–52.

Walker, J. H. Real-world variability, reasonableness judgments, and memory representations for concepts. *Journal of Verbal Learning and Verbal Behavior*, 1975, *14*, 241–252.

Wallsten, T. S., & Budescu, D. V. Additivity and nonadditivity in judging MMPI profiles. *Journal of Experimental Psychology: Human Perception and Performance*, 1981, *7*, 1096–1109.

Warr, P. B., & Knapper, C. *The perception of people and events*. London: Wiley, 1968.

Wegner, D. M., & Vallacher, R. R. *The self in social psychology*. New York: Oxford University Press, 1980.

Wiggins, J. S. A psychological taxonomy of trait-descriptive terms: The interpersonal domain. *Journal of Personality and Social Psychology*, 1979, *37*, 395–412.

Wilder, D. A. Perceiving persons as a group: Categorization and intergroup relations. In D. L. Hamilton (Ed.), *Cognitive processes in stereotyping and intergroup behavior*. Hillsdale, N.J.: Lawrence Erlbaum Associates, 1981.

Wyer, R. S. *Cognitive organization and change: An information-processing approach*. Hillsdale, N.J.: Lawrence Erlbaum Associates, 1974.

Wyer, R. S., & Hartwick, J. The role of information retrieval and conditional inference processes in belief formation and change. In L. Berkowitz (Ed.), *Advances in experimental social psychology* (Vol. 13). New York: Academic Press, 1980.

Wyer, R. S., & Srull, T. K. The processing of social stimulus information: A conceptual integration. In R. Hastie, T. M. Ostrom, E. B. Ebbesen, R. S. Wyer, D. L. Hamilton & D. E. Carlston (Eds.), *Person memory: Cognitive basis for social perception*. Hillsdale, N.J.: Lawrence Erlbaum Associates, 1980.

Wyer, R. S., & Srull, T. K. Category accessibility: Some theoretical and empirical issues concerning the processing of social stimulus information. In E. T. Higgins, C. P. Herman, & M. P. Zanna (Eds.), *Social cognition: The Ontario Symposium* (Vol. 1). Hillsdale, N.J.: Lawrence Erlbaum Associates, 1981.

# 4 The Nature and Functions of Schemas

William F. Brewer
Glenn V. Nakamura
*University of Illinois at Urbana-Champaign*

## Contents

Schema theory is one of the most intellectually exciting areas of current cognitive psychology. There has been such a rapid growth of theories and data on this topic that it is difficult to understand what has been accomplished. In this chapter we attempt to give an analytic account of the nature and functions of schemas in psychological theory and to organize some of the experimental evidence dealing with the operation of schemas in human memory. We restrict ourselves to laboratory studies and theories from cognitive psychology and artificial intelligence and do not cover the schema literature from social psychology.

Much of this chapter is devoted to attempting to understand what schemas are. In brief, they are higher-order cognitive structures that have been hypothesized to underlie many aspects of human knowledge and skill. They serve a crucial role in providing an account of how old knowledge interacts with new knowledge in perception, language, thought, and memory.

This chapter is organized into six sections. The first section is devoted to a detailed examination of the schema concept as formulated by Bartlett. The second section relates Bartlett's theory to the larger issue of the conflict in psychological theory between ideas from British Empiricism and ideas from Continental philosophy. The third section briefly outlines some of the basic theoretical assumptions of information processing psychology in order to serve as a background for our analysis of schema theory. In the fourth section we examine modern schema theory (e.g., Minsky, 1975; Rumelhart & Ortony, 1977; Rumelhart, 1980, reprinted in this volume) and contrast these theories with Bartlett's theory and with the information processing approach. In the fifth section we sketch out our own position. In the final section we develop a framework for analyzing the functions of schemas in the human memory process and then examine a number of recent experiments in terms of this framework.

## BARTLETT'S SCHEMA THEORY

The schema theory Bartlett developed in his book *Remembering* (1932), has been the inspiration for most modern schema theories. Bartlett's work is a particularly powerful presentation of schema theory and on some issues his theory is worked out in more depth than current schema theories, so his work merits careful consideration. In this section we analyze Bartlett's basic assumptions and lay out the conceptual core of his theory.

### Bartlett's Definition of Schemas

Bartlett (1932) defined a schema as "an active organisation of past reactions, or of past experiences, which must always be supposed to be operating in any well-adapted organic response'' (p. 201). His book consists of an elaboration of his schema theory and an application of it to data he had gathered much earlier on memory for figures, pictures, and stories (e.g., Bartlett, 1916, 1920, 1921).

First we would like to know what kind of construct schemas were for Bartlett. In the terms of modern philosophy of science (cf. Suppe, 1977), was Bartlett an instrumentalist (schemas are just constructs used to organize the data) or was he a realist (schemas exist and the schema theory attempts to describe them)? It is clear from Bartlett's text that he was a realist with respect to his schema theory. Given that he is a realist, what kind of entities does he think schemas are? It appears that he assumes they are unconscious mental processes. In a discussion of the neurologist Head's schema theory, Bartlett stated that ''schemata are active, without any awareness at all'' (1932, p. 200), and even more clearly in his autobiography he stated that schemas have the same status as images and ideas but that they are not available to introspection (1936, p. 47).

The hypothesis that schemas are complex unconscious knowledge structures is one of Bartlett's major contributions. In his book, Bartlett generously gave Head credit for developing the schema hypothesis. However, on this issue, as on many others, Bartlett's theory is very different. Head gave only a sketchy account of his approach, but it seems likely that he considered schemas to be physiological entities. Thus, he stated, ''schemata lie for ever outside consciousness; they are physiological processes with no direct psychical equivalent'' (Head, 1918, p. 158). Many psychologists and philosophers have found the concept of an unconscious mental process hard to accept. When the Würzburg psychologists postulated such entities they were attacked by the introspective psychologists, who believed that the data of psychology were restricted to conscious phenomena (see Humphrey, 1951). They were also attacked by behaviorists, who thought that the data of psychology were restricted to observations of overt behavior (Watson, 1913). However, in recent years a number of philosophers have made powerful arguments for the acceptance of unconscious mental processes as proper objects of scientific study (e.g., Fodor, 1968; Putnam, 1973), and these processes form the core of modern information processing psychology.

## Properties of Schemas

Having established that Bartlett took schemas to be unconscious mental structures, we now examine their characteristics. In Bartlett's (1932) abstract definition of schemas he consistently described them as ''organized,'' but gave little further specification. He did state that the term ''pattern'' would not be quite accurate, since it implies more detail than he intended. However, in the analysis of the various memory experiments reported in his book he gave a number of examples that help clarify his use of the term "organized." He probably intended the term to cover the organization involved in such things as: symmetrical visual figures (p. 24); rules (p. 52); the plan of a prose passage (p. 83—he gives the structure of a "cumulative story" as an example, cf. Rumelhart, 1975); and literary conventions (p. 140—he gives ending a story with a moral as an example, cf. Brewer, in press). If this is a correct reading of Bartlett, then it is clear that the term "organized" covers a very wide range of cognitive structures.

Another fundamental aspect of schemas in Bartlett's theory is that they are composed of old knowledge. Thus, he stated that they are "masses of organised past experiences" (1932, pp. 197–198). However, there are a wide variety of ways in which old knowledge could be represented, and Bartlett had a specific hypothesis about the form of representation in schemas. In particular, Bartlett wanted to develop an alternative to the standard British Empiricist view that old knowledge was represented in the form of a collection of specific mental images (e.g., Hobbs, Berkeley, James Mill). Head and Holmes (1911, p. 186) had initially developed schema theory in neurology as an alternative to the image view as applied to body posture and movement. This was one important component of Head's theory that Bartlett wanted to retain. However, he wanted to apply it to all the higher mental processes and he attacked Head for implicitly accepting the image position for other psychological processes (1932, p. 200).

## Operation of Schemas

In adopting the position that much of old knowledge was represented in the form of unconscious mental structures Bartlett had already made a major break with the image view. However, he also wanted to emphasize that knowledge was represented in larger units. Thus, he stated that schemas "operate, not simply as individual members coming one after another, but as a unitary mass" (1932, p. 201). Not only did he believe that schemas operated as larger units of knowledge, but he argued that schemas developed into qualitatively different cognitive structures. He stated that, "the past operates as an organised mass rather than as a group of elements each of which retains its specific character" (1932, p. 197).

By examining Bartlett's account of his memory data it is possible to infer what type of qualitative change Bartlett had in mind. He believed that schemas were generic mental structures. He assumed that in the course of exposure to many particular instances of phenomena the mind abstracted a generic cognitive representation (i.e., a schema). Bartlett often discussed this issue by comparing conventional modes of representing cultural artifacts in societies with conventional modes of representation within individuals. In one analysis of this issue he referred to the "stereotyped modes of representation or of reaction" of individuals and suggested that these "conventionalisations are produced by a combination of innumerable small changes" (1932, p. 95). Overall, a close reading of Bartlett suggests that he hypothesized schemas to be unconscious mental structures organized into generic cognitive representations.

In addition to these structural characteristics of schemas, Bartlett developed a number of proposals about schema processing. His fundamental processing assumption was that all new information interacts with the old information represented in the schema. This is one of the assumptions that Bartlett's theory and Head's theory had in common. In discussing postural change Head and Holmes had stated "Every recognisable change enters into consciousness already charged with its relation to something that has gone before" (Head, 1920, p. 605), and Bartlett quoted this section of their paper with approval. However, this aspect of Bartlett's approach to schemas was present in his earliest work. In his first published experiment Bartlett explained errors made by his subjects in recalling visual figures by the interaction of new and old information. He stated that many of the errors were due to "the tendency to interpret presented material in accordance with the general character of earlier experience" (1916, p. 231).

In his later discussions of the interaction of old schema-based information with new input, Bartlett focused on the active nature of this process. He felt that earlier writers who had considered the role of old knowledge had treated the old information as a passive framework, somewhat like a partially completed jigsaw puzzle capable of accepting the appropriate piece. Bartlett felt that the data in his memory studies were not consistent with a passive schema process. When he presented subjects with material to recall they made a large number of errors. Many of the errors were more regular, more meaningful, and more conventionalized than the original stimuli. Bartlett took these results to indicate that the subjects were actively attempting to relate the new material to old schema information—a process he called "effort after meaning." He stated that to accept the passive view "as if what is accepted and given a place in mental life is always simply a question of what fits into already formed apperception systems is to miss the obvious point that the process of fitting is an active process" (1932, p. 85). Bartlett typically gathered introspective reports during the recall process and on the basis of these protocols he concluded that the active processes were sometimes conscious strategies on the part of the subject (1932, p. 87–89), but more frequently he found them to be active unconscious processes (1932, p. 20).

Bartlett also thought that schema processes were generative, where generative means a process that can deal with an indefinitely large number of new instances. He was particularly clear on this characteristic of schema processing when discussing motor production schemas. Bartlett pointed out that a skilled tennis player is more likely to hit a tennis ball than an unskilled player, even when the ball appears in a new location never before experienced by the skilled player. Thus, he argued that the old information accumulated by the skilled player is not in the form of a set of fixed motor movements, but in the form of a generative motor schema (1932, p. 202).

## Bartlett's Memory Theories

The final aspect of Bartlett's schema theory that we discuss in detail is his theory of the recall process. Bartlett actually had two different theories of recall. When he was talking abstractly and focusing on the mistakes of the storehouse or trace models he adopted a pure reconstructive model. However, when he was explaining his own data he adopted a partial reconstructive model.

*Pure reconstructive recall.* The pure reconstructive model assumes that when an individual is exposed to some new information that new information serves to modify the appropriate schema, but that no specific episodic representation of the new information is retained in memory. Thus, for example, if someone goes into an office that they have never been in before, the information about that office will be integrated with the individual's established office schema and will modify that schema to some extent. Bartlett stated that the recall for a specific event, such as the visit to the office, is carried out by having "the organism . . . turn . . . round upon its own 'schemata' " (1932, p. 202). Many writers have felt that this aspect of Bartlett's theory was incomprehensible. It does not seem so to us. If one reads this section of his memory theory in the context of his earlier published work and recognizes his concern with the issue of personal memory, then the problem Bartlett is dealing with becomes clear. He was concerned with providing an account of how an individual produces a specific memory representation from a generic schema representation. In the section of his book where he developed the pure reconstructive theory, Bartlett stated that an individual attempting to remember a specific event cannot base the recall on specific traces since "the individual details that have built them up have disappeared, but somehow [must] construct or . . . infer from what is present the probable constituents and their order which went to build them up" (1932, p. 202). The pure schema reconstructive theory of recall succeeds admirably in dispensing with specific traces and gives a natural account of schema-based inferential errors in recall. However, it has a fatal flaw—it allows no recall of unique episodic information from the original episode. Thus, in the case of the earlier example of recall of an office, the pure reconstructive theory accounts nicely for the recall of generic schema information (e.g., typewriter, chairs) and provides an explanation of schema-based errors in recall (e.g., recalling books or filing cabinets when none were present—see Brewer & Treyens, 1981). However, the theory cannot account for the recall of specific nongeneric information about the room (e.g., that the typewriter was an Underwood standard or that one of the chairs was made of plastic). Obviously, the pure schema reconstructive theory is in error. This is the natural consequence of combining a schema theory with a memory theory that allows no specific "trace" information whatsoever.

The problem of how specific memories are derived from generic schemas was discussed briefly by Bartlett. He stated that "somehow we have to find a way of individualising some of the characteristics of the total functioning mass of the moment" (1932, p. 208). His solution was to suggest that "images are a device for picking bits out of schemes" (1932, p. 219). Most writers discussing Bartlett's theory have found these comments to be unintelligible. However, again we do not think that this is the case. Bartlett apparently assumed that specific memories are what Brewer and Pani (1983) call personal memories. A personal memory is a recollection of information from an individual's past that is experienced in terms of visual imagery and is typically accompanied by a belief that it represents a memory of a particular time and location (cf. Brewer & Pani, 1983, for additional discussion). If this analysis of Bartlett is correct, then his discussion of the issue makes much more sense. He was attempting to reconcile a memory theory based on unconscious schemas with the phenomenally experienced images of specific personal memories.

In a trace theory of memory, the memory theorist attempts to account for the recall of specific memories by some type of encoding and retrieval mechanism. Within the framework of the pure reconstructive theory Bartlett faces serious difficulties in providing a mechanism that produces specific memories from generic schemas. He stated that "specific recall is, in fact, an achievement of consciousness" (1935, p. 225). Although he gave no more details, he apparently felt that one of the major functions of consciousness was to allow an individual to generate specific phenomenologically experienced representations from unconscious generic schemas. He also suggested that the instantiation process was guided by the individual's "attitudes" (feeling and affect), but gave no clear account of how this process might achieve the desired result (cf., 1932, pp. 206–207). This is one of the only parts of Bartlett's memory theory that has not been followed up by later memory theorists (however, see Spiro, 1980).

*Partial reconstructive recall.* The pure reconstructive schema theory of memory that has been outlined above is Bartlett's "official" theory of memory—the one he presents formally when he is describing the memory process in abstract theoretical terms. However, a close reading of Bartlett's accounts of his actual experiments reveals a partially reconstructive schema theory. This theory assumes that recall is a joint function of a schema component and a specific episodic component. The motivation for the partially reconstructive theory apparently derives from certain aspects of his memory data. In a number of places Bartlett noted that there was recall of specific schema-unrelated material. Thus, in an experiment on memory for visual symbols he stated, "The persistence of certain kinds of novel detail is an undoubted fact" (1932, p. 107). In his experiment on repeated reproduction of stories he noted that "as a rule one or two striking details seemed to recur with as little change as the form itself" (1932, p. 83). In an experiment on the serial reproduction of pictures, he pointed out that some nonschema details were frequently retained and stated that "This constitutes yet another case of that curious preservation of the trivial, the odd, the disconnected, the unimportant detail" (1932, p. 184). While Bartlett never overtly presented a theory that combines memory for specific information with his schema theory, he certainly suggested it in several places. In a discussion of inferences made in a memory-for-faces task he noted "that inferences, based upon judgments of this kind, are mingled unwittingly with the actual recall of perceptual material or patterns" (1932, p. 52). In a general discussion of imagery and schemas he noted that during recall "some part of the event which has to be remembered recurs, and the event is then reconstructed on the basis of the relation of this specific bit of material to the general mass of relevant past experience or reactions" (1932, p. 209). Thus, it seems to us that when Bartlett was attempting to account for his own data and when he was not focusing on his opposition to trace theories, he implicitly held a partially reconstructive schema theory of memory. Almost all later memory theorists adopt a form of Bartlett's unofficial, partially reconstructive theory of memory.

Within the partial reconstruction position, there is a problem of the articulation of data and theory with respect to recall of nonschema information. Bartlett often found that nonschema information was not recalled (1932, p. 99) or was transformed to fit some schema (1932, p. 89); but on other occasions nonschema information was well recalled (1932, p. 90, 184). Clearly, if a schema theory is to be explanatory it must be articulated in ways that give a motivated account of these apparently inconsistent data (see, Thorndyke & Yekovich, 1980, for a similar critique of modern schema theories).

In summary, Bartlett thought schemas were unconscious mental structures. He believed that they were organized generic mental representations that actively incorporated incoming episodic information. On the specific issue of recall, Bartlett's official position was a totally reconstructive theory, but in practice, he also held a partially reconstructive account of recall.

## BARTLETT, BRITISH EMPIRICISM, AND CONTINENTAL PHILOSOPHY

This section attempts to answer the following puzzle: Bartlett's schema theory was published in 1932 and yet contemporary schema theory dates from 1975 (Minsky, 1975; Rumelhart, 1975). What caused the gap from 1932 to 1975? In order to answer this question it is necessary to take a brief metatheoretical detour. Mainstream American psychology in its early introspective form (e.g., Titchener) and its stimulus-response form (e.g., Watson, Hull, Skinner) was a direct descendant from the conceptual framework of British Empiricism.

For our purposes the canonical British Empiricist position concerning the structure of the mind can be characterized as: (a) *Empiricist*—all knowledge derives from the environment; (b) *Atomistic*—the mind is composed of simple elements; (c) *Parsimonious*—the mind is composed of a few basic types of elements; (d) *Associationistic*—the fundamental mental mechanisms are associations which form through spatial and temporal contiguity; (e) *Particularistic*—the basic elements are particulars (not true of Locke). (f) *Passive*—the mind is not active; (g) *Mechanistic*—the mind is not purposive, goal-directed, or intentional; (h) *Finite*—no mechanisms are proposed that would be capable of dealing with an indefinitely large number of new situations. (See Boring, 1950; de Groot, 1965; and Mandler & Mandler, 1964; for a more detailed discussion of these positions.) Continental philosophy (e.g., Leibniz, Kant, Herbart, Lotze, Brentano) has not been as homogeneous as British Empiricism, but has tended to take the opposite side on these issues—thus the classic contrast between Empiricism and Rationalism. We view each of the theoretical paradigms examined in this chapter in terms of these fundamental assumptions. However, in doing this, we do not include the empiricist-nativist issue since it is rarely discussed by the theorists we consider. If we were to impose our own classification on these theories, we would classify all the schema theories as nativistic, since theorists who postulate as much mental machinery as schema theorists do are typically forced into a nativist position (e.g., Chomsky, 1965).

The British Empiricist position has a certain aesthetic appeal and has been the typical choice of the tough-minded theorist. Most behavioral scientists have considered the British Empiricist position to be the more ''scientific'' position. Thus, when American psychology shifted to Behaviorism, there was a drastic shift in the subject matter of psychology (from phenomenal experience to behavior), but no change in each of the assumptions outlined above. On these fundamental issues stimulus-response psychology was in total agreement with British Empiricism.

With this background in mind, it is now possible to examine the reception of Bartlett's schema theory. Bartlett's work had little impact on American psychology. In a review of the *Remembering* book McGeoch (1933) said the experiments were, ''outside the current of contemporary American research upon memory'' (p. 774), and in another review Jenkins (1935) concluded, ''The book will find a place upon the shelves of those who study remembering, but it will not be in the special section reserved for those investigators whose writings have become landmarks in the advance towards the comprehension of this important problem'' (p. 715). In England, Bartlett's schema theory was taken much more seriously (e.g., Oldfield & Zangwill, 1942a, 1942b, 1943a, 1943b). However,

## TABLE 4.1

A Classification of Major Research Paradigms in Terms of the Contrast Between the Assumptions of British Empiricism and Continental Philosophy

| | British Empiricism | Bartlett's Theory | Stimulus-Response | Information Processing | Modern Schema | Revised Schema | Continental Philosophy | |
|---|---|---|---|---|---|---|---|---|
| Atomistic | + | − | + | + | − | − | − | Molar |
| Parsimonious | + | + | + | + | + | − | − | Modular |
| Associationistic | + | − | + | − | − | − | − | Non Associationistic |
| Particularistic | + | − | + | − | − | − | − | Generic/Abstract |
| Passive | + | − | + | +− | − | − | − | Active |
| Mechanistic | + | − | + | +− | − | − | − | Purposive |
| Finite | + | − | + | | − | − | − | Generative |

*Note.* + indicates general acceptance of the British Empiricist assumptions. − indicates general acceptance of the Continental assumptions. +− indicates that some members took one position and some the other. In order to make the contrast clear the description of British Empiricism is of a conservative version of that tradition.

even in England opinion shifted in the British Empiricist direction and by the time Bartlett died his major students considered the theory to have been a total failure (Broadbent, 1970; Oldfield, 1972; Zangwill, 1972).

We think a comparison of the assumptions of Bartlett's schema theory with the assumptions of British Empiricism makes very clear what the problem was— on almost all of the issues discussed above, Bartlett's schema theory adopts the Continental position (see Table 4.1). On the issue of parsimony Bartlett does take the British Empiricist position (one construct, the schema, does most of the work); however, on every one of the remaining issues Bartlett's theory is clearly on the Continental side. The intellectual roots of this heresy are to be found in Bartlett's direct reading of the Continental philosophers, indirectly through the influence of James Ward and G. F. Stout, and through the work of the Würzburg psychologists (see, Bartlett, 1936; Broadbent, 1970; Drever, 1965; Northway, 1940; Zangwill, 1972). Thus, Bartlett's schema theory was simply incompatible with the basic theoretical assumptions of the stimulus-response psychology that was dominant (in the United States) at the time he formulated the theory. In fact, one basic thesis of this chapter is that the history of the shifts from stimulus-response psychology to information processing psychology to schema theory is the history of a succession of psychologists who lust after the British Empiricist position but who have been dragged "kicking and screaming" by the brute facts of nature to the Continental position.

## INFORMATION PROCESSING PSYCHOLOGY

In this section we briefly sketch some of the core theoretical assumptions made by theories in the information processing tradition, as background for the assumptions made by modern schema theories. By information processing theories we mean theories based on a computer metaphor that trace the flow of information in the mind through various stages of processing (e.g., Anderson & Bower, 1973; Atkinson & Shiffrin, 1968; Neisser, 1967; Newell & Simon, 1972). In terms of the contrast between British Empiricism and Continental philosophy, the information processing approach can be seen as a "profane union" (Anderson & Bower, 1973, p. 4) of the two traditions. In shifting from stimulus-response theories to information processing theories, there was a continuing acceptance of some of the tenets of British Empiricism, but a rejection of a number of others.

First, one would like to know what information processing theorists consider their theories to be about (i.e., what ontological assumptions do they make?). This is a difficult question, since many of the constructs used in these theories have been taken from computer science and artificial intelligence, and it is not clear how these borrowed constructs are to be interpreted in psychological theories (see Pylyshyn, 1978, and commentary). Thus, many theorists prefer not to address this issue directly or tend to be ambivalent when they do. Neisser's book, *Cognitive Psychology* (1967), was one of the major forces in molding the information processing paradigm. He argued that the "program analogy" makes it scientifically respectable to study unconscious mental processes (1967, p. 8). Thus, he apparently adopted the realist position that information processing theories are theories about the nature of unconscious mental processes. Quillian (1968) appeared to take a realist position, Collins and Quillian (1969) avoided the issue, but later Collins and Quillian (1972) appeared to take an instrumentalist position. Anderson apparently took a realist position with respect to the entities postulated in Anderson and Bower (1973), but he took a radically instrumentalist position several years later (Anderson, 1976). (See Anderson's discussion of his change of view in Anderson, 1980, p. 85). Clearly the workers in the information processing paradigm have not reached a consensus on these difficult problems.

One of the major changes in the shift from behaviorist theories to information processing theories was the rejection of the assumption that the theories were about particulars. Information processing psychologists did not accept the assumption that psychological theories were restricted to observable behavior, and they included abstract entities in their theories (see Anderson & Bower's 1973 discussion of the "terminal metapostulate" issue).

Through the influence of generative linguistics (Chomsky, 1965), many information processing theorists came to realize that psychological theories need to provide an account of the ability of human beings to deal appropriately with "new instances" in language, perception, thought, and action. The researchers in the information processing tradition came to see that inability to deal with this aspect of human cognition was a fatal flaw in stimulus-response theories, and so they introduced abstract entities to allow some generativity.

Another fundamental shift made by information processing psychology was the abandonment of the belief that all psychological theories could be formulated in terms of associations (see Anderson & Bower, 1973, for a contrary opinion on this point). Information processing theorists replaced the simple association with a wide variety of relational and structural entities: propositions (Kintsch, 1972); semantic relations (Quillian, 1968); and semantic features (Smith, Shoben, & Rips, 1974).

Some of the information processing theories avoided the general tendency of stimulus-response theories to be passive and nonpurposive, but there was not as much agreement on these issues. Thus, Newell and Simon (1972) provided explicit goal-directed problem-solving machinery that gave their theory a purposive component. Anderson and Bower (1973) chose to retain a passive memory representation ("strategy-free"), but included active processes in their executive component.

Two of the British Empiricist assumptions have been retained by the information processing approaches. All of the information processing theories have been atomistic and parsimonious. They have assumed that a complete theory of the mind could be constructed with a small number of basic mental elements. Holding to these assumptions has produced some interesting problems. For example, Anderson's (1976) theory combines the atomistic assumption with interference constructs to produce a "fan" hypothesis—which, put crudely, is that the more you know about a concept the slower and harder it will be to think about an instance related to that concept. While there is some support for this hypothesis in laboratory list-learning tasks it seems highly unlikely that the fan effect occurs for real-world knowledge. If the fan effect does not hold up for real world knowledge (see, Smith, 1981) then it would appear that theorists in this tradition will have to carefully examine their assumptions.

Overall, we think the picture is clear. Information processing psychology was a partial move toward the Continental tradition (see Table 4.1). The information processing theories rejected many of the British Empiricist assumptions of the earlier stimulus-response psychology, but retained a strong belief in atomism and parsimony.

## MODERN SCHEMA THEORY

It is clear that by 1975 there had been a Zeitgeist which prepared the cognitive science community for schema theory. In that one year papers were published arguing for schema theory by researchers in: artificial intelligence (Minsky, 1975); cognitive psychology (Rumelhart, 1975); linguistics (Fillmore, 1975); motor performance (Schmidt, 1975); and several cognitive psychology-artificial intelligence combinations (Bobrow & Norman, 1975; Schank & Abelson, 1975). It appears that the common issue that motivated investigators to look for a new theory was a desire to deal with "complex" tasks. The remarkable convergence of new papers in the same year was probably due to the fact that earlier versions of Minsky's important paper (1975) were widely circulated in the period just before 1975. It is also interesting to note that every one of these papers makes explicit reference to Bartlett's (1932) schema theory—this only a few years after his major biographers had declared the theory to have been a failure (Broadbent, 1970; Oldfield, 1972; Zangwill, 1972).

### Ontological Assumptions

On the issue of the ontological status of schemas it is hard to be sure what many schema theorists believe, and in those cases where the issue is treated clearly there is little consensus. Minsky (1975) and Rumelhart (1980) both define schemas as "data structures," a phrase that certainly has the flavor of a convenient notation to summarize the data (i.e., instrumentalism). Yet, the substance of both papers and Rumelhart's title, "Schemata: The Building Blocks of Cognition," certainly suggest they have more realist leanings. Neisser (1976) apparently takes a realist position and considers schemas to be physiological entities. He states, "a schema is a part of the nervous system. It is some active array of physiological structures and processes" (p. 54). Anderson (1981) takes a strong instrumentalist position. He suggests that the only solution to this problem is to "postulate some set of internal structures and processes that are consistent with the data and don't worry about unique identifiability" (p. 122). Problems concerning the status of theoretical entities are difficult for any science (Suppe, 1977); however, the issue seems particularly acute in current cognitive psychology, since theories must find a solution for the treatment of psychological entities (e.g., images, intentions, thoughts, and unconscious mental processes) and for constructs borrowed from the area of artificial intelligence (e.g., data structures, nodes, arcs, and networks). See Pylyshyn (1978) and Thagard (1982) for a discussion of some of these problems.

Schema theories can be distinguished from information processing theories by one crucial characteristic—all schema theories reject the atomistic assumption. Schema theorists assume that there are some phenomena that cannot be accounted for by a concatenation of smaller theoretical constructs and that it is necessary to develop larger theoretical entities to deal with these phenomena. Aside from this one attribute, schema theories vary widely in the specific structures postulated and the theoretical emphasis given to particular problems. In order to display some of the overall properties of modern schema theories we focus on two of the more general accounts of schemas—those of Minsky (1975) and Rumelhart (Rumelhart, 1980, reprinted in this volume; Rumelhart & Ortony, 1977).

## Minsky's Theory

Minsky (1975) is very clear about the rejection of the atomistic assumption. In the first two sentences of his paper he criticizes earlier theories for being "too minute, [and] local" and argues that theories of the higher mental processes "ought to be larger" (p. 211). The notion of a "larger" theory is hard to explicate purely in terms of the theoretical entities themselves. There is an additional assumption in the reasoning. This approach implicitly assumes that there are "larger phenomena" and larger theories are actually theories that deal with these phenomena. The nature of these "larger phenomena" can be seen from the examples given in Minsky's paper: perception of objects, perception of places, comprehension of discourse, comprehension of actions, and carrying out actions.

Minsky also states that the new theoretical constructs must contain more structure than those of earlier theories. He then goes on to provide some specific proposals about the type of structure needed. He introduces the construct of the frame (a type of schema in the terminology of this chapter). A frame has fixed "nodes" that provide its basic structure. It has "slots" that can be filled by specific information from the environment. This provides additional structure, since a slot will only accept a particular class of instances. If there is no information to the contrary the slots are filled with "default assignments." With this type of theoretical machinery applied to knowledge about rooms, one could give an account of the following phenomena: (a) Someone walking into a room without a ceiling will be surprised. (b) People will not be able to understand the sentence "The ceiling is made of passive transformations." (c) Someone who had just been in a room might state that they had seen the ceiling when eye movement recordings showed that they never looked up high enough to see the ceiling. (d) If asked to guess what a ceiling is made of, people will be much more likely to guess plaster than glass. (e) In a recall study some of the people who had been in a room with acoustic tile on the ceiling will recall that the room had a plaster ceiling (cf. Brewer & Treyens, 1981).

Minsky's theory was, in some sense, intended to be both a psychological theory and a theory in artificial intelligence. For the purposes of this chapter we have emphasized the psychological side of the theory. As a theory in artificial intelligence, the general outline Minsky supplies in his paper has been articulated in much greater detail (e.g., Bobrow & Winograd, 1977; Charniak, 1977). There are very thoughtful discussions of Minsky's theory, the relation of frames to propositions, and the implications of these issues for the philosophy of science in Thagard (1980, 1982).

## Rumelhart's Theory

Rumelhart has provided a specific schema theory for the structure of stories (1975, 1977) and several papers on the general nature and functions of schemas (Rumelhart & Ortony, 1977; Rumelhart, 1980). We focus on his general characterization of schemas. Rumelhart and Ortony (1977) clearly reject the atomistic assumption and explicitly point out that it is the attempt to handle all levels of abstraction including "higher level conceptualizations" (p. 109–110) that most clearly distinguishes schema theories from earlier information processing models. They state that "schemata are data structures for representing the generic concepts stored in memory" (p. 101). Rumelhart and Ortony follow Minsky in postulating that schemas have variables with constraints and that the variables have default values or, to be more precise, a distribution of possible default values. They point out that schemas are frequently defined in terms of other schemas ("schemata embed"). Thus, one's schema for an office building might include an office schema as a subpart. The office schema could function as a schema in its own right with a typewriter schema as a subpart, and the typewriter schema could function as a schema with keys as a subpart. In a more recent paper on schemas, Rumelhart (1980) emphasizes that schemas are active in the ways that procedures and parsers are active processes in computer programs.

In addition to the general characterization of schemas outlined above, Rumelhart has articulated some of the functions of schemas. In particular, he has attempted to clarify the interactions among the incoming episodic information, the generic information in the schema, and the specific nature of the output. Rumelhart and Ortony (1977) state that "once an assignment of variable has been made, either from the environment, from memory, or by default, the schema is said to have been *instantiated*" (p. 105). These ideas are then used to develop a theory of the memory process. Rumelhart and Ortony suggest that what gets stored in memory is an instantiated schema and that during the process of recall generic schema information may be used to further interpret and reconstruct a particular memory from the original instantiated schema record. In applying these ideas to the process of text comprehension, Rumelhart and Ortony focus on the interaction of "top down" schema information and "bottom up" text information. If a reader arrives at the schema intended by the author the text has been correctly comprehended. If the reader can find no schema to accept the text information the text is not comprehended. If the reader finds a schema, but not the one intended by the author, the text is misinterpreted.

## Modern Schema Theory: Summary

Having used Minsky's and Rumelhart's schema theories to instantiate modern schema theory, we now contrast the general characteristics of modern schema theory with the classic assumptions of British Empiricism. Clearly the major defining characteristic of schema theory is its rejection of the atomistic assumption. All schema theorists adopt what we will call the molar assumption. They assume that a schema theory needs to postulate "larger" theoretical entities and that these molar theoretical entities operate as units in the theory (cf., Anderson, 1980, p. 143; Charniak, 1977, p. 359; Minsky, 1975, p. 215; Rumelhart & Ortony, 1977, p. 106). A somewhat more extreme form of anti-atomism would be to argue that schema theories not only need molar theoretical entities, but that these molar entities are qualitatively different from the smaller atomic entities in the theory. We will call this the assumption of "emergent levels." This issue is very similar to the debate about "mental chemistry" within the British Empiricist tradition. Thus, James Mill took a pure atomistic position and assumed that the more complex aspects of the mind were derived from different groupings of the basic mental atoms. However, his son, John Stuart Mill, adopted the emergent levels position and argued that the smaller mental atoms formed qualitatively new mental structures through the mental equivalence of chemical operations (see Boring, 1950, and Mandler & Mandler, 1964, for a discussion of this issue). Anderson (1981, p. 147) makes an explicit argument against the hypothesis of emergent levels. Most schema theorists have not overtly addressed this issue, but it seems to us that the decision to introduce new theoretical entities (frames, problem-solving schemas, etc.) is frequently an implicit acceptance of the hypothesis of emergent levels.

The desire for parsimony is the one characteristic of the British Empiricist paradigm that seems to us is still accepted in modern schema theory. An analysis of these theories gives the impression that many theorists are attempting to employ a particular kind of theoretical entity such as frames (Minsky, 1975), scripts (Abelson, 1981), or propositions (Anderson, 1981) and use them to account for as wide a range of phenomena as possible.

The issue of associationism does not appear to be a live issue in schema theory. It seems highly unlikely that any schema theorists would think of themselves as "neo-associationists" as did Anderson and Bower (1973). The intellectual challenge has shifted from attempting to show that associations can handle everything to attempting to create some form of explicit theoretical machinery powerful enough to deal with the obvious capacities of the human mind (cf. Chomsky, 1965, p. 58 for a similar argument with respect to language acquisition).

One of the obvious characteristics of schema theories is the free use of generic and abstract theoretical constructs. In fact, one might want to argue that in some versions of schema theory the focus on generic information has been so strong that it is hard for the theories to deal with particular information. For example, at one point Neisser states that "perceivers pick up only what they have schemata for" (1976, p. 80).

Schema theories have worked hard to try and give an account of the apparently active aspects of human cognition. Minsky's (1975) frame theory, as originally presented, is more passive than are most other schema theories. However, Goldstein and Papert (1977) introduce the notion of "frame keepers" to deal with some of the more active aspects of the functioning of schemas. Rumelhart's 1980 modification of the earlier Rumelhart and Ortony (1977) approach was an attempt to suggest some general techniques (procedures, parsers) for making schemas more active. Neisser's (1976) schema theory stands out for other recent proposals in that he not only treats the active aspects of schemas, but makes it their most important characteristic.

Typically, the theoretical machinery included in schema theories to deal with the active aspects of cognition also has a purposive flavor. Neisser's (1976) theory puts a strong emphasis on this issue. He states, "schemata are anticipations, they are the medium by which the past affects the future" (p. 22).

Schema theories have clearly recognized the problem of the generativity of cognitive processes (Minsky, 1975, p. 248; Rumelhart & Ortony, 1977, p. 112) and have made some suggestions about how to deal with this difficult issue. However, one has the feeling that most of these proposals are better discussions of the problem than successful solutions.

## Bartlett and Modern Schema Theory

It is interesting to compare Bartlett's schema theory with the more recent schema theories. In terms of underlying motivation and overall structure, the older schema theory and the newer schema theories are very close. Thus, Bartlett wanted a theory that emphasized the role of old knowledge and that dealt with molar cognitive phenomenon. He proposed a theory of organized generic schemas that function in a generative, active, and purposive fashion. Through the influences of linguistics, information processing psychology, and artificial intelligence, modern schema theory has been able to develop more detailed and analytic accounts of the structure of schemas. In addition, these influences have enabled modern schema theory to more successfully deal with abstract, active, and generative theoretical entities. In recognizing the problem of accounting for specific personal memories within the framework of a schema theory Bartlett's position may actually be somewhat in advance of modern schema theories. On the particular issue of reconstructive memory, modern theories have not taken the totally reconstructive approach of Bartlett's "official" theory, but have developed partially reconstructive accounts that closely resemble Bartlett's "unofficial" theory. In summary, modern schema theories are very similar to Bartlett's theory, but have clarified, elaborated, and refined many aspects of his theory.

## Information Processing Psychology and Modern Schema Theory

If one compares modern schema theory with information processing psychology on their basic theoretical assumptions, the overall intellectual trends are obvious (see Table 4.1). Schema theories are closer to the Continental side on these issues. The most striking difference between schema theories and information processing theories is the rejection of the atomistic assumption. On those issues where information processing psychology has shifted toward the Continental position, schema theories have moved even more clearly and more firmly into the Continental camp. The only major British Empiricist assumption retained by schema theory is the assumption of parsimony.

## THE NATURE OF SCHEMAS

### Ontological Assumptions

In this section we discuss what we think schemas are. We believe a straightforward realist view is the correct way to approach the issue of the ontological status of schemas. We think that schema theories are theories about schemas and that schemas are the unconscious cognitive structures and processes that underlie human knowledge and skills. We believe that these mental entities have a physiological base, but that in the ultimate scientific account of things it will always be necessary to provide a scientific explanation at the level of mental entities (cf. Fodor, 1968; Putnam, 1973). We reject the instrumentalist option (Anderson, 1976, 1978) on a variety of grounds: (a) It seems inconsistent with our view that our goal as scientists is to search for Truth. (b) There are good arguments for realism (Suppe, 1977). (c) Realism has worked very well in the mature sciences. (d) As cognitive psychology matures it seems quite likely that there will be enough theoretical, empirical, aesthetic, and pragmatic constraints on our theories to undercut the indeterminacy arguments.

On the issue of the size of the mental "elements" we clearly favor the molar position. However, we think schema theories should explicitly adopt the more extreme view of emergent levels. It seems to us that in human cognition there truly are emergent phenomena. Thus, in trying to give a scientific account of a spoken story, there are qualitatively different phenomena occuring at the level of the phonemes, at the level of syntax, and at the level of the plot; and it will require qualitatively different types of theories to deal with the different levels. Therefore we think the view that molar theories are simply sets of smaller elements operating as units is incorrect.

## Modularity

The one tenet of British Empiricism that schema theories have not abandoned is the assumption of parsimony. We think that schema theories ought to make a clean sweep of the British Empiricist assumptions and adopt a liberal approach to postulating theoretical entities. It simply does not seem to us that a schema theory with a single schema construct can deal with the human abilities to: (a) understand a passage of expository text; (b) hit a tennis ball; (c) remember the shape of a leaf; (d) speak a sentence; and (e) remember the plot of a movie. Thus, we adopt the position that the mind is modular and that it will be necessary to develop different types of theoretical entities to account for the different cognitive processes (see Chomsky, 1980, for a similar argument). We realize that parsimony is an aesthetically pleasing attribute of a scientific theory and agree that it would be pleasing to find a parsimonious theory that accounted for all of the above phenomena. However, given the current primitive state of schema theory, the assertion that a single type of theoretical entity can deal with all of the molar cognitive processes is just contrary to the facts.

It seems to us, that if one examines *specific* schema theories instead of general theoretical statements about schemas, that the many differences in the theoretical entities used in these specific theories is not in keeping with the parsimony assumption, but instead supports the modularity hypothesis. There appear to be strong similarities for the specific theories within a domain or module, but qualitative differences across domains. For example, scripts (Abelson, 1981; Graesser & Nakamura, 1982); plans (Lichtenstein & Brewer, 1980; Schmidt, Sridharan, & Goodson, 1978); scene schemas (Brewer & Treyens, 1981; Mandler & Ritchey, 1977); and motor schemas (Schmidt, 1975). Note also the recent theoretical controversy over the nature of story schemas (Black & Wilensky, 1979; Brewer & Lichtenstein, 1981, 1982; Mandler & Johnson, 1980). Brewer and Lichtenstein (1981, 1982) have argued that the story schemas proposed by researchers in the story grammar tradition (Mandler & Johnson, 1977; Stein & Glenn, 1979; Thorndyke, 1977) have actually been theories of the plan schemas that underlie the goal-directed behavior of the characters in narratives. Brewer and Lichtenstein argue that a theory of the *story* schema must contain theoretical constructs that deal with the discourse organizations that lead to particular affective states (1981, 1982), and must capture culture-specific literary conventions (Brewer, in press). If Brewer and Lichtenstein are correct, then one needs very different types of theories to deal with goal-directed behavior and with the structure of stories. Thus, overall it seems to us that in the actual practice of constructing specific schema theories one finds considerable support for the modularity position.

## Ecological Validity

Many schema theorists have made arguments in favor of "ecological validity" (e.g., Bartlett, 1932, p. 17, 47; Brewer & Treyens, 1981, p. 207; and Neisser, 1976, for a very strong form). The general approach has been to assert that cognitive psychology should not study narrow laboratory tasks, but should study tasks that occur in real life. In the course of developing the analysis of schema theory outlined above, we have come to believe that the argument for ecological validity is not correct as usually stated. It is not that studies of phenomena from everyday life are somehow intrinsically better than narrow laboratory studies. Instead we think the intuition behind the ecological validity position derives from the issues of emergent levels and modularity of mind. If one accepts the argument for emergent levels and/or the modularity thesis, then focusing on a few narrow laboratory tasks becomes a highly dangerous research strategy. If either of these two assumptions is true, then no matter how much effort is put into the study of nonsense syllables or eyelid conditioning it cannot ever result in a comprehensive theory of the mind. On the other hand, if one adopts the research strategy of studying a wide range of everyday tasks, one is much more likely to find phenomena from qualitatively different levels or from different cognitive domains. Thus, the research strategy of focusing on ecologically valid tasks should not be driven by the everyday nature of the task (clearly one can learn much about the mind from some narrow laboratory tasks), but by the recognition of the research implications of accepting the emergent levels and modularity positions. Bartlett worked out part of this logic in his introductory section on methodology (1932, pp. 2–7).

## Phenomenal Experience

A final issue that we think needs to be addressed by schema theory is the relationship between schemas and phenomenal experience. It is clear why this problem has been avoided. For the earlier behaviorists there was no problem, since they explicitly excluded the data of phenomenal experience from a science of behavior. The main focus of information processing psychologists was on unconscious mental processes. Therefore they tended to ignore the data of phenomenal experience, or to argue that the experience itself was of little interest to information processing psychology as compared to the underlying unconscious cognitive processes (e.g., Pylyshyn, 1973). Schema theorists have also focused on the unconscious mental processes of the schema and ignored the problems of consciousness and phenomenal experience (e.g., Rumelhart & Ortony, 1977). Minsky (1975) discusses the problems of imagery and consciousness at various points in his frame paper, but never explicitly relates these issues to the frame construct. The one schema theorist who was an exception to this trend is Bartlett. He concerned himself with these problems at length in his book (1932), and he was particularly concerned with trying to work out a solution to the apparent inconsistency between his pure reconstructive schema theory and the particular experiences that are involved in personal memories (see the discussion of Bartlett in the first section of this chapter).

In a recent paper Brewer and Pani (1983) bite the bullet on this issue. They argue that an ultimate scientific psychology *must* account for the data from phenomenal experience, just as it must account for the data of performance. If, for example, the data from phenomenal experience and from performance on some task are "inconsistent" one does not throw out the phenomenal data because it is somehow less scientific. Instead the science of psychology must aspire to explain all of the data. As an example of the problem in the area of memory, Brewer and Pani (1982, in preparation) show striking differences in the phenomenal reports of imagery for different types of memory tasks. They argue that a complete theory of memory must give an account of this experiential data in addition to the usual memory performance data. The general issue of the relation of conscious and unconscious processes is a pervasive one for cognitive psychology. We discuss three examples that relate directly to schema theory.

*Personal memory.*    First is the problem of personal memory. There is an apparent tension between schema theories and the experience of personal memory. Schema theories focus on generic knowledge and the schematization of incoming episodic information. Yet when one has a personal memory (e.g., "Where were you the last time you spent cash for something?") there is a strong phenomenal experience of imagery and the imagery appears to contain "irrelevant" details of the original experience. Clearly, as Bartlett recognized, schema theory must deal with this problem (see Brewer & Pani, 1983, and Neisser, 1982, for somewhat different ways of approaching this issue).

*Generic images.*    A second problem is that of generic images. Many types of generic knowledge processes appear to operate with little concomitant phenomenal experience (e.g., "What is the opposite of falsehood?"). However, repetitive experience with visual perceptual information leads to generic knowledge structures that have strong visual image properties (e.g., "What hand does the Statue of Liberty hold the torch in?"). How is this fact to be dealt with in schema theory? One could say that the true schema in these cases is an unconscious generic structure and that the phenomenal experience is an epiphenomenon. One could take a strong imagist view and say that the phenomenal experience *is* the schema. Or one could say that it is necessary to postulate both an underlying unconscious schema and a phenomenally accessible generic mental image (cf. Brewer & Pani, 1983). For our purpose here, it is not important to decide which of these is the correct view. The point is that schema theory must overtly address this type of issue.

*Procedural information.*    A final example is the strong phenomenal experience that accompanies the transfer of procedural knowledge into semantic knowledge (two examples: (a) "What is the 8th letter of the alphabet?"; (b) "What finger do you use to type an 'r' with?"). The difference in phenomenal experience is striking. When a skilled task (motor, cognitive, or rote linguistic) is carried out there is little or no phenomenal experience of imagery. Yet, in order to answer a propositional question about the information contained in the procedure there is a strong experience of imagery (cf. Brewer & Pani, 1983). Clearly, the problem is to explain these facts. Why are the production schemas normally unconscious? Why does the propositional task give rise to powerful imagery experiences? Does one want to say that the imagery is causal in the performance of the task?

It seems to us that examples such as these lead to an obvious conclusion. Schema theory must take the data from phenomenal experience seriously and schema theory must be articulated so that there is a graceful fit of the facts from phenomenal experience. These are difficult problems and we cannot provide solutions here, but we do have a suggestion as to the direction of theory development. Perhaps one can adopt the position that the schema structures and the processes operating on the structures are unconscious, but that the products of these operations are conscious. This is similar to a position taken by Lashley (1960) and, of course, somewhat similar to Bartlett's discussion of these issues. The type of conscious product seems specific to the particular cognitive domain involved. Thus, the memory processes relating to particular perceptual inputs seem to give rise to modality specific imagery (e.g., visual imagery for visual perceptual input), whereas the cognitive operations involving abstract thoughts or practiced skills seem to give rise to other types of nonimage conscious products (see Brewer & Pani, 1983, for further discussion).

## Definition of Schema

In light of this analysis of schema theory, what are schemas? Schemas are the unconscious mental structures and processes that underlie the molar aspects of human knowledge and skill. They contain abstract generic knowledge that has been organized to form qualitative new structures. Schemas are modular—different cognitive domains have schemas with different structural characteristics. At input, schemas actively interact with incoming episodic information. This interaction consists of two basic processes: (a) the modification of the generic knowledge in the relevant schema; (b) the construction of a specific instantiated memory representation. An instantiated schema is a cognitive structure that results from the interaction of the old information of the generic schema and the new information from the episodic input. The generic schema contains some fixed structural relations and some slots that accept a range of specific input information from the environment. The unconscious operation of the schema gives rise to the specific conscious contents of the mind. At output, generic production schemas interact with new incoming information to allow appropriate responses to an indefinite number of new situations.

In informal interactions with colleagues from the stimulus-response and information processing traditions it is obvious that they consider schema theory to be a vague and "soft-headed" theory. Why is that? We think that there are several reasons that derive from the world view of the critics and several reasons that derive from the current status of schema theory. The first cause of this attribution is, of course, the result of the wholesale adoption of the Continental position by schema theory. From the British Empiricist point of view the Continental position has always seemed vague and soft-headed. The second reason is a matter of temperament in theory construction (*not* unrelated to the Empiricist-Rationalist issue). Some theorists prefer a precise, completely worked-out theory even if it is obviously wrong. Other theorists prefer a theory that is not obviously false, even if this means having only a sketch of an account of the phenomena at hand. Herbert Feigl once referred to this difference in scientific temperament as the great split between the "nothing but" theorists and the "something more" theorists. Clearly, schema theory falls in the "something more" camp.

The other two reasons for the perception of schema theory as vague arise from true problems with the theories in their current stage of development. First, the attempt to hold to the ideal of parsimony has caused problems in trying to give a general characterization of the nature of schemas. If one rejects the parsimony assumption and accepts the arguments for modularity, then a general account of schemas must look vague. Such an account can only focus on the characteristics that the general class of molar cognitive structures have in common, and so cannot be too precise without running up against obvious counterexamples. On the other hand, consistent with the modularity thesis, it is much harder to accuse specific schema theories in particular domains of being vague compared to other theories in psychology (Graesser & Nakamura, 1982; Lichtenstein & Brewer, 1980; Rumelhart, 1977). Finally, it is obvious that modern schema theory is still immature and in need of further development (see Thorndyke & Yekovich, 1980, for a similar analysis). Clearly, there is much work ahead in this area. In fact, there are some really hard problems for schema theory that we have not even mentioned. For example: How do schemas develop? How does incoming information activate an appropriate schema? What are the correct structures for schemas in different cognitive domains? Nevertheless, even in its current state of development, it seems to us that schema theory is one of the important currents in psychology and the larger cognitive science community. In keeping with this discussion of schema theory we attempt, in the last section of this chapter, to articulate and make more precise one aspect of schema theory—the role of schemas in the memory process.

## THE FUNCTIONS OF SCHEMAS IN THE MEMORY PROCESS

### Basic Schema Findings

First we examine a set of basic empirical findings in the study of human memory that set the stage for our analysis. It is experimental results such as these that seem to require a schema theory account of human memory. We refer to the results of these experiments as the "basic schema findings."

*Memory with and without schemas.*   There are a great variety of different experiments which can be used to show that information which can be instantiated in a schema is better recalled than information which cannot easily be instantiated in a schema. In fact, the very first experiment on human memory shows this effect. Ebbinghaus (1885/1964) found that recall for information from a lyric poem was about ten times better than recall of nonsense material. By 1937 there had been many experiments on this issue, all leading to the general conclusion that recall of meaningful material was much better than recall of meaningless material (Welborn & English, 1937). In these older experiments the meaningful materials are very different from the meaningless materials along many dimensions. In more recent times, experimenters have found techniques to show the schema effect with materials in which the basic elements are the same, or even with the use of only a single passage to yield the schema effects. Examples of modern studies showing that recall is better for material which can be instantiated in a schema are: (a) standard text versus scrambled text (Brent, 1969; Chiesi, Spilich, & Voss, 1979; Lachman & Dooling, 1968; Thorndyke, 1977); (b) picture before opaquely written passage versus picture after the passage (Bransford & Johnson, 1972); (c) title or theme before opaquely written passage versus after the passage (Bransford & Johnson, 1972; Dooling & Lachman, 1971; Dooling & Mullet, 1973); (d) recognition of organized pictures versus disorganized pictures (Mandler & Johnson, 1976; Mandler & Ritchey, 1977); (e) canonical videotaped actions versus scrambled actions (Lichtenstein, 1979).

*Subject knowledge and recall.*   Another way to show the general effects of schemas is to compare the differences in recall for subjects who come to the experiment with different degrees of schema-based knowledge. The basic finding is that subjects with a more developed schema for some body of knowledge show higher recall for materials related to that knowledge. Studies showing this effect include: recall of chess positions by expert chess players versus novice players (Chase & Simon, 1973); recall of a baseball narrative by individuals with high and low knowledge of baseball (Chiesi et al., 1979); recall of narratives about Western and Australian Aboriginal medicine by Western and Australian Aboriginal subjects (Steffensen & Colker, 1982).

*Memory for schema-related information.*   One of Bartlett's (1932) original findings dealing with the recall of text was that information connected with the underlying theme or plot of the passage was more likely to be recalled than was information not connected to the theme. This basic finding, that schema-related information will be recalled better than schema-unrelated information, is a very robust finding and has been replicated many times by a great number of researchers using a wide variety of theories about the nature of the underlying schemas (Brewer & Treyens, 1981; van Dijk & Kintsch, 1978; Gomulicki, 1956; Goodman, 1980; Johnson, 1970; Lichtenstein & Brewer, 1980; Mandler & Johnson, 1977; Meyer & McConkie, 1973; Rumelhart, 1977; Thorndyke, 1977).

## Schemas and the Memory Process

The basic schema findings outlined above can be accounted for by any of the schema theories discussed earlier. The ability to deal with this body of experimental findings is one of the major reasons for the rapid development of schema theory in psychology in recent years. However, it seems to us that accounting for these basic schema findings is not enough. It is necessary to develop much more explicit and precise theories about the operation of schemas in the memory process. We attempt to work out a more detailed understanding of the role of schemas in memory by focusing on two questions: (a) In a given memory task how much of the subject's memory is due to generic schema information and how much is due to episodic information? (The term "episodic" is not intended to carry any theoretical implications, e.g., Tulving, 1972, but is merely a descriptive term used to indicate the information actually obtained from the environment during a particular exposure.) (b) What are the mechanisms through which schemas operate in the memory process?

We propose that there are five basic processes through which schemas could operate during the memory process (these schema-based operations are extensions of the processes outlined in Brewer & Treyens, 1981):

1. Schemas could influence the amount of attention allocated to a particular type of information, with the assumption that more attention leads to better memory.

2. Schemas could operate as a framework in memory that serves to preserve incoming episodic information.
3. Generic schema information could interact with incoming episodic information to produce a memory representation that is a combination of old generic information and new episodic information.
4. Schemas could serve to guide retrieval processes in order to locate episodic information in memory.
5. Schemas could operate to influence what retained information a subject chooses to produce in a memory task.

In the remainder of this section we examine the experimental literature to see if we can find unambiguous evidence to support the position that schemas operate through the mechanisms discussed above. Since the basic schema findings could result from any of the five schema-based processes we will attempt to use a "subtractive logic." For each set of data discussed, we will try to show that the results must have been due to a particular process because we can rule out all of the other alternatives. Note that in our analysis we frequently claim that a particular experiment supports positions quite different from that proposed by the original investigators. We will work our way through the five basic schema processes in the order given above, and for each process we will treat experiments dealing with linguistic materials first and those using nonlinguistic materials second.

## Attention

The basic assumption of the attention mechanism as applied to memory is that increased amounts of attention lead to a stronger memory trace. In order to relate this mechanism to schema-based processes one has to work out the relation between attention and schema-based information. Currently this is an area of some confusion. A number of researchers have postulated that schema-related information receives more attention than schema-unrelated information (Bower, 1976; Cirilo & Foss, 1980; Kintsch & van Dijk, 1978). However, in direct contrast to this position, a number of other researchers have postulated that schema-related information receives less attention than schema-unrelated information (Bobrow & Norman, 1975; Friedman, 1979). Notice that a memory theory that only allows schemas to operate via attention, and makes the assumption that schema-related material receives less attention, cannot account for the basic schema findings, since it would have to predict poorer recall for schema-related material. However, as we will see, it is possible to combine the hypothesis of less attention to schema-related information with other schema-based memory processes to give an account of the basic schema findings. Of all the schema-based memory processes to be discussed the attention mechanism is the hypothesis with the least amount of theoretical and empirical consensus.

*Linguistic materials.* There are empirical studies with text materials that support both positions on the schema-attention issue. Cirilo and Foss (1980) find longer reading time (and thus presumably more attention) for schema-related information, while Shebilske and Reid (1979) find the reverse. This is too complex an issue to analyze here, but it seems to us that the general direction that must be taken is to provide a much more sophisticated account of the interaction between the reader's developing mental model and the structure of the text (see Rumelhart, 1980). In dealing with text one has to take into account the fact that the author has complete freedom to manipulate the text structure by including, omitting, or reordering any aspect of the underlying schema-based information (see Brewer, 1980). Within this framework, a simple analysis into schema-related information and schema-unrelated information (or as frequently described, high in the text hierarchy and low in the text hierarchy) probably does not cut the world in the appropriate fashion. We will present a brief example to illustrate the complexities of this issue. Imagine a story about a racing car driver. First, we will examine schema-related information: If the author has chosen to include in the text schema-based information that is easily available from the reader's schema then one might expect the reader to devote less attention to it. For example, "The driver turned the steering wheel to the right. The car went around the turn to the right." However, for schema-related material that is informative about the plot one would expect the reader to devote more attention, e.g., "The accident had left a huge oil spill on the far turn." Now we will examine schema-unrelated information: If the schema-unrelated information is *irrelevant* to the plot, then one would not expect readers to devote much attention to it, e.g., "The driver put his candy wrapper in the trashcan." However, if the schema-unrelated information is *inconsistent* with the developing mental model about an automobile race, then one would expect the reader to devote considerable attention to the anomalous information in order to try and instantiate it into the developing mental model, e.g., "A man in the stands stood up, pointed his finger at one of the cars, and it turned into a giant Twinkie." Thus, while it appears that there are schema-based attention processes, it also seems that a full analysis of attention and schema relatedness will have to incorporate an account of the relation of text information to schema information, and an analysis of reading that views the reader as using text information to develop a mental model during the course of reading the text.

Even though the current state of our knowledge about schema-based attention processes is poorly developed, there is some reason to believe that the attention process is not the major determiner of the schema-based recall findings. A number of studies using a variety of techniques have attempted to control the attentional processes and have found that this has little effect on schema-based memory findings (Britton, Meyer, Simpson, Holdredge, Curry, 1979; Graesser, Gordon, & Sawyer, 1979; Graesser, Nakamura, Zimmerman, & Riha, 1980; Johnson, 1970; Reynolds, 1979).

*Nonlinguistic materials.*    Several studies have examined the number and duration of eye fixations on schema-related and schema-unrelated information in viewing pictures. The general finding is that subjects devote more attention to schema-unrelated information (Friedman, 1979; Loftus & Mackworth, 1978). Friedman's (1979) study makes an important distinction between schema-irrelevant information and schema-inconsistent information. She finds a strong initial effect of long fixations for schema-inconsistent information and a small tendency for schema-irrelevant information to have longer fixations than schema-relevant information.

Overall, it appears that there is some agreement that subjects direct attention to schema-inconsistent information. It appears that the resolution of the issue of the amount of attention directed at schema-relevant versus schema-irrelevant information may require that this dichotomy be replaced with a much more complex, and perhaps domain-specific analysis of reading text and of viewing the visual world.

## Framework

The framework hypothesis states that schemas can serve as a scaffolding to preserve schema-related episodic information. It is easy to conceptualize this mechanism in terms of Minsky's (1975) theory of a frame with slots that accept a range of possible values. In these terms the framework view states that instantiating a slot with a particular piece of episodic information will tend to preserve the memory trace for that information. The framework hypothesis predicts that new schema-related information will be better retained than new schema-unrelated information. In order to show that this effect is due to a preserved episodic trace one must rule out other schema-based mechanisms such as integration or retrieval. Note that the framework hypothesis, as stated, makes no assumption about the level of information that is preserved by the framework. The preserved episodic information could be fairly low-level perceptual information ("surface information") or much more abstract information.

*Linguistic materials.*    The studies showing the effect of a picture or title on the recall of an opaquely written passage (Bransford & Johnson, 1972; Dooling & Lachman, 1971; Dooling & Mullet, 1973) can be interpreted as supporting the framework hypothesis. In these studies the subjects who received a schema-evoking picture or title before they heard the passage showed much better recall than subjects who received the picture or title after they heard the passage. If the effect had been due to old schema knowledge (integration) or to the schema operating as a retrieval mechanism, then the subjects who received the schema afterward could have used the schema to make inferences or as a retrieval device just as well as the subjects who received it first. Since the data show a large difference in recall between the two conditions, it appears that the schema is operating as a framework to preserve the episodic information contained in the passage.

Another study that can be interpreted as support for the framework hypothesis is a text recall study by Thorndyke (1977). In this study Thorndyke compared recall for two types of embedded goal-based passages, one with the superordinate goal at the beginning and one with the superordinate goal at the end (in texts of this kind, when the goal comes first the reader can understand the purpose of a rather strange sequence of actions). Recall was better for the group that received the goal at the beginning of the passage, and through our subtractive logic we interpret this finding to support the position that schemas can act as a framework to preserve information from texts.

*Nonlinguistic materials.*    There are a number of studies of picture memory by Mandler (Mandler & Johnson, 1976; Mandler & Parker, 1976; Mandler & Ritchey, 1977) which can be interpreted as evidence for the action of schemas as frameworks to preserve episodic picture information. Two types of pictures are used in these studies—organized and unorganized. An organized picture consists of a small number of schema-related objects spatially arranged to make up a schema-consistent visual scene. The unorganized pictures consist of the same objects rearranged to give a schema-inconsistent visual scene (e.g., a desk in the upper part of the picture not resting on any solid surface). Memory for the information in the pictures (objects, spatial relations) was tested with a recognition procedure in which the foils for the organized pictures were changed from the original picture but were schema-consistent. In general, these studies showed that recognition memory was better for organized pictures than for unorganized pictures. The use of schema-consistent foils eliminates the possibility that the subjects are responding on the basis of generic knowledge, and the use of a recognition memory procedure reduces or eliminates the use of schemas as retrieval mechanisms, so we believe this finding can be used to show that schemas operate as frameworks to preserve episodic information.

Thus, overall we find that there is evidence from both linguistic and non-linguistic domains for schemas operating as frameworks to preserve episodic information.

## Integration

The integration hypothesis states that during the process of schema instantiation old schema-based information becomes integrated with new episodic information. Thus, the instantiated memory representation will contain both generic information from the schema and episodic information from the input. The proportion of generic information and episodic information will vary with factors such as the type of schema and time interval before test. The most extreme form of integration would be the case where all the episodic information was lost from memory so that the memory response would be based completely on generic information. If integration occurs, then it will lead to apparently better memory for schema-related information than for schema-unrelated information since the memory for schema-related material will actually be based on a mixture of generic schema information and episodic information. When a subject gives information in recall that comes from the generic schema and was not in the episodic input, then we say that an inference has occurred. The occurrence of inferences in a recall task or false recognition responses to schema-related foils on a recognition task is a qualitative indication that the process of integration has occurred. And when this occurs one can be almost certain that some proportion of the apparent episodic memory for presented schema-related items actually derives from generic schema knowledge. For the purposes of this general definition of integration, it does not matter if the interaction of old and new information occurs during comprehension or during testing or how conscious the subject is of the integration process.

*Linguistic materials.*   Evidence for integration in memory for textual material is widespread. In one of the very first text-memory experiments ever performed, Binet and Henri (1894; translated in Thieman & Brewer, 1978) found examples of integration. They noted, for example, that one child recalled "for her animals" as "for her rabbits" and they argued that these "errors of imagination" were obviously due to the child's background knowledge. Bartlett (1932) also noted the process of integration in his story recall data. He stated that he deliberately chose to use somewhat unusual stories (Kathlamet Indian texts) as materials so that he could look for inferences driven by the schemas that his English undergraduates brought to bear on the texts. He obtained the expected data and gave as an example the fact that one of his English subjects recalled "paddling a canoe" (from the Kathlamet text) as "rowing a boat."

One of the first modern studies to focus on inferences in text memory was the study of Sulin and Dooling (1974). In this study subjects heard a passage and were later given a recognition memory test. Some of the subjects were told that the passage was about Helen Keller and these subjects showed a strong tendency (after one week) to make false recognition responses to nonpresented sentences such as one stating that the main character was blind. In more recent times there have been a number of studies of memory for script-based texts (Bower, Black, & Turner, 1979; Graesser et al., 1979; Graesser, Woll, Kowalski, & Smith, 1980—reviewed in Graesser, 1981 and Graesser & Nakamura, 1982). These studies have shown a very high rate of script-based intrusions and false recognitions of script-based foils. In one of these studies (Graesser, Woll, Kowalski, & Smith, 1980), the researchers used the evidence of script-based inferences to argue that much of the memory advantage for script-related items at one week was due to script-based information and not to episodic information. Another recent study showing evidence for integration is the work of Chiesi et al. (1979)

on memory for texts about baseball games. These researchers found that subjects made many false recognition responses to nonpresented items relating to the baseball schema.

A number of experiments have varied the retention interval to study schema-based memory processes over time. These studies have found that the integration effect becomes stronger over time (van Dijk & Kintsch, 1978; Graesser, Woll, Kowalski, & Smith, 1980; Spiro, 1977; Sulin & Dooling, 1974). Presumably, this effect is due to the differential loss from memory of different types of information. At immediate testing there is apparently some retained information about the particular propositions from the initial text. Over time, this type of "surface" information is lost, leaving the instantiated schema in memory; and after very long time intervals much of the episodic information in the instantiated schema may be lost, leaving predominantly generic schema information.

*Nonlinguistic materials.*    A series of recent studies provide evidence for integration in memory tasks using visual perceptual input. Jenkins, Wald, and Pittenger (1978) presented subjects with a series of pictures that described an event. The subjects showed a large number of false recognition responses to schema-based items that belonged to the event but that had not been shown in the original sequence. Loftus, Miller, and Burns (1978) have shown that giving subjects (false) verbal information about an event previously seen by the subjects can lead subjects to make false recognition responses to pictures that they have never seen before. Brewer and Treyens (1981) obtained evidence for integration in a naturalistic study of memory for rooms. The subjects were asked to wait in an office briefly, on the pretext that the experimental apparatus was not ready. Then the subjects were taken to another location and given a series of recall and recognition tests for information about the room. In recall the subjects reported a number of objects that were not in the experimental office. These inferred objects were all highly related to the office schema. On a verbal recognition test (e.g., "Did you see a typewriter?") there was a high positive correlation between schema-expectancy ratings from a different group of subjects and the verbal-recognition scores for *nonpresented* items from the group of subjects who saw the room. Since this correlation was based on recognition ratings of items the subjects never actually saw, it must have been based on the subject's office schema.

A series of experiments using nonlinguistic materials have investigated the role of the retention interval in schema-based integration processes. These studies, like the linguistic studies discussed earlier, have shown that the integration effect becomes stronger over time (Brewer & Dupree, 1983; Mandler & Parker, 1976; Mandler & Ritchey, 1977). The explanation for these effects is essentially like that proposed for the studies using linguistic materials. Different types of information are apparently lost from memory at different rates over time. Thus, at short time intervals, there is some retained perceptual information about the visual scene, and over time this specific episodic information is lost and memory performance is increasingly based on the instantiated schema and generic schema information. Brewer and Dupree (1983) suggested that for hierarchically organized plan schemas the information is lost from the bottom up, leaving successively more abstract information about plans and goals in memory at longer time intervals.

Overall, there is much evidence for integration in memory for both linguistic and nonlinguistic material. The size of the effect seems to vary widely depending on the "strength" of the particular schema. Thus, scripts seem particularly powerful in producing inferences. In all of these domains there is a tendency for integration to be much stronger at longer time intervals. As the specific episodic information is lost over time, the underlying generic information plays a larger role in the memory task.

## Retrieval

The retrieval hypothesis states that schemas may operate to guide the memory search for schema-related episodic information. This hypothesis predicts better recall of schema-related than of schema-unrelated information. For a schema-related item and a schema-unrelated item of equivalent memory strength (as tested by recognition memory) the retrieval hypothesis predicts that the schema-related item is more likely to be given in a free recall task.

*Linguistic materials.*   Two studies by Anderson and Pichert (1978) and by Pichert and Anderson (1977) can be interpreted as support for the use of schemas as retrieval devices. Subjects in these studies read a text that could be viewed from two different viewpoints (schemas). Thus, for example, one text was about a house and its contents and could be viewed from the point of view of a home buyer or a burglar. Subjects who took a particular perspective (burglar) tended to recall more schema-related information (e.g., location of the family silver). After recall from one perspective, subjects were asked to recall the story a second time from the other perspective, and under this schema-based perspective, they recalled some of the now schema-related information that had previously been schema-irrelevant. Thus, it looks as if the perspective manipulation acts to provide a schema-based retrieval plan. There have been other interpretations of these findings (Wyer, Srull, Gordon, & Hartwick, 1982).

*Nonlinguistic materials.*   Lichtenstein and Brewer (1980) carried out a series of studies showing that plan schemas have powerful effects on the recall of goal-directed actions (i.e., actions that are part of a plan schema are recalled better than actions that are not part of a plan schema). However, Lichtenstein and Brewer only used recall measures which, by themselves, are not sufficient to establish what mechanism was producing the facilitation in recall for plan schema items. Brewer and Dupree (1983) used a variety of recall and recognition tasks to attempt to give a more analytic account of the findings of Lichtenstein and Brewer (1980). They compared recall of actions that were seen embedded in a plan schema (e.g., *reached up with a ruler to adjust the hands of a high clock*) with the same actions not embedded in a plan schema (e.g., *reached up with a ruler*). They found that immediate recall for an action was more than twice as good if it occurred in a plan schema. However, they also found that on an immediate visual recognition test the two types of actions were recognized equally well. Thus, for actions equally well recognized many more of the schema-related items were given on the recall task. Brewer and Dupree argued that this pattern of results indicates that the plan schemas were operating as a retrieval mechanism to allow access to a greater portion of the plan-related episodic information.

Brewer and Treyens (1981) have used similar logic to investigate memory for places. For the objects in a room that were strongly recognized in a verbal recognition task, the schema-related objects were much more likely to have been written down in recall than were schema-unrelated objects. Brewer and Treyens argued that this result indicated that some of the better recall for schema-related items must have been due to the office schema being used as a retrieval device. Thus, our analysis of these studies indicates that schemas can function as retrieval mechanisms.

## Editing

The editing hypothesis states that schemas may operate outside of the memory mechanism itself to determine which information the subject chooses to communicate to the experimenter. Thus, if the experimenter instructs the subject to recall "just the basic ideas," the subject might use schema knowledge to identify the schema-relevant information and choose to write down only the schema-relevant information. This use of schemas to edit memory output gives the appearance of better recall for schema-related material.

*Linguistic material.*    In terms of the actual experiments there is evidence for schema-based editing, but it operates to *reduce* recall of very high schema-related information. Graesser, Woll, Kowalski, and Smith (1980) found that subjects in a script generation task tended not to produce very typical script actions. Brewer and Treyens (1981) argue that this type of finding follows from an analysis of the recall task as one in which the subject is communicating with the experimenter. The subjects apparently are following a conversational maxim (Grice, 1975) that one should not tell someone information that is completely obvious.

Within the story grammar tradition (Mandler, 1978; Mandler & Johnson, 1977; Stein & Glenn, 1979) there is a recall finding that can be given a similar interpretation. In producing texts to fit particular theoretical models the researchers in this tradition have often violated the maxim that an author should not include in the text information that is obvious to the reader. In particular, a number of story grammar researchers have included in their texts a category called "reaction" or "internal response" or "internal plan." By including these categories one can obtain texts such as, "After the argument with his boss Joe was angry [reaction] so he decided to slam the door as he left the office [internal plan]. He slammed the door as he left the office," instead of the more natural, "After the argument with his boss Joe slammed the door as he left the office." One of the major empirical findings of the story grammar tradition (Mandler, 1978; Mandler & Johnson, 1977; Stein & Glenn, 1979) has been that information relating to reactions or internal plans is very frequently lost in story recall tasks. It seems to us that this memory data is actually produced by the operation of schemas to edit information that is redundant with the actions described in the narratives (see Black & Wilensky, 1979; Brewer & Treyens, 1981, on communication; and van Dijk, 1980, p. 262, for further discussion of this editing process in recall tasks).

*Nonlinguistic materials.*    Brewer and Treyens (1981) found evidence that schemas were being used to edit out some of the very high schema-related information in their naturalistic room memory study. Subjects rarely recalled information such as, "the room had a ceiling," since this very high schema-related information can be assumed for any room.

Overall, it is clear that schemas can operate to edit the information that is recalled. It may be that the editing procedure is sometimes used to edit out schema-unrelated information (in fact, if the demand characteristics for total recall are not too severe, one would think that a principle of least effort would tend to produce some editing of schema-unrelated information). However, the current experimental findings suggest schema-based editing serves to eliminate very high schema-related information, and thus this process operates in a direction opposed to the basic schema findings.

## Functions of Schemas in Memory

Our analysis of the literature suggests that there is evidence for schemas operating in all five schema-based processes. Schemas have been shown to affect memory through attention processes, through acting as a framework to preserve episodic information, through integration of old and new knowledge, through a retrieval process, and through an output editing process. While the evidence is not completely clear, it would appear that the basic schema findings are due to a mixture of: schemas operating as a framework to preserve schema-related information; schemas operating to integrate old schema-based information with new episodic information to give the appearance of increased memory for schema-based episodic information; and schemas operating in retrieval to facilitate the location of schema-related information. Currently the evidence does not suggest that schemas operating to direct attention or operating as output editors are major factors in the memory process.

## Memory for Schema-Related and Schema-Unrelated Information

A number of researchers have pointed out that there appear to be some major inconsistencies in schema theory approaches to the issue of memory for schema-related and schema-unrelated information (e.g., Thorndyke & Yekovich, 1980). In this last section we formulate the problem, and attempt to use the framework developed earlier to resolve some of the apparently conflicting data. The basic problem is that there are a number of studies that do not give the basic schema effects described earlier in the chapter. Thus, some studies of script memory (Graesser et al., 1979; Graesser, Woll, Kowalski, & Smith, 1980) and some studies of picture memory (Friedman, 1979) find memory for schema-unrelated information to be better than memory for schema-related information.

*Recall versus recognition.*    The first step in working out these problems is to distinguish the type of memory test involved. There is essentially total agreement that for recall tasks the basic schema effect is found: schema-related information is better recalled than schema-unrelated information. In terms of our analysis this general finding is due to the powerful schema-based processes of integration and retrieval during recall.

However, for recognition memory the studies give apparently mixed results. Thus, some experiments with text found that recognition memory for schema-related information is better (Bower et al., 1979) while other experiments found that recognition for schema-related information is worse (Graesser et al., 1979; Graesser, Woll, Kowalski, & Smith, 1980). There is a similar divergence in results for studies using recognition memory and nonlinguistic materials. Some studies found that recognition memory for schema-related material is better (Brewer & Dupree, 1983; Goodman, 1980) while other studies find it to be worse (Friedman, 1979). Some of these difficulties can be resolved by taking into account the time interval before test, the types of "schema-unrelated" information used, and the relative contributions of episodic and generic information.

*Delay of memory test.*    Within the set of studies on the schema-related/schema-unrelated issue there is a tendency for memory tasks that use relatively short time intervals to find schema-unrelated information to be equal or better than schema-related information (Brewer & Dupree, 1983; Friedman, 1979; Graesser et al., 1979), whereas memory tasks that involve a longer time interval tend to show schema-related information recognized better than schema-unrelated (Brewer & Dupree, 1983; Goodman, 1980; Graesser, Woll, Kowalski, & Smith, 1980). Thus, it appears that part of the apparent conflict between these studies is due to good recognition for "surface" information after short time intervals and the loss of this information after longer time intervals, leading to an advantage for schema-based information. While this analysis accounts for much of the conflicting data, there still remains some theoretical and empirical disagreement about the strength of the episodic memory for schema-related and schema-unrelated information.

*Relative contributions of episodic and generic information.* In attempting to analyze the results of experiments in this area, one should also use the analysis of the different types of memory processes to distinguish the relative contribution of episodic and generic information in a particular experiment. Bower et al. (1979) found that script-relevant items were better recalled than script-irrelevant items, whereas in direct contrast Graesser, Woll, Kowalski, and Smith (1980) arrived at the opposite conclusion. The difference between these studies is that Bower et al. (1979) based their conclusion on the overall correct recall data, which included contributions of both episodic and generic information. On the other hand, Graesser, Woll, Kowalski, and Smith (1980) used the intrusion rate to estimate the amount of generic information. Then they subtracted this estimate from the overall correct recall to obtain an estimate of the amount of episodic information. If one combines the data in the Graesser study for both episodic and generic contributions, the overall recall data are in good agreement with the Bower data. Thus, in attempting to compare studies in this area one must be careful to analyze the findings in terms of the relative contributions of episodic and generic information.

*Type of schema-related and schema-unrelated information.* A final factor to be considered is the nature of the schema-unrelated information in these studies. As discussed earlier, one must distinguish between schema-irrelevant information and schema-inconsistent information. For schema-irrelevant versus schema-relevant information it still seems to us that there is some conflict, both in theory and in data, that cannot be accounted for by our analysis. We clearly need more detailed experiments to determine the relative strength of memory for these types of information in different domains. For schema-inconsistent information the issue seems simpler. Most theorists who have explicitly discussed this type of information have hypothesized that it will show high recognition and perhaps high recall. The usual line of reasoning is that much attention will be devoted to schema-inconsistent information, leading to a stronger memory representation and also that more effort will be devoted to attempting to force schema instantiation, thus giving rise to a more elaborated memory representation. There is some experimental evidence to support these assumptions (Bower et al., 1979; Friedman, 1979).

## CONCLUSION

We think that an understanding of how new knowledge interacts with old knowledge will play a major role in the development of a scientific theory of the human mind. In this chapter we have attempted to show how schema theory has been formulated to deal with the relationships between old and new knowledge. We have argued that the rise of schema theory represents a continuation of a general trend in the study of the mind away from the assumptions of British Empiricism toward those of Continental philosophy. We have proposed that an understanding of the mind will require a number of very different types of schema theories and have pointed out the problems involved in relating the unconscious mental structures and processes of the schema to the phenomena of conscious experience. Finally, we have attempted to develop a more explicit account of the operations of schemas in the memory process and reanalyze the experimental literature in terms of this framework. Our analysis suggests that schema-based processes operate to: (a) direct attention, (b) serve as a framework to preserve episodic information, (c) combine generic information with episodic information to form instantiated schema memory representations, (d) act as a retrieval mechanism in recall, and (e) act as a mechanism to edit memory output.

## ACKNOWLEDGMENTS

This research was supported in part by the National Institute of Education under Contract No. HEW-NIE-C-400-76-0116. We would like to thank Don Dulany, Brian Ross, Ellen Brewer, and our editors for comments on an earlier version of this chapter.

## REFERENCES

Abelson, R. P. Psychological status of the script concept. *American Psychologist*, 1981, *36*, 715–729.

Anderson, J. R. *Language, memory, and thought*. Hillsdale, N.J.: Lawrence Erlbaum Associates, 1976.

Anderson, J. R. Arguments concerning representations for mental imagery. *Psychological Review*, 1978, *85*, 249–277.

Anderson, J. R. On the merits of ACT and information-processing psychology: A response to Wexler's review. *Cognition*, 1980, *8*, 73–88.

Anderson, J. R. Concepts, propositions, and schemata: What are the cognitive units? In H. E. Howe, Jr. & J. H. Flowers (Eds.), *Nebraska Symposium on Motivation* (Vol. 28). Lincoln: University of Nebraska Press, 1981.

Anderson, J. R., & Bower, G. H. *Human associative memory*. Washington, D.C.: V. H. Winston, 1973.

Anderson, R. C., & Pichert, J. W. Recall of previously unrecallable information following a shift in perspective. *Journal of Verbal Learning and Verbal Behavior*, 1978, *17*, 1–12.

Atkinson, R. C., & Shiffrin, R. M. Human memory: A proposed system and its control processes.

In K. W. Spence & J. T. Spence (Eds.), *The psychology of learning and motivation: Advances in research and theory* (Vol. 2). New York: Academic Press, 1968.

Bartlett, F. C. An experimental study of some problems of perceiving and imaging. *British Journal of Psychology*, 1916, *8*, 222–266.

Bartlett, F. C. Some experiments on the reproduction of folk-stories. *Folklore*, 1920, *31*, 30–47.

Bartlett, F. C. The functions of images. *British Journal of Psychology*, 1921, *11*, 320–337.

Bartlett, F. C. *Remembering*. London: Cambridge University Press, 1932.

Bartlett, F. C. Remembering. *Scientia*, 1935, *52*, 221–226.

Bartlett, F. C. Autobiography. In C. Murchison (Ed.), *A history of psychology in autobiography* (Vol. 3). Worcester, Mass.: Clark University Press, 1936.

Binet, A., & Henri, V. La mémoire des phrases (Mémoire des idées). *L'Anée Psychologique*, 1894, *1*, 24–59.

Black, J. B., & Wilensky, R. An evaluation of story grammars. *Cognitive Science*, 1979, *3*, 213–230.

Bobrow, D. G., & Norman, D. A. Some principles of memory schemata. In D. G. Bobrow & A. Collins (Eds.), *Representation and understanding*. New York: Academic Press, 1975.

Bobrow, D. G., & Winograd, T. An overview of KLR, a knowledge representation language. *Cognitive Science*, 1977, *1*, 3–46.

Boring, E. G. *A history of experimental psychology* (2nd ed.). New York: Appleton-Century-Crofts, 1950.

Bower, G. H. Experiments on story understanding and recall. *Quarterly Journal of Experimental Psychology*, 1976, *28*, 511–534.

Bower, G. H., Black, J. B., & Turner, T. J. Scripts in memory for text. *Cognitive Psychology*, 1979, *11*, 177–220.

Bransford, J. D., & Johnson, M. K. Contextual prerequisites for understanding: Some investigations of comprehension and recall. *Journal of Verbal Learning and Verbal Behavior*, 1972, *11*, 717–726.

Brent, S. G. Linguistic unity, list length, and rate of presentation in serial anticipation learning. *Journal of Verbal Learning and Verbal Behavior*, 1969, *8*, 70–79.

Brewer, W. F. Literary theory, rhetoric, and stylistics: Implications for psychology. In R. J. Spiro, B. C. Bruce, & W. F. Brewer (Eds.), *Theoretical issues in reading comprehension: Perspectives from cognitive psychology, linguistics, artificial intelligence, and education*. Hillsdale, N.J.: Lawrence Erlbaum Associates, 1980.

Brewer, W. F. The story schema: Universal and culture-specific properties. In D. Olson, N. Torrance, & A. Hildyard (Eds.), *Literacy, language, and learning: The nature and consequences of reading and writing*, in press.

Brewer, W. F., & Dupree, D. A. Use of plan schemata in the recall and recognition of goal-directed actions. *Journal of Experimental Psychology: Learning, Memory, and Cognition*, 1983, *9*, 117–129.

Brewer, W. F., & Lichtenstein, E. H. Event schemas, story schemas, and story grammars. In J. Long & A. Baddeley (Eds.), *Attention and performance IX*. Hillsdale, N.J.: Lawrence Erlbaum Associates, 1981.

Brewer, W. F., & Lichtenstein, E. H. Stories are to entertain: A structural-affect theory of stories. *Journal of Pragmatics*, 1982, *6*, 473–486.

Brewer, W. F., & Pani, J. R. The structure of human memory. In G. H. Bower (Ed.), *The psychology of learning and motivation: Advances in research and theory* (Vol. 17). New York: Academic Press, 1983.

Brewer, W. F., & Pani, J. R. *Personal memory, generic memory, and skill: An empirical study*. Paper presented at the meetings of the Psychonomic Society, Minneapolis, November 1982.

Brewer, W. F., & Pani, J. R. *Phenomenal reports during memory recall*. In preparation.

Brewer, W. F., & Treyens, J. C. Role of schemata in memory for places. *Cognitive Psychology,* 1981, *13,* 207–230.

Britton, B. K., Meyer, B. J. F., Simpson, R., Holdredge, T. S., & Curry, C. Effects of the organization of text on memory: Tests of two implications of a selective attention hypothesis. *Journal of Experimental Psychology: Human Learning and Memory,* 1979, *5,* 496–506.

Broadbent, D. E. Frederic Charles Bartlett: 1886–1969. *Biographical Memoirs of Fellows of the Royal Society,* 1970, *16,* 1–13.

Charniak, E. A framed PAINTING: The representation of a common sense knowledge fragment. *Cognitive Science,* 1977, *1,* 355–394.

Chase, W. G., & Simon, H. A. The mind's eye in chess. In W. G. Chase (Ed.), *Visual information processing.* New York: Academic Press, 1973.

Chiesi, H. L., Spilich, G. J., & Voss, J. F. Acquisition of domain-related information in relation to high and low domain knowledge. *Journal of Verbal Learning and Verbal Behavior,* 1979, *18,* 257–273.

Chomsky, N. *Aspects of the theory of syntax.* Cambridge, Mass.: M.I.T. Press, 1965.

Chomsky, N. *Rules and representations.* New York: Columbia University Press, 1980.

Cirilo, R. K., & Foss, D. J. Text structure and reading time for sentences. *Journal of Verbal Learning and Verbal Behavior,* 1980, *19,* 96–109.

Collins, A. M., & Quillian, M. R. Retrieval time from semantic memory. *Journal of Verbal Learning and Verbal Behavior,* 1969, *8,* 240–247.

Collins, A. M., & Quillian, M. R. How to make a language user. In E. Tulving & W. Donaldson (Eds.), *Organization of memory.* New York: Academic Press, 1972.

de Groot, A. D. *Thought and choice in chess.* The Hague: Mouton, 1965.

van Dijk, T. A. *Macrostructures.* Hillsdale, N. J.: Lawrence Erlbaum Associates, 1980.

van Dijk, T. A., & Kintsch, W. Cognitive psychology and discourse: Recalling and summarizing stories. In W. U. Dressler (Ed.), *Current trends in textlinguistics.* Berlin: Walter de Gruyter, 1978.

Dooling, D. J., & Lachman, R. Effects of comprehension on retention of prose. *Journal of Experimental Psychology,* 1971, *88,* 216–222.

Dooling, D. J., & Mullet, R. L. Locus of thematic effects in retention of prose. *Journal of Experimental Psychology,* 1973, *97,* 404–406.

Drever, J. The historical background for national trends in psychology: On the non-existence of English associationism. *Journal of the History of the Behavioral Sciences,* 1965, *1,* 123–130.

Ebbinghaus, H. *Memory.* New York: Dover, 1964. (Originally published, 1885.)

Fillmore, C. J. An alternative to checklist theories of meaning. In *Proceedings of the first annual meeting of the Berkeley Linguistics Society,* 1975 (University of California, Berkeley).

Fodor, J. A. The appeal to tacit knowledge in psychological explanation. *Journal of Philosophy,* 1968, *65,* 627–640.

Friedman, A. Framing pictures: The role of knowledge in automatized encoding and memory for gist. *Journal of Experimental Psychology: General,* 1979, *108,* 316–355.

Goldstein, I., & Papert, S. Artificial intelligence, language, and the study of knowledge. *Cognitive Science,* 1977, *1,* 84–123.

Gomulicki, B. R. Recall as an abstractive process. *Acta Psychologica,* 1956, *12,* 77–94.

Goodman, G. S. Picture memory: How the action schema affects retention. *Cognitive Psychology,* 1980, *12,* 473–495.

Graesser, A. C. *Prose comprehension beyond the word.* New York: Springer-Verlag, 1981.

Graesser, A. C., Gordon, S. E., & Sawyer, J. D. Recognition memory for typical and atypical actions in scripted activities: Tests of a script pointer + tag hypothesis. *Journal of Verbal Learning and Verbal Behavior,* 1979, *18,* 319–332.

Graesser, A. C., & Nakamura, G. V. The impact of a schema on comprehension and memory. In G.

H. Bower (Ed.), *The psychology of learning and motivation: Advances in research and theory* (Vol. 16). New York: Academic Press, 1982.

Graesser, A. C., Nakamura, G. V., Zimmerman, J. A., & Riha, J. *Recognition memory for script-relevant versus irrelevant actions as a function of encoding conditions.* Unpublished manuscript, California State University Fullerton, 1980.

Graesser, A. C., Woll, S. B., Kowalski, D. J., & Smith, D. A. Memory for typical and atypical actions in scripted activities. *Journal of Experimental Psychology: Human Learning and Memory,* 1980, *6,* 503–515.

Grice, H. P. Logic and conversation. In P. Cole & J. L. Morgan (Eds.), *Syntax and semantics* (Vol. 3), *Speech acts.* New York: Seminar Press, 1975.

Head, H. Sensation and the cerebral cortex. *Brain,* 1918, *41,* 57–253.

Head, H. *Studies in neurology* (Vol. 2). London: Hodder & Stoughton, 1920.

Head, H., & Holmes, G. Sensory disturbances from cerebral lesions. *Brain,* 1911, *34,* 102–254.

Humphrey, G. *Thinking.* New York: Wiley, 1951.

Jenkins, J. G. Review of *Remembering* by F. C. Bartlett. *American Journal of Psychology,* 1935, *47,* 712–715.

Jenkins, J. J., Wald, J., & Pittenger, J. B. Apprehending pictorial events: An instance of psychological cohesion. In C. W. Savage (Ed.), *Minnesota studies in the philosophy of science* (Vol. 9). Minneapolis: University of Minnesota Press, 1978.

Johnson, R. E. Recall of prose as a function of the structural importance of the lingustic units. *Journal of Verbal Learning and Verbal Behavior,* 1970, *9,* 12–20.

Kintsch, W. Notes on the structure of semantic memory. In E. Tulving & W. Donaldson (Eds.), *Organization of memory.* New York: Academic Press, 1972.

Kintsch, W., & van Dijk, T. A. Toward a model of text comprehension and production. *Psychological Review,* 1978, *85,* 363–394.

Lachman, R., & Dooling, D. J. Connected discourse and random strings: Effects of number of inputs on recognition and recall. *Journal of Experimental Psychology,* 1968, *77,* 517–522.

Lashley, K. S. Cerebral organization and behavior. In F. A. Beach, D. O. Hebb, C. T. Morgan, & H. W. Nissen (Eds.), *The neuropsychology of Lashley.* New York: McGraw-Hill, 1960.

Lichtenstein, E. H. *Memory for goal-directed events.* Unpublished doctoral dissertation, University of Illinois, 1979.

Lichtenstein, E. H., & Brewer, W. F. Memory for goal-directed events. *Cognitive Psychology,* 1980, *12,* 412–445.

Loftus, G. R., & Mackworth, N. H. Cognitive determinants of fixation location during picture viewing. *Journal of Experimental Psychology: Human Perception and Performance,* 1978, *4,* 565–572.

Loftus, E. F., Miller, D. G., & Burns, H. G. Semantic integration of verbal information into a visual memory. *Journal of Experimental Psychology: Human Learning and Memory,* 1978, *4,* 19–31.

Mandler, J. M. A code in the node: The use of a story schema in retrieval. *Discourse Processes,* 1978, *1,* 14–35.

Mandler, J. M., & Johnson, N.S. Some of the thousand words a picture is worth. *Journal of Experimental Psychology: Human Learning and Memory,* 1976, *2,* 529–540.

Mandler, J. M., & Johnson, N. S. Remembrance of things parsed: Story structure and recall. *Cognitive Psychology,* 1977, *9,* 111–151.

Mandler, J. M., & Johnson, N. S. On throwing out the baby with the bathwater: A reply to Black and Wilensky's evaluation of story grammars. *Cognitive Science,* 1980, *4,* 305–312.

Mandler, J. M., & Mandler, G. *Thinking: From association to gestalt.* New York: Wiley, 1964.

Mandler, J. M., & Parker, R. E. Memory for descriptive and spatial information in complex pictures. *Journal of Experimental Psychology: Human Learning and Memory,* 1976, *2,* 38–48.

Mandler, J. M., & Ritchey, G. H. Long-term memory for pictures. *Journal of Experimental Psychology: Human Learning and Memory*, 1977, *3*, 386–396.

McGeoch, J. A. Review of *Remembering* by F. C. Bartlett. *Psychological Bulletin*, 1933, *30*, 774–776.

Meyer, B. J. F., & McConkie, G. W. What is recalled after hearing a passage? *Journal of Educational Psychology*, 1973, *65*, 109–117.

Minsky, M. A framework for representing knowledge. In P. H. Winston (Ed.), *The psychology of computer vision*. New York: McGraw-Hill, 1975.

Neisser, U. *Cognitive psychology*. New York: Appleton-Century-Crofts, 1967.

Neisser, U. *Cognition and reality*. San Francisco: W. H. Freeman, 1976.

Neisser, U. *Memory observed*. San Francisco: W. H. Freeman, 1982.

Newell, A., & Simon, H. A. *Human problem solving*. Englewood Cliffs, N.J.: Prentice-Hall, 1972.

Northway, M. L. The concept of the 'schema'. *British Journal of Psychology*, 1940, *30*, 316–325.

Oldfield, R. C. Frederic Charles Bartlett: 1886–1969. *American Journal of Psychology*, 1972, *85*, 133–140.

Oldfield, R. C., & Zangwill, O. L. Head's concept of the schema and its application in contemporary British psychology. Part I. Head's concept of the schema. *British Journal of Psychology*, 1942, *32*, 267–286. (a)

Oldfield, R. C., & Zangwill, O. L. Head's concept of the schema and its application in contemporary British psychology. Part II. Critical analysis of Head's theory. *British Journal of Psychology*, 1942, *33*, 58–64. (b)

Oldfield, R. C., & Zangwill, O. L. Head's concept of the schema and its application in contemporary British psychology. Part III. Bartlett's theory of memory. *British Journal of Psychology*, 1943, *33*, 113–129. (a)

Oldfield, R. C., & Zangwill, O. L. Head's concept of the schema and its application in contemporary British psychology. Part IV. Wolters' theory of thinking. *British Journal of Psychology*, 1943, *33*, 143–149. (b)

Pichert, J. W., & Anderson, R. C. Taking different perspectives on a story. *Journal of Educational Psychology*, 1977, *69*, 309–315.

Putnam, H. Reductionism and the nature of psychology. *Cognition*, 1973, *2*, 131–146.

Pylyshyn, Z. W. What the mind's eye tells the mind's brain: A critique of mental imagery. *Psychological Bulletin*, 1973, *80*, 1–24.

Pylyshyn, Z. W. Computational models and empirical constraints. *Behavioral and Brain Science*, 1978, *1*, 93–127.

Quillian, M. R. Semantic memory. In M. Minsky (Ed.), *Semantic information processing*. Cambridge, Mass.: M.I.T. Press, 1968.

Reynolds, R. E. *The effect of attention on the learning and recall of important text elements*. Unpublished doctoral dissertation, University of Illinois, 1979.

Rumelhart, D. E. Notes on a schema for stories. In D. G. Bobrow & A. Collins (Eds.), *Representation and understanding*. New York: Academic Press, 1975.

Rumelhart, D. E. Understanding and summarizing brief stories. In D. LaBerge & S. J. Samuels (Eds.), *Basic processes in reading: Perception and comprehension*. Hillsdale, N.J.: Lawrence Erlbaum Associates, 1977.

Rumelhart, D. E. Schemata: The building blocks of cognition. In R. J. Spiro, B. C. Bruce, & W. F. Brewer (Eds.), *Theoretical issues in reading comprehension: Perspectives from cognitive psychology, linguistics, artificial intelligence, and education*. Hillsdale, N.J.: Lawrence Erlbaum Associates, 1980.

Rumelhart, D. E., & Ortony, A. The representation of knowledge in memory. In R. C. Anderson, R. J. Spiro, & W. E. Montague (Eds.), *Schooling and the acquisition of knowledge*. Hillsdale, N.J.: Lawrence Erlbaum Associates, 1977.

Schank, R. C., & Abelson, R. P. Scripts, plans, and knowledge. *Advance Papers of the Fourth International Joint Conference on Artificial Intelligence,* Tbilisi, 1975, 151–157.

Schmidt, C. F., Sridharan, N. S., & Goodson, J. L. The plan recognition problem: An intersection of psychology and artificial intelligence. *Artificial Intelligence,* 1978, *11,* 45–83.

Schmidt, R. A. A schema theory of discrete motor skill learning. *Psychological Review,* 1975, *82,* 225–260.

Shebilske, W. L., & Reid, L. S. Reading eye movements, macro-structure and the comprehension processes. In P. A. Kolers, M. E. Wrolstad, & H. Bouma (Eds.), *Processing of visual language.* New York: Plenum Press, 1979.

Smith, E. E. Organization of factual knowledge. In H. E. Howe, Jr. & J. H. Flowers (Eds.), *Nebraska Symposium on Motivation* (Vol. 28). Lincoln: University of Nebraska Press, 1981.

Smith, E. E., Shoben, E. J., & Rips, L. J. Structure and process in semantic memory: A featural model for semantic decisions. *Psychological Review,* 1974, *81,* 214–241.

Spiro, R. J. Remembering information from text: The 'state of schema' approach. In R. C. Anderson, R. J. Spiro, & W. E. Montague (Eds.), *Schooling and the acquisition of knowledge.* Hillsdale, N.J.: Lawrence Erlbaum Associates, 1977.

Spiro, R. J. Constructive processes in prose comprehension and recall. In R. J. Spiro, B. C. Bruce, & W. F. Brewer (Eds.), *Theoretical issues in reading comprehension: Perspectives from cognitive psychology, linguistics, artificial intelligence, and education.* Hillsdale, N.J.: Lawrence Erlbaum Associates, 1980.

Steffensen, M. S., & Colker, L. Intercultural misunderstandings about health care: Recall of descriptions of illness and treatment. *Social Science & Medicine,* 1982, *16,* 1949–1954.

Stein, N. L., & Glenn, C. G. An analysis of story comprehension in elementary school children. In R. O. Freedle (Ed.), *New directions in discourse processing.* Norwood, N.J.: Ablex, 1979.

Sulin, R. A., & Dooling, D. J. Intrusion of a thematic idea in retention of prose. *Journal of Experimental Psychology,* 1974, *103,* 255–262.

Suppe, F. (Ed.). *The structure of scientific theories* (2nd ed.). Urbana: University of Illinois Press, 1977.

Thagard, P. *The representation of knowledge in frame systems.* Unpublished manuscript, University of Michigan-Dearborn, January 1980.

Thagard, P. *Scientific theories as frame systems.* Unpublished manuscript, University of Michigan-Dearborn, May 1982.

Thieman, T. J., & Brewer, W. F. Alfred Binet on memory for ideas. *Genetic Psychology Monographs,* 1978, *97,* 243–264.

Thorndyke, P. W. Cognitive structures in comprehension and memory of narrative discourse. *Cognitive Psychology, 1977, 9,* 77–110.

Thorndyke, P. W., & Yekovich, F. R. A critique of schema-based theories of human story memory. *Poetics,* 1980, *9,* 23–49.

Tulving, E. Episodic and semantic memory. In E. Tulving & W. Donaldson (Eds.), *Organization of memory.* New York: Academic Press, 1972.

Watson, J. B. Psychology as the behaviorist views it. *Psychological Review,* 1913, *20,* 158–177.

Welborn, E. L., & English, H. Logical learning and retention: A general review of experiments with meaningful verbal materials. *Psychological Bulletin,* 1937, *34,* 1–20.

Wyer, R. S., Srull, T. K., Gordon, S. E., & Hartwick, J. Effects of processing objectives on the recall of prose material. *Journal of Personality and Social Psychology,* 1982, *43,* 674–688.

Zangwill, O. L. *Remembering* revisited. *Quarterly Journal of Experimental Psychology,* 1972, *24,* 123–138.

# 5 Schemata and the Cognitive System*

**David E. Rumelhart**
*University of California, San Diego*

**Contents**

## INTRODUCTION

The notion of a schema is an old one in cognitive psychology. It goes back at least to the work of Bartlett (1932) and Piaget (1952). Indeed, many of the aspects of the schema idea were already present in Kant's use of the concept.

---

*This paper is an adaptation of a paper entitled "Schemata: The Building Blocks of Cognition" In R. Spiro, B. Bruce, & W. Brewer (Eds.), *Theoretical issues in reading comprehension*. Hillsdale, New Jersey: Lawrence Erlbaum Associates, 1980.

Nevertheless, it played little role in the mainstream of psychology for many years. Primarily, the concept has been seen as vague and endowed with mysterious powers by its promulgators. Beginning in about 1975, however, the concept has been revived and received a new currency in the field of Cognitive Science (c f. Bobrow & Norman, 1975; Chafe, 1976; Fillmore, 1975; Minsky, 1975; Moore & Newell, 1973; Rumelhart, 1975; Schank & Abelson, 1975; Winograd, 1975). It is my intent, in this paper, to develop the concept of a schema in its modern reincarnation, to show why this idea has seemed powerful, and to show how a schema theory can help make sense of a number of cognitive processes. One important reason why people once again feel comfortable with the idea of a schema is because we now understand how to build computer systems that employ schema-like entities as a fundamental part of their operations. In this sense, the schema idea has become more precise and it has become easier to see what the basic properties of the schema are.

There are many related formulations of the idea of the schema. Schema-like concepts have been variously referred to as frames, schemata, beta structures, scripts, mops knowledge units, and various other names. These various terms have been used by different authors to refer to any of a set of interrelated concepts. They are *not all synonymous*. Different authors have different things in mind when they use these different terms. Nevertheless, the various concepts are closely enough related that a discussion of any one of them will serve as an introduction to the others. I will thus focus my discussion on the one I know best: *schemata* (the singular is schema) as developed in Rumelhart and Ortony (1977).

The term schema comes into cognitive psychology most directly from Bartlett (1932). Bartlett himself attributes his use of the term to Head (1926). However, it would appear that Kant's use of the term already anticipated its major conceptual content. The Oxford English Dictionary gives the following definition of the term:

> In Kant: Any one of certain forms of rules of ''productive imagination'' through which the understanding is able to apply its ''categories'' to the manifold of sense-perception in the process of realizing knowledge or experience.

Some further discussion of Kant's view is given in Rumelhart and Ortony (1977). It is because of this historical precedence that I have chosen to retain the term schema.

For all of the authors mentioned above, schemata truly are the fundamental elements upon which all information processing depends. Schemata are employed in the process of interpreting sensory data, in retrieving information from memory, in organizing actions, in the determining of goals and subgoals, in the allocation of resources and generally in guiding the flow of processing in the system. Clearly, any device capable of all these wondrous things must be powerful indeed. Moreover, since our understanding of these tasks which schemata are supposed to carry out has not reached maturity, it is little wonder that a definitive explication of schemata does not yet exist and that skeptics view theories based on them with some suspicion. In this paper, I hope to spell out, as clearly as possible, the nature of schemata and the kinds of problems they were devised to solve. In addition, I hope to present a convincing case that indeed the framework provided by schemata and allied concepts does, in fact, form the basis for a reasonable theory of human information processing.

Although the theoretical developments I discuss have not been directly formulated in terms of issues of social cognition, it is clear that all of the writers in this field have assumed that schemata, frames, scripts, and the like form the basis for our social perceptions as much as for our perceptions of simpler objects and events. Indeed, it seems likely that the inherent richness of social situations make social perceptions even more dependent on the learned schemata. I will return to this discussion at the end of the chapter. I turn now to a discussion of the abstract nature of the schema.

## WHAT IS A SCHEMA?

A schema theory is basically a theory about knowledge. It is a theory about how knowledge is represented and about how that representation facilitates the *use* of the knowledge in particular ways. According to "schema theories" all knowledge is packaged into units. These units are the schemata. Embedded in these packets of knowledge is, in addition to the knowledge itself, information about how this knowledge is to be used.

A schema, then, is a data structure for representing the generic concepts stored in memory. There are schemata representing our knowledge about all concepts: those underlying objects, social situations, events, sequences of events, actions and sequences of actions. A schema contains, as part of its specification, the network of interrelations that is believed to normally hold among the constituents of the concept in question. A schema theory embodies a *prototype* theory of meaning. That is, inasmuch as a schema underlying a concept stored in memory corresponds to the *meaning* of that concept, meanings are encoded in terms of the typical or normal situations or events which instantiate that concept.

Rather than attempting a formal description of schemata and their characteristics at this point, I turn instead to some useful analogies in hopes of giving the reader a more concrete notion of the nature of schemata as I understand them. I turn first to one of the more fruitful analogies, that of a play.

### Schemata are like plays

The internal structure of a schema corresponds, in many ways, to the script of a play. Just as a play has characters that can be played by different actors at different times without changing the essential nature of the play, so a schema has *variables that can be associated with (bound to) different aspects of* the environment on different instantiations of the schema. As an example, consider the schema for the concept *buy*. One can imagine a playwright having written a most mundane play in which the entire play consisted of one person purchasing some object from another person. At minimum, such a play must have two people, some merchandise and some medium of exchange. Whatever else happens, at the outset of the play one character (call him/her the **purchaser**) must possess the medium of exchange (call it the **money**). The second person, the **seller** must possess the object in question, the **merchandise.** Then, by some interaction (**bargaining**) a bargain is struck and the **seller** agrees to give the **merchandise** to the **purchaser** in exchange for a quantity of the **money.** There would, of course, be many ways of playing this little play. The **merchandise** could vary from a trinket of little value to an object of incalculable worth. The **seller** and the **purchaser** could vary in status, occupation, sex, nationality, age, and so forth, and the **money** could vary in amount, and whether it was actually money or clam shells, and the **bargaining** could vary in form. Still, through all of this variation, as long as the fundamental plot remained the same we could say that the **buy** play was being performed.

Now, this little play is very much like the schema that I believe underlies our understanding of the concept *buy* or that for *sell.* There are variables, corresponding to the characters in the play. We have the **purchaser,** the **seller,** the **money,** the **merchandise** and the **bargaining.** When we understand a situation to be a case of **buying,** we come to associate persons, objects, and subevents with the various variables of our schema. Upon having made these associations, we can determine to what degree the situation we are observing corresponds to this *prototype* case of **buying.**

Just as a playwright often specifies characteristics of the characters in his play, (age, sex, disposition etc.), so too, as part of the specification of a schema, we have associated knowledge about the variables of the schema. We know, for example, that the **purchaser** and **seller** are normally people and that the **money** is normally money. Moreover, we know that the value of the **money** in question will co-vary with the value of the **merchandise,** and so on. Such knowledge about the typical values of the variables and their interrelationships is called the *variable constraints.*

These constraints serve two important functions in a schema theory. In the first place, variable constraints help in the identification of the various aspects of the situation with the variables of the schema. If we know that we are observing a case of **buying,** we are not going to map the **purchaser** variable into the object in the world which should serve as the **money.** We know this, in part, because we know that the **purchaser** is normally an animate being whereas the **money** is normally money or some other inanimate object. In the second place, variable constraints can help by serving as *default values,* (c.f. Minsky, 1975) or initial "guesses" for variables whose values we have not yet observed. Thus, for example, if we take a certain transaction to be one of **buying,** but do not notice the **money,** we can *infer* that there was **money** and that, in fact, the **money** probably *was money* amounting in value to about the value of the **merchandise.** In this way, the schema can help us make inferences about unobserved aspects of a situation.

It is perhaps useful to note here that variable constraints offer default values for unobserved variables *conditional on the values of the observed variables.* Moreover, the constraints are not *all-or-none* constraints which *require* that certain variables have a fixed range of values. Rather, they are merely specifications of the *normal* range of values for each variable and how this normal range varies with the specification of various combinations of other values on the other variables. Thus, as Rumelhart and Ortony (1977) suggest, it is perhaps most useful to think of variable constraints as forming a kind of *multivariate distribution* with correlations among the several variables.

There is also the notion of an *instantiation of a schema* which corresponds to an *enactment of a play.* A play is enacted whenever particular actors, speaking particular lines perform at a particular time and place. Similarly, a schema is *instantiated* whenever a particular configuration of values are bound to a particular configuration of variables at a particular moment in time. Interpreting a situation to be an instance of some concept, such as an instance of buying, involves, according to the present view, the instantiation of an appropriate schema, say the **buy** schema, by associating the various variables of the schema with the various aspects of the situation. Such a schema along with its variable bindings is called an instantiated schema. Just as we could, say, take a movie of an enactment of a play and thereby save for posterity a trace of the enactment, likewise it is the traces of our instantiated schemata which serve as the basis of our recollections.

Before leaving the analogy between the script of a play and a schema, it is useful to note that neither is a complete specification of every detail—both allow room for irrelevant variation and creative interpretation. The script of a play, no matter how meticulous the playwright, allows for an infinity of variations each of which can properly be considered an enactment of the play. Certain lines composed by the playwright are sometimes changed to suit the interpretation of the director. Nevertheless, within limits, it is the same play. So it is with schemata. A schema is not so rigidly applied that no variation is allowed. The schema only provides the skeleton around which the situation is interpreted. Variations orthogonal to the specifications of the schema have no bearing on the quality with which the schema is said to account for the situation. Moreover, even minor aspects of the situation which might be considered central to the schema can undergo some variation before we completely reject the interpretation provided by the schema.

Finally, despite all of the ways in which a schema is like a play, there are also numerous ways in which a schema is unlike a play. Perhaps most important of these is degree of abstraction. In our example of the **buy** schema we imagined a play that was more abstract than one that any playwright would ever compose. Normally, the playwright would determine the *kind* of buying involved, as well as more detail about the characters and more constraints on the dialog. The **buy** schema, on the other hand, must be applicable to *any* case of buying and thus must, necessarily, be more abstract than any actual play would ever be. Moreover, whereas a play is normally about people and their actions, a schema may be about events and objects of any sort. Indeed, a schema may merely be about the nature of a wholly inactive object such as a chair. In this case, the schema specifies not action or event sequences, but rather spatial and functional relationships characteristic of chairs. Finally, although a play may contain acts each with their own structure, a script for a play exists really only on one level. A script does not consist of a configuration of sub-scripts. A schema, on the other hand, should be viewed as consisting of a configuration of sub-schemata corresponding to the constituents of the concept being represented. These points will be made clearer in the following sections when I draw analogies between schemata and other familiar concepts.

## Schemata are like theories

Perhaps the central function of schemata is in the construction of an interpretation of an event, object or situation—that is, in the process of comprehension. In all of this, it is useful to think of a schema as a kind of informal, private, unarticulated theory about the nature of the events, objects or situations which we face. The total set of schemata we have available for interpreting our world in a sense constitutes our private theory of the nature of reality. The total set of schemata instantiated at a particular moment in time constitutes our internal model of the situation we face at that moment in time.

Thus, just as the activity surrounding a theory is often focused on the evaluation of the theory and the comparison of the theory with observations we have made, so it is that the primary activity associated with a schema is the determination whether it gives an adequate account for some aspect of our current situation. Just as the determination that a particular theory accounts for some observed results involves the determinations of the *parameters of the theory,* so the determination that a particular configuration of schemata accounts for the data presently available at our senses requires the determination of the values of the *variables of the schemata.* If a promising schema fails to account for some aspect of a situation, one has the options of accepting the schema as adequate in spite of its flawed account or of rejecting the schema as inadequate and looking for another possibility. Therefore, the fundamental processes of comprehension are taken to be analogous to hypothesis testing, evaluation of goodness of fit and parameter estimation. Thus, one is presumably constantly evaluating hypotheses about the most plausible interpretation of the situation at hand. We can be said to have understood a situation when we are able to find a configuration of hypotheses (schemata) which offer a coherent account for the various aspects of that situation. To the degree to which we fail to find such a configuration, the situation will appear confusing and uncomprehensible.

Schemata are like theories in another important respect. Theories, once they are moderately successful, become a source of predictions about unobserved events. Not all experiments are carried out. Not all possible observations are made. Instead, we use our theories to make inferences with some confidence about these unobserved events. So it is with schemata. We need not observe all aspects of a situation before we are willing to assume that some particular configuration of schemata offers a satisfactory account for that situation. Once we have accepted a configuration of schemata, the schemata themselves provide a richness which goes far beyond our observations. Upon deciding that we have seen an automobile, we assume that it has an engine, headlights, and all of the standard characteristics of an automobile. We do this without the slightest hesitation. We have complete confidence in our little theory. This allows our interpretations to far outstrip our sensory observations. In fact, once we have determined that a particular schema accounts for some event we may not be able to determine which aspects of our beliefs are based on direct sensory information and which are merely consequences of our interpretation.

## Schemata are like procedures

There are at least two inadequacies of the analogies presented above. In the first place, plays and theories are passive. Schemata are active processes. In the second place, the relationship between a theory and its constituent sub-theories or between a play and its constituent sub-plays are not always evident. Schemata, on the other hand, have a very well defined constituent structure.

In both of these ways, schemata resemble procedures or computer programs. Schemata are active computational devices capable of evaluating the quality of their own fit to the available data. That is, a schema should be viewed as a procedure whose function it is to determine whether, and to what degree, it accounts for the pattern of observations. This includes, among other things, associating its variables to the appropriate aspects of its environment—i.e., binding its own variables. Thus, to the degree that schemata underlying concepts are identified with *meaning of those concepts,* a schema theory is *both* a *prototype theory and* a *procedural theory* of meaning. Obviously, the degree to which a schema theory of human information processing can work depends on the degree to which procedures can actually be constructed to carry out the tasks I have just assigned to them. I believe they can, and address this issue in the following sections.

The second characteristic which schemata share with procedures is a structural one. Procedures normally consist of a network (or a tree) of sub-procedures.

A particular procedure normally carries out its task by invoking a pattern of sub-procedures each of which in turn operates by invoking its sub-procedures. Each procedure or sub-procedure can return values which can serve as conditions determining which, if any further sub-procedures are to be invoked. So it is with schemata. A schema is a network (or possibly a tree) of sub-schemata, each of which carries out its assigned task of evaluating its goodness of fit whenever activated. These sub-schemata represent the conceptual constituents of the concept being represented.

Thus, for example, suppose we had a schema for a **face.** This would consist of a certain configuration of sub-schemata each representing a different constituent of a face. For example, there would presumably be a sub-schema representing the **mouth,** one for the **nose,** and one for each **ear** and each **eye.** These sub-schemata in turn would consist of a configuration of constituents. The **eye** schema, for example, would consist of a configuration of sub-schemata including, perhaps, an **iris, eyelashes,** an **eyebrow,** and so forth.

Just as a procedure uses results produced by its sub-procedures to carry out its task, so too a schema uses results produced by its sub-schemata to carry out its tasks. As I indicated above, the primary activity of a schema is the evaluation of its goodness of fit. An important mechanism of this evaluation involves the evaluation of the goodness of fit of each of its constituent parts. Thus, if a good **eye** is found and a good **mouth** is found, the **face** schema can use this information along with its own evaluation of whether the entire *configuration* is right for a face to generate an overall evaluation of its goodness of fit.

To summarize then, just as a procedure consists of sub-procedures and those sub-procedures, in turn, consist of more sub-procedures etc., so a schema consists of sub-schemata each of which, in turn, is specified as a configuration of its sub-schemata, and so on. One may be struck by the fact that this process must stop somewhere. If each and every schema were merely a configuration of sub-schemata the process would never end. The solution to this dilemma for schemata is identical to the solution for procedures. When a computer program is written, this embedding process does not continue indefinitely. Eventually, some sub-procedure consists entirely of a configuration of *elementary instructions* for the machine in question. Likewise, with schemata, there must be a set of schemata that are elementary, in the sense that they do not consist of a further breakdown in terms of sub-schemata. Such elementary schemata correspond to what Norman and Rumelhart (1975) call *primitives.*

## Schemata are like parsers

A parser is a device that, given a sequence of symbols, determines whether that sequence forms a legal sentence (according to the rules of some grammar) and, if it does, determines the *constituent structure* of the sentence. That is, it determines which symbols in the sequence correspond to which constituents of the sentence. The process of finding and verifying appropriate schemata is thus a kind of parsing process which works with conceptual elements—finding constituents and sub-constituents among the data currently impinging on the system in much the same way that a sentence parser must find the proper parse for the input string of words.

One particularly useful aspect of this analogy is the substantial body of work carried out in computational linguistics on various parsing procedures. I believe that the processing strategies developed for some of the most sophisticated of these will carry over nicely in their application to schemata generally. As I discuss below, I have in mind here especially the work of Kaplan (1973) and his development of the general syntactic processor (GSP).

## Summary of the Major Features of Schemata

Rumelhart and Ortony (1977) listed four major characteristics of schemata. These were:

1. Schemata have variables.
2. Schemata can embed, one within another.
3. Schemata represent knowledge at all levels of abstraction.
4. Schemata represent *knowledge* rather than definitions.

The analogies presented above illustrate all of these features. Whereas schemata have variables, plays have roles, theories have parameters, and procedures have arguments. The embedding characteristic of schemata is best illustrated by the analogy between schemata and procedures. Schemata consist of sub-schemata as procedures consist of sub-procedures. Just as theories can be about the grand and the small, so schemata can represent knowledge at all levels—from ideologies and cultural truths to knowledge about what constitutes an appropriate sentence in our language to knowledge about the meaning of a particular word to knowledge about what patterns of excitations are associated with what letters of the alphabet. We have schemata to represent all levels of our experience, at all levels of abstraction. Finally, our schemata *are* our knowledge. All of our generic knowledge is embedded in schemata.

In addition to these four features, the analogies presented here indicate at least two more general features of schemata.

5. Schemata are active processes.
6. Schemata are recognition devices whose processing is aimed at the evaluation of their goodness of fit to the data being processed.

## THE CONTROL STRUCTURE OF SCHEMATA

Perhaps the central questions in the development of a schema based model of perception and comprehension are: first, how is an adequate configuration of schemata discovered and, secondly, how is the goodness of fit evaluated. These are largely problems of *control structures*. There are many schemata. Not all of them can be evaluated at once. Somehow, there must be a scheme for activating just those schemata which are most promising. There are two basic sources of activation for schemata. These are usually referred to as *top-down* and *bottom-up* activation. These two directions correspond to what Bobrow and Norman (1975) have called *conceptually-driven* and *data-driven* processing.

### Conceptually-Driven and Data-Driven Processing

A schema may activate a sub-schema in the way a procedure invokes its sub-procedures. This is called *conceptual-driven* processing. In a sense, conceptually-driven processing is *expectation-driven* processing. That is, when a schema is activated and it, in turn, activates its sub-schemata the activation of these sub-schemata derive from a sort of expectation that they will be able to account for some portion of the input data. For example, suppose that, through some mechanism, the **face** schema is considered a promising account for the input and thereby activated and set about evaluating its goodness of fit. The *promise* of the **face** schema is, in a sense, transferred to its **mouth, nose, eye, ear,** sub-schemata.

A second mechanism for schema activation is bottom-up or *data-driven* activation. A schema is said to be activated from the bottom-up whenever a sub-schema which has been somehow activated causes the various schemata of which it is a part to be activated. If the activation of the **face** schema led to the activation of the **person** schema we would say that the activation of the **person** schema was data-driven. Thus, where *conceptually-driven* activation goes from *whole to part,* data-driven activation goes from *part to whole.* In schema directed processing activation goes in *both* directions.

Schema directed processing is assumed to proceed in roughly the following way: Some event occurs at the sensory system. The occurrence of this event "automatically" activates certain "low-level" schemata (such schemata might be called *feature detectors*). These low level schemata, in turn, activate (in a data-driven fashion) certain of the "higher-level" schemata (the most probable ones) of which they are constituents. These "higher-level" schemata then initiate conceptually-driven processing by activating the sub-schemata not already activated in an attempt to evaluate their goodness of fit.

At some point, when one of these higher level schemata began to get further positive results about its goodness of fit (i.e., it found evidence for other of its constituents), it activates still higher level schemata which look for still larger constituents.

This higher, more abstract schema then activates, from the top-down still other of its constituent schemata and this activation flows through its sub-schemata back down to lower-level schemata which eventually make contact with either other schemata which have been activated from the bottom-up or they initiate a search for the "predicted" sensory inputs.

Whenever a schema initiates a search for sensory data that are not present, that counts as evidence against that schema and also as evidence against all of those schemata that require the presence of that schema as a constituent sub-schema. When sufficient evidence is accumulated against a schema, processing of that schema is suspended and processing resources are allocated to other currently more promising schemata. Whenever enough evidence is gained in favor of a schema that schema is taken as an adequate account for the relevant aspect of the input and the interpretation offered by that schema is taken as the "correct" interpretation of the relevant event. Later processing, on other, higher-level schemata may eventually disconfirm a temporarily accepted schema and we will have the phenomenon of the "double-take."

The discussion of the processing system to this point has been rather abstract. In the following section I examine, in some detail, an example of this mixed initiative processing system.

## An Example

Consider the following brief passage:

> Business had been slow since the oil crisis. Nobody seemed to want anything really elegant anymore. Suddenly the door opened and a well dressed man entered the showroom floor. John put on his friendliest and most sincere expression and walked toward the man.

Although merely a fragment, most people generate a rather clear interpretation of this story. Apparently, John is a car salesman fallen on hard times. He probably sells rather large elegant cars—most likely Cadillacs. Suddenly a good prospect enters the showroom where John works. John wants to make a sale. To do that he must make a good impression on the man, therefore he tries to appear friendly and sincere. He also wants to talk to the man to deliver his sales pitch. Thus, he makes his way over to the man. Presumably, had the story continued John would have made the sales pitch and, if all went well, sold the man a car.

How do people arrive at such an interpretation? Clearly, people do not arrive at it all at once. As the sentences are read, schemata are activated, evaluated and refined or discarded. When people are asked to describe their various hypotheses as they read through the story, a remarkably consistent pattern of hypothesis generation and evaluation emerges. The first sentence is usually interpreted to mean that business is low *because* of the oil crisis. Thus, people are led to see the story as about a business which is somehow dependent on oil as suffering. Frequent hypotheses involve either the selling of cars, or of gasoline. A few interpret the sentence as being about the economy in general. The second sentence, about people not wanting elegant things anymore, leads people with the gas station hypothesis into a quandary. Elegance just doesn't fit with gas stations. The gas station hypothesis is weakened, but not always rejected. On the other hand, people with hypotheses about the general economy or about cars have no trouble incorporating this sentence into their emerging interpretation. In the former case they conclude it means that people don't buy luxury items and in the latter they assume it means that people don't buy large elegant cars—Cadillacs—much anymore. The third sentence clinches the car interpretation for nearly all readers. They are already looking for a business interpretation—that most probably means a **selling** interpretation—and when a *well dressed man* enters the door he is immediately labeled as someone with **money**—a prospective **buyer.** The phrase *showroom floor* clearly invalidates the gas station interpretation and strongly implicates automobiles which are often sold from a showroom. Moreover, the occurrence of a specific event doesn't fit at all well with the view that the passage is a general discussion of the state of the economy. Finally, with the introduction of John, we have an ideal candidate for the **seller.** John's actions are clearly those stereotypic of a salesman. John wants to make a sale and his "putting on" is clearly an attempt on his part to "make a good impression." His movement toward the man fits nicely into this interpretation. If he is a salesman, he must make contact with the man and deliver the stereotypic "pitch."

Qualitatively, this little account (which was derived from an analysis of a number of readers describing their current interpretation of the story after each sentence (see Rumelhart, 1981, for a more detailed account of this data) fits well with the general approach I have been outlining. The process of comprehension is very much like the process of constructing a theory, testing it against the data currently available, and as more data becomes available, specifying the theory further—i.e., refining the default values (as perhaps was the case when those holding the "car hypothesis" from the beginning encountered the sentence about nobody wanting anything elegant anymore). If the account becomes sufficiently strained, it is given up and a new one constructed, or, alternatively, if a new theory presents itself which obviously gives a more cogent account, the old one can be dropped and the new one accepted.

But where do these theories come from? The theories are, of course, schemata. Presumably, through experience we have built up a vast repertoire of such schemata. We have schemata for salesmen, the kinds of motives they have and the kinds of techniques they employ. We have schemata for automobiles, including how and where they are sold. We have built up schemata for the "oil crisis," what kinds of effects it has on what kinds of business. We have schemata about business people, the kinds of motives they have and the kinds of responses they make to these motives. The knowledge embedded in these schemata form the framework for our theories. It is some configuration of these schemata which ultimately form the basis for our understanding.

But how does a relevant schema suggest itself? It is here that the control structures discussed above play an essential role. Presumably, it is the "bottom-up" observation that a certain concept has been referenced that leads to the suggestion of the initial hypotheses. The notion that business was slow, suggests schemata about business and the economy. Since the slowness was dated from the occurrence of the oil crisis, it is a natural inference that the oil crisis was the *cause* of the slowness. Thus, a **business** schema is activated. The particular **type** of business is presumably a variable which must be filled. The information about the oil crisis suggests that it may be an oil related business. Thus, readers are led to restrict the **type** variable of the **business** schema to oil related businesses.

At this point, after the bottom-up activation of the high level **business** schema has occurred, this schema would generate a top-down activation of the various possible oil related businesses. Prime candidates for these are, of course, automobile related businesses. Of these, selling gasoline and automobiles are the two most salient possibilities.

When the second sentence is encountered, an attempt is made to fit it into the schemata currently considered most promising. As I discussed above, this information could serve to further restrict the **type** variable in the automobile **business** schema, but doesn't fit well with the gasoline business schema.

The **business** schema presumably has, as part of its specification, a reference to the **buy** or **sell** schema discussed earlier. Once activated, these schemata search for potential variable bindings. In the case of the automobile business, the **merchandise** variable is bound to an automobile. The second sentence suggests an elegant automobile. The reader has, when the third sentence is encountered, not yet found a candidate for **buyer** or **seller.** The sentence about a well-dressed man immediately suggests a potential **buyer.** The phrase "showroom floor" offers additional bottom-up support for the automobile hypothesis. In fact, it is a strong enough clue itself that it can suggest automobile sales to a reader who currently considers an alternative schema more likely. We thus have a **buyer** and some **merchandise.** The well-dressed quality of the **buyer** is consistent with our view that the **merchandise** is elegant and therefore expensive—being well-dressed suggests **money.** We need only a **seller**—i.e., an automobile salesman. Readers probably already bring a relatively complete characterization of the "default value" for car salesman. We need but little additional information to generate a rather detailed description of his goals and motives.

In spite of the length of this example, it should be noted that I have provided only a sketch of the elaborate processing which must occur in the comprehension of even so simple and direct a story as this. The problem is indeed a complex one and no one yet has been able to construct a model capable of actually carrying out the tasks involved. It is the conviction that the concept of the *schema* is the most promising route to the solution to these problems that has led to its current popularity.

## THE MAJOR FUNCTIONS OF SCHEMATA

My intent to this point has been primarily definitional. I have tried to show what schemata are generally and how they generally are supposed to work. In this section I give a few examples of phenomena for which schemata appear to offer promising accounts. I first turn to a discussion of *perception*.

### Schemata and Perceiving

There are numerous examples in the psychological literature which suggest a schema-like theory to account for them. I will mention just a few here. Perception, like language comprehension, is an interactive process. Information comes in from our sense organs, which suggest but do not determine, appropriate schemata for the interpretation of the sense data. It is often only in the context of the whole that the individual parts of an object can be identified. Similarly, the whole itself cannot be identified apart from its parts. The interpretation of parts and wholes must proceed jointly. Our final interpretation is determined both by the local clues and by consistency among the various levels of analysis. Consider, as an example, Figure 5.1 taken from Palmer (1975). The object on the left is clearly recognizable as a face, but its parts (series B) are not recognizable out of context. Thus, it cannot be that we first perceive the parts and then construct an interpretation of the whole. Rather, the various shapes of the lines *suggest,* but do not determine, possible interpretations (the wiggly line suggests a possible nose, the acute angle suggests a possible eye, etc.). Lower-level **nose** and **eye** schemata may be activated which in turn may activate higher-level schemata such as the **face** schema. The **face** schema then activates schemata for all parts of the **face** not receiving bottom-up activation. (For example, the lips may not be close enough to **lips** to activate this schema at all out of context. In this case, the **lips** schema would be activated by the **face** schema and find sufficient evidence to serve—in context—to count as **lips.**)

As can be noted from series C of the figure, it is not that parts of a face cannot *ever* be recognized without the face as a context. But, in order to be recognized out of context, they too much have an internal structure. If enough data is available about its internal structure, a schema like the **nose** schema can serve the function of an organizing whole perfectly well.

A    in context                    B    out of context

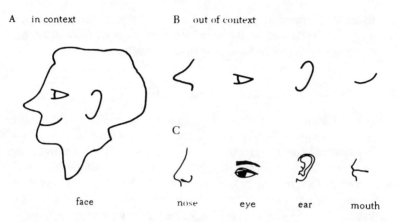

face                    nose          eye          ear          mouth

FIG. 5.1.    An illustration of part-whole context. Facial features recognizable in
the context of a profile (A) are not recognizable out of context (B). When the
internal part structure of the facial features is differentiated (C), however, the
features become recognizable out of context.

There is ample evidence of similar processes in reading. It is well known, for
example, that strings of characters that form words are more easily apprehended
than strings that do not form words. The reason for this presumably stems from
the fact that we have schemata corresponding to words and none for random
letter strings. Just as evidence for a **nose** indirectly constitutes evidence for **lips**
through the **face** schema, so too evidence for one letter can constitute evidence
for other letters through the schema for the word in question. Thus, for example,
evidence favoring a **t** in the first position and an **e** in the third position of a three
letter word indirectly constitutes evidence for a **h** in the second position through
activation of the **the** schema. The use of such information is presumably the
mechanism whereby words are easier to see than random letter strings. (See
McClelland & Rumelhart, 1981 and Rumelhart & McClelland, 1982 for a detailed model of this process in word perception.)

It is interesting that schemata not only *contribute* towards the development of
an accurate percept, but by the same token, they can sometimes cause a distortion. An experiment by Bruner and Potter (1964) illustrates the debilitating effect
of premature commitment to a particular schema. In their study subjects were
presented with defocused slides of familiar objects. The slides were slowly
brought into focus. At each step along the way, as the slides were brought into
focus, subjects were to report their best guess as to what the slide was of. Under
these conditions subjects continued to mis-identify the object long after naive
subjects (those started with less severe amounts of defocusing) were able to
readily identify the object in question.

This result is presumably due to the fact that subjects became committed to their early interpretations of the slide and then required more information to disconfirm their original hypothesis than is normally required.

## Schemata and Understanding Discourse

As discussed above, the process of understanding discourse is the process of finding a configuration of schemata that offers an adequate account of the passage in question. The analysis of the "oil crisis story" given above illustrates generally how such a process is supposed to operate. Clues from the story suggest possible interpretations (instantiations of schemata) which are then evaluated against the successive sentences of the story until finally a consistent interpretation is discovered. Sometimes, we fail to understand a situation correctly. There are at least three reasons implicit in schema-theory as to why this might occur:

1. We may not have the appropriate schemata. In this case we simply cannot understand the concept being communicated.
2. We may have the appropriate schemata, but the clues provided by the situation may be insufficient to suggest them. Here again we will not understand the situation, but, with appropriate additional clues, we may come to understand it.
3. We may find a consistent interpretation of the situation, but may not find a veridical one. In this case, we will "comprehend" the situation, but will be incorrect in our interpretation.

There are numerous examples of these three phenomena in the literature. Perhaps the most interesting set of studies along these lines were carried out by Bransford and Johnson (1973). They studied the comprehension of texts in which subjects lacked the appropriate schemata, ones in which the schemata were potentially available, but there were not sufficient clues to suggest the correct ones as well as ones in which subjects were led to choose a "wrong" interpretation. Consider, as an example, the following paragraph used in one of their studies.

The procedure is actually quite simple. First you arrange things into different groups. Of course, one pile may be sufficient depending on how much there is to do. If you have to go somewhere else due to lack of facilities that is the next step, otherwise you are pretty well set. It is important not to overdo things. That is, it is better to do too few things at once than too many. In the short run this may not seem important but complications can easily arise. A mistake can be expensive as well. At first the whole procedure will seem complicated. Soon, however, it will become just another facet of life. It is difficult to foresee any end to the necessity for this task in the immediate future, but then one can never tell. After the procedure is completed one arranges the materials into different groups again. Then they can be put into their appropriate places. Eventually they will be used once more and the whole cycle will then have to be repeated. However, that is part of life. (p. 400)

Most readers find this passage extremely difficult to understand. However, once they are told that it is about washing clothes, they are able to bring their clothes washing schema to the fore and make sense out of the story. The difficulty with this passage is thus not that readers don't have the appropriate schemata, rather, it stems from the fact that the clues in the story never seem to *suggest* the appropriate schemata in the first place. The "bottom-up" information is inadequate to initiate the comprehension process appropriately. Once the appropriate schemata are suggested, most people have no trouble understanding the text.

Although most readers simply find the passage incomprehensible, some find alternative schemata to account for it and thus render it comprehensible. Perhaps the most interesting interpretation I have collected was from a Washington bureaucrat who had no difficulty with the passage. He was able to interpret the passage as a clear description of his job. He was, in fact, surprised to find that it was supposed to be about "washing clothes" and not about "pushing papers." Here then, we have an example of the third kind of comprehension failure, "understanding the story," but "misunderstanding the author."

Obviously, a detailed account of the comprehension process requires a detailed description of the schemata people have available as well as an account of the conditions under which certain of these schemata are activated. A number of researchers have been developing such specific models of specific schemata (cf. Rumelhart, 1975, 1977; Schank & Abelson, 1977)

## Schemata and Remembering

In addition to the important role assigned to schemata in comprehension and perception, schemata are assumed to be the guiding forces behind remembering as well. Perhaps the clearest way to see this is to consider some of the commonalities between remembering and apprehension. Rumelhart and Ortony (1977) suggest that the process of remembering is essentially similar to the process of perceiving, except that in remembering, the data source is no longer sensorial, but memorial. To quote,

There is thus a kind of continuum between understanding and remembering where in the former we have the imposition of an interpretation primarily on incoming 'sensory fragments,' and in the latter we have the imposition of an interpretation primarily on 'memorial fragments.' In both cases schemata are employed. It should be emphasized that although remembering can be thought of as perceiving with memory as the modality, the episodic memories on which it is usually based are not merely fragments of the initial sensory input, but a fragmentary representation of our interpretation of that input. (p. 27)

Thus, important aspects of the memory process can be seen as identical to the process of comprehension. I have thus, implicitly, alluded to two ways in which schemata affect recollection. First, they are the mechanisms whereby initial interpretations are formed and, as such, they determine the *form* of the memorial fragments. Second, schemata are used to *re-interpret* the stored data in order to *reconstruct* the original interpretation. There is ample evidence for both of these roles. The first point suggests that we remember our *interpretations* of an event rather than the event itself. Bartlett's (1932) original finding that we remember the *gist* of a story rather than the details suggests this conclusion. Tulving and Thomson's (1973) arguments about encoding specificity, would seem to require the same conclusion. Perhaps the most convincing results, however, come from some experiments by Bransford and his associates (c f. Barclay, Bransford, Franks, McCarrell, & Nitsch, 1974; or Bransford, Barclay, & Franks, 1972). In one of their experiments (Bransford, Barclay & Franks, 1972), they presented subjects with sentences drawn from pairs like

(1a)  The woman stood *on* the stool and the mouse sat on the floor beneath *it*.
(1b)  The woman stood *on* the stool and the mouse sat on the floor beneath *her*.

or drawn from pairs like

(2a)  The woman stood *beside* the stool and the mouse sat on the floor beneath *it*.
(2b)  The woman stood *beside* the stool and the mouse sat on the floor beneath *her*.

They found that on subsequent recognition tests subjects could not tell which of the first pair of sentences had been presented to them, but those given sentences drawn from the second pair had no difficulty recognizing which had been presented. Since the two pairs differ by exactly the same number of words, it cannot be a difference in memory for the sentences per se that accounts for the difference in recognizability, but rather differences in *interpretation* which account for the differential distinguishability between the two pairs.

The second role of schemata in remembering involves their use in reconstructing the original interpretation. Here, perhaps the best evidence comes from an experiment reported by Spiro (1977). Spiro designed his experiment to carefully discriminate between those inferences drawn at time of comprehension and those drawn at time of recall. In his experiment subjects read stories which they were led to believe were true. Then, after reading the stories subjects were given an additional piece of information which was either *consistent with the implications* of the story or *inconsistent with the implications* of the story. On later recall of the story, there was a general tendency for those with information inconsistent with the thrust of the story to *distort* their recall of the story so as to make it consistent with the later information. Moreover, this cannot entirely be due to a reinterpretation of the story at the time they received the additional information, since the longer the delay between the addition of the information and the recall test the greater the degree of distortion. In terms of the framework under discussion in this paper, this suggests that the longer between presentation and recall the fewer memorial fragments are available and the more the subjects must rely on their generic knowledge of what situations like those for which they have memorial fragments are like—that is, their schemata. The less consistent their original information from the typical, the more room (and need) for distortion.

Thus just as comprehension is presumed to be identical to the process of selecting and verifying conceptual schemata to account for the situation to be understood, so, the process of remembering involves as a major component the process of selecting and verifying an appropriate configuration of schemata to account for the memorial fragments found in memory. Such an account constitutes a recollection.

There is an important omission in this account of remembering. Note, it has been tacitly assumed in our account of perception (and therefore in that for remembering), that data present themselves passively to the sensory system directly exciting certain low-level "features" and that comprehension (or perception) involves the discovery of an adequate account of the spatio-temporal pattern of excitation of these low-level feature detectors. Similarly, in this account of remembering, it sounds as if there is, somehow, a set of memorial fragments which are presenting themselves to the memory system for interpretation and that the process of interpretation (selecting potential configurations of schemata and verifying that they are consistent with the stored data—memory fragments) is simply all there is to remembering. *This is quite obviously false for both understanding and remembering.* First consider the case of perception, then I will show how this extends to remembering.

Perception is goal directed. We do not passively wait for some stimuli to arrive and then, at that late date, attempt an interpretation. Instead, we actively seek information relevant to our current needs and goals. When we want a phone number we do not merely interpret our current sensory input as if it were a phone number but we actively *seek* information to be so interpreted. This "information seeking" process must go hand in hand with the information interpretation process. Just as expectations (embodied by certain activated schemata) can serve an important function in guiding our process of interpreting input which happens to reach our sensory organs, so too, do these same schemata guide our *informa-*

*tion seeking.* Not only do schemata tell us *what to see,* but they also tell us *where to see it.* I have not emphasized this aspect of the comprehension process.

If perception is goal directed, then remembering is even more so. In remembering, we are not merely perusing around our memories making sense about what "happens to come to mind." The ordinary case of memory is probably more akin to the process of looking for a phone number than watching a TV program or reading a text. Here the "search" problem is severe. Whatever memory probe or question we have available will bring some fragments of memory to mind (activate some of the appropriate memory structures). Perhaps sometimes this is enough—the interpretation of this fragment of memory is enough to respond to the question at hand. More often, however, this is probably not the case. The appropriate fragments are just not "in front of us" impinging on our memory interpretation system. In these cases, we must instigate a *search.* Just as in the case of looking for a telephone number, the search is not random. Rather, it must be guided by schemata, which represent the layout of our memories in the same way as schemata encode the layout of our homes or our telephone books. When we want a phone number, we realize we might be able to use a phone book. We thus might search our house for the phone book. Knowing the layout of our house, we know the typical location of the phone book and will immediately go there to find it. Note the location of the phone book is a sub-goal in the search for the phone number in much the same way that a "retrieval context" is a sub-goal in a memory search. When we find the phone book we use our knowledge of the structure of the phone book to guide us to the appropriate region of the book. Finally, once there, we use our expectations about the structure and meaning of phone numbers to construct an appropriate interpretation of the symbols on the page. Not much work has been done on mapping out the search paths through memory while trying to recollect events after a long delay. Work by Williams (1977) would seem to be a promising approach along these lines.

## Schemata and Learning

One of the central problems of a schema theory is a specification of the process (or processes) whereby new schemata are developed. Even if it is granted that a set of "hand-crafted" procedures *could* carry out the tasks assigned to them by schema theories, it remains to be shown that plausible learning procedures could result in such a set of schemata. There is currently very little known about what kinds of learning principles would be necessary for such a development. From a logical point of view, three basically different modes of learning are possible in a schema based system.

1. Traces of comprehension processes form a sort of learning inasmuch as upon having understood some situation or perceived some event, we can

retrieve stored information about that situation or event. Such learning corresponds roughly to "fact learning." Rumelhart and Norman (1978) have called this learning *accretion*.

2. Existing schemata may *evolve* or undergo change to make that more in tune with experience. Our concepts presumably undergo continual change as we gain more experience with new exemplars. This corresponds to the elaboration and refinement of concepts through continued experience. Rumelhart and Norman (1978) have called this sort of learning *tuning*.

3. The third sort of learning involves the *creation* of new schemata. This involves the actual development of new concepts. There are, in a schema theory, at least two ways in which new concepts can be generated: they can be patterned on existing schemata or they can (in principle) be induced from experience. Rumelhart and Norman call learning of new schemata *restructuring*.

I now turn to a discussion of these three modes of learning and the conditions under which they occur.

*Accretion.* Learning by accretion is probably the most common sort of learning. It is also the sort of learning that has least effect on the operation of the system. Whenever new information is encountered there is assumed to be some trace of the comprehension process laid down in memory. This memory trace is the basis for recollections. Generally, these traces are assumed to be partial copies of the original instantiated schemata. Thus, memory traces are assumed to be very much like schemata themselves. They differ only inasmuch as they are fragmentary and they have representations for particular aspects of the original situation in place of the variables of the original schemata. Thus, as we experience the world, we store, as a natural side effect of comprehension, traces that can serve as the basis of future recall. Later, during retrieval, we can use this information to reconstruct an interpretation of the original experience—thereby remembering the experience.

Such an accumulation of knowledge is the normal sort of learning. Although the accumulation of a substantial body of knowledge may be necessary for more fundamental kinds of learning, it causes no new schemata to be formed. Such learning occurs whenever our schemata available at the time of the original experience are deemed adequate for the interpretation of the experience. When we encounter a situation in which currently available schemata do not prove adequate, there is the possibility of schema change and thus a modification of the very devices through which we experience the world.

*Tuning.* Tuning involves the actual modification or evolution of existing schemata. There are essentially three ways in which schemata can evolve. First, our knowledge of the variable constraints and default values can be upgraded continuously as we continue to use the schemata. Whenever we find a case in which we determine that a certain schema offers an adequate account of a particular situation, we can modify the variable constraints and default values in the direction of the current experience. This will make the schema sensitive to slow changes in the population of cases to which the schema is applied. As this process continues it will continue to sharpen the variables and default values to make the schema better represent the population of situation to which it is applied. Note, however, that this sort of tuning will only occur when the schema is deemed to offer an adequate account of the situation at hand. This change must be slow because cases which deviate widely from the appropriate variable constraints and default values will not be accommodated by the schema in question.

The second sort of tuning involves replacing a constant portion of a schema with a variable one—that is, adding a new variable to a schema. This sort of schema modification amounts to *concept generalization*—making a schema more generally applicable. Presumably, the occasion for such learning is the discovery, at some point in time, that a particular schema would offer a good account for a particular situation if only some presumably constant feature of the schema were allowed to vary. To the degree that a constant is merely a variable with very tight constraints, this can be seen as a special case of the previous kind of tuning, namely one in which the change is from a variable with highly constrained constraints becoming one with somewhat more relaxed constraints.

The third sort of tuning is, in a sense, the opposite of the last one, namely, the process of making a variable into a constant, or specializing the use of the concept. One occasion for such learning would be the discovery that certain "outlier" situations are better accounted for by other schemata and thus that the apparent variable is better thought of as a constant. As before, this can also be thought of as a special case of changing variable constraints—in this case tightening them.

*Restructuring.*   If accretion and tuning were the only learning mechanisms, no new schemata could be created. The third learning mode discussed above involves the creation of new schemata. There are basically two ways in which new schemata can be formed. Rumelhart and Norman (1978) term these *patterned generation* and *schema induction*.

Patterned generation involves the creation of a new schema by copying an old one with a few modifications. Such learning is, in essence, learning by analogy. We learn that some new concept is like an old one except for a few differences. New schemata can differ from old ones by having variables where the old one had constants (a generalization of the old schema), by having constants where an old schema had variables (a further specification of the old schema), or by substituting a new variable or constant for an old variable or constant of the original schema. Once a new schema is created by such processes, the process of tuning will continue to modify the newly created schema to bring it more into line with experience. Rumelhart and Norman (1981) have given a more detailed account of learning new schemata by analogy with old ones.

The second way in which new schemata can be formed is through the process of schema induction. The notion here is that if a certain spatio-temporal configuration of schemata occur repeatedly, there is reason to assume that the particular configuration forms a meaningful concept and a schema can be formed which consists of just that configuration. This, of course, is the classical continguity learning. It is interesting, that in spite of the ubiquity of the notion of contiguity learning in learning theories of the past, there is no real *need* for it in a schema based system. Provided we begin with a sufficiently general set of schemata, the processes of tuning, accretion and patterned generation can carry us a long way. Schema induction does cause some difficulty for the notion of schemata as I have outlined them. In order for schema induction to work properly, we must posit some aspect of the system sensitive to the recurrence of configurations of schemata which do not, at the time they occurred, match any existing schemata. Such a system is not a natural part of a schema based system.

## Schemata and Solving Problems

Schemata play a central role in all of our reasoning processes. Most of the reasoning we do apparently *does not* involve the application of general purpose reasoning skills. Rather, it seems that most of our reasoning ability is tied to particular schemata related to particular bodies of knowledge.

One of my favorite demonstrations of the critical role of schemata in reasoning comes from the work of Wason and Johnson-Laird (1972) and some more recent replications and extensions of their work carried out by Roy D'Andrade.[1] Subjects in D'Andrade's experiments were given one of two formally equivalent problems to solve. Half of the subjects were given the task illustrated in Figure 5.2. Subjects were shown the four cards illustrated in the figure and told that

> All labels made at Pica's Custom Label Factory have a letter printed on one side, and a number printed on the other side. As part of your job as a label checker at Pica's Custom Label Factory, you have the job of making sure that all labels with a vowel printed on one side have an odd number printed on the other side. Which of the labels . . . would you have to turn over to make sure the label was printed correctly?

Only 13% of the subjects correctly indicated that cards 2 and 4 (the cards marked with an 8 and an E, respectively) must be checked. Card 4 must, of course, be checked because it may have an even number on the back. Card 2 must also be checked since it might have a vowel on the back and thus violate rule. No other cards must be checked.

---

[1]Roy D'Andrade has kindly given me access to the data from his as yet unpublished experiment.

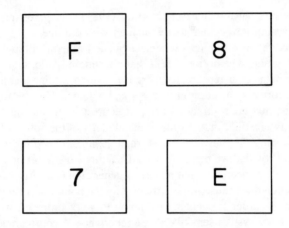

FIG. 5.2.   Stimuli presented to the "Label Factory" subjects.

Here we have a classical failure of human reasoning. It has been argued that this is a case of our interpreting the simple conditional as a bi-conditional. In any case, results like these are often used to illustrate the weakness of the human reasoning system. However, the results of the second part of D'Andrade's experiment point up the fallacy in this conclusion. Figure 5.3 illustrates the stimuli for these subjects. Subjects were told that

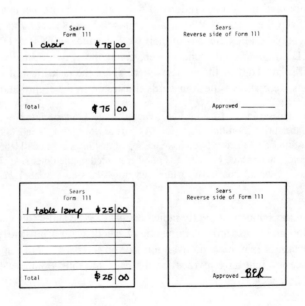

FIG. 5.3.   Stimuli for the "Sears" subjects.

As part of your job as an assistant at Sears, you have the job of checking sales receipts to make sure that any sale of over $30.00 has been approved by the section manager. (This is a rule of the store.) The amount of the sale is written on the front of the form. Which of the forms . . . would you have to turn over to make sure the sales clerks had followed the regulation?

In this case nearly 70% indicated the correct forms, forms 1 and 2, the $75 and the unsigned forms. Formally, these two problems are identical. Yet, when phrased in terms of the familiar setting of the Sears store, over five times as many subjects were able to correctly solve the problem. What is the difference here? Why do people appear not to understand the meaning of "if" in the first case and understand it nearly perfectly in the second? In terms of schema theory the answer is rather straightforward. The first case is unfamiliar and subjects have no schemata into which to incorporate the problem and therefore can bring only very general problem solving strategies to bear on the problem. The second case more nearly approximates a "real life" problem solving situation. Once we can "understand" the situation by encoding it in terms of a relatively rich set of schemata, the conceptual constraints of the schemata can be brought into play and the problem readily solved. It is as if the schema already contains all of the reasoning mechanism ordinarily required in the use of the schemata. Thus, understanding the problem and solving it it nearly the same thing.

## Schemata and Social Cognition

Although I have not yet directly addressed the social psychological issues with which this book is primarily concerned, it should be obvious that I assume that the same principles of perception, comprehension, remembering, learning and thinking apply as well to the social world as to any other aspects of the world. Social knowledge, beliefs and attitudes cannot be separated from knowledge and beliefs about the world in general. Thus, I assume that social knowledge, like all other forms of knowledge, exists in the form of schemata. For example, our perceptions of people are, I assume, determined in much the same way as our perception of other objects. We observe certain characteristics of an individual, on the basis of those characteristics certain schemata are activated, these schemata, in turn, make predictions about the motives of the person's actions and other aspects of the person's behavior. If one of the active schemata offers a satisfactory account of the person's behavior, it is assumed that, indeed, the schema offers the correct account—even if there are many other possible interpretations of the person's behavior. In this way, we *see* people perform motivated actions—even though the motivations are not directly observed.

Similarly, our schemata shape our memories of social events in much the same way that they shape our memories of other events. Thus, for example, we are more likely to remember that a librarian wears glasses than that a waitress wears glasses whether or not the individual in question was wearing glasses when we observed them. This is presumably because the default for a librarian is to wear glasses, whereas the default for a waitress is not to wear glasses. We should expect similar "distortions" in our memory for all social events.

Social learning should also occur according to the same principles of schema learning that I have discussed above. In general, when we enter a new social situation in which no existing schema exists, I would expect that a new schema would be created by analogy with existing schemata. Thus, there should be a propensity to view new situations as variations on older ones. I would also expect that certain aspects of our older schemata, irrelevant to the newer situation, would nevertheless be carried over to the newer schemata and applied to the new situation. Thus, for example, a new social situation interpreted as variation on a *formal* situation might well accrue attitudes developed toward the older situation even though there is nothing in the newer situation to account for such attitudes. This follows because when new schemata are created by analogy much of the internal structure of the old schema is just "copied" over to the new schema. In time, if the evidence in the new situation contradicts those aspects due to the older schema the new schema will evolve and become *tuned* to the new situation.

## CONCLUSION

It was my intent in this paper to give the reader unfamiliar with schemata an intuition with which he/she could interpret the increasing number of papers employing these conceptualizations. I have aimed from generality rather than specificity in my account. I have tried to show the many domains to which the concept of a schema has been applied and the heuristic value of thinking about psychological problems in terms of schemata. The papers cited above provide a more detailed account of schemata and more definite examples of their applicability. Although the development of schema based theories such as the ones I mention above is not yet mature and these ideas have not yet proved their usefulness, I believe that they offer the most promising leads for those of us interested in the difficult problems posed when we try to apply psychological theories directly to socially relevant domains.

## REFERENCES

Barclay, J. R., Bransford, J. D., Franks, J. J., McCarrell, N. S., & Nitsch, K. Comprehension and semantic flexibility. *Journal of Verbal Learning and Verbal Behavior*, 1974, *13*, 471–481.

Bartlett, F. C. *Remembering*. Cambridge: Cambridge University Press, 1932.

Bobrow, D. G., & Norman, D. A. Some principles of memory schemata. In D. G. Bobrow & A. M. Collins (Eds.), *Representation and understanding: Studies in cognitive science*. New York: Academic Press, 1975.

Bransford, J. D., Barclay, J. R., & Franks, J. J. Sentence memory: A constructive versus interpretive approach. *Cognitive Psychology*, 1972, *3*, 193–209.

Bransford, J. D., & Johnson, M. K. Considerations of some problems of comprehension. In W. G. Chase (Ed.), *Visual information processing*. New York: Academic Press, 1973.

Bruner, J. S., & Potter, M. Inference in visual recognition, *Science*, 1964, *144*, 424–425.

Chafe, W. L. Givenness, contrastiveness, definiteness, subjects, topics, and point of view. In C. N. Li (Ed.), *Subject and topic*. New York: Academic Press, 1976.

Fillmore, C. J. An alternative to checklist theories of meaning. *Proceedings of the First Annual Meeting of the Berkeley Linguistics Society*, 1975, *1*, 123–131.

Head, H. *Aphasia and kindred disorders of speech*. Cambridge, 1926.

Kaplan, R. M. A general syntactic processor. In R. Rustin (Ed.), *Natural language processing*. New York: Algorithmics Press, 1973.

McClelland, J. L., & Rumelhart, D. E. An interactive activation model of context effects in letter perception, Part I: An account of basic findings. *Psychological Review*, 1981, 375–407.

Minsky, M. A framework for representing knowledge. In P. H. Winston (Ed.), *The psychology of computer vision*. New York: McGraw-Hill, 1975.

Moore, J., & Newell, A. How can MERLIN understand? In L. W. Gregg (Ed.), *Knowledge and cognition*. Hillsdale, N.J.: Lawrence Erlbaum Associates, 1973.

Norman, D. A., & Rumelhart, D. E. Memory and knowledge. In D. A. Norman, D. E. Rumelhart, & The LNR Research Group, *Explorations in cognition*. San Francisco: Freeman, 1975.

Palmer, S. E. Visual perception and world knowledge: Notes on a model of sensory-cognitive interaction. In D. A. Norman, D. E. Rumelhart, & The LNR Research Group, *Explorations in cognition*. San Francisco: Freeman, 1975.

Piaget, J. [*The origins of intelligence in children*] (M. Cook, trans.). New York: International Universities Press, 1952.

Rumelhart, D. E. Notes on a schema for stories. In D. G. Bobrow & A. M. Collins (Eds.), *Representation and understanding: Studies in cognitive science*. New York: Academic Press, 1975.

Rumelhart, D. E. Toward an interactive model of reading. In S. Dornic (Ed.), *Attention and performance VI*. Hillsdale, N.J.: Lawrence Erlbaum Associates, 1977.

Rumelhart, D. E. Understanding understanding. University of California San Diego Center for Human Information Processing, Technical Report 100, 1981.

Rumelhart, D. E., & McClelland, J. L. An interactive activation model of context effects in letter perception, Part II: The contextual enhancement effect and some tests and extensions of the model. *Psychological Review*, 1982, in press.

Rumelhart, D. E., & Norman, D. A. Accretion, tuning and restructuring: Three modes of learning. In J. W. Cotton & R. Klatzky (Eds.), *Semantic factors in cognition*. Hillsdale, New Jersey: Lawrence Erlbaum Associates, 1978.

Rumelhart, D. E., & Norman, D. A. Analogical processes in learning. In J. R. Anderson (Ed.), *Cognitive skills and their acquisition*. Hillsdale, N.J.: Lawrence Erlbaum Associates, 1981.

Rumelhart, D. E., & Ortony, A. The representation of knowledge in memory. In R. C. Anderson, R. J. Spiro, & W. E. Montague (Eds.), *Schooling and the acquisition of knowledge*. Hillsdale, N.J.: Lawrence Erlbaum Associates, 1977.

Schank, R. C., & Abelson, R. P. Scripts, plans, and knowledge. *Advance Papers of the Fourth International Joint Conference on Artificial Intelligence*. Tbilisi, Georgia, USSR, 1975, pp. 151–157.

Schank, R., & Abelson, R. *Scripts, plans, goals and understanding: An inquiry into human knowledge structures*. Hillsdale, New Jersey: Lawrence Erlbaum Associates, 1977.

Spiro, R. J. Inferential reconstruction in memory for connected discourse. In R. C. Anderson, R. J. Spiro & W. E. Montague (Eds.), *Schooling and the acquisition of knowledge*. Hillsdale, N.J.: Lawrence Erlbaum Associates, 1977.

Tulving, E., & Thomson, D. M. Encoding specificity and retrieval processes in episodic memory. *Psychological Review*, 1973, *80*, 352–373.

Wason, P., & Johnson-Laird, P. N. *Psychology of reasoning: Structure and content*. Cambridge: Harvard University Press, 1972.

Williams, M. D. Some observations on the process of retrieval from very long term memory (Doctoral dissertation, University of California, San Diego, 1977). *Dissertation Abstracts International*, 1977.

Winograd, T. Frame representations and the declarative/procedural controversy. In D. Bobrow & A. Collins (Eds.), *Representation and understanding: Studies in cognitive science*. New York: Academic Press, 1975.

# 6

## Cognitive Heuristics*

Steven J. Sherman
Eric Corty
*Indiana University*

**Contents**

---

*The authors would like to thank Reid Hastie and John Castellan for their helpful comments and advice.

**189**

The study of decision making is an area in which new understandings can be of great importance. Everyday we are faced with decisions both large ("Should I buy that house?") and small ("Should I bring an umbrella today?") under conditions of uncertainty. Those in positions of power are typically faced with decisions that have great consequences. Obviously, different choices may have different outcomes, and it is important for our well-being that the best choice possible be made. By understanding the decision-making process one can learn what errors are made or biases are followed and then, it is hoped, correct them in the future.

## HISTORICAL APPROACHES TO DECISION MAKING

Over the years, several different approaches have been taken to arrive at an understanding of human judgment and decision making. Early work was dominated by a formal model approach usually employing linear and normative models of judgment (see Slovic & Lichtenstein, 1971 for a review). In this approach, statistical decision models are applied to human judgment. For example, the Bayesian model normatively describes what the rational or statistically optimal response should be in a judgmental situation. In approaches such as this, some model of judgment is used as a standard against which to measure the success of a judge.

Other formal approaches have attempted to develop models not of what people ought to do but of what they do. Brunswik (1940) used a multiple linear regression model to describe judgments, and more recent work (e.g., Dawes & Corrigan, 1974; Zeleny, 1976) has discussed similar multiattribute utility models of judgment.

Several problems have been pointed out in discussions of these formal models of judgment. Wallsten (1980) sees three basic shortcomings of such models: They are demonstrably false in that they don't always describe what people do; many of the models are too robust to be falsified; the models aren't concerned with the intervening process underlying judgments.

It is basically in response to this third criticism that alternative approaches began to emerge. Anderson (1974a, 1974b) developed information integration theory as a unified, general approach to judgment. According to this approach, judges first evaluate relevant stimuli and then combine or integrate them into an overall judgment. The processes for integrating information follow simple rules of ordinary algebra, and Anderson has used adding, averaging, and multiplying models of information integration. The Anderson approach presents a conception of the human judge as an integrator of stimulus information and uses simple algebraic models to describe the integration process. As such, it goes beyond the normative models in trying to describe the psychological processes underlying judgments. While Anderson does provide ways to assess the weights of various kinds of information and to determine when information is combined in an additive or averaging manner, there is little in the way of theoretical content. The description is basically in terms of the input-output relations of decision behavior and not in terms of underlying process.

Much of the more recent work in decision theory has been guided by a different kind of approach—cognitive and information processing theories. The conception of the decision maker that is assumed by this approach is that of a general information processing system with limited capacity. The major concern here is with the process of decision making and with the limitations of decision makers. Judgmental heuristic use is characteristic of this kind of approach. It proposes that people rely on a few simplifying rules or heuristic principles in making judgments, and it is this approach that will be the focus of the present chapter.

This approach may be thought of as similar to other recent cognitive information processing approaches (e.g., Anderson & Bower, 1973; Anderson, 1976). While all these approaches share a view of human judgment that involves attention, information extraction, encoding, retrieval, and the like, the judgmental heuristic approach is less committed to specifics. There are no precise rules of capacity or exact models of information retrieval. As such, it has all the advantages and disadvantages of a looser approach. Often such a flexible approach allows great latitude in thinking and research so that the end result is a level of understanding that is greater than when one starts with a rigid and precise model. Witness the contribution of dissonance theory (as opposed to congruity or balance theory) to understanding attitude change.

The judgmental heuristic approach has several general advantages. As a data driven approach, it is sensitive to what people do as they make judgments. By analyzing the kind of information that judges use, this approach does have the potential for identifying the processes that underlie decision making. In addition, by describing what people do as they make judgments and the kind of information used, the judgmental heuristic approach has the potential for making suggestions to solve problems in decision making and to improve judgments.

Yet there are also problems. Formal theories and normative approaches to decision making suffer from being too specific, too limited in scope, and too hard to generalize. The judgmental heuristic approach (and other similar process oriented approaches) does provide a general understanding of human judgment, but it is too vague and difficult to test in a rigorous way. While, as we shall see, the implications are compelling, they are typically not stated in a precise fashion. Thus, the heuristic approach often has little predictive value. There are rarely suggestions for the independent assessment of key aspects of judgments (e.g., availability or representativeness), and there are few guidelines to tell us when and under what conditions each heuristic will be applied. One goal of the present chapter is to point out some of these problems and limitations of the judgmental heuristic approach and to suggest ways to improve it by further specifying the principles and processes.

It should be mentioned that a most desirable approach to human judgment would be one that combines a formal model and a processing focus. In recent years, some gains have been made in this direction. Both Castellan and Edgell (1973) and Wallsten (1977) have developed models of judgment in a probability learning task that are based on a sampling approach to processing uncertain information. Castellan and Edgell present a scanning model with two stages involving hypotheses about the appropriate cue dimension and about which response will be correct given that cue dimension. It suggests that only part of the total information is attended to. Attention is a function of the validity of the information. Wallsten proposes a similar model, but suggests that judges attend to information as a function of its salience and that they search until some criterion is reached. Both Castellan and Edgell (1973) and Wallsten (1977) take their general information processing assumptions and use them in a more formal model that is then evaluated. It would appear that models such as these, which combine an emphasis on general information processing principles and processes in judgment and on the specificity of a formal model, will be necessary for a complete understanding of human judgment and decision making.

The recent work in decision making that focuses on the processes underlying judgment owes much to the work of Kahneman and Tversky. Instead of approaching decision making by stating normative principles and seeing whether people were adequate intuitive statisticians, Kahneman and Tversky adopted a problem solving approach. They sought to understand decisions and judgments in terms of general principles of information processing. In part, this involves identifying and analyzing typical judgmental biases and errors. The assumption that people are rational and would conform to normative theories gave way to an approach that considered the dynamics and limitations of the decision approach. There was concern not only with what decisions were made but how these decisions were generated. Following their seminal work (Kahneman & Tversky, 1972, 1973; Tversky & Kahneman, 1973), the field of decision making research has burgeoned. Prior to 1973, very few books and articles on human judgment and decision making were written. Since that time, the number has been growing at an increasing rate. Kahneman and Tversky identified the errors that people made in decision tasks. From the consistency of error and bias that they saw, they were able to describe a set of heuristics or rules of thumb that seemed to govern the process of decision making.

Rules to guide decisions may be very specific, such as the rules of thumb that guide game-playing. For example, "sacrifice bunt in the bottom of the last inning with the score tied, no outs, and a man at first base" is a principle that guides managerial strategy in baseball. "Finesse the queen missing 5, but don't finesse missing 4" is a rule for bridge players trying to handle a suit. Students have specific test-taking rules of thumb for multiple choice exams, e.g., "answers with 'always' or 'never' in them are wrong." Aside from rules that guide specific judgments and decisions, there are more general principles that are involved in a wide variety of judgments. These are the judgmental heuristics that will be analyzed in this chapter. Heuristics may be thought of as general purpose judgmental tools that can be applied in a wide variety of decision-making circumstances. As general principles for reducing complex tasks to simpler judgmental operations, heuristics do not involve a formal or exhaustive analysis of the information at hand. They are judgmental procedures that overemphasize particular properties of the data and ignore other properties in order to make decisions or to generate probability estimates or estimates of population parameters. For example, judges may use the ease of accessibility of a category as an indicator of its frequency (the availability heuristic). They may thus decide that more states begin with the letter N than M because examples of the former come to mind more quickly and easily. Judges may also use the similarity of a sample to various populations in order to decide on category membership (the representativeness heuristic). Thus, a faculty member described as quiet, shy, and interested in poetry will be judged as more likely to be in the fine arts department than in the physics department since he fits more closely the typical fine arts professor.

As an approach to decision making that emerged from the development of cognitive psychology as a discipline, research on judgmental heuristics is concerned with internal processes, cognitive limitations, and how the internal processes are shaped by these limitations. There are many general information processing principles that are important in understanding the use and consequences of judgmental heuristics. In making any judgment or evaluation, people rarely attend to all available information or draw upon all possible information from memory. Instead, there is selectivity in attentional, processing, and retrieval phases of decision making. Heuristic principles involve such selectivity. The particular type of information drawn upon will, of course, depend on the type of judgment to be made (e.g., comprehension, similarity, inference, categorization) and on the relative accessibility of information. The various heuristic principles can be categorized in terms of the kind of selective accessing of information and the kind of cognitive processing involved. For example, the representativeness heuristic involves judgments of similarity and matching sample information to an abstracted prototype. The availability heuristic is concerned with issues of the determinants and implications of information accessibility. Anchoring and adjustment is a heuristic principle involving the weighting of information processed at various times and the interpretation of later information in light of previous impressions. Finally, the simulation heuristic can be understood as an instance of script processing.

It is important to realize that the use of heuristics should be viewed in this broader conceptual and theoretical cognitive context rather than being considered mystical bases for decisions that have little in common with other kinds of cognitive functioning. As we shall see, heuristic use is concerned with all the general characteristics and stages of information processing. Attention, encoding, retrieval, reconstruction, and the use of schematic or configural representations of events are all involved in heuristic principles. Thus, heuristic use is consistent with the contemporary models of information processing.

In focusing on the biases and errors that result from using heuristic principles, this approach to understanding decision making is similar to that which underlies other research in cognitive psychology. The general approach of focusing on errors to understand process has, for example, been used in studies of memory. Visually presented items tend to produce errors that are acoustically related in short-term memory studies (e.g., substituting B for P or bad for mad). This has led to the conclusion that items are acoustically encoded (Baddeley, 1966; Conrad, 1964, 1970). On the other hand, semantic errors (e.g., substituting angry for mad) emerge in long-term memory studies. This evidence is used to support general propositional models that suggest that meaning is retained while surface features are lost (Anisfeld & Knapp, 1968; Baddeley, 1966, 1970).

The impact of Kahneman and Tversky is not solely due to the putative correctness of their findings. As Pitz (1977) points out, some of Kahneman and Tversky's experiments and examples seem almost magical. Both the subject and the reader of the experiment give a seemingly reasonable answer to an apparently innocuous question only to learn, mirabile visu, that their answer is wrong. The impact is often humbling. The cleverness of Kahneman and Tversky's examples make them both highly memorable and useful for purposes of teaching. This in no small way has accounted for the popularity of both their general approach and their specific work.

With the rise of research on heuristics, the early view of humans as rational information processors has changed. Rather it has become apparent that in making judgments of categorization, probability, or quantity estimation we rely on simplifying rules. These rules are often successful in reducing complex judgments to simpler tasks, but they can also leave us victims of characteristic errors.

Heuristics are useful because humans are limited information processors. Hogarth (1980) points out several such information-processing limitations. (1) Humans are selective in the information that they perceive. Obviously, if a piece of information is necessary for solving a problem but it has not been selected out of all the impinging information, problem solving will be limited. (2) Humans generally process their selected information in a sequential manner. The consequences of this for information processing ability are twofold. First of all, the order in which information is processed can affect our perceptions as in primacy and recency effects (Jones & Goethals, 1972). Secondly, when information is presented sequentially people come to see some relation between events. In fact, people often infer a causal relationship where none exists. (3) Not only is our attention selective, but so is our memory. Not all of that which we perceive is remembered and not all of that remembered is remembered accurately. Memory is an active process in which reconstructions can take place to yield a more unified, schematic whole (Bransford & Franks, 1971; Jenkins, 1974). At the time of recall we can also be influenced to remember events non-veridically. For example, Loftus and Palmer (1974) showed that after presenting information about an accident they could cause subjects to increase their estimates of the speed of the autos at the time of impact by asking how fast they were going when they *smashed* into one another as opposed to when they *bumped* into one another. Clearly, when a decision is based on inaccurate information it cannot be an optimal one.

A fourth limitation of which Hogarth (1980) speaks is the topic of the present chapter—heuristics. Heuristics are simplifying procedures for processing information. Under some conditions they allow one to make reasonable decisions with little effort. But when they are applied indiscriminately, they lead to characteristic errors. And heuristics do get applied indiscriminately. Unlike algorithms, heuristics are informal and intuitive and get applied, often without awareness, to decision-making situations. In a sense, we apply heuristics in the same way that a good chess player or carpenter apply their skills. They would be hardpressed to state the rules governing their decisions, yet the outcome is generally as desired. An algorithm, on the other hand, is a step by step procedure that is invoked for solving a problem. An algorithm, unlike a heuristic, is a consciously applied problem-solving technique. In addition, heuristics are applied in a more unpredictable way. Different heuristics may be applied to the exact same problem or to the same problem type as the time and context change.

The prevailing view of heuristics is that they involve errors of cold (ir)rationality rather than errors due to motivational factors. Instead of indicating ego-defensive or self-enhancing processes, heuristics lead to characteristic biases because, as simplifying rules of thumb, they often lead decision makers to ignore relevant information. Heuristic use, and their associated errors, have been characterized as almost unavoidable. Heuristics are used when they are penalized directly, when they lead to poor decisions with negative long-term outcomes, and when the decision maker is knowledgeable. It is this almost mechanical and instinctive use that makes heuristics of interest. The study of heuristics can lead to a better understanding of human cognitive processes and potentially to better decision making. By mapping the errors that people make, it should become possible to expose limitations and to help people correct them. In fact, attention is being turned to this very area (Kahneman & Tversky, 1979b; Nisbett, Krantz, Jepson, & Fong, 1982; Nisbett & Ross, 1980).

## ORGANIZATION OF THE CHAPTER

The goals of the present chapter are to review the relevant literature and, more importantly, to provide some conceptual integration by identifying common and general themes and specifying the functions served by heuristics. In doing this, new perspectives on the operation and limitations of using heuristic principles will be spelled out as well as suggestions for directions of future work.

The chapter will begin by reviewing the conceptions of and research related to four heuristic principles: Representativeness, availability, simulation, and anchoring and adjustment. Work from a variety of substantive areas of social psychology will be interpreted in terms of the operation of these principles of judgment, and the operation of these principles will be demonstrated in gambling decisions. Following this review, we attempt to provide a framework within which to understand in general terms the principles of operation and characteristic errors associated with heuristic use.

One of the problems in treatments of heuristic principles has been a failure to specify in a clear manner the distinctions among the various heuristic principles and to specify the conditions under which each will be used. As a way to begin to resolve this problem, we spell out the distinction between availability and representativeness, and draw a parallel between the use of these principles and the distinction between exemplar matching and prototype matching in categorical judgments. This is used as a way to understand the conditions under which each heuristic principle will be the predominant choice for judgments.

Another important and unresolved issue with respect to the use of heuristic principles in judgment is a specification of the conditions under which heuristic principles are likely to be adopted. One issue involves the kinds of decisions and situations that typically lead a judge to rely on heuristic principles. A second issue concerns the level of cognitive functioning necessary for the use of these principles. Are they simplifying rules and short-cuts used mostly by the beginning and unsophisticated decision maker, or are they advanced tools that sophisticated judges use as a way to handle complex decision problems? A section of the chapter is devoted to this issue of whether heuristic use represents a primitive or advanced stage of functioning, and speculation about the development of heuristic principles in children is made.

Finally, the issue of the errors associated with heuristic use is addressed. Are there ways to reduce or eliminate such errors? Why do we continue to use these principles if they lead to such widespread errors of judgment? Answers to these questions will ultimately get us back again to the issue of the functions served by using heuristic principles.

## A REVIEW OF HEURISTIC PRINCIPLES

Tversky and Kahneman (1974) outlined the important heuristic principles that are employed for reducing complex judgments to simpler operations. In all cases, these judgmental heuristics allow the decision maker to focus on a limited set of the properties of the information to arrive at decisions.

## Representativeness

In judging the probability that object A belongs to class B or that event A originates from process B, people typically don't use a full analysis of the information at hand. Rather, an object is judged as likely to belong to a category by the extent to which it represents the essential features of the parent population or the generating process. The degree to which any sample event or sample statistic is similar to the perceived population parameter describes the representativeness of that event or statistic. Kahneman and Tversky (1972) have delighted us with many examples of the representativeness heuristic.

1. "All families of six children in a city were surveyed. In 72 families the exact order of births of boys and girls was G B G B B G.

What is your estimate of the number of families surveyed in which the exact order of births was B G B B B B?" (p. 432)

While the 2 sequences are equally likely, they aren't equally representative of the assumed population proportion (50% boys and girls). Over 80% of the subjects judged the first sequence as more likely.

2. "There are two programs in a high school. Boys are a majority (65%) in Program A, and a minority (45%) in program B. There is an equal number of classes in each of the two programs.

You enter a class at random, and observe that 55% of the students are boys. What is your best guess—does the class belong to program A or to program B?" (p. 433)

Since boys are a majority in program A and since 55% represents this majority relationship, the given class is more representative of A than B. Over 75% of subjects judged the class as belonging to A (it is actually slightly more likely to belong to B).

3. On each round of a game, 20 marbles are distributed at random among five children: Alan, Ben, Carl, Dan, and Ed. Consider the following distributions:

|      | I |      | II |
|------|---|------|----|
| Alan | 4 | Alan | 4  |
| Ben  | 4 | Ben  | 4  |
| Carl | 5 | Carl | 4  |
| Dan  | 4 | Dan  | 4  |
| Ed   | 3 | Ed   | 4  |

In many rounds of the game, will there be more results of type I or type II? (p. 434)

While the equal distribution of marbles is more likely, it appears too lawful— not representative of a random process. A distribution that departs somewhat from perfect equality appears to capture the random process better. Thus, nearly 70% of subjects wrongly viewed the unequal distribution as more probable.

## Overlooked and misused features of information

As with the use of most heuristic principles, representativeness may be a useful and effort-saving strategy. In general, more representative outcomes and samples are more probable. However, by focusing solely on the similarity of the sample to the parent population, other essential features of the information are often overlooked. Similarity between sample and population isn't always related to its likelihood, for other factors affect likelihood that have nothing to do with similarity. Much discussion of the use of the representativeness heuristic has focused on the kinds of information that are ignored in applying the principle and the kinds of errors that are commonly committed.

*Base rates.*    One factor that has a great effect on the likelihood of an event, but no effect on the representativeness of that event, is the prior probability of the outcome. When judgments are made primarily on the basis of representativeness, outcomes that "look like" a target category will be judged as likely members even when the prior probability of any outcome being a member of that category is extremely small. This insensitivity to base rates has been well documented by Kahneman and Tversky (1973). In one such demonstration, subjects were shown personality descriptions of individuals supposedly drawn at random from a group of 100 lawyers and engineers. Subjects estimated the likelihood that each person described was a lawyer or engineer. In one condition, subjects were told that the population consisted of 70 lawyers and 30 engineers. In the other case, the population was described as 30 lawyers and 70 engineers. Unless a description is perfectly valid or diagnostic, the likelihood of the person described being a lawyer is higher in the former case. However, subjects ignored base rates and gave identical estimates in the two cases. Category membership was decided solely on the basis of the extent to which a description was representative of a lawyer or an engineer. Even when the description was almost completely unin- formative and undiagnostic of either profession, subjects ignored the prior proba- bility in their judgments. Lyon and Slovic (1976) varied the problem setting, the distribution of prior probabilities, and the presentation and response formats and found that in all cases judges neglected prior probabilities and concentrated on the characteristics of the evidence.

More recently, Locksley, Hepburn, and Ortiz (1982) investigated the effects of social stereotypes on judgments of individuals. Since stereotypes are beliefs about the characteristics of a group, they correspond to base rate information that may be used in the judgments of individuals. Locksley et al. found evidence for the base rate fallacy. That is, individuating target information (even if weakly diagnostic) induced subjects to ignore their own stereotypic (base rate) beliefs.

Borgida and Brekke (1981) have written a recent review of the base rate fallacy in both attribution and prediction tasks. Aside from reviewing the many articles that report the base rate fallacy, Borgida and Brekke discuss the limiting conditions of this bias and the processes underlying it.

*Sample size.*    Another aspect of a sample that is unrelated to its representativeness, but is related to its likelihood, is its size. Sample size is a normatively important determinant of likelihood, but is irrelevant to how much a sample resembles the population. However, if people judge only by the similarity of the sample to the population parameter, this insensitivity to sample size will lead to errors of judgment. Thus, subjects erroneously believe that it is no more likely for a small hospital (with 15 births per day) to deliver as many as 60% boys on any day as it is for a large hospital with 45 births per day. Likewise, subjects believe that picking 4 out of 5 red balls is a better indicator that the actual distribution of balls was 2/3 red (as opposed to 2/3 white) than is picking 12 out of 20 red balls. This is because the proportion is larger in the former case and is more representative of a majority of red balls. Kahneman and Tversky (1972) also showed that in judgments of posterior probability, subjects ignored both population proportions and sample differences (two useful pieces of information) and based their estimates on sample ratios. It doesn't fit people's intuitions that sampling variation diminishes as sample size increases. Thus, the increase in murders in a city from 4 to 6 in a year is coded as a 50% increase and is seen as an important change requiring explanation and action. Even statisticians are not immune from this "belief in the law of small numbers." They, too, feel that small samples will be and should be quite representative of the parent population. Uecker and Kinney (1977) showed that external auditors failed to understand sampling error. They frequently chose a sample based on the error rate and ignored the number of observations on which the rate was based.

*Regression effects.*    The scores of subjects initially selected for extremely high or low values will fall closer to the mean on subsequent observations, and thus very good performers will appear to get worse, while poor performers will improve. Since subjects believe that the final predicted outcome should be highly representative of the initial input, they feel that the best estimates of later scores are the earlier scores, however extreme. Regression to the mean is thus interpreted as a real change requiring explanation. The coach who takes a team with a 1 and 20 won-loss record and wins the next 2 of 6 games is given credit for this "turnaround" since the outcome is not representative of the initial value.

*Gambler's fallacy.*    With regression effects, judges ignore initial expected values (based on the group mean) and expect any initial outcome, however extreme, to be repeated. The gambler's fallacy, another error based on application of the representativeness heuristic, is in a sense the opposite kind of error. In this case, judges strongly believe that the initial expected value will be achieved in the long run so that the final value will be representative of the initial expected value. Any early deviation from expectation will thus be followed by deviations in the opposite direction. By ignoring regression effects, subjects believe too much that deviations will be repeated. With the gambler's fallacy error, deviations are expected to be balanced out. Of course, in both cases the initial outcomes are given too much weight in predicting later outcomes. By ignoring regression effects, subjects base predictions entirely on initial outcomes and fail to regress them toward initial expectations. In the case of the gambler's fallacy, initial outcomes are used to determine what the future outcomes should be in order to balance out any deviations from expected value.

The gambler's fallacy is usually discussed in situations where judges predict randomly determined outcomes. If the first 4 (of 100) coin tosses are heads, subjects still believe that the final count after 100 flips will be 50-50, the number most representative of the expected value. Initial deviations must be balanced out for the final outcome to be maximally representative of the population value. Subjects also expect short sequences of coin flips to be representative of the expected outcome and to represent the randomness of the process by which they are generated. Thus, subjects believe that the sequence H T T H T H is more likely than H H H H H H (which isn't representative of the expected outcome) or H H H T T T (which isn't representative of the random process). While judges expect sample outcomes to represent population values and are overly surprised at violations of expectancy, they do not expect a perfect fit between expectancy and outcome. Thus, 50 heads and 50 tails in 100 flips seems more surprising than 51 heads and 49 tails. The latter better represents both the fairness of the coin and the randomness involved in tossing a coin. Similar errors are seen when subjects try to generate their own sequences of random events. Their sequences are always too representative and contain too many alternations of heads and tails and too few long runs.

*Reliability and validity.*    Sample size is one contributor to the reliability of evidence, and we have already seen that judgments are too insensitive to sample size. More confidence should be given to evidence based on many observations and smaller deviations should be expected with large samples. However, judges fail to do this. Likewise, when judges predict simply by matching prediction to impression, they fail to take the uncertainty of the evidence into account. Predictions should also be moderated by considerations of reliability. Even when both the reliability and validity of information is known to be low, it has been shown that judges will make much use of it. Kahneman and Tversky (1973) gave subjects a description of a college freshman. Two types of questions were asked: (1) an evaluation of the input (e.g., what percent of descriptions of freshmen would impress you more?); (2) prediction (e.g., what percent of freshmen will get a higher G.P.A.?). Since there is greater uncertainty associated with the latter kind of question, predictions should be more regressive than evaluations. Kahneman and Tversky suggest that unreliability or lack of validity of the descriptions shouldn't affect evaluations, but should affect predictions. However, subjects picked the most representative scores for both evaluation and prediction, showing a neglect of the confidence that could be placed in the information.

Trope (1978) also showed that judges employ the representativeness heuristic to the extent of ignoring the reliability of relevant information. Subjects made inferences about a target's attributes on the basis of information retrieved from memory. In making the inferences, subjects relied only on the diagnosticity of the information retrieved. Although subjects were aware of the unreliability of their memory, this had little effect on their inferences. Thus, judgments were far more extreme than those justified by normative considerations. This neglect of reliability has the additional effect of making people overconfident in their judgments. Overconfidence seems to be a characteristic outcome of using a variety of heuristic principles (Slovic, Fischhoff, & Lichtenstein, 1977).

In another demonstration of overreliance on representativeness, Kahneman and Tversky (1973) showed that predictions of a variable were no more regressive than mere translation of the variable from one scale to another. Subjects predicted the Grade Point Averages (G.P.A.s) of 10 students on the basis of a single percentage score. The percentile score was said to represent either the percentile G.P.A., the scores on a mental concentration test that was related to G.P.A. but gave different results from test to retest (i.e., had low reliability), or the scores on a humor test that was not very much related to G.P.A. (i.e., had low validity). Predictions in the last two cases should have been regressive. However, estimates from the mental concentration test were no more regressive than mere translation from percentile G.P.A. Predictions from the humor test were also insufficiently regressive.

Just as judgments and predictions are made by judgments of similarity of the input to the outcomes, so is degree of confidence in a prediction related to the extent to which an outcome is representative of the input (Kahneman & Tversky, 1973). Confidence is high, for example, when the input variables are highly correlated and thus appear representative. The marginal explanatory power of adding highly correlated cues is actually negligible. High intercorrelations among inputs should have less predictive validity than uncorrelated inputs. Yet more confidence is placed in correlated inputs. Similarly, subjects wrongly express more confidence in extreme outcomes for making predictions.

Ross, Amabile, and Steinmetz (1977) have recently reported another interesting bias in judgment that reflects the tendency for judges to focus on the representativeness of a behavior and ignore its validity. Subjects were assigned to a role as quizmaster or contestant. The quizmaster was to try to stump the contestant by asking any questions he liked (barring personalistic information). Since any subject has a large store of esoteric knowledge, it was quite easy to stump the contestant. In attributing general knowledge to both the quizmaster and the contestant, observers, quizmasters, and contestants all rated the quizmaster higher. All failed to take into account the role advantage of the quizmaster. Stumping someone is representative of being knowledgeable while failing to answer 10 of 10 questions is representative of not being well informed. The fact that this information was an invalid indicator of general knowledge was not taken into account.

*Conjunctional probability.*    Any event or outcome may have many different aspects. It is in the judgment and evaluation of such compound events that the greatest contrast between probability and representativeness arises. Often one aspect of an event will be so representative of an outcome or class that judgments of likelihood are based on this single aspect. Other dimensions will be ignored. Specificity of any information about an event often makes it more representative of an outcome while at the same time making it less likely to be true. Thus, errors of judgment will arise because estimates are generally made on the basis of representativeness. A man may be described as sporty, athletic, wealthy, and a member of a country club. One might estimate the likelihood that such a person is democrat. One might also estimate the probability that he is both a democrat and a tennis player. The probability of the conjunction must necessarily be lower than the probability that he is a democrat; the more specific must be less probable. Yet, since the description is so highly representative of a tennis player, subjects will judge the conjunctive event as more likely. The focus on representativeness information leads subjects to ignore other pertinent aspects of the information. In a study reported by Kahneman and Tversky (1982a), subjects were given a description of "Linda" that was representative of an active feminist and unrepresentative of a bank teller. One group of subjects ranked the extent to which Linda was typical of (1) one active in the feminist movement, (2) a bank teller, (3) a bank teller who was active in the feminist movement. As expected, subjects ordered the similarity rankings such that Linda was seen as most like one active in the feminist movement and least like a bank teller. Other subjects (some in a within-subject design and some in a between-subject design) judged the likelihood of Linda's being in the three categories. The conjunctive effect emerged. In opposition to actual probabilities, subjects judged it more likely that Linda was both a feminist and a bank teller than she was a bank teller. Slovic, Fischhoff, and Lichtenstein (1976) also reported violations of the conjunctive rule. Subjects read a sketch of Tom W., who resembled the stereotypic engineer but not the typical journalist. Subjects judged it less likely that he would select Journalism as his major than that he would select Journalism as his major and switch to Engineering.

While the violation of the conjunctive rule is clearly untenable from a statistical point of view, it is compelling even when one is aware of the representativeness heuristic and the tendency to misjudge compound events. Consider the following Tversky and Kahneman (1982a) example, which traps even sophisti-cated judges. Imagine that Bjorn Borg (or whoever happens to be the number one seeded player) reaches the finals of an important tennis match. (a) What is the likelihood that he will win the match? (b) What is the likelihood that he will lose the first set? (c) What is the likelihood that he will lose the first set but win the match? Few judges set the probability of the conjunctive event as lower than the likelihood that he will lose the first set.

Thus, subjects judge the likelihood of compound events by the degree to which they are representative of a relevant model. They use only similarity information rather than other relevant information, principles of representative-ness rather than laws of probability. Lichtenstein, Earle, and Slovic (1975) also examined judgments using compound cues. Subjects were asked to predict a criterion number given two cue numbers that were independent but both were correlated with the criterion. Since they were independent, the cues should have had additive impact on judgments. They shouldn't have been averaged. Howev-er, the average of the cues is the most representative feature. Subjects showed their reliance on the representativeness heuristic by averaging the regressed cues rather than by adding their effects. In some cases, the normative model can predict a value more extreme than either cue. Take the case where the cue values were from two sets, each with a mean of 50 and a standard deviation of 10. The sets were independent, and they correlated .8 and .4 with the criterion. When the first cue is 64, the normative response is 61.2. When the first cue is 64 and the second cue is 54, the normative response is 62.8—a value more extreme than for the first alone. Since subjects used a representativeness criterion and since the average of two cues is smaller than the first cue alone, *all* guesses for the combined cues were less extreme than for the first cue alone.

*Resemblance criteria and causal analysis.*    People have a propensity for causal analysis (Michotte, 1963). Work on attribution theory has outlined the factors important in the observer's assignment of causality for an event (Heider, 1958; Kelley, 1967). In judging causal relationships, Nisbett and Ross (1980) claim that people pick out the most representative reasons as causes for any consequence. Great and complex events are thought to have great and complex causes (e.g., Rothbart & Fulero, 1978). Shweder (1977) points out that prescien-tific medicine was dominated by the resemblance criterion. Bright yellow drugs were used for jaundice; epilepsy was treated by a drug derived from a monkey whose movements were epileptic in appearance.

The use of resemblance criteria for causal assessment can help us understand many findings in the social psychology literature. The "fundamental attribution error" refers to the general tendency to overestimate the importance of personal or dispositional factors in determining behavior relative to environmental factors. This bias is explicable in terms of the use of the representativeness heuristic since people's implicit theories about the causes of behavior give too much weight to dispositional causes (Nisbett & Ross, 1980). Thus, attributors will overemphasize the role of these representative dispositional causes in accounting for behavior. In addition, since the normal presumption is that people cause their actions, the correspondent inference is the anchor or starting point. Adjustments are made, but as we shall see, insufficient adjustment is another heuristic principle. Thus, the initial inference will remain stronger than it should (see Jones, 1979, for a discussion of this process). Jones also suggests that the actor-act unit is a natural and salient one, and thus that the availability heuristic might also be involved in the "fundamental attribution error."

Nisbett and Wilson (1977) proposed that the use of representative causes to explain events was widespread, and that people often lacked the ability to report or analyze the actual causes of their behavior. Their "causal analyses" were fortuitously correct only when the representative causes happened to be the operative factors in the situation. And, in that case, an observer could do just as well as the actor in "understanding" the causal factors. Weiss and Brown (1977), for example, studied the accuracy of women's accounts of their mood fluctuations. Subjects kept track of their moods and of several potential influences (e.g., weather, day of the week). At the end, subjects gave their perceptions of the importance of various factors. Objective weights were derived from multiple regression analyses. Subjects' accounts were quite inaccurate. In fact, the weights assigned by subjects were almost identical to the weights predicted by a group of observers. These findings are consistent with Nisbett and Wilson's (1977) notion that representative theories and causal accounts are given as people analyze their own and others' behavior.

It should be pointed out that Nisbett and Wilson's notion that people use implicit theories to generate conclusions isn't exactly the same as employing the representativeness heuristic. As we shall see, representativeness depends on similarity judgments. It isn't the underlying theory per se that is important but the features that the theory points to and the use of these features in making similarity judgments that is the key to representativeness.

People's implicit causal theories are also relevant for estimates of covariation. Work by Chapman and Chapman (1967, 1969) shows that beliefs about the covariation between events are based on a priori theories that specify the degree of association between events. Their research has demonstrated that practicing clinicians have strong preconceptions about which responses on diagnostic tests are associated with which clinical symptoms. For example, seeing genitalia on the Rorschach is thought to indicate homosexuality, although this is not a valid indicator. These a priori theories are held by laypersons as well as clinicians. After Chapman and Chapman had assessed the theories held by clinicians, naive subjects were given a set of clinical data—a series of Rorschach cards with client's responses and their symptoms. There was no relationship between symptoms and responses. Yet subjects reported seeing the same relationships that clinicians had indicated in their theories. Even when the pairings were rigged so that actually valid signs (but signs which didn't fit naive theories) were paired with the appropriate diagnosis, subjects continued to believe they had seen the sign-symptom associations specified by their a priori theories. Representative relationships are seen even where they don't exist. People's implicit theories have a stronger effect on judgments of covariance than do the actual data. They are "prepared" to see certain kinds of relationships.

This notion of preparedness has been used to understand certain operant and classical conditioning effects in animal research. Rats seem especially well-prepared to learn associations between distinctive tastes and later gastric pain (Garcia, McGowan, & Green, 1972). Covariations between spatial cues and somatic pain are also easily learned. Such relationships may fit the rat's "implicit theories" about environmental associations. Seligman (1970) also believes that animals have expectations about the causal relationships between their behavior and the outcomes that follow. Cats can learn to press levers to escape, but have trouble learning to kick or scratch in order to escape. Pigeons seem prepared to learn to peck for rewards. Preparedness, in terms of implicit causal theories, has also been proposed as underlying certain human phobias. The fact that people readily become phobic about heights or snakes but not tulips or cardboard may say something about their a priori theories of causal relationships.

Implicit theories about personality traits and the relationship between traits and behavior underlies person perception. Mischel (1968, 1969, 1973) has proposed that the consistency which people see in the traits of others and between their traits and behavior is more a reflection of their a priori theories than a reflection of the reality of those relationships. Once again, implicit theories of covariation overwhelm actual data. Representative reasons are detected more easily and are constructed in our analysis of events.

There are thus two ways in which causal analyses are affected by the representativeness heuristic. In the first place, we saw that people use resemblance criteria in causal analyses—the features of any cause are thought to resemble (be representative of) the features of the outcome. Secondly, we saw that causal factors are perceived to the extent that they fit a priori theories of causality and association.

The propensity for people to engage in causal analysis affects the way in which they use evidence in judging probabilities. Tversky and Kahneman (1980) have recently analyzed the role of causal reasoning in judgments under uncertainty and have identified certain biases associated with such judgments. They were concerned with judgments of the conditional probability of some event X given some data D (P(X/D)). D might be a potential cause of X (D as a causal datum) or X might be a cause of D (D as a diagnostic datum). For example, personality is usually seen as causing behavior, while behavior is diagnostic of personality. Tversky and Kahneman argue that it is more natural, and it fits better with people's implicit understanding of events to reason from causes to consequences than vice versa. Thus, people should give greater impact to causal data than to equally informative diagnostic data. They should be more confident in inferring effects from causes rather than vice versa even when cause and effect provide equal information about each other. This asymmetry between causal and diagnostic inference was demonstrated in Tversky and Kahneman's work. Subjects judged it more likely that a girl would have blue eyes if her mother had blue eyes than that a mother would have blue eyes if her daughter had blue eyes. They were likewise more confident in predicting a son's height from his father's height rather than vice versa.

This tendency for causal analysis to dominate over diagnostic information leads to characteristic errors of judgment. Consider the following problem (from Tversky & Kahneman, 1980, p. 55).

> "Let A be the event that before the end of next year, Peter will have installed a burglar alarm system in his home. Let B denote the event that Peter's home will be burglarized before the end of next year. Let $\bar{A}$ and $\bar{B}$ denote the negations of A and B, respectively.
>
> Question: Which of the two conditional probabilities, $P(A/B)$ or $P(A/\bar{B})$, is higher?
>
> Question: Which of the two conditional probabilities, $P(B/A)$ or $P(B/\bar{A})$, is higher?"

Nearly 82% of subjects stated both that $P(A/B) > P(A/\bar{B})$ and $P(B/A) < P(B/\bar{B})$. This is contrary to the laws of probability. The fact that $P(A/B) > P(A/\bar{B})$ reflects the tendency of subjects to focus on the causal impact of the burglary. Considering $P(A/B)$, a burglary can cause an alarm system to be installed. Subjects give less weight to the diagnostic significance of the burglary—the house had not been equipped with an alarm system at the time of the burglary. Likewise, causal thinking dominates the judgment that $P(B/A) < P(B/\bar{A})$. The causal impact of A (an alarm system reduces burglary) dominates over its diagnostic impact. (The occurrence of a burglary prompted the installation of an alarm system.)

A priori causal theories dominate judgments under uncertainty, again demonstrating that the representativeness of information rather than normative considerations often do a better job of accounting for judgments.

This broad review of the situations in which representativeness is employed as a judgmental heuristic indicates the generality of this principle and the breadth of the research program itself. By identifying the kinds of information that are used in making decisions, this approach has allowed us to predict when errors of judgment might be made across a wide variety of problem solving situations. Unlike many analyses of cognitive processes that provide a rigorous understanding of thinking in one or a few kinds of tasks, work on judgmental heuristics allows contact with so many kinds of tasks. It is thus an extremely compelling approach. While any one example or area of application might be attacked, one would be hardpressed to account for all the phenomena (e.g., ignoring base rates, failures to regress sufficiently) by any other principle.

## Judging the representativeness of an event or sample

As we shall see in more detail later, the essence of judgments of representativeness involves a matching of an event or outcome to some abstraction or prototype of the model or population. The more similar the event to the abstraction, the greater its likelihood of being seen as a member of that category. Bar-Hillel (1974) showed in a direct way that judgments using the representativeness heuristic were based on judgments of similarity between sample and population. She found high correspondence between people's judgments of similarity and their judgments of probability. Three kinds of judgments were made: (a) the similarity of two bar graphs to a standard; (b) the likelihood of the two bar graphs yielding the standard as a sample; and (c) the likelihood of the two bar graphs emerging as samples from the standard as a population. The correlations among the judgments were very high, indicating the judgments of similarity (representativeness) and likelihood are essentially identical judgments.

The fact that people expect samples to be similar to the population or to reflect the generating process has helped us understand the gambler's fallacy and why people ignore base rates and sample size. However, in order to understand fully judgments involving representativeness, we must know not only how people use representativeness to make judgments, but how they came to judge the representativeness of any event or sample. We know that people judge the probability of an event by "the degree to which it is similar in essential properties to the parent population or the generating process," but how do people first decide the extent to which an event *is* representative of the population? Since judgments of representativeness are similarity judgments, Tversky's (1977) exciting paper on feature similarity has much to offer in the way of helping us to understand judgments of representativeness. However, while Tversky's paper has been of great importance in choice research, it has not been linked sufficiently to heuristic principles such as representativeness. The issues that underlie similarity judgments will be crucial for understanding heuristic processes and their associated biases.

*Feature matching.*   Rather than a geometric or dimensional approach to similarity, Tversky (1977) takes a feature matching approach. The similarity of A to B is a function of the common features of A and B; features in A but not B; and features in B but not A. (While Tversky suggests that the noncommon features are more critical, results such as those by Ward and Jenkins, 1965, suggest that the common features will play a greater role in such judgments.) Features are assumed to vary in their salience. The more salient a feature, the greater the contribution to judgments of similarity. A key aspect of Tversky's analysis is that similarity is not a symmetric relation. In judging the extent to which "A is similar to B," A is the subject and B the referent. Since the focus is on the subject, the features of the subject are weighed more heavily. Thus, similarity is reduced more by distinctive features of the subject than by distinctive features of the referent. The variant (the less salient stimulus) will thus be judged as more similar to a prototype than vice versa. North Korea is seen as more similar to Red China than Red China is to North Korea. In judgments of representativeness, the typical direction of similarity is from the event to the model or prototype (e.g., how closely does this person match my prototypic lawyer). However, Kahneman and Tversky (1972) suggest that the process could go the other way. That is, we may judge the degree to which the typical lawyer is similar to our image of a particular person. According to Tversky's (1977) analysis, the judgment of representativeness (and all the ensuing effects) should be less when judging the similarity of the prototype to the event.

Tversky presents empirical evidence that similarity judgments involve a contrast of measures of common and distinctive features. For example, in judgments of similarity among vehicles, the multiple correlation between similarity judgments and the listing of common and distinctive features was .72. In addition, changes in judgments of similarity come about as different features become more or less salient through intensity, priming, or diagnostic significance.

Judgments of representativeness will involve these propositions about similarity. The number of common versus distinctive features between model and prototype, the direction of the comparison, and the salience of the various features will all affect assessments of representativeness and thus will affect judgments that employ this heuristic.

Tversky has given us a framework for relating in a formal manner the concepts of similarity and prototypicality to that of representativeness. As stated, representativeness is a relation between some model or abstraction and an event associated with the model. Tversky and Kahneman (1982a) distinguish four cases in which the concept of representativeness is invoked: (a) M is a class, and X is a value of a variable defined in this class; (b) M is a class, and X is an instance of that class; (c) M is a class, and X is a subset of M; (d) M is a causal system, and X is a possible consequence. Representativeness can thus be defined for a value and a distribution, an instance and a category, a sample and a population, or an effect and a cause. In all cases, representativeness involves the level of correspondence between X and M. In case (a), representativeness is determined by perceived relative frequency or association; in case (d), it is determined by causal beliefs (as discussed earlier). It is primarily in cases (b) and (c) that similarity plays a major role. An instance or sample will be representative of a category if its salient features are shared by other members and if it doesn't have distinctive features not shared by other members. While judgments of representativeness usually involve the comparison of an instance with the abstracted central tendency, there is another sense in which an instance can be representative of a category. It can be representative of the ideal type (rather than the modal type)—the type that embodies the essence of the category (Tversky & Kahneman, 1982a). While Tversky and Kahneman have referred to this ideal type as the prototype and to the abstracted central tendency as the typical, we have stuck with the more usual terminology and referred to the abstracted central tendency as the prototype.

Furthermore, a set of instances can be representative of a population not only with respect to its central tendency, but also with respect to its variability or range. One can talk about the representativeness of an instance or subset in terms of any dimension. It isn't always possible ahead of time to identify the dimensions that will be used for judgments of representativeness. It also may not be easy to assess the nature of the prototype that is used for similarity matching. However, these issues must be resolved before our understanding of the representativeness heuristic is complete. Representativeness must be independently defined, and we must understand judgments of representativeness as well as judgments by representativeness.

## Availability

In judging the frequency of a category, the likelihood of an event, or the frequency of co-occurrence of two or more events, people often use the ease with which specific instances can be brought to mind as a primary basis for judgment. This heuristic is called availability. Since instances of larger classes and more likely events are typically more available, this is a useful and often appropriate rule. However, factors aside from frequency and probability can affect availability. Thus, characteristic errors of judgment will be made when availability is relied on too heavily in judgments of frequency or probability.

### Sampling and sampling errors

The essence of making judgments of likelihood and number from an assessment of availability lies in the notion of sampling. When asked to judge the frequency or probability of an event, one rarely has the time or resources to conduct an exhaustive search of all cases. Instead, one does mentally what all basic books of research methodology tell us to do—generate a sample of evidence and use it as a basis of judgment. The sample is then taken as a fair representation of the population. Of course, if the sample is a random and representative one, the procedure is sound and no systematic errors of judgment will be made. However, if the sample is biased and unrepresentative in some way, errors of judgment will follow. The unrepresentative sample will be used as a basis for inferring population values. The problem is, of course, that the most available cases may not be random or unbiased. In survey research work, a sampling procedure that uses the most available people (e.g., only those with telephones or those at a shopping mall) will yield a biased sample. Likewise, obtaining a sample from memory by generating the most available examples will be biased if all possibilities from the population aren't represented in memory. Just as the names of all people in a city aren't in the phone book, not all instances of a category are represented in memory. For example, deaths by fire and shooting are generally in memory because one reads about them. Deaths due to emphysema or cancer usually aren't reported in the newspaper. Thus, one may judge deaths by fire to be more frequent than deaths by emphysema because examples are easily available. However, the sample isn't a representative one. Instances may be unavailable in memory because they were never presented.

In support of this suggestion, Lichtenstein, Slovic, Fischhoff, Layman, and Combs (1978) found that there were great misconceptions in judgments of the frequency of death from various causes. For example, strokes cause 85% more deaths than accidents; yet only 20% of subjects judged death by stroke as more likely. One clear reason for the bias had to do with the frequency with which various causes of death appeared in newspaper articles. This proved to be an excellent predictor of subjects' estimates. Thus, unrepresentative media coverage leads to inadequate and misleading information upon which subjects make judgments. In addition, availability of instances may not reflect actual cases because instances are initially attended to in a biased way or forgotten in a selective way. Furthermore, instances may be made more or less available by procedures unrelated to their frequency or likelihood. As we shall see, priming procedures are well-known and can be used to make certain instances or categories more available and thus more likely to be accessed.

Another factor that will lead to a nonrandom sample as the most available information has to do with the way in which things are stored in memory. There is a certain structure and organization to memory; this structure means that some things will be more accessible, independent of frequency. For example, Rosch (1978) has proposed that our memory organization for words involves a tree-like structure while Collins and Quillian (1969) discuss a hierarchical network structure. Either type of organization implies that in accessing words we may turn to the first letter and "read out" a long list of words. Given this memory organization, it isn't surprising that words that begin with the letter K are more available and accessible than those with K as the third letter (no dictionary is organized like that), and thus are judged as more frequent (Tversky & Kahneman, 1973).

Hogarth (1980) points out that in making judgments of frequency or probability on the basis of readily available instances, we are likely to be influenced by the absolute number of occurrences brought to mind and to ignore the relative number of occurrences. In judging whether psychologists or insurance salesmen are more likely to exercise, the reader of this chapter may well try to think of the psychologists and insurance salesmen that he or she knows who exercise. This ignores the total number of psychologists and insurance salesmen known by the reader. Since there should be more of the former, the reader is likely to conclude wrongly that psychologists are more likely to exercise (or to do almost anything else) than are insurance salesmen. Research by Estes (1976) in fact indicates that people estimate probabilities or frequencies more on the basis of their experience with absolute numbers rather than with relative frequencies.

*Salience and vividness.*    The salience of an instance is clearly related to its availability. Things that have been primed recently become salient and are used in judgments involving ambiguous events. Higgins, Rholes, and Jones (1977) unobtrusively primed either positive or negative trait terms (e.g., self-confident or conceited) and found that subsequent evaluations of an ambiguously described target were in line with the primed categories. Identical behaviors by the target were interpreted as indicating a self-confident or a conceited person depending on which traits had been primed earlier. Likewise, Srull and Wyer (1979, 1980) showed that the likelihood of a behavior being encoded in terms of a particular trait category depended on the accessibility of that category as determined by previous activation. Subjects first performed a sentence construction task that primed the hostility trait. In a seemingly unrelated experiment, they then read an ambiguous description of an actor. Ratings along the primed dimension increased with the frequency and recency of priming.

The influence of priming on availability has been interpreted in two ways. According to Wyer and Srull's (1980) "storage bin" model, frequent or recent activation of a category leads to its being stored on top of the memory bin after its use. It is thus the first thing picked from the bin at subsequent memory search. Higgins and King (1981) proposed an "energy cell" model in which frequent or recent priming increases the energy of the cells associated with the activated category. Highly energized cells are more available for use in processing information.

The influence of perspective on availability and judgments shows effects of a similar nature. Giving subjects a perspective prior to exposure to information makes certain categories more available and leads to selective attention and biased interpretation. Zadny and Gerard (1974) had subjects observe a skit. Some were given the perspective that the skit involved a burglary while others were told that it concerned some friends removing drugs from an apartment prior to a drug bust. There was also a group told that the skit involved people waiting in an apartment. Perspective affected what was recalled. Anderson and Pichert (1978) also found that perspective altered the availability of certain categories and affected the understanding and recall of a story. Finally, Fiske, Taylor, Etcoff, and Laufer (1979) report that perspective or vantage point leads to differential recall of facts, but interestingly not to variable attributions of causality.

Vivid instances are also highly available for use in judgments (see Taylor & Thompson, 1982 for a recent review). Reyes, Thompson, and Bower (1980) have shown that evidence in a criminal case that was presented more vividly was recalled better and was used more as a basis for judgment than equally probative but less vivid evidence. A defendant who "staggered against a serving table, knocking a bowl of guacamole dip to the floor and splattering guacamole on the white shag carpet" is more likely to be judged guilty at a later time than a defendant who "staggered against a serving table, knocking a bowl to the floor." Similarly, Enzle, Hanson, and Lowe (1975) have shown that information that leads to imagery has a great impact on inferences.

Just as unrepresentative media coverage can lead to the differential availability of causes of death and thus create biases in judgments, so can the vividness and salience of various causes of death contribute to the bias by affecting availability. Causes of death that are catastrophic and lethal should thus be overestimated. In fact, Lichtenstein et al. (1978) reported that the most overestimated causes of death were all sensational events—botulism, tornado, flood, homicide, motor vehicle accidents. Most of the causes of death that were underestimated were undramatic, quiet killers—asthma, tuberculosis, diabetes, stomach cancer, stroke.

Concrete and direct experience with objects also makes them highly available. Regan and Fazio (1977) showed the role of direct experience in the attitude-behavior relation. In a field study, students who had been personally involved in a housing crisis demonstrated greater consistency between their attitudes and their behavioral attempts to alleviate the crisis than did students with similar attitudes but no prior direct experience. Likewise, in a laboratory study, subjects who formed attitudes toward 5 types of puzzles by actually playing with them showed higher correlations between attitudes and behavior in a free-play situation than subjects who passively received information about the puzzles. Fazio, Chen, McDonel, and Sherman (1982) now have evidence that this effect of direct experience on attitude-behavior consistency is mediated by the increased accessibility of attitudes based on direct experience. The effects of direct experience paralleled those of frequency of occurrence. This is a particularly good example of how other procedures (in this case direct experience) can have the same effect on availability as does frequency of occurrence. Thus, judgments of frequency based on availability may be faulty.

The fact that occurrences are used more in judgments than are nonoccurrences is related to this notion of salience affecting availability independently of frequency or probability. Both people and animals seem to have some difficulty in processing negative information and in using nonoccurrences as positive cues for making judgments and solving problems. Jenkins and Sainsbury (1969, 1970) used the term *Feature Positive Effect* to describe this phenomenon. First applied to animal behavior, the feature-positive effect described a strong asymmetry in pigeon's ability to learn a discrimination based on the presence versus absence of a single distinguishing feature. Birds were involved in a discrimination task where a response key was illuminated on each trial. On half the trials, a black dot was present on the key, and on the other half it was absent. For some birds, the presence of the dot constituted the food-reinforced trials (S+), and there was no reward on trials without the dot (S−). This is the feature positive case. In the feature negative condition, the black dot was present only on the nonreinforced S− trials, while the absence of the dot indicated an S+ trial. Pigeons in the feature positive case quickly acquired a discrimination between S+ and S− trials whereas pigeons in the feature negative condition rarely showed much sign of learning.

Newman, Wolff, and Hearst (1980) have shown the pervasiveness of the feature-positive effect. In one of their experiments, human subjects were shown a series of cards, each with two trigrams on it. Subjects were told that one of the trigrams was "good," and they had to try to pick the right one on each trial. In the feature-positive case, the presence of a feature (e.g., the letter T) indicated the "good" trigram. For feature-negative subjects, the absence of the feature (e.g., the letter T) indicated the "good" trigram. Feature-positive subjects required an average of 34.6 trials to arrive at the correct solution. *Not one* of the 8 subjects in the feature negative case ever found the solution over 60 trials. Other experiments showed the feature positive effect across a variety of stimulus materials, procedures, feedback, pacing, and instructions.

Other work also suggests that people have difficulty in dealing with nonoccurrences. Research on judgments of contingency has shown repeatedly that human subjects will estimate the level of contingency between an event and an outcome (e.g., cloud seeding and rain) mainly by the number of positive confirming instances. In other words, only cases where cloud seeding is followed by rain are used heavily in the judgment of contingency (Jenkins & Ward, 1965; Ward & Jenkins, 1965).

The literature on hypothesis testing further indicates that people generally do not seek out disconfirming information. They have a distinct bias to search for positive instances of a hypothesis, and they fail to search for negative instances that might disconfirm a hypothesis. Wason (1968) demonstrated in a simple yet dramatic way how people fail to seek out disconfirming evidence in hypothesis testing. Subjects were shown four cards on which one letter or number appeared (A, B, 2, or 3) and were asked to test the hypothesis that "all cards with a vowel on one side have an even number on the other." They were to test this hypothesis by turning over any or all of the 4 cards. The card with a 3 on it (a useful choice providing possible disconfirmation) was almost never chosen. Snyder and Swann (1978) also have evidence of a hypothesis confirmation bias. Their subjects overlooked the importance of information indicating the nonoccurrence of a predicted outcome. When subjects were testing the hypothesis that a target was an extrovert, they asked few questions about the target engaging in introverted behavior. In a similar way, Mynatt, Doherty, and Tweney (1977, 1978) found a confirmation bias as a general process when subjects tested hypotheses.

Not only do subjects fail to look for disconfirming evidence, but they also fail to use it sufficiently when it is available. Einhorn and Hogarth (1978) showed that subjects making judgments discounted both nonoccurrences of an action and instances of incorrect prediction. In an interesting application of this failure to process nonoccurrences sufficiently, Wells and Lindsay (1980) showed how nonidentifications in eyewitness testimony ("this is not the man") are considered uninformative and are not often used in court trials. While such nonidentifications do have diagnostic value and should be used in judgments of innocence and guilt, they are treated as irrelevant.

Fazio, Sherman, and Herr (1982) have recently demonstrated that there is a tendency to make less of failures to do something than of equally informative active behaviors in making self-inferences. Positive occurrences are more available and thus more likely to be used by people in answering questions about their knowledge or attitudes.

Nisbett, Borgida, Crandall, and Reed (1976) have presented convincing evidence that individual cases, which are usually vivid and concrete, are overused in making inferences, while highly informative data summaries are relatively ignored. Hamill, Wilson, and Nisbett (1980) also show how a single striking instance can affect attitudes while pallid statistics have little or no effect. The detailed presentation of a single welfare case affected attitudes toward welfare recipients more than did the presentation of compelling but dull statistics. It is likely the enhanced availability and memorability of detailed single case information that makes it so important in the judgment process. Borgida and Nisbett (1977) likewise showed that face-to-face information from a student about a course had a bigger effect on course preferences than did complete summaries of course evaluations. Anyone who has taught an introductory psychology course can attest to the tendency of people to use concrete and vivid single case instances in making judgments. It never fails that after an hour of brilliant presentation of a general principle in psychology, a student will deny the generalization by claiming, "But I have a sister who . . ." Others nod in agreement.

Another kind of vivid case that will be highly available and thus overused in making inferences of frequency and probability is the extreme case. Kahneman and Tversky (1972) had subjects read lists of people and subsequently asked them to estimate the proportion of men and women on the list. Subjects overestimated the proportion of whichever sex had been represented by extremely famous people (e.g., Richard Nixon, Elizabeth Taylor). These names were more available and constituted the sample that subjects used for their frequency judgments. Rothbart, Fulero, Jensen, Howard, and Birrell (1978) also introduced extreme cases into lists. Subjects were presented with the heights of each of 50 men in a group. For half the subjects, the 20% of members who were over 6 feet were only slightly so. In the other case, the men over 6 feet were extremely tall. After presentation, subjects estimated the proportion of men over 6 feet. As expected, the extreme individuals were more salient and available. Subjects used this availability as a cue for frequency and overestimated the number of 6-footers in the group with extreme cases. A similar result was reported for estimations of social behaviors depicted by extreme instances.

The role of vivid, noteworthy, and memorable events has been proposed by Ross, Greene, and House (1977) to underlie the false consensus effect. People judge the number of others who share with them a trait or behavioral tendency as relatively high. For example, shy people judge that there is more shyness in the world than do people who aren't shy. False consensus effects were noted for a variety of beliefs ranging from personal preferences to problems to political beliefs. Availability is related to the false consensus effect in two ways. On the one hand, we do interact more with those who share our beliefs and values and traits. Thus, when we judge frequency from the availability of instances, we tend to overestimate the number who share some attribute with us. In addition, our own choices and behaviors and those of our closest friends and relatives (and they are likely to feel and act as we do) are most available to us. Ross and Sicoly (1979) support this view with their finding that one's own experiences and actions are particularly vivid and thus cloud one's judgments about contributions to joint enterprises. Both husbands and wives take more credit for doing certain joint chores, since their own behavior is more memorable and available to them. Similar effects emerged for players assigning responsibility to a loss in a basketball game and for contributions to group discussion during brainstorming. The bias is interpreted as reflecting selective retrieval of one's own behavior due to its availability. One's own efforts and actions during interaction are particularly memorable. Brenner (1973) found that, as subjects sat around a table and took turns reading words out loud, they had better memory for words they themselves read.

So pervasive is the effect on judgments of the vividness of specific cases that even when subjects are warned of the atypicality of such cases, the effects persist. Hamill et al. (1980) presented subjects with a videotape of an interview with a prison guard. The guard was depicted as either very decent and caring or as brutal. Some subjects were told nothing about the guard's typicality; others were told either that the guard was very typical or atypical. Subjects subsequently gave their impressions of prison guards. The logical judgment is clear— typicality information should have had a major effect on judgments. Yet typicality information had no effect. A humane guard led subjects to believe that guards were nice, while a brutish guard led to negative impressions. Even atypical vivid instances are overemphasized in judgments.

*Ease of generation.*    When people estimate values, they do so by extrapolation from some initial impression. Ease of generation of examples is thus a critical element in judgment. We might, for example, judge that more states begin with the letter N than M simply because the former are at first easier to generate. Likewise, instances that are shorter, smaller, or consist of fewer elements are easier to generate than instances that are long or large. It thus appears to subjects that there are many more committees of two members that can be formed in a group of ten members than committees of eight members (Tversky & Kahneman, 1973).

*Causal analysis and focus of attention.*    Just as representativeness plays a major role in people's understanding of the causes of events, availability is also relevant. Any manipulation that focuses the perceiver's attention on a potential cause will render that cause more available and make it a more likely candidate. This focus of attention can be achieved in several ways. Pryor and Kriss (1977) did it by linguistic structure. They proposed that the subject of a sentence was more focal than the object and would thus be seen as a more likely causal agent. Thus, Sue was more likely to be seen as the cause of the relationship when "Sue liked the restaurant," than when "the restaurant was liked by Sue." To show that such a causal analysis was mediated by the availability heuristic, Pryor and Kriss also collected recall data. Sentence structure affected availability for recall in exactly the same way as it affected causal ascriptions. Kiesler, Nisbett, and Zanna (1969) and Salancik (1974, 1976) also manipulated the language of information presentation in order to make certain causal possibilities more available. Both were successful in affecting causal inferences.

Focus of attention can also be manipulated by making an actor distinctive in some way. Taylor, Fiske, Close, Anderson, and Ruderman (1974) made actors unique by representing them in a solo status (e.g., the only black person or only woman in a group). Solo status individuals (who were most salient and available) were judged as more influential in group discussion. Studies of objective self-awareness (Duval & Wicklund, 1972) report effects of availability on actors' perceptions of their own behavior. Actors who are made to focus on themselves (as by looking in a mirror) make more self-attributions for their behavior. McArthur and Post (1977) report parallel effects when others are made the focus of attention. Simply shining a light on an actor makes one more likely to attribute his or her behavior to dispositional causes.

Attributing causality to highly available potential causes is the basis for actor versus observer attributions according to Jones and Nisbett (1972). Actors are focused outward on situational factors and thus tend to use situational explanations for their behavior. Observers are highly focused on the actor and his or her qualities and employ more dispositional explanations of behavior. As one might expect from an availability explanation of causal inference, when the perspective or focus of attention of actors and observers are altered, causal ascriptions change. Storms (1973) used videotapes to alter the perspectives of actors and observers. When perspectives were reversed such that actors were focused on themselves and observers looked over the shoulder of actors at the situation, typical differences in causal attributions were reversed. Actors attributed more causality to dispositions, and observers to the situation.

Availability judgments are also implicit in Bem's (1967) self-perception theory, which is based on the assumption that one's self-judgment relies predominantly on perceptions of recent available behavior and ignores other information in memory that is less available.

*Illusory correlation.*   We saw how estimates of covariation were affected by the degree to which the associations were representative of a priori theories of association. Availability also plays an important role in judgments of covariation. When subjects are asked to estimate the frequency of co-occurrence of a pair of items, they use the strength of association between members of a pair as a basis for the judgment. The frequency of co-occurrence of related words (e.g., lion-tiger; bacon-eggs) was greatly overestimated (Chapman, 1967). Chapman and Chapman (1967, 1969) also showed how illusory correlation enters into clinical judgment. Evaluations of the frequency of co-occurrence of various signs and symptoms were based on the associative value of the sign and symptom. Tversky and Kahneman (1973) suggest availability as an explanation for this phenomenon. They propose that the assessment of the strength of the associative bond between items mediates the judgment of co-occurrence. Since association between items is strengthened by co-occurrence, judges conclude from a strong association (one easily accessed and remembered) that the items must have been frequently paired in recent experience. Unfortunately, strength of association or availability doesn't guarantee a large frequency of recent co-occurrence.

Tversky and Kahneman (1973) demonstrated illusory correlation in the judgment of personality correlates. They constructed pairs of personality traits. Some pairs were highly related (e.g., selfish-greed); some were unrelated (e.g., eager-careful). Subjects heard a series of pairs. Some were then asked to recall the second member of each pair given the first. Some assessed how well they would have been able to recall each pair. Finally, a third group was given all the pairs and was asked to judge the frequency of occurrence of each pair. Highly related pairs were recalled better, were judged as being more recallable, and were judged as appearing significantly more frequently. This supports the notion that judgments of frequency are made on the basis of availability of associations.

Another methodology for assessing judgments of covariation has been used by Smedslund (1963) and Ward and Jenkins (1965). Subjects estimated associations between events from fourfold present-absent tables. For example, they estimated the relationship between a disease and a symptom by studying the number of times the disease and symptom occurred together, one occurred without the other, or neither occurred. As we saw earlier, subjects did poorly at this task because of excessive reliance on the present-present cell. Instances of this type are most available and are easiest to construct in considering a relationship between two variables. Since covariation estimation is a complex and difficult task, it is no wonder that people simplify it by focusing on one kind of information.

In general, learning about the covariation between stimuli requires that the linkage be highly available. Nisbett and Ross (1980) point out four ways in which the availability of the linkage can be increased as a way to increase judgments of covariation: (a) the interval between the stimuli should be short; (b) the interval between event pairings should be short; (c) the items to be associated should be salient and distinctive (as in Hamilton & Gifford, 1976) or have high initial association value (as in Chapman & Chapman, 1967, 1969); and (d) the covariation should be strong (ideally 100%).

One implication of employing the availability heuristic for making judgments of frequency, probability, and covariation is that these judgments will be highly unstable. The judgments will change depending on what stimuli happen to be most salient and available at any point in time. By appropriate priming or focus of attention techniques, different members of a category or different categories can be made available. Such manipulations will then affect category judgments or frequency estimates. The notion that judgments based on availability will be unstable is consistent with Salancik and Conway's (1975) proposal that attitudes are not stable and enduring predispositions, but are inferences drawn from whatever relevant information is salient at the time. By asking questions about past religious behaviors in different ways (whether subjects had done things occasionally or often), Salancik and Conway were able to make either past pro-religious or anti-religious behaviors available for subjects. When subjects were subsequently asked to state their attitudes toward religion, these available behaviors were accessed first and served as a basis for judgment. In the same way, one could alter subjects' judgments of whether there were more words that began with K or had K as the third letter, whether Bostonians or New Yorkers had more stable marriages, or whether certain symptoms covaried with certain diseases by altering the context of the judgment and by making certain specific examples more or less available.

An important and related point is that the judgments which psychologists ask subjects to make don't passively tap into or elicit thoughts that are already in the subject's head. Whether subjects are asked to make frequency or probability estimates or are asked to judge their attitude to an object, it is often the case that the judgment is developed at the time the question is asked. Whatever information is available at the time and whatever principle of judgment happens to be employed will determine the nature of the judgment (see Cook & Flay, 1978; Nuttin, 1975). Many judgments can thus be considered constructions to a particular question posed at a particular time rather than reflections of underlying and stable beliefs of the judge. Instability is an important and pervasive feature of human judgment. While people may believe their assessments, judgments, and attitudes are stable and rather permanent, the use of heuristics such as availability in making such judgments ensures that these judgments will change as the conditions and context of evaluation change.

## Simulation

The simulation heuristic is in a sense related to the availability heuristic. Availability refers to the ease with which specific instances are brought to mind. The simulation heuristic uses as a basis for judgment the ease with which examples or scenarios can be constructed. Since recall and construction are quite different ways of bringing things to mind, there are different rules and principles involved. Kahneman and Tversky (1982b) have outlined the operation of the simulation heuristic. It applies when questions about the likelihood or frequency of some event is approached by the judge's running a simulation model of the event. The output of the simulation is a judgment of the ease with which the model produces various outcomes. The simulation thus yields a measure of the model's ability to generate the possible outcomes, and the ease of simulation of any outcome is used as a basis for likelihood judgment. Kahneman and Tversky list five judg-mental tasks in which simulation is a likely heuristic for problem solving: pre-dicting a future event; assessing the probability of a specific event; assessing conditional probabilities (e.g., if war breaks out in the Middle East, what will the economic consequences be?); counterfactual assessments (e.g., if Kennedy hadn't been assassinated, what would the economy be like now?); and assess-ments of causality.

Some preliminary but illuminating work on counterfactual judgments has been reported by Kahneman and Tversky (1982b). They find that the easier it is for subjects to imagine that an alternative outcome could have occurred the more they act as though the actual outcome shouldn't have occurred and could have been avoided. In an example, they ask readers to consider a passenger who is caught in a traffic jam and arrives at the airport 30 minutes late. He finds the plane left on time, and he missed it by half an hour. Another passenger, booked on another flight, was also 30 minutes late, but his flight was delayed 25 minutes, and he missed it by only 5 minutes. Kahneman and Tversky suggest that both passengers would engage in counterfactual construction and try to simulate alternative actions that might have allowed them to be on time. Since it is easier to imagine how to save 5 minutes in travel time than 30 minutes, the second passenger should be more disappointed—even though they had the same expec-tations at the time of arrival at the airport. The basketball team that loses by one point in overtime can construct numerous scenarios involving minor changes in reality that would have led to a different outcome. The team that loses by 30 points can construct few, if any, such scenarios. The closer one is to any goal at the final outcome, the easier to construct counterfactual scenarios and the less necessary does the actual outcome appear. Because it seems more possible to have achieved an alternative outcome, those who come closer to reaching a desirable goal will naturally feel worse.

Other work in this area suggests that for simulation activity that tries to undo the past (e.g., how could a fatal accident have been avoided?), subjects introduce alternatives that remove a surprising or unexpected event rather than add some unexpected event. In addition, mental simulation follows the focus rule in that stories are reworked by changing some aspect of the main object of attention (e.g., the driver of the car in the fatal accident when the subject is asked to empathize with the driver's family), rather than some noncentral object (e.g., aspects of the weather or other person).

### Biases due to simulation

The simulation heuristic works to help assess the probability of events by constructing scenarios. The ease or difficulty with which the simulation reaches end states is used to judge the likelihood of those states being reached. As with the use of other heuristics, reliance on simulation should lead to certain errors and biases. The most easily constructed scenarios or paths to an outcome don't necessarily correspond to the most likely set of events. Ease of construction is related to things other than likelihood. Kahneman and Tversky (1982b) suggest several biases that should emerge as the simulation heuristic is applied.

1. Because naive judges don't combine substages of scenarios in a normatively prescribed manner, the apparent goodness of a scenario will depend more on plausibility of the weakest link than on the number of links. Thus, a single stage scenario where the single necessary occurrence has a .25 probability may seem far less likely than a five stage scenario where each stage has a probability of .75.
2. Judges will be biased in favor of events for which there is one plausible scenario and biased against events that can be produced by several alternative but unlikely routes. An outcome for which the single possible path has a probability of occurrence of .7 will seem more likely than an outcome with six independent possible paths, each with a .2 likelihood. These two biases are expressions of the tendency to overestimate the likelihood of conjunctive events and underestimate the likelihood of disjunctive events. These biases will be discussed in greater detail under the anchoring heuristic.
3. There will be a bias toward scenarios where dramatic events make causal transitions. Events that are produced by slow incremental changes will be underestimated.

Biases from reliance on the simulation heuristic arise because the most available scenarios aren't necessarily the most likely. Several areas of social psychological research have yielded findings that are explicable by the operation of the simulation heuristic. Several years ago, Ross, Lepper, Strack, and Steinmetz (1977) identified what they termed the explanation effect. Once subjects explain some hypothetical future outcome, their subjective likelihood for this outcome increases. Presumably, in judging the probabilities of future events, subjects go through a simulation procedure. The scenarios used in the explanation task become highly available and easy to construct. Paths to the explained outcome are thus numerous and quickly generated. The probability of the explained outcome is thus judged as high. Once subjects go through a dry run simulating a particular outcome, that outcome appears likely due to the presence of scenarios implying the event. In their work, Ross et al. (1977) asked subjects to read a clinical case study with an eye toward explaining some possible outcome (e.g., the suicide of the client). Subjects were aware that the outcome explained was purely hypothetical. When later asked to judge the actual likelihood of various outcomes, subjects showed inflated subjective probabilities for the events explained. Carroll (1978a) found that imagining future events led to similar effects. Sherman, Skov, Hervitz, and Stock (1981) showed that once hypothetical events are explained, they not only become subjectively more likely but actually increase in their likelihood of occurrence. Subjects explained their own hypothetical success or failure on an upcoming anagram test. Those who explained hypothetical failure not only then expected to do more poorly on the task, but actually solved fewer anagrams than subjects who explained hypothetical success. Sherman, Zehner, Johnson, and Hirt (1983) showed that the effects of explaining hypothetical outcomes on judgments are mediated by making available in memory certain facts and scenarios. However, if information has already been organized and some global impressions or scenarios formed, introduction of an explanation task has no effect on later judgments.

Even when the information base for the construction of scenarios is invalidated, as long as the scenarios themselves seem plausible and continue to imply a particular outcome, that outcome will be judged as likely to occur. Ross, Lepper, and Hubbard (1975) falsely led subjects to believe that they were doing very well or very poorly at a task where they had to pick out an authentic suicide note. Presumably, as subjects got feedback, they tried to explain their extreme outcomes of success ("I am usually called on to solve people's problems because I'm socially sensitive"; "I once got my sister out of a severely depressed state") or failure ("I never seem to be aware when people feel badly"; "I didn't realize how my roommate felt after her engagement was broken.") Later, subjects were told that the success-failure feedback had all been rigged; it was totally phony. They were then asked how they thought they might actually do on the task. Those who had initially been led to believe they had succeeded persevered in their belief that they were sensitive and would do well. Those led to expect failure prior to dehoaxing believed they would do poorly. Evidently the reasons subjects had generated to explain the supposed outcomes remained as viable links to those outcomes even though the reason for generating the scenarios had been identified as invalid. The outcome of the initial simulation procedure left certain paths easy to access.

Just as the explanation of hypothetical future events biases the simulation process and the output for judging the likelihood of outcomes, people's propensity for explaining events that have already occurred leads them to construct plausible scenarios for known outcomes. These constructions give actually occurring events the appearance of having been highly plausible or inevitable. This process has been studied by Fischhoff and his colleagues (Fischhoff, 1975; Fischhoff & Beyth, 1975) and has been called the "I knew it would happen" phenomenon. Once people know the outcome of an uncertain situation, several things happen. One can see a direct relationship between certain events and what actually happened. This allows interpretation and understanding of why things turned out as they did. Fischhoff (1975) has referred to this as creeping determinism, where what happens seems to have flowed naturally from preceding events. In hindsight, the outcome seems inevitable. In his work, Fischhoff (1975) tested these hindsight biases by presenting subjects with unfamiliar historical passages such as the description of the British-Gurka war. Some subjects were asked to make probabilistic predictions of various outcomes. This was the foresight group. Several hindsight groups were also included in which subjects were told prior to their judgments that some particular outcome had occurred. All subjects judged the probability that each outcome was going to occur (based on the description information) and judged the relevance of various facts. The most dramatic result was that hindsight subjects perceived whatever outcome they were told had occurred as having been more likely than did foresight subjects. Knowing that something *had* occurred doubled the odds that it had been likely to occur.

Further experiments were designed to determine whether judges were aware of this "creeping determinism." Subjects were given the same information as the hindsight subjects described above. They were asked to answer "as if they had not known what really happened." Subjects believed they would have seen the inevitability of the event. Other subjects were asked to judge what a group of people who did *not* know the true outcome would choose as likelihood estimates. When the subjects themselves did know the outcome, they believed that the others would (and should) be able to see the inevitability of what happened. In a final study, subjects were asked to make their own predictions about Nixon's then upcoming trip to China. After the trip (when subjects knew what really happened), they were asked to remember their predictions. Subjects remembered having given higher estimates than they actually had for events which later occurred. They perceived a past without surprises—no events to which they remembered assigning low probabilities were perceived as having occurred.

In summary, finding out what has happened makes it appear inevitable. Yet people are unaware of this bias and believe that they would have known what was coming before it happened, that they *did* know in foresight, and that others should know in foresight. The process underlying these results involves the construction of plausible scenarios and explanations for events known to have occurred. Such an outcome will thus appear inevitable when we apply a simulation model. Routes to the actual outcome become numerous as past data are interpreted in such a way as to be consistent with the outcome. While such a bias makes people feel omniscient, it has harmful effects. As Fischhoff and Beyth (1975) point out, we become overly harsh in judging our own or others' decisions that turn out badly. Since the outcome appears predictable in retrospect, we feel people should have known and should be responsible for the bad outcomes. In addition, the bias keeps us from learning from the past. When we see a past that appears unsurprising and predictable, we don't learn from it and change our thinking. This will, of course, insure that our future will be full of more surprises.

Both the explanation of hypothetical future events and the post hoc understanding of actually occurring events involve causal analysis of outcomes. A causal structure is imposed on either a set of past events or a set of events that would predict a future outcome. Both lead to the generation of scenarios and links between antecedents and outcomes that bias judgments when the simulation heuristic is later applied to make probablistic judgments of various outcomes. Whatever outcomes were considered in the causal analysis become more likely. When particular scenarios are available and many alternative routes to the same outcome come to mind, that outcome is judged as probable. Once a situation is conceived in one way, it is hard to see anything else as possible. Bruner and Potter (1964) showed how the generation of a certain scenario limits future thinking and renders the generation of other scenarios more difficult.

Biases thus creep into both our understanding of the past and our understanding of the uncertain future. In both cases, it is the construction and subsequent availability of certain scenarios that underlies the effect. Just as events that one explains take on a quality of inevitability, hypothetical future events (or actually occurring events) that defy explanation or for which no good scenario comes to mind should appear highly improbable. The plausibility of the scenarios generated and the ease or difficulty one has in their construction should be used by subjects as cues for judging the likelihood of outcomes.

Recent work by Sherman, Cialdini, Schwartzman, and Reynolds (1982) indicates that manipulations designed to affect the ease or difficulty of imagining certain events renders judgments of those events more or less probable. Thus, a disease with easy to imagine symptoms is seen as more likely to afflict subjects than an equally prevalent disease with hard to imagine symptoms. Similarly, when a good mood is induced in subjects, positive life events (e.g., winning a lottery) are judged as more likely, presumably because a positive mood makes it easier to imagine positive events (see Isen, Clark, Shalker, & Karp, 1978).

Simulation is also involved when people are asked to predict their own future behavior. A simulation is run in which links are developed between existing present conditions (or conditions assumed to exist at some future time) and various alternative behaviors. Consider the case of a person predicting what he would do if he were called on the phone and asked to donate an afternoon to collecting money for charity. In trying to predict his response, he would construct scenarios consistent with agreeing with the request or refusing. The ease of construction of each type of scenario and the number constructed for each alternative response would be used as a basis for prediction. Unfortunately, as we have seen, the ease of construction of a scenario may be a biased indicator of its likelihood. Thus, there will be times when people's predictions of what they would do in certain situations will be badly amiss. Sherman (1980) showed that people were quite unable to predict what they would do in several behavioral compliance situations. They overpredicted desirable behaviors and under-predicted undesirable social behaviors. Presumably, this was because of the ease with which acceptable behavior scenarios can be brought to mind and con-structed. In making predictions about behaviors to which they will have no actual obligation, it is easier for people to activate the "good person" script (Abelson, 1978) than the "polite refusal" script.

The identification of the simulation heuristic as distinct from availability is fairly recent. Thus, not much work has been done to understand the operation of this principle of judgment. Future work will have to address the issue of what the simulator is like (e.g., like a sampler, a computer program, an algebraic model?). In addition, just as it is necessary to assess the representativeness of a sample independently of the judgments that are presumed to be based on representative-ness, it is also necessary to assess the availability of instances independently of its effects. Only when the degree of availability of a set of objects or outcomes is known can we be certain that judgmental effects can be attributed to availability. Thus, work must be done to assess the content of scenarios and simulations and to determine when and how they are, in fact, constructed.

## Anchoring and Adjustment

For many kinds of judgments, people make estimates by beginning with some starting value and adjusting this value until a final judgment is made. Whether this starting value is dictated by the problem, arrived at by reasoned decision making, or chosen arbitrarily, adjustments are generally not sufficient. Final judgments are biased toward initially considered values. This heuristic is referred to as anchoring by Tversky and Kahneman (1974). Demonstrations of this ten-dency are quite striking. For example, subjects asked to estimate the percentage of African countries in the United Nations were "randomly" given a starting point and were asked to make judgments with respect to that point. Subjects given a starting point of 10% arrived at a final judgment of 25%, while those given 65% as a starting point ended at 45% (Tversky & Kahneman, 1974).

Anchoring is also seen when subjects generate their own initial values and use them as an initial basis for judgment. Thus, estimates of the product $8 \times 7 \times 6 \times 5 \times 4 \times 3 \times 2 \times 1$ are much higher than estimates of $1 \times 2 \times 3 \times 4 \times 5 \times 6 \times 7 \times 8$ because subjects generate initial values by multiplying the first few numbers and don't adjust sufficiently for the rest (Tversky & Kahneman, 1974). In a similar demonstration of anchoring effects, Lichtenstein, Earle, and Slovic (1975) found that subjects were far too conservative in using cues to predict a criterion. They stuck to initial expected values much more than they should have. The gambler's fallacy appears to have an element of anchoring in it. People continue to believe that initial expected values over a series of trials will eventu-ate despite the occurrence of initially inconsistent outcomes.

## Biases due to anchoring and adjustment

This tendency to use initial and partial estimates without sufficient adjustments for later possibilities explains people's overestimation of the occurrence of conjunctive events and their underestimation of disjunctive events. For a conjunctive event (the probability that several independent outcomes will all occur), one must assess the likelihood of a series of successful outcomes. Each elementary event may have a rather high likelihood, so that the probability of success for the first one or two events is quite high. With this high value as an initial estimate and with insufficient adjustment for later events, conjunctive events will appear overly likely. On the other hand, for disjunctive events (the likelihood of at least one of many events), the probability of each may be quite small. As a consequence of anchoring, the final likelihood will be underestimated. These biases may have severe consequences. People may fail to enter into important endeavors where there are many possible independent routes to success, but each has a very small likelihood. On the other hand, projects (such as nuclear reactors) where there is a high probability of success of any part but which require all parts to work in order to avoid disaster will appear overly likely to succeed and will be undertaken.

Another consequence of the anchoring heuristic is that people will construct confidence limits that are too narrow. In selecting confidence limits, a judge will start with the most likely value and adjust outward. Insufficient adjustments ensure that the extreme values (e.g., the 1% and 99% limits) won't be extreme enough. Winkler (1967) reports that the actual values fall outside estimates of the 98% confidence limits about 30% of the time. Of course, one could construct confidence limits by starting at the extreme values and asking for the likelihood of those values. This procedure will anchor judges at the extremes and make such outcomes appear too likely. With this procedure, subjects appear too conservative, assigning higher probabilities to extreme events than they should.

Several social psychological phenomena discussed earlier involve anchoring effects. The perseverance of initial impressions (Ross et al., 1975) and the effects of explanations of hypothetical future events (both discussed under simulation) demonstrate the impact and importance of initial judgments. Once some initial understanding of an event is arrived at, subsequent analysis, even in the light of new and contradictory information, doesn't lead to sufficient adjustment. Too little weight is given to new information. Initial judgments are remarkable in their resistance to reanalysis and reinterpretation. Once a causal analysis is undertaken, subjects are more likely to assimilate new information to this construction than to accommodate the analysis to the new information. Kahneman and Tversky (1973) and Tversky and Kahneman (1980) report that initial impressions from a personal sketch are not revised in the light of new information regardless of the unreliability of the initial information. Even when the new facts are highly unexpected, subjects are quite good at finding causal accounts that allow the maintenance of initial judgments.

Lord, Ross, and Lepper (1979) showed this striking tendency of people to stick to initial views and to assimilate evidence toward these views. Subjects were exposed to two studies of the deterrent effects of capital punishment, one which supported their views and one which opposed them. After reading both studies, subjects were more favorable toward their initial position than they had been. The introduction of mixed evidence led to even greater attitude polarization. Subjects' prior beliefs had effects on their consideration of subsequent evidence.

The primacy effect in impression formation is, of course, an expression of the anchoring phenomenon. Information received early allows initial inferences about what an object or person is like. These inferences bias the interpretation of subsequent information, and they aren't revised or adjusted sufficiently in the light of new information (Jones & Goethals, 1972). Whether the primacy effect is due to a differential weighting mechanism (Anderson, 1971, 1974a, 1974b), a change of meaning (Wyer, 1974; Wyer & Watson, 1969), or a change of referent (Higgins & Rholes, 1976), the fact is that insufficient adjustment from an initial judgment is made.

## Gambling: An Application of Heuristic Principles

We have demonstrated the many biases that result from reliance on cognitive heuristics. Judgments will at times be systematically and predictably amiss when representativeness, availability, simulation, or anchoring are involved. While the judges themselves aren't usually aware of these biases and errors, an understanding of such biases would benefit those whose livelihoods depend on the judgments of others. For example, casino owners and bookmakers would do well to pay attention to the heuristic strategies used in gambling judgments and the errors associated with such strategies. Not surprisingly, a look at the various games and procedures found in gambling houses indicates that the owners of these establishments take advantage of the biases in human judgment.

Ellen Langer (1975) has written about the "illusion of control," a phenomenon relevant to gambling decisions. Although not discussed in terms of cognitive heuristics, the illusion of control can be considered a special instance of application of the representativeness heuristic. To the extent that a chance situation is representative of or contains features that are typical of a skill task, people will act as though skill is involved. Thus, the belief that one has some control over the outcome will lead a judge to have higher expectations of success than the actual (chance) probabilities warrant. In her work, Langer introduced several features into chance settings that make them representative of skill situations. In one such study, she made interpersonal competition, a typical feature of skill tasks, part of a randomly determined outcome. Subjects competed in a purely chance card drawing contest against either a dapper and confident opponent or against a poorly dressed and bumbling schnook. Since a skill orientation had been elicited, subjects should have judged their likelihood of winning by the characteristics of the opponent. The fact that they bet significantly more on the likelihood of winning against the schnook shows that this occurred. In another study, chance tasks were made to have characteristics representative of skill situations by introducing an element of choice. Lottery tickets were either assigned randomly to players, or players were allowed to choose their own ticket. An illusion of control should have led high choice subjects to feel more likely to win. Indeed, these subjects valued their tickets more highly and requested more money when asked to sell them. In other studies, Langer found that the introduction of familiarity and involvement into chance situations also elicited the illusion of control and led subjects to be overly optimistic about their chances of winning.

To the extent that casinos introduce into their games features that make them representative of skill tasks, gamblers will maintain an illusion of control, overestimate their chances to win, and be more likely to gamble. Most games have such features. Choice is, of course, a part of many games. In fact, the most popular games at Las Vegas, craps and blackjack, have the strongest elements of choice. Games that have little choice, such as roulette or baccarat (whether extra cards are taken is determined by fixed rules), are not as popular. Recently, several states have introduced choice into their lottery system so that players can pick their number rather than having the numbers handed to them. In addition to choice, craps has another aspect that gives it the appearance of a skill task. There is active participation by the player. The actual rolling of the dice is an important feature of craps. Players believe they can affect the roll by blowing on the dice, rolling hard for high numbers and soft for low numbers, and so forth. Strickland, Lewicki, and Katz (1966) showed that subjects were willing to bet more money on the outcome of a dice roll before the roll than after the roll but before the outcome was disclosed.

The dealers and stickmen for gambling establishments also behave in ways designed to induce an illusion of control in the players. While they must be competent, they are warned against appearing too sophisticated or confident. For example, dealers do not shuffle the cards in fancy ways.

Those who take bets on sporting events such as football games, basketball games, or horse races also take advantage of biases in judgment induced by the application of cognitive heuristics. Again, the illusion of control is evident as players sift through all the past data and statistics (e.g., in the racing form) to help them make a choice.

We have also seen how application of the representativeness heuristic leads to the gambler's fallacy, a belief that in the long run outcomes will balance out and initial expectancies will be met. Since this bias is likely to affect betting decisions, odds-makers can take advantage in setting the odds. When a team with a winning streak meets a team with a long losing streak, the bettor should overestimate the chances of the underdog. Howard Cosell is forever telling us how the "law of averages will catch up." By setting the odds lower than they really should be, gambling houses can take advantage of this bias.

Kaplan (1980) has presented an interesting comparison of the strategy used by oddsmakers to set the point spread of a football game and the strategy used by fans to judge the quality of teams. When fans judge abstract team information without knowing the names of the teams, they use information in the same way that oddsmakers do. However, when team identities are given, fans make different judgments. They mistakenly take into account their prior expectations about the teams and past information from previous years. This information is not so relevant for predicting current performance, and thus fans are less successful than oddsmakers in predicting outcomes. In other words, fans overuse background information and expectancies and underuse data from recent games.

We have seen earlier that people tend to overestimate the likelihood of conjunctive events. Bettors should thus be eager to choose bets involving the conjunction of two or more outcomes. In fact, many of the bets offered to the gambler involve conjunctive events. Daily Doubles, Quinellas, Perfectas, Exactas, and Trifectas all require that the bettor be correct on multiple decisions, any one of which doesn't seem that difficult. Parlay cards in football betting are extremely popular. They pay far less than a fair price, but players see them as easy ways to make a lot of money.

One kind of football bet, the teaser, seems especially suited to the bias of seeing conjunctive events as too likely. In a teaser, the bettor picks two (or more) football games on which to bet. In each game he gets six more points than the official line, whichever way he chooses. The only thing he has to do is get *both* games right. He can take, for example, two six-point favorites as even point bets. It sounds easy since either event alone appears so likely and the bias toward overestimating conjunctive events operates. There is also another heuristic bias operating. When the correct line is Dallas by seven points, the bettor of a teaser wins this part of the bet if he takes Dallas and Dallas wins by at least one point. Since the expectation is Dallas by seven points and since people set overly narrow confidence limits (see the anchoring heuristic), it appears to be more of a certainty than it really is that Dallas will win by at least one point. The combination of overestimating the probability of conjunctive events and setting overly narrow confidence limits makes the teaser an especially attractive bet. No doubt many bettors are poorer because of these biases associated with heuristic principles.

As judges will also underestimate the likelihood of disjunctive events, it is not surprising that no such bets are available to the gambler. There would be no takers for bets of the following nature: You bet five football games and must be correct on just one (or more) to win your bet. However, for each game, you must give away nine points from the actual betting line (e.g., if your chosen team is actually favored by three points, you must give away twelve points). Since winning any game will appear very unlikely, and subjects won't adjust sufficiently for the fact that there are five possibilities, such a bet will seem worse than it really is.

Another heuristic that affects gamblers' decisions is the simulation heuristic. Gamblers' constructions of scenarios and various routes to different outcomes is an important part of the decision process. The "I knew it would happen" phenomenon is probably what keeps gamblers gambling more than anything else. Fischhoff's (1975) work tells us that after the outcomes of any gamble are known, they will appear inevitable. In retrospect, gamblers will see all the reasons for the outcome, will feel they should have been able to choose correctly, and will even believe they knew it all along (but were diverted by an irrational friend). Counter-factual construction also plays a part in gamblers' analyses. As we saw earlier, when one doesn't reach the desired outcome, the closer one is to that outcome (e.g., missing a plane by 5 minutes instead of an hour), the more easily one can generate scenarios of how the desired outcome could have been reached. This will keep future expectations high and ensure more gambling. It is thus in the "house's" better interest for the gambler to see how close he was to his goal. Thus, sports announcers (trying to keep T.V. viewers interested) who talk about how a lopsided game is really pretty close and how it "could turn around," and "anything might happen," and "there's a long way to go yet" are giving losing bettors scenarios that make their bet not so silly or unlikely. Photo-finishes at race tracks are used in similar ways. The pictures are displayed where bettors can study them. Losers can see how close they were and can imagine minor changes in the race that would have given them a win. This keeps their future expectations for success high and maintains their belief in their decision making ability.

To stress that a desired event nearly occurred does make such an event appear to have been more likely from the start. The one point loser in a basketball game, the photo-finish loser at the horse track, and the football bettor who loses to the spread by a last second meaningless fieldgoal are all examples of "close but 'no cigar" losers. However, in some instances there is a numerical or spatial aspect to closeness in gambling that does not, in a real sense, indicate almost winning. However, numerical or spatial closeness may have the same psychologically compelling effect. For example, the person whose lottery number is 45782 feels he almost won when the winning ticket picked is 45781. The roulette player who bets on 34 feels he was close when 33 comes out, even though the two numbers aren't near each other on the wheel. This is a likely reason why the numbers on the wheel aren't consecutive—there are more ways for a loser to be close, numerically and according to spatial proximity on the wheel. Likewise, the keno player feels close to winning (with all the resultant effects on future gambling) when a number that is physically adjacent to his lights up. Kozielecki (1981) suggests that a player who picks 10 on a keno bet will feel more like a winner when 9 lights up than when 11 lights up (the keno grid is 10 columns × 8 rows; thus 9 and 10 are adjacent, while 10 and 11 aren't). Perhaps the keno operators understand the effects of being spatially close. When any number lights up, it also casts light on a large part of all adjacent numbers, and thus may give the players of adjacent numbers an even stronger feeling of being close and raise their subsequent expectations.

## A GENERAL FRAMEWORK FOR THE UNDERSTANDING OF HEURISTIC PRINCIPLES

While lists of heuristics and intriguing examples of them can be found in the literature, what is missing is a framework within which to place the various heuristics and to understand in general terms their principles of operation and their characteristic errors. When we are called upon to make judgments about some individual case (whether it be to categorize an instance, to judge its likelihood, or to estimate some characteristic value), there are three kinds of information that can be used. First, there is some background information in the form of expectations, base rates, or population parameters. This is typically information that is in long term memory and has become available due to either the context of the judgment or recent activation. We often have a priori expectations about the category, probability, or value of something due to previous experience or information. For example, we may expect that George Brett will hit .357 in an upcoming baseball season based on his performance in past years. We could look at appropriate tables to arrive at the expectation that the probability of rain on a November day in Indianapolis is .19. In many problems, base rates are simply given. The percentage of lawyers and engineers in the population or the average I.Q. in a class are given in certain Kahneman and Tversky problems. For other problems, the population parameters are already well known by the judges (e.g., the fact that 50% of the time a coin will turn up heads). In the judgment of any individual case, a priori expectations and base rates should of course be used.

A second source of information for judgments of a specific case is the data available about outcomes from other occurrences. In being asked to predict what George Brett will do at one particular time at bat, we may be told that up to this point in the season he is only 20 for 80 (batting .250). Or we may be told that on the first 10 flips of a fair coin, nine were heads and may be asked to predict the next one (or 10) flips. In the lawyer-engineer problem, subjects might be told that six people were looked at in the population and all were lawyers. They can then be given a description of Tom and be asked what his occupation is likely to be. Data from other occurrences may or may not be useful in making decisions about some specific instance. In the case of coin tosses the fact that any number of heads are observed on the first 10 tosses of a fair coin should be irrelevant to the judgment of the likelihood of a head on the eleventh toss. Only when the distribution of outcomes of other occurrences is so odd that it might cause one to question the fairness of the coin (and thus the initial expectation) should this information be considered. The fact that the first seven people picked from a population of 70% lawyers and 30% engineers are lawyers may or may not be important information in deciding the occupation of the next case. If the population is extremely large, this information is as irrelevant as the coin toss information. On the other hand, if the population is small, the knowledge of other occurrences will, of course, alter one's expectations. In the extreme case, with only 10 people in the population, any individual case presented after the seven lawyers must be an engineer. The data from George Brett's first 80 at-bats in a season is a piece of information that should be used in the judgment of his next at-bat. The indication is that something about Brett has changed and that the .357 expectation is too high.

A third source of information to be used in case judgment is individuating information. This kind of information would include the description of the particular person to be judged as a lawyer or an engineer or the circumstances of a particular George Brett at-bat (who the pitcher is, men on base, ballpark, etc.). Even specific information about a particular coin toss could be useful if it included facts about whether the coin was on heads or tails at the time of the flip, the force of the flip, the wind velocity, and so forth.

In arriving at any decision or judgment, one should, of course, take all these relevant sources of information into account. Appropriate weight should be assigned to each kind of evidence, which should be combined. Normative approaches such as Bayes Theorem or multiple regression models do exactly this. In using heuristic principles, however, the decision maker does not deal properly and fully with all the available information. Not as much power is extracted from the information because the decision maker ignores useful information, attends to useless information, or misweighs or miscombines the available categories of information. All characteristic errors and biases associated with heuristic use can be understood in terms of the use and misuse of the three kinds of information described above.

A word might be noted at this point about the notion that errors and irrationality are typically and inevitably associated with heuristic use. As we shall see in a later section, many of the so-called errors thought to stem from reliance on heuristic principles can be understood in terms of subjects' representations of the problems or in terms of the particular framing of problems. What might appear as irrationality is often a sensible decision making strategy given the subject's goals and understanding of the information. In addition, the very notion of error or irrationality implies an objective criterion of appropriateness. Such a criterion is often nonexistent for problems used in the study of heuristic use. Who can say how diagnostic any particular piece of personalistic information is or how much faith to put in the belief that any base rate given is based on adequate sampling procedures? The point is that our major interest in judgments based on heuristic principles is not on the rationality or irrationality of such judgments but rather on understanding and delineating the processes underlying human judgment and decision making. The identification of possible errors of judgment should not be our only concern.

Giving too little weight to initial expectations, population parameters, and base rates has already been shown to underlie many judgmental biases. In both the lawyer-engineer problem and in the prediction of coin tosses, base rates are ignored as other information is given too much weight. The two cases differ, however, in terms of what information is used for judgments and in terms of how the base rate data are treated. In the case of the lawyer-engineer problem, it is the individuating information about the specific case that is weighted too heavily. The extent to which the description is representative of a typical lawyer or engineer is used as the major basis for judgment regardless of the validity of such information and regardless of the base rates. In the coin toss problem, the classic gambler's fallacy error is committed. Judges continue to believe that the population parameter (50% heads) will be the final outcome of a series of tosses. They fail to apply the 50% judgment to each and every toss. This distinction between the prediction for any single flip and the overall proportion of heads and tails across a series of tosses is an important one. Sample information from previous tosses should have no effect on the prediction of any single independent toss, but should very much affect one's estimate of the number of heads and tails across a series of trials. Unfortunately, the former judgments are affected by sample data, while the latter estimate remains 50% despite an initially biased sample. The data from other tosses and the deviation of these from the expected 50% is thus used as a basis of judgment for individual tosses. Subjects believe that any toss will bring the overall level closer to the initial expected value of 50%. The likelihood of heads thus increases as the proportion of prior tails increases.

In the case of predicting George Brett's likelihood of a base hit at his next at-bat, it is also possible to ignore or misuse the a priori expectation of .357. One could focus entirely on the current season's 20 for 80 and predict a .25 probability of a base hit. This is, of course, a failure to regress adequately (as in predicting that any extreme score will be maintained). Alternatively, one could commit the gambler's fallacy error and predict a likelihood of greater than .357 on the assumption that his final season's average will be .357. In the case of prediction about Brett, it really isn't clear what weights should be given to the initial expectations, to the outcome of the other recent occurrences, or to any individuating information about a specific at-bat situation.

In general, both the representativeness and the availability heuristics may be viewed as the tendency to pay too much attention to individuating information or data from other occurrences at the expense of initial expectations and base rates. In the case of representativeness, the extent to which individuating information is similar to aspects of the population may dominate the judgment (as in the lawyer-engineer case). Alternatively, the extent to which prior occurrences are representative of the population may determine the judgment of some new event (as in the judgment of a coin toss). Judgments based on availability depend on the strength of association of individuating information with specific examples or on the number of specific other occurrences that can be brought to mind easily.

Just as it is possible to over-weigh data from other occurrences and from individuating information as base rate information is relatively ignored, it is also possible to under-weigh these other sources of data as initial expectations are given too much weight in judgments. Anchoring and insufficient adjustment is a case in point. Here, initial expectancies (whether derived from early observations or assigned arbitrarily) are used more than they should be. New data from subsequent occurrences or individuating information about a particular case are insufficiently attended to. In a sense, the gambler's fallacy error in the judgment of coin tosses may be considered an insufficient adjustment of the initial expectations for the percentage of heads across a series of trials. Despite early deviations from this expectation, it is maintained.

Due to our limited information processing capacity, we generally attend only to one source of evidence at a time, and this leads to characteristic errors. Though better decision making may depend upon using and properly weighting all sources of information, it is not always clear what the optimal weights should be. One important determinant of the weights is the reliability and validity of the data. If any information is neither reliable nor valid, even though it is available for use, it should be ignored. Individuating information may range from being totally diagnostic to being quite irrelevant. In a population of 97% women, the individuating information that a person chosen at random has a beard should lead one to ignore the base rate when guessing the sex of that person. Alternatively, the information that a man is near-sighted and works in a hardware store should have no bearing on the judgment of his likelihood of being a child-abuser.

The optimal combination of sample and base rate information also depends upon the degree to which the base rate is seen as static. In the earlier example of a coin toss, it is clear that the expectation for any single toss should remain constant within very wide ranges of the sample data (unless these data make it clear that the coin is rigged). However, in the case of George Brett's likelihood of getting a base-hit, the initial expectation of .357 is not seen as fixed. It is quite possible that he has become a poorer hitter (in light of his 20 for 80 performance) and that the consideration of recent trials should lead to a re-evaluation of the expectancy. Likewise, the individuating circumstances of a specific time at bat should lead to judgments that deviate from the general expectancy. Within wide limits of circumstances (e.g., the coin was held heads up ¼″ from a table top and dropped), coin flip estimates should be unaffected by individuating information.

It is clear that for many kinds of judgments base rates do shift, and subsequent expectations and judgments should take this into account. Bayes Theorem, of course, provides a way to assess how judges should revise their estimates in the light of changing base rates. However, little research has been done which investigates subjects' ability to track moving probabilities or to revise judgments as probability levels shift. Primacy effects in judgment would predict that judges will fail to take into account actual changes in underlying probability levels. When early events favor one hypothesis and later events favor an alternative, subjective revision of probability estimates will fail to reflect this change until later than is normative (Peterson & DuCharme, 1967). Pitz and his colleagues (Pitz, 1969; Pitz, Downing, & Reinhold, 1967) also showed that subjects' estimates of which of two bags of chips a sample was being drawn from weren't revised sufficiently following disconfirming information. Brown and Bane (1975) also report that judges fail to revise estimates accurately when the underlying probability levels change. Subjects from time to time estimated the probability of a focal color being drawn from a bag containing two colors of chips. The color with the lower probability was focal, and its probability increased over trials. Subjective probabilities consistently were higher than objective probabilities. This overestimation of increasing probabilities (in a sense, the opposite of a primacy effect) is thought to underlie people's overconfidence in skilled performance, where judges are estimating the likelihood of an increasingly probable occurrence (success). Surely more work is needed to understand the kinds of judgments (and errors) associated with tasks where the initial probability levels are changing.

## AVAILABILITY VERSUS REPRESENTATIVENESS: EXEMPLAR MATCHING VERSUS PROTOTYPE MATCHING

In foregoing sections, we have shown that people do employ a set of heuristic principles in making judgments, categorizing objects, assessing the probability of uncertain events, or estimating the values of uncertain quantities. When such heuristics are applied, the decision process is neither random nor does it involve a formal or exhaustive analysis of the information. Rather, the use of heuristic principles means that only a subset of available information is used and that this subset is considered in light of the principles outlined earlier. Given that heuristic principles often enter into decision making, the question remains as to what the differences among these principles are and which particular heuristic will be elicited for any specific judgment.

One of the main problems in our understanding of heuristic principles has been a failure to specify clearly the distinctions among the various heuristics. This has been especially true for the use of availability and representativeness. At times the description of the use of one of these principles in such judgments sounds very much like the use of the other. For example, discussions of illusory correlation (see earlier sections) have been made in terms of both availability and representativeness, and the differences in either process or outcome that are to be expected from using one or the other principle aren't spelled out. Related to the problem of specifying the differences among the various heuristic principles is the issue of specifying the conditions under which one principle rather than another will be used. The key distinction to be made here is between the choice of representativeness or availability as a principle for judgment. Both are heuristic principles used in assessing the likelihood of some particular event.

For judgments such as the class membership of some object (e.g., is Tom a lawyer or an engineer?) or the probability of some uncertain event (e.g., the likelihood of rain on a November day) both representativeness and availability are applicable judgmental principles. The difference between these heuristics is seen in the nature of the judgmental process. The representativeness heuristic involves judgments of the correspondence or similarity between the sample event and some model representation, or prototype, of the population. As Kahneman and Tversky (1972) point out, representativeness judgments stress the general features or connotation of the event. Judgments employing the availability heuristic, on the other hand, involve the association of the sample with some particular population instance or involve the ease of retrieval or construction of such a specific instance. In other words, the denotation of the event is critical. For judgments employing representativeness, events are characterized by their general, abstracted, and modal properties. Availability is used as events are considered in terms of associations with specific examples and occurrences. Kahneman and Tversky (1972) further point out that both heuristics involve judgments of the amount of mental effort used in order to judge the probability of events. It is hard to imagine an uncertain process yielding a nonrepresentative outcome, and it is hard to retrieve or construct unavailable instances of an event. In both cases, the greater effort is associated with low judged probability of the events in question.

Several authors have recently discussed either the simultaneous or sequential use of representativeness and availability in making judgments. Kubovy (1977) asked people to give the first digit that came to mind. He suggests that in making such a choice subjects first consider the most available digit. At a second stage, they judge whether the digit first generated is representative of a spontaneous act. If it is judged as spontaneous, then it is given as a response. If not, the subject will generate a new digit. To show that the two heuristics (availability and representativeness) are used sequentially, Kubovy made certain digits more available by priming them. When the priming was subtle (e.g., "Give the *first* digit that comes to mind" to prime 1), the primed digit became more available, was judged as representative of a spontaneous act, and was given more often. When the priming was unsubtle (e.g., "Write down the first number that comes to mind . . . like 1''), the primed digit became more available, but was not emitted more often because it was judged to be nonrepresentative of a spontaneous act. Thus, increased availability wasn't sufficient to increase a digit's selection. It also had to meet the representativeness requirement.

There is a broader sense in which representativeness is involved in any decision based on the availability of information. In making judgments of frequency or probability by the availability of instances (as in the judgment of the relative frequency of words that start with K or have K as the third letter), subjects generate specific examples. Of course, those most available are more likely to be generated. However, once this sample set is generated, subjects look at it, may assume the sample is representative of the population and thus may ignore any selection bias. Even if the sample is biased due to the artificially increased availability of odd instances, the sample is seen as reflecting the essential properties of the population and is thus used for making judgments. Any information that the available instances were biased, nonrandom, or nonrepresentative should lead subjects not to use availability as an indicator of frequency.

One can also point to decisions where *either* representativeness or availability might be used for making the judgment. Consider the judgment of the likelihood that a couple you know, John and Mary, will get divorced within the next 2 years. This judgment can be made in one of two ways. You could judge the similarity of John and Mary to your idea of the typical couple that gets divorced. Do they have the features or characteristics representative of the causes of divorce or the characteristics that are generally present in couples that split up? Such a judgment employs the representativeness heuristic. Alternatively, you could search memory for specific similar couples you have known. Divorce for John and Mary will seem likely if there is a large number of divorces among the couples called to mind. Or, one could search memory for specific couples that have been divorced and then judge the similarity of these specific cases to John and Mary. Either of these latter strategies involves the availability heuristic—the judgment of a case at hand by reference to or association with the number or ease of specific instances generated.

When the distinction between representativeness and availability is made in these terms, the difference between the two heuristics parallels another important distinction that has been of much concern recently. There has been interest in the concept of natural categories and how people both learn such categories and make category judgments. The two major category learning models are the prototype or independent cue model and the exemplar or interactive cue model. According to the prototype model (e.g., Posner & Keele, 1968), people abstract a measure of central tendency of a category and base their categorical judgments on this central tendency or prototype. The closer a stimulus is to this abstracted prototype, the greater the likelihood that it will be judged as an instance of that category. Several sources of evidence support this model. Subjects classify prototype patterns they have never seen before as quickly and accurately as old training patterns (Homa & Chambliss, 1975; Strange, Kenney, Kessel, & Jenkins, 1970). Transfer performance is well predicted by distance of the stimulus from the prototype rather than by the frequency of similar features to training stimuli (Franks & Bransford, 1971). In addition, with long delays between learning and transfer, there is greater forgetting of old training stimuli than of prototypes (Goldman & Homa, 1977). This implies that subjects actively abstract the central tendency or prototype of a category at the time the exemplars are presented and learned.

The alternative is the exemplar model, or context theory of classification, proposed by Medin (Medin & Schaffer, 1978; Medin & Smith, 1981; Smith & Medin, 1981). According to this view, a stimulus item to be classified acts as a retrieval cue to access information associated with similar stored exemplars. This specific exemplar information serves as the basis for category judgments. Thus, the component stimulus dimensions aren't treated independently, and no category information enters into judgments independently of specific item information. As the similarity of the stimulus to specific retrieved exemplars increases so does the probability of classifying the stimulus into the category. To use an example from Medin and Smith, an animal might be classified as a rodent not by comparison with the prototype rodent, but because it is very similar to a rabbit, a known rodent. Support for the exemplar model is given by Medin and Schaffer and by Medin and Smith, who show that component dimensions aren't independent. They find that strong similarity to specific exemplars is more important to categorization and to its speed and confidence than is overall similarity to the average or prototypic representation of a category.

The crux of the difference between the prototype versus exemplar matching models can be captured as follows: Imagine two categories, A and B. In category A, X is a member, but is unlike most other members. X is an atypical instance (e.g., the ostrich is a bird; the fellow down the hall is very weird and unlike most psychologists, but he is a member of your department). X is not anything like the prototype of A. In category B, the prototype or abstracted modal instance is very much like X, but no actual category member is very much like X. Imagine that we show all members of categories A and B to a subject and then show him item Y. Y is very much like X in appearance and action. The subject must classify Y as an A or a B. A prototype model would predict classification as a B, while an exemplar matching model would predict classification as an A.

There would seem to be great similarity between the prototype versus exemplar matching models on the one hand and the representativeness versus availability heuristic on the other. Representativeness involves matching to an abstracted central model while availability involves association, accessing, and matching to specific instances. Thus, a consideration of the category learning and natural category literature might be helpful in understanding which of the two major prototypes is more likely to be used and under what conditions each might be chosen. We have cited evidence in support of both the prototype and the exemplar matching models.

Research in the area of cognitive heuristics is consistent with this view that both prototype matching (representativeness) and exemplar matching (availability) are used in judgments. Tversky and Kahneman (1973) present a judgmental problem that vividly demonstrates how different presentations of the same formal problem can elicit either the representativeness or the availability heuristic. Some subjects were given the following problem:

Form 1:    "Consider the following diagram:

| | | | | | |
|---|---|---|---|---|---|
| X | X | O | X | X | X |
| X | X | X | X | O | X |
| X | O | X | X | X | X |
| X | X | X | O | X | X |
| X | X | X | X | X | O |
| O | X | X | X | X | X |

A Path in this diagram is any descending line which starts at the top row, ends at the bottom row, and passes through exactly one symbol (X or O) in each row.

What do you think is the percentage of paths which contain:

6 X's & 0 O's    _____%
5 X's & 1 O      _____%
4 X's & 2 O's    _____%

.

.

.

.

0 X's & 6 O's    _____%

Note that these include all possible path-types and hence your estimates should add to 100%.

Of 73 subjects, 54 erroneously judged more paths of 6 X's and no O's than paths of 5 X's and one O. The problem elicited an availability heuristic. Due to the sequential character of the definition of a path, subjects were likely to judge frequency by generating individual paths. At every step, there are more X's than O's so it is easier to construct paths with all X's.

Other subjects received an alternative, but formally identical version of the problem:

Form 2:    "Six players participate in a card game. On each round of the game, each player receives a single card drawn blindly from a well-shuffled deck. In the deck, 5/6 of the cards are marked X and the remaining 1/6 are marked O. In many rounds of the game, what is the percentage of rounds in which:

6 players receive X and no player receives O    _____%
5 players receive X and 1 player receives O    _____%

.

.

.

.

No player receives X and 6 players receive O    _____%

Note that these include all the possible outcomes and hence your estimates should add to 100%.

While the Form 1 version stresses individual instances (specific exemplars) by
its display, Form 2 makes the population proportion (5/6; the central tendency)
explicit and salient. In this case, outcomes were likely to have been judged by the
degree to which they were representative of the central tendency value rather
than by the ease of availability of individual instances. By using this representativeness heuristic, 5/6 X's was judged as more likely than 6 of 6 X's by 71 of
the 82 subjects. The fact that the same formal problem can be approached by
different heuristics has also been noted by Wallsten (1980). He points out that
people generally organize problems by content rather than structure, and thus the
same formal problem presented with different content may lead to different rules
and tactics for solution.

Pitz (1980) has dealt with the issue of what aspects from a sample of information are used in making predictions and judgments (Hamilos & Pitz, 1977; Pitz,
Leung, Hamilos, & Terpening, 1976). In particular, subjects were given sample
information in the form of a sequence of numbers that were part of a set. They
were shown several values, each of which consisted of a three-digit number.
Subjects were told to learn as much as they could about the sample information.
Finally, they were given a prediction task in which two three-digit numbers were
given, and they were asked which was more likely to occur as an outcome. Pitz
et al. (1976) found that subjects made a great deal of use of abstracted information. The central tendency of the sample distribution was employed accurately,
as were the variability, skewness, and bimodality. Hamilos and Pitz (1977) used
a recognition task. After sample information was presented, they showed further
values to subjects and asked whether or not these numbers had been presented in
the original sample. The belief that an item had been seen before increased as
values got closer to the middle of the sample distribution. This again shows
abstraction of a central tendency as a prototypic value and use of the representativeness of a value to this central tendency in making judgments. Subjects also
abstracted variability information as seen by the fact that a decline in confidence
of having seen any particular item depended on the variability of the sample
distribution. The relationship between recognition confidence and the deviation

of an item from the sample median (in terms of standard units) was constant. Aside from abstracting summarizing prototypic information (central tendency and variability), subjects also used specific exemplars in making judgments. In particular, extreme values were quite available for use. The ability to discriminate old from new information was greatest at the extremes of the distribution. Both Potts (1972) and DeSoto and Bosley (1962) have also shown how important the extreme values of a category set are. Thus, subjects remember some specific sample values (the extremes) and use them to define a framework. In addition, they abstract the central tendency, represented as a range of values, as part of the prototypic member. Pitz's results are consistent with the view that judgments of category membership involve both judgments of representativeness (similarity to abstracted prototype) and judgments of availability (associations with specific exemplars). Likewise, Slovic, Kunreuther, and White (1974) show that flood plain residents misperceive the probability of floods in ways explained by both availability and representativeness heuristics.

Whether or not representativeness or availability (matching to prototype or association with specific exemplars) will be used in probability or category judgments depends on how the original category information is encoded and stored in memory. Information about any person, object, or set of objects can be processed in terms of some abstracted prototype or schematic representation or in terms of specific features or members, especially those most distinctive and salient. The social psychological literature is filled with examples of both types of encoding. Cantor and Mischel (1979) showed how information about a particular person is processed and stored in terms of some abstracted prototype. When a target person was described in mainly extraverted terms, this trait was abstracted and information was organized around the prototype. Qualities that were presented and were consistent with extraversion were well remembered, while traits irrelevant to or inconsistent with the prototype were badly remembered. Since the prototype, and not necessarily specific instances, was used for judgments, traits not seen before but consistent with extraversion were also (mis)remembered as having been seen. In other words, having been labelled as a category member, a target comes to fit the image of the "ideal" member. However, while the traits functioned as prototypes and similarity to this prototype was used for judgments, subjects also stored individual items. In a recognition task, they distinguished between presented, prototypic traits and nonpresented, prototypic traits by remembering more of the former (Cantor & Mischel, 1977). Work by Tsujimoto, Wilde, and Robertson (1978) also showed that subjects abstracted a prototypic linear ordering from a set of athletic dominance data. In that study, slides that were new but consistent with the abstracted ordering were remembered just as well as actually presented old slides. Their data could thus be accounted for entirely in terms of prototype abstraction and comparison to prototype with no memory of or comparison to individual acquisition exemplars. Thus, when information is stored in terms of a schematic representation, specific items of information will be lost and representativeness rather than availability of instances will be used in making judgments. Lingle and Ostrom (1981) make a similar point about the effects of making global evaluative judgments. Once such a judgment is made, the specific items of information that went into making the judgment will be lost, and subsequent decisions will be based solely on the stored global representation. On the other hand, memory for specific items has been found to be important in work by Anderson and Bower (1973) and Reitman and Bower (1973).

## When Availability and When Representativeness?

Thus, research indicates that subjects can and do use both abstracted prototypes or central tendencies and associations to specific exemplars in storing material and making judgments. Both prototype and exemplar models are supported; both representativeness and availability are used. The question is when and under what conditions is each most likely to be used. One answer has to do with the relative salience of each kind of information at any given point in time. Regardless of how a set of information is encoded, any aspects of that information (be it the abstracted prototype or specific exemplars) can be made more or less salient at any time. Priming procedures such as those used by Srull and Wyer (1980) or Higgins et al. (1977) can, of course, make salient either the generic features of a set or specific instances. The weird professor in the department (or *any* particular faculty member) can be made salient by recent or frequent activation. Gilovich (1981) shows how the priming of one specific value or association can have a great effect on judgments. Subjects rated the potential of hypothetical football players. Descriptions of the players were rated as having higher potential when they contained information irrelevant to ability but which made salient and available an association to some current football star (e.g., is from the same home town as Gene Upshaw). Availability of associations to specific exemplars thus affected judgments. In another demonstration, subjects' recommendations about how to solve hypothetical international crises were affected by making available specific actual historical crises (e.g., Vietnam was made available by using terms like "quickstrike" and "chinook helicopters" and by having the president from Texas and the briefing room as Dean Rusk Hall).

Alternatively, the central tendency of any category can be made salient by having observers think in "average" terms. Judgments of suitability of a new stimulus for the category will be made in terms of whichever properties, prototype or specific exemplars, have been activated. In the earlier example (X is a weird member of category A; and X is the prototype of category B), the judgment of whether Y (an item similar to X) is an A or a B will depend on whether the judge has been primed to think in prototypic terms or whether the weird Mr. X from category A has been made salient.

Individual instances, rather than abstracted prototypes, will be used for judgment whenever those instances are attention-getting in some way. We saw how extreme instances are used in judgments of category membership (e.g., Hamilos & Pitz, 1977). Particular items become distinctive and memorable either when (a) they fit some pre-existing schema, have high association value, and are expected or (b) when they are inconsistent with existing structures, are distinctive, and are highly unexpected. Social structures that are balanced and thus fit with the balance schema are easier to learn and remember (Picek, Sherman, & Shiffrin, 1975; Zajonc & Burnstein, 1965). On the other hand, there is evidence that imbalanced social structures, which are highly distinctive and unexpected, are memorable (Cottrell, Ingraham, & Monfort, 1971; Gerard & Fleischer, 1967). Hastie and Kumar (1979) also found that subjects showed highest recall for items incongruent with expectations. Subjects studied sentences describing a person. Some sentences were consistent with an implied prototype or personality type, some were neutral with respect to the prototype, and some were incongruent with the personality type. In a memory task, the inconsistent information had a significant advantage. In the present volume, Wyer and Gordon discuss the role of inconsistency in recall.

Chapman (1967) reported that pairs of stimuli with high association value (e.g., knife-fork) were recalled as having been seen often and were used in characterizing a set of information more than were pairs with low association value. Hamilton (1979), on the other hand, demonstrated that subjects strongly encoded associations between distinctive, low association value stimuli (e.g., minority people and minority traits). He used this as a basis for understanding stereotypes. It thus appears that both very expected and schema-fitting objects or very unexpected and distinctive exemplars are accessible from memory. Whether expected or distinctive objects become stored in a way that makes them highly available seems to depend on both the processing load and the pre-existence of schematic structure. Under high information load, subjects encode only expected or schema-consistent information (Reyes et al., 1980). Without cognitive strain, subjects are more likely to focus on and encode unexpected instances (Hastie & Kumar, 1979). In addition, when an existing cognitive structure or schema is present for processing information, subjects will attend to and easily store expected and schema consistent information (as in Chapman & Chapman, 1967, 1969). However, without an existing schema (as in Hamilton, 1979), distinctive information is easily noted and deeply encoded. Associations to whichever exemplars are stored will be used in making probability and category judgments about new items of information.

Judges are likely to use matching to a prototypic representation for making category judgments unless specific exemplars are especially salient or are elicited by the item to be judged. The item to be judged may be described in such a way that no specific exemplars are called up. Representativeness will then be used as a basis for judgment. In fact, an item may be described twice by different partial features so that in neither case is a specific exemplar brought to mind. However, a single description consisting of the combination of these partial descriptors may evoke some particular example, leading subjects to use availability in their judgments. This could result in decisions that are quite different from those made when no example was elicited and judgments were made by representativeness. Consider the following example: One set of subjects is asked who is likely to be a better basketball player, a 6'6" black man or a 6'6" white man. Based on this partial description, subjects may access their prototypic basketball star and conclude that the odds favor the black man. A second set of subjects is asked who is likely to be a better basketball player, a midwesterner or an easterner. Again, a quick search for the prototype leads to the easterner as a choice. A third set of subjects is asked whether a white, 6'6" midwesterner or a black, 6'6" easterner is more likely to be a better basketball player. The former description may now be complete enough to call Larry Bird quickly to mind. Based on the availability of this instance, the white midwesterner will be chosen. Thus, when a description does call to mind a specific example or examples, judgments will be based on availability. If not, the abstracted prototype will be accessed and the representativeness heuristic used.

Judgments using the representativeness of an instance to an abstracted prototype may also be necessary when specific exemplars are simply unavailable for judgment. A long time after information is first received and organized in memory, only an abstracted representation rather than any specific exemplars may remain. Consistent with this idea is the finding of Srull and Wyer (1980) that once a prototypic representation of a set of information is achieved, it has greater and greater effects on judgments as time goes by. When the summary representation can easily be achieved and no items in the set are inconsistent with it (as in Potts, 1972; or Tsujimoto et al., 1978), it is likely that only the abstracted representation and not specific exemplars will remain for use in judgment.

Another factor that determines whether information will be encoded and used in prototype or exemplar form is the time initially available for information processing. Under time pressure and cognitive overload, subjects may be forced to abstract some central tendency from a set of items and ignore inconsistent exemplars. At a more leisurely pace (as in Hastie & Kumar, 1979), subjects can reflect on any specific item and see its relationship to other examples or to an abstracted prototype. Rothbart et al. (1978) have reached a similar conclusion in their study of heuristic use in stereotype formation. They proposed that information about a group could be organized either around individual members or around the group "as a whole." The former would prompt the availability heuristic for making group judgments while the latter would foster the use of an abstracted central tendency for making judgments. The authors presented trait information about group members and found that under low memory load subjects organized their perceptions of the group around specific individual members. However, under high memory load, perceptions were organized around the group as a whole, and specific cases were not represented in memory.

It is also important to consider the task set given to subjects at the time the information is presented for processing. Impression sets foster a prototypic representation of the objects while a recall set leads subjects to treat the objects one by one and encode exemplars separately (Hamilton, Katz, & Leirer, 1980; Hartwick, 1979). Thus, an impression set should lead to category judgments based on the representativeness heuristic while a recall set should lead to the use of availability of specific exemplars for making judgments.

A recent study by Hanson (1982) indicates that category judgments will be made in terms of prototype matching only when it has been easy for subjects to abstract a prototype from the information set. When prototype abstraction is difficult, exemplar matching for judgments is more the rule. In particular, prototype abstraction was made likely or unlikely through task instructions. In one case, subjects were shown objects of various shapes and asked to which of three categories each belonged. Feedback was given after each item. In this case, prototype abstraction would be likely. Another group was told to look at the items and try to remember them. They were given no feedback and were told only that there would be some categorization later. A transfer task was given to both groups after presentation of all items. All new items and prototypic items were given, and subjects were asked to categorize them. The items could be scaled according to similarity to any prototype or to specific exemplars. The group for which prototype abstraction was likely did show strong prototype matching in their categorization. The other group exhibited exemplar matching. Two other groups, for whom prototype abstraction could be achieved to a lesser extent, showed intermediate results. One of these groups guessed the category of each initial object but got no feedback. The other group was told the category of each item and didn't have to abstract the prototypes in an active way. Past studies that support exemplar matching (e.g., Medin & Schaffer, 1978) have in fact used categories that were poorly formed so that prototype abstraction would be difficult. On the other hand, categories were well defined and prototypes easy to abstract in the work by Posner and Keele (1968). Olson (1976) also suggests that representativeness won't be used in judgments when the prototype isn't well articulated. He also raises important issues about what are the representative features of any information set.

Individual differences in the ability to abstract prototypes may also prove to be an important factor. Tesser and Leone (1977) have shown that there are individual differences in schematicity for certain kinds of information sets. Walker (1976) found reliable sex differences in the use of social schemas. Females tended to employ and maintain horizontal schemas (based on interpersonal symmetry) in processing social information, while males preferred vertical schemas (asymmetrical and transitive relations as in dominance hierarchies). We would expect highly schematic subjects to make category judgments by representativeness while weakly schematic subjects should use availability and association to specific exemplars more.

The indication is that people may use either the representativeness heuristic or the availability heuristic in making judgments about the likelihood or the category identity of any event or object. Associations to specific and available exemplars or matching to well defined prototypes, to fuzzy abstractions, or to ideal types have all been demonstrated. Any and all of these principles may be used depending on the relative salience of the exemplars or the prototypic representation. Even when prototype matching is demonstrated, however, this doesn't necessarily mean that a stable and lasting prototype exists for judgment. One's prototypic representation of a category may change depending on which specific exemplars have been recently primed and are salient. The stability and precise form of the prototype is an important issue that awaits further work.

## CONDITIONS UNDER WHICH HEURISTIC PRINCIPLES ARE LIKELY TO BE USED

Of course, heuristic principles are not used in every decision-making situation or for every kind of judgment. Whether these principles are being used appropriately so that more accurate and efficient judgments are made or whether they are being used inappropriately so that judgments will involve characteristic errors and biases, there are certain conditions that make it more likely that judges will rely on heuristic principles. We deal here with two such conditions—the extent to which the decision is important and involving, and the extent to which the decision maker is a novice or an advanced judge. We will deal with this latter issue both in terms of the decision making stage of the judge (whether the judge is experienced or not) and in terms of the judge's age (the development of judgmental principles in children).

### Importance and Involvement

We have seen that cognitive heuristics are useful judgmental principles in that they reduce complex tasks to simpler judgmental operations and usually achieve reasonable approximations. Heuristics, rather than more complete and formal analyses, are employed most when there is great time pressure or when one's cognitive processing system is taxed or overloaded. Because of the cost-effectiveness of applying rules of thumb, heuristics will tend to be used more for unimportant or uninvolving judgments. Decisions such as what to order at the fast-food restaurant or which magazine to read while waiting at the doctor's office should not be approached with formal inferential methods. When the decision is important and errors of judgment can be costly, however, decision makers generally should and do adopt more formal and complete analyses. Gabrenya and Arkin (1979) showed that, when the consequences of information processing were low in hedonic relevance, subjects adopted nonvigilant low-level processing that involved the use of heuristics and scripts. Processing deficits may thus be seen as due, in part, to motivational and arousal states of the judge rather than to any inherent limitations in processing. Langer (1978) also suggests that mindless processing will cease when the consequences of decisions become meaningful. Finally, Chaiken (1980) showed that subjects who were highly involved in a persuasive message situation used a systematic information processing strategy in which message-based cognitions mediated persuasion. Uninvolved subjects, on the other hand, employed a heuristic processing strategy where simple decision rules mediated persuasion.

Nisbett and Ross (1980) point out that there may be an exception to the general principle that more formal analyses and normative considerations are used for important and meaningful judgments. They speculate that decisions of especially high personal involvement will not be approached in a formal and rational way. They give examples of people irrationally blaming themselves for being unable to breast feed a baby successfully due to an inverted nipple or for causing someone's death by suggesting a particular airplane flight. Observers of these events don't make such irrational judgments. Perhaps inferences about matters that involve the self in a significant way evoke more primitive cognitive structures and principles.

In support of Nisbett and Ross' suggestion, Alloy and Abramson (1979) found that subjects could correctly judge contingencies between responses and outcomes unless the task was important. When outcomes were relevant and involvement was high, subjects failed to use the differential effectiveness of responses in judging contingencies. They instead resorted to more primitive heuristic principles. Only depressed subjects were immune from the tendency to fall back on simplifying strategies.

In a proposition suggesting another factor that might be relevant in determining whether or not heuristic strategies will be adopted, Isen (1981) maintains that positive affect will lead to simplified problem solving techniques. Since people in a good mood might be more likely to avoid cognitive overload and try to maintain their positive state, they ought to reduce decision-making complexity by falling back on heuristic principles. Isen reports that subjects put in a good mood by getting juice and cookies or a one dollar gift were more likely to make errors in a frequency estimation task by adopting the availability heuristic.

## Heuristic Principles: Primitive or Advanced Decision Making Tools?

Questions have arisen concerning the level of cognitive functioning necessary for the development of heuristic principles and the level of sophistication at which heuristics are relied on most. Are heuristics a primitive or an advanced decision-making tool? Do they develop early in childhood or are they an adult acquisition? Do they predominate in early or late stages of experience with particular kinds of complex judgments? It is certainly important to understand how and when people acquire and learn when to use the heuristic principles that so dominate their decision making. As yet, no theory of cognitive development, either in terms of ages or stages, has dealt specifically with the issue of judgmental heuristics and their associated biases. However they develop, it seems clear that neither age nor experience fully eliminates these biases in judgment. We have seen that experts as well as laypersons are subject to similar kinds of errors of judgment.

## The stage of the decision maker

One might speculate about the issue of whether heuristic development and use represent a primitive or advanced level of functioning. Since there are systematic and (seemingly) obvious errors associated with their use, heuristic principles are usually considered as representing an early and unsophisticated level of decision making. However, it is also possible to consider heuristics as a tool of the very advanced decision maker. Heuristic use may represent major judgmental principles of both very primitive and very advanced levels of cognitive functioning. The very young and uninitiated may rely on simplifying principles because the world is too complex and confusing for them to deal fully with all available information. Heuristics are needed to allow the unpracticed to make judgments and decisions with minimal confusion and cognitive strain. The very advanced and sophisticated may rely on heuristic principles because their knowledge and experience has allowed them to structure, organize, and simplify their worlds. This experience has allowed the development of schemas, scripts, and principles of judgment that can reduce complex decision making to an almost routine and automatic task.

The recent ideas of several theorists are consistent with the notion that heuristic use may be prevalent in very advanced (as well as primitive) levels of thinking. Hayes-Roth (1977) discussed the evolution of cognitive structures and processes. Her knowledge assembly theory proposes that both the representation and processing of knowledge change qualitatively with learning and experience. For example, consider a study where subjects learn noun-noun pairs in an A-B A-C transfer paradigm. According to Hayes-Roth, when the A-B pair is learned minimally, it is represented as unrelated A and B cognitive unit (cogit) representations. The A representation is available for use in learning the A-C pair, which should thus be enhanced. With moderate A-B learning, the pair is represented as an assembly of two associated A and B cogit representations. In this case, activation of A will activate B, and A-C learning will suffer. However, if A-B has been overlearned and is a unitized memory representation, it should no longer interfere with A-C learning. The point is that as learning proceeds to advanced levels, component representations get unitized and function as single elements in memory. Complex information can be dealt with in a simple and straightforward way. New information is approached through these integrated structures and when the information is consistent with the unitized package, great savings in processing time are achieved. However, when new information is inconsistent with the structures (and with the rules and principles implied by them) or when the unitized structures must be broken down into their component parts, processing will be inefficient.

An implication of Hayes-Roth's thinking is that once schemas and rules exist for organizing information, any schema-consistent information will be represented in memory as a unitary whole and will be processed as a whole according to the rules. The principle will be automatically applied in processing rule-relevant information. The balance principle (Heider, 1958) is such a rule. It is a coherent conceptual framework for representing liking relationships among social stimuli. Both Picek et al. (1975) and Sentis and Burnstein (1979) suggest that once the balance rule has been fully developed (that is, at advanced stages of experience), it is applied automatically to relevant social structural information. Since the information must be filtered through this rule or principle which treats the social structure as a whole, people should have a hard time dealing with individual parts of the integrated representation. Sentis and Burnstein (1979) had subjects study balanced or imbalanced three relation structures. They then answered questions that required retrieval of either one, two, or all three of the relations. For imbalanced structures, the information is not organized by a rule and must be represented relation by relation. In this case, reaction time increased as subjects dealt with more relations. However, for balanced structures, the information is represented as a unified whole according to the balance rule, and it took subjects less time to verify all three relations than two or one. Organizing information according to a simplifying principle means that, when only part of the information is needed, subjects will have to undo the organization that the rule has imposed on the information. Hayes-Roth (1977) has presented comparable data showing the difficulty of processing component parts of unitized structures.

Carroll (1980) agrees with the notion that it is often the very experienced and knowledgeable decision maker who relies most heavily on simplifying heuristic principles. In analyzing the decision processes of expert parole decision makers, Carroll (1978b) found that they did not exhaustively weigh the implications of all the facts in accordance with normative models. Rather they used simplifying principles and schematic rules, and demonstrated strong confirmatory biases. Nonexperts, on the other hand, had fewer and less detailed rules.

Once a rule or principle is highly developed and available, it becomes difficult to escape its use. It is applied automatically when activated by relevant information. This inescapability can be demonstrated by again considering the balance principle. Sherman (1975) asked people to think not about relations between people (which usually follow the balance principle), but about relations between magnetic poles. Here, the laws of magnetic attraction and repulsion are well-known (like poles repel; unlike poles attract); but, unfortunately, what is a sensible set of relations among three magnetic poles ($---$, $++-$) is exactly what is unbalanced in personal relationships. Since the balance principle is difficult not to apply when thinking about relations of attraction, it should be very hard for people to make judgments about magnets. Sherman has measured reaction time and errors for questions such as: "Among poles of magnets, A and B repel each other, B and C repel each other, what will A and C do?" or ". . . A and B attract each other, B and C repel each other, what will A and C do?" Aside from taking very long to answer, subjects make errors more than 35% of the time. It would appear that it is the development of a strong and available balance principle that makes these judgments so difficult. Once rules are highly developed, they interfere with the processing of any information that is incompatible with the application of the rule.

Langer (1978) has also proposed that, when information is overlearned, people respond automatically and mindlessly on the basis of simplified rules and principles. When scripts are well-learned, they control behavior and lead to thoughtless action. This, of course, occurs only after much experience in the domain at hand. At relatively early stages of learning, all information is attended to and decisions aren't made in a mindless manner. Langer's own research supports her ideas. By setting up situations that fit a well learned behavioral rule, Langer, Blank, and Chanowitz (1978) demonstrated that subjects mindlessly followed the rule even though it was not the reasonable thing to do. In one case, confederates asked to break into line to use a xerox machine "because they had to make copies." The reason, of course, is silly and adds nothing to the request itself. Yet the presence of any reason activates the "favor x $\rightarrow$ reason y $\rightarrow$ comply" script, and subjects in this condition complied 93% of the time.

The research cited in this section indicates that at advanced levels of knowledge, heuristic driven, automatic processing is the rule rather than active and complete processing of incoming information. It is reasonable, then, that simplifying rules are used both early in learning when the information processing load is too heavy to allow full information processing and late in learning when structures and principles have been well developed and direct the process of making judgments. Of course, it is likely that the rules used at advanced levels of experience are better and incorporate more information so that biases and errors are less likely than at early levels.

One way to understand the development of simplifying rules or heuristic principles as one gains experience in a particular domain of judgment is to study the development of expertise. There is now a rather extensive literature on changes in thinking and judgment as expertise develops. Much of this work has been done on the acquisition of skill in chess. For example, Simon and Chase (1973) recount several years of such research. An early finding (deGroot, 1965) was that chess grandmasters, when presented with a chess problem and asked to pick the next move, chose stronger moves than less experienced players. Yet on other indices, for example the number of moves examined or the speed of the decision, the two types of players could not be differentiated. DeGroot went on to discover that grandmasters, when shown a logical chess array and then asked to reconstruct it, were very much more accurate than were the lesser players. However, both groups did equally poorly when asked to reconstruct random arrays. Chase and Simon posit that over years of play and study of chess, players build up a vocabulary of patterns that they can recognize and for which they have stock moves that they consider using in response. In other words, advanced chess players have abstracted prototypes of various kinds of games (e.g., queen-side attack) and judge the similarity of any specific game to these prototypes. Of course, representativeness cannot be used in judgments unless one has developed a category system for a collection of objects, has abstracted a prototype of each category, and has developed ways to judge similarity to the prototype. These require experience. This might suggest that representativeness is a heuristic principle that is developed and used rather late in the course of one's experience in an area of judgment. On the other hand, availability requires only a judgment of the ease with which specific instances are brought to mind. Such a principle might be employed early in one's experience as a more primitive heuristic. It would certainly be worth finding out whether in fact the predominance of availability and representativeness as principles of judgment change over the course of development and experience.

The extent to which a chess game is representative of any prototype will determine the range of moves considered. The availability and simulation heuristics will also play a role in the decisions of expert chess players. As one considers a move and its implications, the ease with which a move can be brought to mind and the number of ways in which any move might lead to a favorable position in the future will be assessed and used in choosing a move. Non-expert players would not be capable of simulating multiple paths from any move to a future game position. One possibility for chess players (and this may be true for other kinds of judgments as well) is that novice players use very simple rules and principles that are subject to many kinds of errors. More advanced players may abandon such principles and treat each game and position independently. Experts again develop simplifying principles, only these are effective ways of organizing information and lead to effective decision making.

It thus appears that both representativeness and simulation begin to play major roles in the judgments of chess players as expertise develops. The judgmental processes of experts in areas other than chess have also been examined (e.g., audit program planning (Joyce, 1976), literary-critical judgment (Einhorn & Koelb, 1982), and medical pathology (Einhorn, 1974). Einhorn (1974) has proposed that the task of the expert is to identify information or cues from the relevant multidimensional stimuli that are encountered. These cues are diagnostic about the judgment or decision. The expert must typically extract, identify, and measure several cues at once. In so doing, errors based on heuristic principles may emerge. For example, Einhorn suggests that once an expert has developed an assessment of the extent to which cues covary (a judgment that requires some degree of experience), the measurement of one of these cues may affect the measurement of the other. On the other hand, Einhorn also suggests that with the development of expertise many biases to which non-experts fall prey will be avoided. He has demonstrated that expert decision makers do not typically commit biases such as leniency or halo effects. This is presumably because experience has taught experts to extract the critical cues for judgment (and to ignore the more irrelevant cues) and to measure these cues more accurately even in the absence of objective tools. In addition, the real expert can discern cues that the non-expert is oblivious to and can discern complex interactions among cues. Einhorn (1974) believes that these aspects of cue formation and utilization are at the heart of expertise.

Expert judgment would thus seem to involve a combination of heuristic principles and more creative and complex cue utilization. However, even the heuristic principles used are likely to be more sophisticated and advanced than those used by non-experts and are less likely to be prone to characteristic errors and biases. Even in using the common representativeness or simulation heuristics, experts are likely to be more accurate in making judgments of similarity or in assessing the number and likelihood of links between antecedent and consequent states.

## The age of the decision maker

Regardless of whether heuristic principles predominate in the judgment of primitive or advanced decision makers, the question still remains about how these principles develop. Clearly, basic principles of learning are involved. Strategies and simplifying principles that are used in chess and lead to wins will be abstracted and codified. Imitation of other players and attention to principles proposed in books are other avenues to developing simplifying strategies. Perhaps the best way to understand the development of heuristic principles is to consider the use of heuristics by children and the changes in use as children develop. Several important questions arise. Do children use heuristics? If so, is the use innate or does it develop at a certain age? If heuristics do develop, what determines their development and use? Is there a developmental sequence in the use of heuristic principles?

Obviously, the standard Kahneman and Tversky problems that have been used with adults (e.g., "Imagine a population composed of 70 lawyers and 30 engineers . . .") are not useful for studying heuristics in young children. In fact, research that directly addresses the use of the standard heuristic principles by children does not seem to exist. Thus we are forced to generalize to heuristics from research in a seemingly related area—problem solving and the development of logical thinking. This generalization or extrapolation is possible because of the definition of and framework for heuristics that we have been espousing. Briefly, we consider a heuristic to be a judgmental principle that reduces complex tasks to simpler judgmental operations by emphasizing certain properties of the data.

Such a procedure may lead to characteristic errors and biases as a result of a misweighing or a miscombination of relevant sources of information.

The first question to be addressed is whether children use heuristics. Many studies, especially of Piagetian tasks, can be taken to suggest that, by our definition, children do use heuristics. In a standard Piagetian task a child is shown two rows of objects. Each row contains an equal number of objects, but the spacing of the objects is different. Row A, for example, is spread out ("X X X") while Row B is packed more tightly ("XXX"). The child is then asked which row contains more objects. Up until a certain age the child will focus on the length of the display and determine that Row A, since it is longer, contains more objects. That is, the child ignores, or gives zero weight to, the relevant dimension of numerosity. Given two sources of information, numerosity and length, the child makes a decision entirely on the basis of one dimension. In many cases this simple decision rule does work—the ice cream cone with three scoops is longer than the one with two scoops, and it does contain more ice cream.

Given that children do use simplifying decision rules, are they innate or do they develop? Siegler (1978) has taken simple tasks and looked at cross-sectional differences in performance in children of different ages. One of the tasks Siegler used was the balance scale task. It consists of an arm balanced at its midpoint on a fulcrum. On each side of the fulcrum there are four evenly spaced pegs on which weights can be placed. The pegs are spaced on a ratio scale so that the fourth peg is four times as far from the fulcrum as is the first peg. The task that faces the children is the following. The arm is locked in a level, balanced position and weights are placed on the pegs. The child observes this and is then asked to guess what would happen were the arm to be released—would the left side go down, would the right side go down, or would the arm remain balanced?

To answer this question correctly there are two sources of information that have to be considered. One has to consider both the amount of weight placed on a side and the distance of the weights from the fulcrum. (Of course, the interaction between these two "main effects" is also important.) Siegler (1978) suggests that there are several stages of increasingly complex rules that children might use. At the lowest level, responding is random and no rule is used. That is, the child responds in such a way that the experimenter cannot generate a rule that explains it. At the next level, what Siegler calls Rule I, the child focuses only on weight and thus will guess that whichever side has the greater weight will go down. A more complex rule, Rule II, focuses both on weight and distance. Rules III and IV take increasingly accurate account of the interactions between weight and distance.

Siegler (1978) tested 3, 4, and 5-year-olds on a series of problems on this task. The 24 problems in the test sequence were varied on the two dimensions of interest so that it would become clear by the errors that the child made what rule he or she was following. He found that basically none of the 3-year-olds used Rule I (i.e., their responses did not seem to be rule based), about half of the four-year-olds used Rule I, and virtually all of the 5-year-olds used Rule I. Thus, there seems to be a development over time of the use of a decision rule. That is, these cross sectional data suggest that decision rules (i.e., heuristics) are not innate but developed.

The question now becomes what determines the development of simplifying principles of judgment? What is it that half of the 4-year-olds and all of the 5-year-olds have that the 3-year-olds don't? Siegler (1978) tried to see if experience with the problem would lead to the generation of a rule. He used the balance scale task again and first pre-tested 3 and 4-year-olds on it in order to select subjects who were not yet using Rule I. He then gave them an experience session where the lever was released after the child had made a guess. As well as this visual feedback, the experimenter prompted the child, if he or she had guessed wrong, to try to determine what it was that caused the balance scale to react as it did. Following this experience session there was a post-test. Siegler found that none of the ten 3-year-olds advanced to Rule I after experience sessions but six of the ten 4-year-olds did. Again it is apparent that decision rules develop, and now it is apparent that experience may be a necessary but not sufficient condition for a rule's development.

Siegler then started to explore how 3-year-olds and 4-year-olds encoded the balance scale problem. He posited that 3-year-olds did not encode or abstract the dimension of weight while the 4-year-olds did. Thus, being given feedback as in the previous experience experiment would be meaningless for 3-year olds as they are not aware of the relevant dimension. Four-year-olds, however, being aware of the weight dimension, could abstract the relation between the level of the weights and the positive or negative feedback. To start investigating this, Siegler (1978) showed children a balance scale with weights on each side of the fulcrum then hid it from their view and asked them to reproduce, on a second scale, the configuration they had been shown. Neither 3-year-olds nor 4-year-olds correctly encoded the distance dimension. The weight dimension was correctly encoded on 73% of the items by the 4-year-olds and on only 35% of the items by the 3-year-olds. Thus, it seemed likely that the rule applied to the balance scale problem that was exhibited by 4-year-olds and not 3-year-olds was due, at least in part, to their encoding of a relevant dimension.

The obvious next step was to try to teach the relevance of the weight dimension to 3-year-olds and then see if they performed more like 4-year-olds. This is exactly what Siegler did. He first taught the subjects to attend to the weight dimension when trying to reproduce the balance scale configuration. He then tested them to see how well they had learned to encode weight; the 3-year-olds encoded it correctly on 69% of the items and the 4-year-olds on 82%. Penultimately, Siegler gave the subjects some training that was intended to make the weight dimension salient when making balance scale predictions. Finally, he gave the subjects the standard series of 24 balance scale problems. It turned out that the 3-year-olds, after having been trained to encode the relevant dimension of weight and after having been given feedback as to its importance in the balance scale task, behaved in a rule governed manner on the post-test. That is, they made errors that were consistent with the simplifying rule that they (and the 4-year-olds) appeared to be following.

Heuristic development, to extrapolate, seems to be dependent on several factors. First of all, a person needs to be able to abstract the relevant dimension(s). Then a person has to be aware that the abstracted dimension is relevant. And then, possibly, the person needs experience with the problem in order to generate a rule. The balance scale example has been very simple and has focused on a rule that is determined by attending to only one dimension. To go beyond this state a person would need more complex cognitive capacity. A person would need to be able to abstract several relevant dimensions, to represent one or several of them in memory, and then to manipulate them.

As children grow, they advance from simple rules to more complex principles. Several studies have shown that under certain conditions it is possible to make a child retreat to using an earlier rule. This is especially interesting when the child retreats from using a normatively correct decision-making strategy to one that is more likely to yield errors. Gelman (1972) has shown this quite nicely. She presented nursery school, kindergarten, and second-grade children with a series of three sets of objects and asked them to pick out the two that were equal in number. She varied the sets in length and density as well as number and thus was able to infer, from the errors the children made, what the dimensions were on which the children based their decisions regarding numerosity. The most accurate approach, obviously, is to focus on number, ignore length and density, and count the objects. By second grade all of the children did this. For the younger children the story was different. As long as the numbers were small, they counted; as the numbers got too big for them they resorted to basing their judgments on the length of the display. Thus it seems that when their cognitive capacity was reached they resorted to an earlier, simpler decision-making rule—one that leads to characteristic errors.

Thus, it seems that children do use decision-making rules that could be called heuristics. They seem to develop with knowledge; that is as a child becomes aware of relevant dimensions he or she becomes able to abstract and generate decision-making rules. And even though a child may possess a normatively correct rule there are conditions of cognitive overload in which retreat to an earlier, less accurate rule occurs.

## ARE THE ERRORS ASSOCIATED WITH HEURISTIC USE INEVITABLE?

The issue of whether the use of heuristic principles inevitably leads to errors of judgment is often raised in the context of criticisms of the usefulness of judgmental heuristics for understanding decision making. As we shall see, some of these criticisms are of the one-shot variety in that they pick a specific kind of error or even a specific problem used in research and try to point to a flaw in its use (e.g., Evans & Dusoir, 1977; Olson, 1976). Other kinds of criticism (e.g., Cohen, 1979, 1981) are more general and argue that the heuristic principle approach is flawed because it misrepresents the way in which people understand the problems and the sytem of reasoning that they apply. Still others point out that the errors of judgmental heuristics can be reduced by framing the problems differently (e.g., Pitz, 1977) or by using judgments in continuous rather than discrete situations (Hogarth, 1980).

Whether or not these criticisms are valid (and many of them are), we should repeat a point made earlier. The presence or absence of errors of judgment should not be the ultimate test of the usefulness of the heuristic principle approach to decision making. It is only important that the approach identifies the kinds of information used in making judgments and the general kinds of strategies that predominate. Whether or not errors occur or which errors occur should be a secondary consideration.

### Are They Really Errors?

Nevertheless, heuristics are studied largely because of the errors produced by their use. But all the errors which are blamed on heuristics are not due only to an inappropriately applied rule of thumb. The application of the decision rule is but one step in the decision process. Errors can occur at other stages in the process. Thus, an error could occur when a decision maker perceives the task, when he or she selects information to be processed, when the information is processed, or when the outcome is interpreted.

In a problem like the lawyer/engineer base rate problem there is a normative rule which should be applied. But in order to use this rule two conditions must obtain. First, the decision maker faced with the problem must know the normative rule, and second he or she must recognize this as a situation in which to apply it. If the person does not know the normative rule then the representativeness heuristic will be applied and an incorrect decision made. This sort of error can be called an error of comprehension (Kahneman & Tversky, 1982a), for a normative rule that is not known or comprehended cannot be applied. But if the decision maker knows that such a rule exists, an error can still be made if he or she does not perceive this as a problem in which the rule should be applied. Kahneman and Tversky (1982a) call this an error of application.

In errors of application, a person may be aware that the decision process being undertaken will not be accurate but may prefer a quick and dirty estimate to the expense of a full and formal analysis. Consider the Tversky and Kahneman (1973) problem of availability in which subjects are asked if there are more words with "K" in first or third position. One might be aware that the best way of deciding this would be to go to a dictionary and start counting. But this is a tedious task and it is much easier, unless the stakes are very high, simply to estimate.

Before it can be concluded with certainty that reliance on heuristic principles does inevitably lead to characteristic biases, we must be sure that subjects truly understand the problems and are applying the heuristics as proposed. In some cases, problems developed by Kahneman and Tversky and others may not be understood as the experimenters intended. For example, Kahneman and Tversky (1982a) used the following problem which was considered earlier: Suppose Bjorn Borg reaches the Wimbledon finals. Please rank order the following outcomes from most to least likely: (a) Borg will win the match. (b) Borg will lose the first set. (c) Borg will win the first set but lose the match. (d) Borg will lose the first set but win the match. Subjects showed the characteristic bias called the conjunction effect by ranking (d) as more likely than (b). Assuming subjects understood the differences between a set and a match, this is certainly an error in judgment *if* subjects understood (d) as asking for the likelihood that Borg would lose the first set *and* win the match. What if they interpreted it to mean that given Borg loses the first set, how likely is he to win the match? If subjects read (d) as a conditional probability estimate, it is not an error to rank it higher than (b)—especially given Borg's reputation as a slow starter.

Another problem presented by Kahneman and Tversky (1982a; adopted from Casscells, Schoenberger, & Grayboys, 1978) reads as follows: "If a test to detect a disease whose prevalence is 1/1000 has a false positive rate of 5%, what is the chance that a person found to have a positive result actually has the disease, assuming you know nothing about the person's symptoms or signs?"

Only 11 of 60 expert subjects gave the correct response of 2%. But did subjects truly understand the meaning of "false positive"? Perhaps the many subjects who answered 95% believed that 5% false positive rate meant that whenever the test showed up positive, it was wrong 5% of the time. Then, of course, the correct answer *is* 95%. The error is not due to ignoring base rates, but due to a misunderstanding of the terms in the problem.

It is also the case that before one claims that a subject is not following "normative" rules, one has to determine the subject's norms. Though psychologists may be aware that global personality descriptions are not good predictors of behavior (Mischel, 1968), many people are not. Thus, in the lawyer/engineer problem the subject believes that he or she is being given useful information because of conversational rules. That is, subjects expect that *any* information given to them must be useful and relevant for solving the problem (Kahneman & Tversky, 1982a). Why else would the experimenter present the information? In addition, the information given may also fit into his or her implicit personality theory. To a subject, the fact that the target, Jack, likes mathematical puzzles may have great diagnostic value and imply that Jack is more likely to be an engineer. In a situation where the sample information is valid (i.e., has diagnostic value), the correct answer of course no longer mirrors the base rates. Gabrenya and Arkin (1979) did determine the subjective diagnostic value of the individuating information. From this they calculated the Bayesian probability that Jack was an engineer and found that it was 35.3%, significantly higher than the base rate of 30%.

Kahneman and Tversky themselves (1982a) acknowledge that not all non-normative responses indicate a bias or judgmental error. Subjects do misunderstand questions and give answers that are reasonable (although normatively wrong) based on their constructions of the problem at hand.

It has also been suggested that many errors and biases attributed to reliance on heuristic principles are not errors at all. Cohen (1979, 1981) believes that in many cases subjects are applying a sound normative system (the Baconian system of reasoning) to the problems. They are not applying heuristic principles as such, but rather are arriving at reasonable solutions to many Kahneman and Tversky problems when these solutions are viewed within the Baconian system. Cohen proposes that the Pascalian notion of probability (from which Kahneman & Tversky derive their normative standards) is not the only valid notion of probability. Biases and errors can exist only when judges are applying an unreasonable system or when they are misapplying a system. In Cohen's view (a view not, however, shared by Kahneman & Tversky, 1979a), subjects are correctly applying a reasonable system. Judgments are not biased or in error with respect to that system. Within Baconian reasoning (detailed in Cohen, 1970), neglect of base-rates, insensitivity to sample size, and other so-called errors of judgment are in fact the appropriate things to do.

One of the problems in evaluating Cohen's claims is that there can be disagreement in many cases about what state of affairs actually is normative. One can argue for many of the problems employed in evaluating judgmental heuristics what is true and what isn't (as in the lawyer/engineer problem). Yet sometimes the problems ask for things that can be measured in the real world, and we can compare judgments to actual standards (e.g., whether K appears more as a first or third letter). In these cases, it should be clear that errors are being made, and no ideas about a different form of representation indicate that these are not errors. In addition, Cohen's ideas on how to determine the representativeness of any sample are no more compelling or intuitive than those of Kahneman and Tversky.

## When Base Rates are Considered

Be that as it may, reliance on heuristics will typically lead to certain specifiable errors and biases. Hogarth (1980) has generated a list of the kinds of decision situations that should be most subject to these judgmental biases. These are situations involving one or more of the following features: task complexity, procedural uncertainty (e.g., no formal rule or schema for solution exists), absence of psychological regret (care in judgment won't be taken when the judge feels little responsibility if a mistake is made), and emotional stress. The question remains whether such errors are inevitable or whether people can learn to make better use of heuristics and not overuse them or fall into the common traps.

Most errors resulting from reliance on heuristic principles are due to the fact that relevant and important information is ignored (e.g., base rates, sample size). Such errors are not inevitable. Many researchers and theorists have specified certain conditions that lead subjects not to make the errors typically associated with heuristic use. Much of this work concerns the use of base rates. As we saw before, use of the representativeness heuristic can be associated with a tendency to ignore base rates. When judges rely on similarity to make judgments of frequency or likelihood, the prior probability is typically ignored since it has no relationship to the representativeness of the event. Tversky and Kahneman's (1980) cab example demonstrates this bias:

> "A cab was involved in a hit-and-run accident at night. Two cab companies, the Green and the Blue, operate in the city. Eighty-five percent of the cabs in the city are Green and 15% are Blue. A witness identified the cab as a Blue cab. The court tested his ability to identify cabs under appropriate visibility conditions. When presented with a sample of cabs (half of which were Blue and half of which were Green) the witness made correct identifications in 80% of the cases and erred in 20% of the cases." (p. 62)

Subjects were asked to judge the probability that the cab involved in the accident was Blue rather than Green. The correct answer, using Bayes' Rule, is .41. The cab is more likely to be Green because the base rate (85-15) is more extreme than the witness is credible. Yet subjects typically answer that the likelihood of the cab being Blue is 80%—corresponding to the credibility of the witness. The base rate is ignored. Bar-Hillel (1975) showed how robust this tendency to ignore base rates is. She found that people ignore base rates regardless of when in the problem they are presented, regardless of whether judges agree or disagree with the data, and regardless of whether the problem is presented in verbal or numerical form. Nisbett and Borgida (1975) and Nisbett et al. (1976) found the neglect of base rate information in a large variety of judgment tasks (e.g., trait inference, causal attribution, and behavioral prediction).

Despite the widespread tendency to ignore base rates, there are certain factors and conditions that, when introduced into the decision-making task, will lead subjects to attend to base rate data. People will, of course, use base rate information if there are no specific case data available. If a judge knows only that 85% of the cabs in the city are Green and knows nothing about the witness' identification or the reliability of the witness, he or she will naturally report the base rate as his(her) judgment of the likelihood of a Green cab being involved in the accident.

A more interesting factor that is related to the use of base rate data is whether those data have causal meaning. When people see no causal link between the base rate data and the case data, they don't combine the two kinds of information. However, when the base rates appear to have some meaningful causal relationship to the outcome, they are not ignored. Consider an alternative formulation of the cab problem:

> "A cab was involved in a hit-and-run accident at night. Two cab companies, the Green and the Blue, operate in the city. Although the two companies are roughly equal in size, 85% of the cab accidents in the city involve Green cabs, and 15% involve Blue cabs. A witness identified the cab as a Blue cab. The court tested his ability to identify cabs under the appropriate visibility conditions. When presented with a sample of cabs (half of which were Blue and half of which were Green) the witness made correct identifications in 80% of the cases and erred in 20% of the cases." (p. 63)

This is formally the same problem as before. However, people make far greater use of the base rate data in this case. The average response is now 55% rather than 80%. The key difference between the problems is that, in the second form, involvement in the accident is correlated with the target variable, whereas in the original problem cab color is uncorrelated with number of accidents. This difference in structure is critical. The second form readily elicits a causal explanation—drivers of Green cabs are more reckless. This property is then applied to all Green cabs and increases the subjective probability that a Green cab would be involved in any accident. A mere difference in the original proportion of Green and Blue cabs doesn't elicit a causal explanation of why more accidents involve Green cabs.

Ajzen (1977) has also proposed that only when base rate evidence fits into a causal schema will it be used. Equally informative but non-causal information is neglected. Here is an example of two forms of one of his problems (p. 308):

Form 1:   Two years ago, a final exam was given in a course at Yale University. About 75% of the students failed the exam.

Form 2:   Two years ago, a final exam was given in a course at Yale University. An educational psychologist interested in scholastic achievement interviewed a large number of students who had taken the course. Since he was primarily concerned with reactions to failure, he selected mostly students who had failed the exam. Specifically, about 75% of the students in his sample had failed the exam.

Subjects were asked to assess the probability that a particular student, who was described briefly, passed the exam. Form 1 has base rate information that is causal—the judge infers that the exam was difficult, and that this was the cause of the high rate of failure. This can be used to predict individual cases. Form 2 allows no such causal inference. Estimates varied greatly. Probability of success in Form 1 was only .39, while it was .55 with Form 2. Zuckerman (1978) has also proposed that judges will use base rate information about behavior when this information elicits a meaningful script to account for the behavior and the script can then be used to predict behavior.

However, even base rate data that can be seen as causally related to an outcome may be ignored if the causal relationship is incompatible with a judge's prior causal schema. Nisbett and Borgida (1975) presented base rates about how many people in an emergency situation actually helped. This proportion was given as quite small in some cases, indicating that people are callous and unfeeling. This conflicted with subjects' general view of what people are like and how they act. The knowledge that helping had a low base rate didn't decrease predictions of the likelihood that a particular participant, briefly described, actually helped. Subjects evidently continued to judge by their initial causal schema rather than by the view implied by the base rate data. They likely viewed the subjects who didn't help as weird and unrepresentative. The subject described wasn't weird and awful, and thus subjects judged that he was one who helped.

Bar-Hillel (1980) suggests that it is not causality per se that is important, but the judged relevance of the information at hand to the problem in question. Specificity is one aspect of information that determines its perceived relevance. Information about a population base rate will thus be seen as less relevant than information about a specific subset of the population and will be utilized less. In addition, individuating and causal base rates relate more specifically to the individual case and will be judged as more relevant. Bar-Hillel thus proposes that making a base rate causally relevant is but one means of increasing its relevance. In fact, when she presented a judgment problem that juxtaposed two causal base rates, judgments were based entirely on the causal base rate that related more specifically to a sub-population rather than to the entire population.

Tversky and Kahneman (1982b) discuss the importance of internal versus external attributions in the use of base rate information. When a base rate is given a situational interpretation, it can be used to predict the outcome of other cases. For example, in the Ajzen (1977) study, the information in Form 1 indicates that the difficulty of the exam (a situational factor) determined the base rate. This allows for the prediction of other individual cases. When a base rate is understood in terms of an accident of sampling (internal characteristics of the particular respondents), as in Nisbett and Borgida (1975), it can be ignored in the prediction of others' behavior.

Base rate information has been shown to affect judgments even when it is not causally related to the outcome. Manis, Dovalina, Avis, and Cardoze (1980) presented base rate information on a case by case basis and had subjects make predictions in a discrete response format rather than a continuous evaluation of category membership probabilities. Predictions in this case were strongly affected by variations in base rate, as Bayesian analysis implies (see Bar-Hillel & Fischhoff, 1981 for an alternative interpretation of these results in terms of representativeness). Feldman, Higgins, Karlovas, and Ruble (1976) also report that sequentially presented base rates are utilized more than those given in a simultaneous presentation. In a study investigating causal attributions for an actor's choice behaviors, consensus information (the base rate of people in the population who engage in a behavior) was used more when it was presented sequentially.

Ginosar and Trope (1980) suggest that, when the individuating information itself is inconsistent in some way and can't be interpreted in terms of stored prototypic representations, a more deliberate mode of thinking will be elicited. In such a case, the individual will attend to base rates. In their work, Ginosar and Trope found that judgments became responsive even to abstract and noncausal base rates when the individuating information was not consistent, was not related to the outcome categories, or when the outcome categories were hard to distinguish. For example, in an alteration of the Kahneman and Tversky lawyer/engineer problem, some subjects read about a target who had qualities of both lawyers and engineers; others had to distinguish between categories of electrical engineer and aeronautical engineer. These subjects were quite responsive to base rate information.

Finally, Kassin's work (1979) shows that when base rate information is extreme or otherwise salient, it will not be ignored. Sequential rather than simultaneous presentation of data may be important in this regard. Subjects' belief in the validity of the base rate information also affects its use (Wells & Harvey [1978] make a similar point).

In summary, biases in judgment due to ignoring base rates is avoided when the base rates are concrete, salient, causally meaningful, specific to the individual case, and valid, or when the usefulness of the individuating information for diagnosing category membership is especially low.

## The Framing of the Problem

A key to whether heuristic principles will be relied on to the extent of exclusion of relevant information and whether the use of heuristics will lead to characteristic errors and biases is how the problem to be solved in presented and structured. As we saw in the cab example, the same formal problem can be framed in several ways, only some of which will lead to correct encoding and solving. Pitz (1977) believes that the representation of the problem is extremely important. To demonstrate this, he asked subjects to choose which of two samples was more likely to have been chosen from a population of numbers with a mean of 50 and a standard deviation of 12. The two samples were: (a) 47, 49, 49, and 49; (b) 45, 48, 52, and 54. When the samples were simply presented, the majority of subjects chose (b). This is because subjects abstract the central tendency (50) and judge by similarity to this abstraction. What subjects ignore by using this representativeness heuristic is the likelihood of each individual value. To make this feature salient, Pitz asked the question in a slightly different way. He first asked subjects to make item by item judgments (e.g., which is more likely 47 or 45, 49 or 48, etc.). Finally, they were asked which of the two samples was more likely. For nearly all subjects, the experience of thinking in terms of individual items was enough to prevent reliance on the representativeness heuristic. Pitz (1977) also demonstrated how other Kahneman and Tversky problems to which subjects fall prey to heuristic biases can be framed in such a way as to improve judgments. Consider the following problem that leads to a characteristic bias:

"The mean I.Q. of the population of eighth-graders in a city is known to be 100. You have selected a random sample of 50 children for a study of educational achievements. The first child tested had an I.Q. of 150. What do you expect the mean to be for the whole sample?" (Tversky & Kahneman, 1971, p. 106)

Tversky and Kahneman found that many subjects guessed 100, exhibiting the gambler's fallacy and implying that they expect the last 49 members to have an I.Q. that averages below 100. When Pitz (1977, p. 7) framed the problem in a different way, the gambler's fallacy was not apparent.

The mean I.Q. of the population of eighth-graders in a city is known to be 100. You have selected a random sample of 50 children for a study of educational achievements. The first child tested has an I.Q. of 150. What do you expect the mean I.Q. to be for the remaining 49 children?

Only 5 of 29 students gave answers of less than 100. These examples illustrate that subjects may indeed have the appropriate problem solving approaches in their repertoires, but need help in encoding the problems in the appropriate manner. With this in mind, Pitz suggests that heuristics aren't an inescapable source of bias that inevitably lead to distorted judgments in the way that perceptual illusions do. Rather, heuristics involve a particular way of encoding a problem and can be considered a set of solutions based on certain strategic considerations. With better problem presentation, judges can achieve more appropriate encoding and avoid many of the characteristic biases associated with heuristic use.

Others have also pointed out that alternative ways of posing judgmental problems can reduce or eliminate certain biases associated with heuristic use. Peterson (1977) has eliminated typical heuristic biases in judging random sequences simply by providing subjects with instructions that random events may be present or by giving them a comparison level of nonrandomness. Fischhoff, Slovic, and Lichtenstein (1979) used a within subject design to induce subjects not to ignore base rates or predictive validity information. Each subject made several judgments as either base rates or preditive validity varied over a wide range of values. This method of presenting problems tuned subjects in to the relevant information and diminished judgmental biases. For example, when subjects were asked to judge grade point average from GPA distributions, a test of mental concentration, *and* a humor test, they took into account the reliability and the validity of the information base. Kahneman and Tversky (1973) had found that the validity and reliability of the information had minimal impact on judgments when a comparable study had been done with a between subject design.

Both Kassin (1979) and Evans and DuSoir (1977) presented problems in such a way that subjects took sample size into account in their judgments. Kahneman and Tversky's work (1972) had shown that people don't understand the principle that sampling variance decreases as sample size increases. They judge likelihood primarily by the degree to which the outcome is representative of the expected value. However, Kassin (1979) asked subjects about the generalizability of results from a given sample of data and found that they took sample size into account in making predictions that went beyond the data. Evans and DuSoir (1977) argued that Kahneman and Tversky's (1972) presentation of the sample size problems was unnecessarily complex and made proportionality rather than sample size salient. They also suggested that Kahneman and Tversky based their results on median scores, thus overlooking many individuals who understood the importance of sample size. By presenting analyses for individuals, Evans and DuSoir found that one third of their subjects gave more weight to sample size than to proportionality. When the problem was presented in an alternative simplified form, the majority of subjects showed insight into the role of sample size.

An example by Pitz (1977, p. 33) also demonstrates how the formulation of a problem can reduce the tendency to ignore sample size. Seventy-one percent of subjects correctly solved the following problem:

> Potential punters for a football team are being evaluated. Each player was asked to kick the ball several times and the distance of each kick was measured. Player P kicked the ball 9 times, averaging 42 yards per punt. Player Q kicked the ball 34 times, averaging 40 yards per punt. Which of the two players would you select for the team?''

Thus, when the formal structure of the problem allows sample size to be seen as a critical factor, subjects do take it into account in making judgments. The choice of response mode can also influence how subjects approach a problem and the principles they apply to solve it. Lichtenstein and Slovic (1971, 1973) showed how different cognitive processes were used when subjects evaluated the worth of gambles by comparing them (''which would you rather play?'') than when they judged each gamble for its worth separately. The different response modes led to reversals of preferences in identical problems. The comparison mode made the probability of winning salient while the individual judgment mode focused subjects on the payoff.

Einhorn and Hogarth (1981) make the point that task representation is more important in understanding errors in judgment than the rules that are used within the representation. They consider the case of the paranoid who processes information and acts with great consistency. It is only his representation of the world as hostile and evil that is at fault, not the rules and information processing techniques used within that representation. Researchers have recently begun to realize the importance of problem representation and have been studying the problem construction and editing that are involved in the initial stages of response to a decision situation. Hayes and Simon (1976) and Hayes, Waterman, and Robinson (1977) have used a process-tracing approach which involves collecting data from the time a subject hears the task instructions to the time work begins on the task. This helps clarify how subjects generate a problem space. In one procedure, subjects are asked to give verbal protocols, which are then compared with protocols from subjects given formally equivalent but differently worded problems (Hayes & Simon, 1976). An alternative method is to ask subjects to make relevance judgments about the instructions as they read one sentence at a time (Hayes et al., 1977).

Tversky and Kahneman (1981), of course, also understand the importance of the form of problem presentation and its effect on representation. They use the term "decision frame" to refer to the judge's conception of the acts, outcomes, and contingencies of a decision. The frame that is adopted is assumed to depend, in part, on the formulation of the problem. Rational decision making requires that the preference between options shouldn't vary with changes in frame. Yet Tversky and Kahneman (1981, p. 453) show that variation in problem presentation can have great effects on judgments. The following example demonstrates this:

> "Problem 1: Imagine that the U.S. is preparing for the outbreak of an unusual Asian disease, which is expected to kill 600 people. Two alternative programs to combat the disease have been proposed. Assume that the exact scientific estimate of the consequences of the programs are as follows:
> If Program A is adopted, 200 people will be saved.
> If Program B is adopted, there is one third probability that 600 people will be saved, and two thirds probability that no people will be saved.
> Which of the two programs would you favor?"

A second version of the problem was presented (p. 453) to other subjects. The initial part of the problem was the same, but the formulation of alternative programs differed:

> "Problem 2:
> If Program C is adopted, 400 people will die.
> If Program D is adopted, there is one third probability that nobody will die, and two thirds probability that 600 people will die.
> Which of the two programs would you favor?"

In Problem 1, 72% chose Program A, the risk aversive alternative. In the formally identical Problem 2, 78% preferred Program D, the risky alternative. The change in wording led subjects to focus on different factors and principles in making their decisions.

Tversky and Kahneman (1981) assume that people will generally evaluate acts in terms of a minimal account—they employ some simplifying heuristic which includes only the direct consequences of the act. This approach has the advantages of simplifying the decision making and of adopting criteria that fit with people's implicit theory that consequences should be causally linked to acts. Yet, certain modes of presentation of a problem can lead judges to evaluate in more inclusive terms, by taking into account earlier outcomes. This can be illustrated by comparing decisions in the following two problems (from Tversky & Kahneman, 1981, p. 457):

"Problem 1:   Imagine that you have decided to see a play where admission is $10 per ticket. As you enter the theater you discover that you have lost a $10 bill. Would you still pay $10 for a ticket for the play?"

"Problem 2:   Imagine that you have decided to see a play and paid the admission price of $10 per ticket. As you enter the theater you discover that you have lost the ticket. The seat was not marked and the ticket cannot be recovered.
   Would you pay $10 for another ticket?"

While 88% of subjects answered "yes" to Problem 1, only 46% answered "yes" to Problem 2. The difference is that the loss of $10 is not linked to the ticket purchase in Problem 1 and thus has little effect on the decision. As in previous examples, a seemingly minor change in formulating the problem led to different decision rules and strategies. Different formulations elicit different problem solving frames. Specific heuristic principles may or may not be applied depending upon the particular presentation format and its association to problem solving frames.

Kahneman and Tversky (1982c) further point out that the key to whether different presentation formats of formally equivalent problems are easy or hard to solve is the mental model or schema evoked by the problem. Different rules and operations are more or less available in different contexts (Hayes & Simon, 1976), so that the reasoning process can't be described in terms of some absolute set of rules. The principles that are applied depend very much on the content and context of the presentation.

The point is that errors and biases usually associated with heuristic use are not inevitable. In the first place, many of these errors are not inherent in the application of heuristic principles. Rather it is the faulty representation or understanding of the problem that underlies the errors of judgment. However, even when the bias is based on the heuristic principle itself, it can often be avoided by alternative forms of problem presentation, which render certain kinds of relevant information more salient.

## Teaching Judges to be Better Decision Makers

Fischhoff (1977) has tried another approach—directly pointing out pitfalls—to try to eliminate judgmental bias. He warned subjects about the biases due to the knowledge of outcomes. Unfortunately, the warning had no effect on the degree of hindsight bias—subjects persisted in assimilating facts as consistent with their preceding notions and continued to believe they "knew it would happen."

Lichtenstein et al. (1978) also tried to eliminate biases in judgment by the direct approach. They had found that subjects grossly misjudged the frequency of death from various causes. The basis for the biases was the differential availability based either on nonrepresentative media reporting or differential salience or vividness of the causes. In order to debias subjects, they were told about availability and were told not to let their judgments be biased by factors such as imaginability, memorability, or media coverage. This technique had no effect on judgments, nor did a technique where subjects were told of the biases and could actually see and try to improve on the estimates of other subjects.

However, others have been more successful in debiasing judgments by directly pointing out the pitfalls of heuristic use or by including procedures designed to eliminate the biases. Ross et al. (1975) eliminated the perseverance effect, a bias due to availability of unrepresentative information. They achieved this by "process" debriefing, in which explicit discussion of the perseverance effect and its causes was included. Beyth-Marom and Fischhoff (1977) reduced the availability bias by having people work very hard to produce examples of classes of events prior to estimating the frequencies of the classes. Another successful technique was reported by Armstrong, Denniston, and Gordon (1975). They improved subjects' performance on a difficult estimation task by decomposing the initial question into a number of smaller questions that were easier to answer. These answers could then be integrated to give a better answer to the original question.

Slovic and Fischhoff (1977) used a different approach to eliminating the bias of outcome knowledge. They first gave subjects false information (presented as true) about the outcomes of experiments. Once subjects had considered these, they were told of the deception and given the true results. This was quite successful in overcoming hindsight bias. The initial false outcome had evidently led subjects to assimilate this false outcome to their prior ideas. Later knowledge of the true outcome couldn't undo this initial construction. This finding suggests that the biasing effects of explaining hypothetical outcomes (Ross et al., 1977; Sherman et al., 1981; Sherman et al., 1983) might be eliminated by having subjects explain multiple rather than single outcomes. Research into the effects of explaining multiple outcomes is now going on in our laboratory.

We have seen that alternative problem presentations, increasing the salience of certain factors, and using within subject designs can be effective ways to eliminate or reduce some of the errors that are characteristic of heuristic use. It has also been suggested that simply motivating subjects to think more carefully by offering incentives would improve judgments. However, since judges may not always be aware of the biases involved in heuristic use, it isn't clear that incentives will help. In fact, there is evidence that decision makers do not improve substantially when incentives are offered. Chapman and Chapman (1967) reported that illusory correlations continued even when subjects were offered large amounts of money for accuracy. The tendency of judges to provide overly narrow confidence limits has also not been eliminated by offers of money (Tversky & Kahneman, 1974). Nor did payoffs eliminate anchoring effects brought on by the assignment of initial arbitrary values (Tversky & Kahneman, 1974). Lichtenstein and Slovic (1971, 1973), Grether (1979), and Grether and Plott (1979) have also failed to eliminate errors of judgment by the offer of incentives. These findings are consistent with the view that the errors associated with heuristic use are of a cognitive rather than a motivational nature and can't be "willed away" by subjects' greater efforts.

The fact that greater effort may not allow judges to avoid the errors associated with heuristic use forces us to think that heuristics are not simply "shortcuts" that are consciously undertaken to reduce the amount of effort necessary to make a judgment. Yet, in some cases it is clear that heuristics are nothing more than shortcuts, and that subjects could employ more complex and complete strategies and arrive at better solutions if the incentives were there. For example, subjects could obtain the correct answer to the product of $10 \times 9 \times 8 \times 7 \times 6 \times 5 \times 4 \times 3 \times 2 \times 1$ (or $1 \times 2 \times 3 \times 4 \times 5 \times 6 \times 7 \times 8 \times 9 \times 10$) by putting out a little effort. It appears, however, that in other tasks even the willingless to expend considerable effort doesn't improve performance. This might indicate that there are two types of heuristics—a consciously applied shortcut procedure and an automatically applied and unavoidable set of strategies. Such a distinction might be important in understanding the processes underlying the use of heuristic strategies.

The whole issue of debiasing judges and thus improving their inductive inferences and judgments has recently been addressed by several writers. Specifically, training people to be better decision makers has been suggested (as opposed to reframing problems or motivating judges). Nisbett and Ross (1980) believe that judgments can be improved by having people learn certain inferential maxims. "Okay, what do the other three cells look like" and "which hat did you draw the sample out of" are examples of such maxims. Nisbett and Ross also believe that the quality of judgments can be improved by educational programs and suggest that elementary statistics and probability theory (with a focus on intuitive strategies and their shortcomings) be taught as early as elementary school. The importance of the distinction between intuitive and formal strategies in decision making would then be available for all.

Nisbett et al. (1982) also believe that inferential errors can be reduced by teaching rough inferential guides (heuristics for eliminating the errors of heuristics?). They do point to several difficulties with such a program. For example, it can be difficult to know which model or inferential procedure is called for in any problem; even when errors occur, it is hard to know why; it may be hard to translate statistical considerations into guides for everyday reasoning. However, they hold hope that statistical heuristics can replace informal heuristics. Statistical heuristics would simply encourage people to think about information in terms of important data properties such as base rates, reliability, and validity. Their optimism is based on the fact that advances in human judgment have occurred in the last 300 years at an impressive rate and that principles of statistical reasoning are really quite modern. In addition, the statistical heuristics they have in mind are in many ways simpler to use than the faulty reasoning underlying many errors.

Kahneman and Tversky (1979b) also suggest corrective procedures for errors of judgment such that principles of statistical prediction would be met. They deal specifically with the failure of intuitive predictions to be sufficiently regressive. Rather than taking the uncertainty of evidence into account, judges typically make predictions according to a simple matching rule, the representativeness heuristic. The corrective procedure involves teaching the judge a five-step technique of proper inference for making a prediction about an act that has uncertain values (e.g., the length of time it will take to write a book chapter).

1. Selection of a reference class; that is, identification of a class to which the case at hand can be referred and for which the distribution of outcomes can be known.
2. Assessment of the distribution for the reference class.
3. Intuitive estimation about the particular case at hand.
4. Assessment of the predictability of the outcome (e.g., how easy is it to predict the length of time to write a book chapter?).
5. Correction of the intuitive estimate by adjusting the value toward that of the reference class.

Suggestions are also given by Kahneman and Tversky (1979b) for debiasing the faulty estimates of the size of credible confidence intervals. Their strategy of debiasing involves eliciting from the judge certain information that is already available but normally neglected.

Direct analysis of judgmental errors has also been suggested as a way of reducing or eliminating them. Kahneman and Tversky (1982a) distinguish between positive and negative analyses. A positive analysis focuses on the factors that lead to a certain error, while a negative analysis explains why the correct response wasn't made. Positive analyses are concerned with the heuristics that people use to make judgments and are useful when the same heuristic explains judgments in a variety of problems where different rules are violated. Negative analyses are concerned with the problems in understanding and applying elementary rules of reasoning and are useful when people consistently violate a rule in different problems, but not by applying only one heuristic. Kahneman and Tversky show how both a positive and a negative analysis can help us understand and correct the tendency for predictions to be insufficiently regressive. This dual analysis can explain both why any particular heuristic is chosen and why the normatively correct rule was not applied.

Decision aids for correcting judgmental deficiencies can speak to any and all steps in the decision-making process. Hogarth (1980) presents suggestions to the sophisticated decision maker for overcoming errors and biases in structuring the problem, assessing consequences, assessing uncertainties, evaluating alternatives, sensitivity analyses, information gathering, and choice. In addition, he outlines eight key issues that naive judges should consider in the process of making any judgment:

1.  Think in terms of variation around the arithmetic average. The amount of variation depends upon (a) the "true" variation of the phenomena and (b) lack of reliability/measurement error (see also point 5 below).
2.  Averages of data show less variation than the data averaged. Furthermore, variation of averages is reduced as the number of observations averaged increases. (Variation of averages is affected both by the amount of variability in the data averaged—upwards—and by the number of items of data averaged—downwards.)
3.  What is the base-rate? (Recall Thurber's: "Compared to what?")
4.  What is the validity of the information source? How does it relate to the predictive target?
5.  What is the reliability of the information source? Recall that imperfect reliability implies lowered predictive validity, e.g., measurement error in economic statistics. Assess the "signal/noise" ratio (margin of error). Avoid extreme predictions based on extreme observations from data sources that are not perfectly reliable (the "regression" fallacy).
6.  When predicting from several items of information, distinguish between:
    (a) redundancy (extent to which different sources overlap/can be predicted from each other); and
    (b) validity of different data sources vis-a-vis the target. Remember, consistency between data sources is only a valid cue to confidence in prediction to the extent that sources are not redundant/overlapping.

7. To what extent could a "random hypothesis" account for your data?

8. Is it possible to test your predictions?

While it is possible to reduce or eliminate errors associated with heuristic use, we shall see in the next section that there are many reasons for the persistence of reliance on simplifying heuristic principles. Whether it is worth replacing these principles with more normatively correct approaches and how this might be done most effectively is not yet entirely clear.

## EXPLAINING THE PERSISTENCE OF HEURISTIC PRINCIPLES

The application of heuristic principles rather than a formal and normative analysis is the rule rather than the exception for many kinds of judgments under uncertainty. It is clear that the employment of these cognitive heuristic principles is accompanied by characteristic biases and errors of judgment that can have costly and embarrassing effects. One may then reasonably ask why heuristics continue to be used as frequently as they are. Don't people learn from their errors of judgment and their biased predictions? There are a number of reasons for the persistence of heuristic use:

1. In the first place, although the examples in the literature dwell on biases, it isn't the case that reliance on heuristic principles leads to errors of judgment all the time or even most of the time. Representativeness and availability *are* reasonable rules of thumb in most instances. People who look like and act like lawyers usually are lawyers. Samples that resemble the population are generally more likely than atypical samples. The instances that come most quickly and easily to mind are often frequent and probable. Heuristics are thus used because they have more than a modicum of success. It is mainly when clever psychologists construct problems where reliance on heuristics leads people astray that we are struck by the glaring errors and biases. In addition, while judgmental heuristics lead decision makers astray, they can also help generate ways to become better decision makers and to overcome biases in decision making. By aiding in decision making and determining judgments that can then be evaluated, their use will ultimately improve the decision making process—as long as judges maintain some skepticism about their judgmental capacities and are willing to seek out and evaluate feedback.

2. Even with the costs of errors, heuristic use has many benefits that in the long run might outweigh these costs. Heuristics tend to be used most when the judge is under cognitive strain or overload. Since people are limited in their information processing capacities, heuristics or other simplifying principles must

be used to reduce complex or impossible judgments to operations that can be applied. As Nisbett and Ross (1980) point out, people must solve problems, not discover truth. If cognitive heuristics help us to arrive at decisions and to function as efficiently as possible, they must be used. And it is usually an easy matter to judge by heuristics. Both the representativeness and availability of any instance can be readily judged. People can assess the similarity of an event to a model or the availability of instances simply and almost automatically. Tversky and Kahneman (1973) reported that the correlation between estimates of the number of words that could be made from nine letter matrices and actual construction of words from the matrices was .96. Whether or not it is appropriate to apply representativeness or availability, those features of a sample of data can be evaluated quickly and accurately.

3. The very use of heuristics leads us to maintain confidence in our judgments. The belief that samples are representative of the population or that availability is an indicator of frequency leads people to overestimate the correlations between frequency and representativeness or frequency and availability. This can be thought of as an instance of illusory correlation. In addition, the process of making judgments is often followed by an attempt to judge our judgments. In the act of judging our judgments, we tend to use the very same heuristics that we used in the judgments themselves. These heuristics simplify the job of judging our judgments. In addition, they are likely to be biased in ways that make those judgments appear better than they were. The "I knew it would happen" phenomenon of course makes us believe in the correctness of our judgments. Once an outcome occurs, we believe we knew it all along. Errors of judgment aren't detected. We don't learn of our errors and thus continue to employ the same principles of judgment and to repeat the same mistakes again and again.

In judging our judgments, we are also subject to other heuristics and their characteristic biases. We use mainly positive confirming instances in our judgments and focus on the frequency of successes rather than the proportion. Since heuristics do often lead to correct decisions, we focus on the times we used them and were successful and thus judge them to be good principles. We ignore the times that we used the rule and were wrong or the times we didn't use the rule and were right. As we have seen in discussing the availability heuristic, people ignore disconfirmation and bias their search toward confirmatory instances (Einhorn & Hogarth, 1978; Mynatt et al., 1977, 1978).

The fact that base rates are ignored in judgments is another reason why we continue to over-value our principles of judgment. Many decisions that we are called on to make would have a high base rate of success even if no formal or informal rules were applied. For example, applicants to graduate school in psychology are already a selected group. Advice from teachers, interest in the area, and so forth make it reasonable to suggest that 70% of those who apply to a graduate program would be successful. A formal model for admissions (or even a simple rule of thumb) that led to selection of candidates such that 73% were successful would not be very impressive. Yet our tendency to ignore the base rate would lead us to be quite impressed with our principle of judgment.

One aspect of the availability heuristic principle is the tendency to focus on salient outcomes. The same tendency exists when we judge our judgments. Successes are highly salient and available. Whether through motivational or cognitive factors, failures should impress us less and be less available in memory. Such a bias will lead us to believe that our judgments (and the principles underlying them) are better than they really are.

It is paradoxical that the very heuristics that lead to biases and errors in the first place can keep us from recognizing and appreciating the nature and extent of those errors. Yet the use of heuristics in judging our judgments will lead us to be overconfident in our ability to judge and to judge our principles of judgment as too good.

4. Another reason for the widespread use of heuristic principles despite their tendency to lead us astray is that corrective feedback is not always available, is not always sought, and is not always useful. Sometimes it is simply impossible or infeasible to collect the information that could be used for judging one's decision making rules. For example, when we apply a rule of thumb to select employees or graduate students, we would have to follow up all candidates who weren't hired or accepted for admission (as well as those to whom offers were made but who didn't accept) in order to assess the rule properly. Such information would be impossible to come by.

Even when corrective feedback is potentially available, it may not be worth one's while to seek it out. Judges may simply lack the cognitive capacity to think about and code outcomes in such a way as to assess the goodness of the decision rule. The information may also be costly. Einhorn (1980) gives the example of the waiter who hasn't the time to give everyone good service, so he saves good service for those he predicts will leave big tips (given good service). If the quality of the service is then related to the size of the tip, it could be that the waiter's rule for predicting potentially good tippers is a useful one. It may also be the case that tip size is affected by the quality of service. He would have to perform the experiment to assess the truth (e.g., give poor service to some customers judged as good tippers and good service to some judged as poor tippers). Aside from taking time and effort, it isn't clear what good the information would do.

Einhorn (1980) further points out that even with outcome information, unless one has knowledge of the task structure, that information can be irrelevant for providing self-correcting feedback about heuristics. Since people rarely organize problems by the structure of the task, outcome feedback alone will rarely help improve the goodness of a decision rule.

Furthermore, most research on heuristic processes has involved judgments in discrete incidents. In this case, feedback is useless since a commitment has already been made. Hogarth (1980) maintains that researchers should focus more on judgments in continuous tasks, where there is the possibility of using outcome feedback in a self-correcting manner.

5. Nisbett et al. (1982) make the point that errors of judgment are often difficult to notice. It is hard to establish that any inference is erroneous since it is hard to know which model and which inferential procedures are called for. In addition, even if one establishes that an error has occurred, it will be difficult to know how and why it occurred. Recall that people lack awareness of their cognitive processes (Nisbett & Wilson, 1977) and would be hard pressed to determine whether an error was due to bad reasoning or bad models.

There is yet another reason why errors associated with reliance on heuristic principles may go unnoticed. In complex judgment tasks which require the simultaneous or sequential processing of different kinds of information, it is possible that more than one heuristic will be involved in the judgment. If each heuristic involves a characteristic error, it is possible that these errors will cancel each other out. In such a case, the final judgment may turn out to be normatively correct, indicating an error free judgmental process. The dilution effect, described by Nisbett, Zukier, and Lemley (1981) involves such a cancellation of errors. We have seen that, when subjects are given diagnostic information about a target case (e.g., Tom has little interest in politics and enjoys mathematical puzzles) and are asked to make predictions about Tom's occupation or his other traits, they fail to take base rates into account. That is, they are insufficiently regressive in their judgments. This is due to a bias inherent in the representativeness heuristic. If Tom "looks like" an engineer, he will be seen as likely to be an engineer and to have other traits associated with an engineer even if there are few engineers in the population. Nisbett et al. (1981) presented a mixture of diagnostic and nondiagnostic information. Subjects were, for example, given information about a social work case that was diagnostic of a child abuser (e.g., "has severe financial obligations and unpaid debts"). When only such diagnostic information was presented, subjects made overly extreme estimates of the likelihood that the client was a child abuser. This effect was diluted by adding nondiagnostic items such as "he manages a hardware store." Thus, a man who wanted his wife to have an abortion is seen as a less likely child abuser if he also is a shoe salesman and has a hearing defect. Items judged as worthless for the purpose of prediction dilute the biasing effects of diagnostic items.

The reason for the dilution effect in no way indicates that subjects suddenly understood the concept of regression. Rather the errors from the representativeness heuristic that led to overly extreme judgments with only diagnostic information were compensated for by further errors of the representativeness heuristic. Nondiagnostic information made the target look less similar to the prototypic child beater, who isn't a hardware store manager and isn't hard of hearing. Thus, two errors of judgment are involved, both concerning similarity of a description to a prototype. One error leads to biased judgments in one direction while the other leads to a bias in the other direction. The diagnostic information is treated nonregressively, while the nondiagnostic information is treated as though it were diagnostic of the target being average on the relevant dimension. The overall effect is that the judgments appear quite reasonable, and the errors in the process aren't seen. Thus, the principles of judgment will continue.

In a similar way, Nisbett and Ross (1980) discuss how the fundamental attribution error may be compensated for by a gambler's fallacy error. The fundamental attribution error leads judges to infer stable dispositions of an actor and thus predict a future too much like the past. Gambler's fallacy predictions see too many changes in the future to compensate for nonrepresentative outcomes in the past. Thus, an overly stable judgment can be compensated for by a belief that things will even out. The net result will be a reasonable prediction which seems to reflect the use of appropriate judgmental principles.

6. In seeking to assess causality or to evaluate judgments, people typically seek out a single "satisfactory" answer and then stop searching. Kanouse (1972) points out that individuals are content with one sufficient explanation for any phenomenon or one reasonable answer to any problem. This tendency to stop at the first sense of understanding has been used by Nisbett and Ross (1980) to explain the overjustification effect. Once the most salient and available reason for doing something (e.g., the offer of money) has been examined and accepted, the attributor stops and looks no further for other possible causes, perhaps of an intrinsic nature. Shaklee and Fischhoff (1982) have demonstrated this tendency for people to ascertain and clarify the role of one cause for an event without proceeding to consider other possible causes. Subjects were told about an event and two or three possible causes. They also received a fact implicating one of those causes. When asked to generate a question to help them explain the event, subjects overwhelmingly preferred to clarify the role of the implicated cause. In addition, this preference for information related to an already known cause was demonstrated as subjects were allowed an extended search for information. In the same way, a heuristic is a reasonably simple way to arrive at a "satisficing" solution to a problem. Once a first answer is arrived at, it is likely that people stop the search for solutions and thus fail to see that there may be better approaches available.

7. Once predictions or judgments are made and an outcome occurs, it is typical that a judge will evaluate the outcome in light of the prediction. Even if the initial prediction isn't misremembered (the "I knew it would happen" phenomenon), it is likely that the judgment will be perceived as better than it really was. The social psychology literature is filled with research demonstrating biased perception and selective retrieval. While it is beyond the scope of this chapter to detail such research, work by Asch, 1946; Lord et al. 1979; Mahoney, 1976; and Zadny and Gerard, 1974 amply demonstrate that prior beliefs, expectations, and judgments very much affect the impact and interpretation of outcomes and new information. Information consistent with one's prior beliefs and judgments is

attended to, given much weight, and seen as reliable. Inconsistent information is challenged, discounted, and even ignored. Thus, one's belief in the ability to make good judgments and predictions can be maintained. The errors associated with heuristic use may appear small since the outcomes are seen as generally consistent with the judgment. Gilovich (1983) has shown that decisions made by gamblers are viewed in this way. Outcome information is processed in a biased fashion such that the original judgment, and the process upon which it was based, look good. For example, the occurrence of a fluke play is seen as much more important for bettors of the losing team than for bettors of the winner. In this way, losers can maintain the highest possible level of belief in their judgmental rules. Even when the outcome is not seen as consistent with judgments, dissonance reduction processes allow people to convince themselves that the outcome is not so bad. Thus, the need to analyze and change the judgmental process is less acute.

8. A final aspect of the judgment process that leads to the maintenance of biased judgmental strategies is the fact that judgments themselves (even if normatively incorrect) can play an important role in affecting outcomes. This is, of course, an example of self-fulfilling prophecy. Judgments and predictions of others' behavior can cause their behavior to fit the predictions (Meichenbaum, Bowers, & Ross, 1969; Rosenthal & Jacobson, 1968; Zanna, Sheras, Cooper, & Shaw, 1975). Self-fulfilling prophecies have also been implicated in the confirmation of social stereotypes (Synder, Tanke, & Berscheid, 1977; Zanna & Pack, 1975). Judgments about the self also can help confirm themselves. Research on the relationship between prior levels of expectation and subsequent task performance (Feather, 1968; Zajonc & Brickman, 1969) has shown such effects. It is reasonable to suppose that judgments based on simplifying heuristic principles, although systematically biased, will lead to strongly held expectations. These expectations can fulfill themselves by the processes known to underlie self-fulfilling prophecies. In this way, people will be deluded into believing that their judgmental principles and decision-making rules are adequate, and even superior. People rarely recognize the role of their expectations and prior predictions on outcomes. An example of a biased expectation that was arrived at through heuristic principles and was then fulfilled is seen in the study by Sherman et al. (1981). Subjects who explained hypothetical failure or success on an upcoming anagram task showed expectations that were biased in the direction of the outcome explained. Presumably, the availability of such an outcome and the ease of simulating paths to that outcome was the basis for the biased expectations. Once arrived at and expressed, those expectations were in fact fulfilled. Subjects who expected to fail did poorly, while those expecting success did very well on the anagram task. In reviewing the entire sequence of events and judgments, subjects could look back and congratulate themselves for knowing themselves so well and for making such good judgments. In Merton's (1957) words, "self-fulfilling prophecies guarantee a reign of error." Biased judgmental processes, often

based on reliance on heuristic principles, will not be seen as biased and will persist in future decision-making.

In summary, there is a contradiction between the fallibility of people's judgments and the confidence that they show in their judgmental abilities (accompanied by the continued use of the fallible principles). Einhorn and Hogarth (1978) have addressed this contradiction. They trace the difficulty to three major factors: (1) people's unwillingness to search for or use disconfirming evidence; (2) people's lack of awareness of environmental effects on outcomes; (3) the use of unaided memory for coding, storing, and retrieving outcome information. They proceed to develop a model for understanding how people learn and maintain unwarranted confidence in their judgments. In it, they stress the role of experience and the frequency and importance of both positive and negative feedback.

While we can now understand why heuristic principles persist, the question still remains whether it is desirable to teach people not to use them. If they are not replaced with simple and adequate decision-making principles, nothing is gained. Perhaps the best we can do is teach people to be more cautious in applying rules of judgment or to improve inductive inference by supplanting intuitive heuristics with other simple rules that are still subject to some errors but which include more of the available information.

## REFERENCES

Abelson, R. P. *Scripts*. Paper presented at the annual meeting of the Midwest Psychological Association, Chicago, May, 1978.

Ajzen, I. Intuitive theories of events and the effects of base-rate information on prediction. *Journal of Personality and Social Psychology*, 1977, *35*, 303–314.

Alloy, L. B., & Abramson, L. Y. Judgment of contingency in depressed and nondepressed students: Sadder but wiser? *Journal of Experimental Psychology: General*, 1979, *108*, 441–485.

Anderson, J. R. *Language, memory, and thought*. Hillsdale, N.J.: Lawrence Erlbaum Associates, 1976.

Anderson, J. R., & Bower, G. H. *Human associative memory*. Washington, D.C.: Winston, 1973.

Anderson, N. H. Two more tests against change of meaning in adjective combinations. *Journal of Verbal Learning and Verbal Behavior*, 1971, *10*, 75–85.

Anderson, N. H Information integration theory: A brief review. In D. H. Krantz, R. C. Atkinson, and P. Suppes (Eds.), *Contemporary developments in mathematical psychology (Vol. 2)*. San Francisco, Freeman, 1974. (a)

Anderson, N. H Cognitive algebra: Integration theory applied to social attribution. In L. Berkowitz (Ed.), *Advances in experimental social psychology (Vol. 7)*. New York, Academic Press, 1974. (b)

Anderson, R. C., & Pichert, J. W. Recall of previously unrecallable information following a shift in perspective. *Journal of Verbal Learning and Verbal Behavior*, 1978, *17*, 1–12.

Anisfeld, M., & Knapp, M. Association, synonymity, and directionality in false recognition. *Journal of Experimental Psychology*, 1968, *77*, 171–179.

Armstrong, J. S., Denniston, W. B., & Gordon, M. M. The use of the decomposition principle in making judgments. *Organizational Behavior and Human Performance*, 1975, *14*, 257–263.

Asch, S. E. Forming impressions of personalities. *Journal of Abnormal and Social Psychology,* 1946, *41,* 258–290.

Baddeley, A. D. The influence of acoustic and semantic similarity on long-term memory for word sequences. *Quarterly Journal of Experimental Psychology,* 1966, *18,* 302–309.

Baddeley, A. D. Effects of acoustic and semantic similarity on short-term paired-associate learning. *British Journal of Psychology,* 1970, *61,* 335–343.

Bar-Hillel, M. Similarity and probability. *Organizational Behavior and Human Performance,* 1974, *11,* 277–282.

Bar-Hillel, M. *The base-rate fallacy in subjective judgments of probability.* Unpublished doctoral dissertation, Hebrew University, 1975.

Bar-Hillel, M. The base-rate fallacy in probability judgments. *Acta Psychologica,* 1980, *44,* 211–233.

Bar-Hillel, M., & Fischhoff, B. When do base rates affect predictions? *Journal of Personality and Social Psychology,* 1981, *41,* 671–680.

Bem, D. J. Self-perception: An alternative interpretation of cognitive dissonance phenomenon. *Psychological Review,* 1967, *74,* 183–200.

Beyth-Marom, R., & Fischhoff, B. Direct measures of availability and frequency judgments. *Bulletin of the Psychonomic Society,* 1977, *9,* 236–238.

Borgida, E., & Brekke, N. The base rate fallacy in attribution and prediction. In J. H. Harvey, W. J. Ickes, & R. E. Kidd (Eds.), *New directions in attribution research (Vol. 3).* Hillsdale, N.J.: Lawrence Erlbaum Associates, 1981.

Borgida, E., & Nisbett, R. E. The differential impact of abstract versus concrete information on decisions. *Journal of Applied Social Psychology,* 1977, *7,* 258–271.

Bransford, J. D., & Franks, J. J. The abstraction of linguistic ideas. *Cognitive Psychology,* 1971, *2,* 331–350.

Brenner, M. The next-in-line effect. *Journal of Verbal Learning and Verbal Behavior,* 1973, *12,* 320–323.

Brown, E. R., & Bane, A. L. Probability estimation in a chance task with changing probabilities. *Journal of Experimental Psychology: Human Perception and Performance,* 1975, *104,* 183–187.

Bruner, J. S., & Potter, M. C. Interference in visual recognition. *Science,* 1964, *144,* 424–425.

Brunswik, E. Thing consistency measured by correlation coefficients. *Psychological Review,* 1940, *47,* 69–78.

Cantor, N., & Mischel, W. Traits as prototypes: Effects on recognition memory. *Journal of Personality and Social Psychology,* 1977, *35,* 38–48.

Cantor, N., & Mischel, W. Prototypicality and personality: Effects on free recall and personality impressions. *Journal of Research in Personality,* 1979, *13,* 187–205.

Carroll, J. S. The effect of imagining an event on expectations for the event: An interpretation in terms of the availability heuristic. *Journal of Experimental Social Psychology,* 1978, *14,* 88–96. (a)

Carroll, J. S. Causal attributions in expert parole decisions. *Journal of Personality and Social Psychology,* 1978, *36,* 1501–1511. (b)

Carroll, J. S. Analyzing decision behavior: The magician's audience. In T. S. Wallsten (Ed.), *Cognitive processes in choice and decision behavior.* Hillsdale, N.J.: Lawrence Erlbaum Associates, 1980.

Casscells, W., Schoenberger, A., & Grayboys, T. Interpretation by physicians of clinical laboratory results. *New England Journal of Medicine,* 1978, *299,* 999–1000.

Castellan, N. J., & Edgell, S. E. An hypothesis generation model for judgment in nonmetric multiple-cue probability learning. *Journal of Mathematical Psychology,* 1973, *10,* 204–222.

Chaiken, S. Heuristic versus systematic information processing and the use of source versus message cues in persuasion. *Journal of Personality and Social Psychology,* 1980, *39,* 752–766.

Chapman, L. J. Illusory correlations in observational report. *Journal of Verbal Learning and Verbal Behavior*, 1967, *6*, 151–155.

Chapman, L. J., & Chapman, J. P. The genesis of popular but erroneous psychodiagnostic observations. *Journal of Abnormal Psychology*, 1967, *72*, 193–204.

Chapman, L. J., & Chapman, J. P. Illusory correlation as an obstacle to the use of valid psychodiagnostic signs. *Journal of Abnormal Psychology*, 1969, *74*, 271–280.

Cohen, L. J. *The implications of induction*. London: Methuen, 1970.

Cohen, L. J. On the psychology of prediction: Whose is the fallacy? *Cognition*, 1979, *7*, 385–407.

Cohen, L. J. Can human irrationality be experimentally demonstrated? *The Behavioral and Brain Sciences*, 1981, *4*, 317–370.

Collins, A. M., & Quillian, M. R. Retrieval from semantic memory. *Journal of Verbal Learning and Verbal Behavior*, 1969, *8*, 240–247.

Conrad, R. Acoustic confusion in immediate memory. *British Journal of Psychology*, 1964, *55*, 75–84.

Conrad, R. Short-term memory processes in the deaf. *British Journal of Psychology*, 1970, *61*, 179–195.

Cook, T. D., & Flay, B. R. The persistence of experimentally induced attitude change. In L. Berkowitz (Ed.), *Advances in experimental social psychology (Vol. 11)*. New York: Academic Press, 1978.

Cottrell, N. B., Ingraham, L. H., & Monfort, F. W. The retention of balanced and unbalanced cognitive structures. *Journal of Personality*, 1971, *39*, 112–131.

Dawes, R., & Corrigan, B. Linear models in decision making. *Psychological Bulletin*, 1974, *81*, 95–106.

deGroot, A. D. *Thought and choice in chess*. The Hague: Mouton & Co., 1965.

DeSoto, C. B., & Bosley, J. J. The cognitive structure of a social structure. *Journal of Abnormal and Social Psychology*, 1962, *64*, 303–307.

Duval, S., & Wicklund, R. A. *A theory of objective self-awareness*. New York: Academic ress, 1972.

Einhorn, H. J. Expert judgment: Some necessary conditions and an example. *Journal of Applied Psychology*, 1974, *59*, 562–571.

Einhorn, H. J. Learning from experience and suboptimal rules in decision making. In T. S. Wallsten (Eds.), *Cognitive processes in choice and decision behavior*. Hillsdale, N.J.: Lawrence Erlbaum Associates, 1980.

Einhorn, H. J., & Hogarth, R. M. Confidence in judgment: Persistence of the illusion of validity. *Psychological Review*, 1978, *85*, 395–416.

Einhorn, H. J., & Hogarth, R. M. Behavioral decision theory: Processes of judgment and choice. *Annual Review of Psychology*, 1981, *32*, 53–88.

Einhorn, H. J., & Koelb, C. T. *A psychometric study of literary-critical judgment*. Unpublished manuscript, University of Chicago, 1982.

Enzle, M. E., Hansen, R. D., & Lowe, L. A. Humanizing the mixed motive paradigm: Methodological implications from attribution theory. *Simulation and Games*, 1975, *11*, 592–613.

Estes, W. K. The cognitive side of probability learning. *Psychological Review*, 1976, *83*, 37–64.

Evans, J. St. B. T., & Dusoir, A. E. Proportionality and sample size as factors in intuitive statistical judgment. *Acta Psychologica*, 1977, *41*, 129–137.

Fazio, R. H., Chen, J., McDonel, E. C., & Sherman, S. J. Attitude accessibility, attitude behavior consistency, and the strength of the object-evaluation association. *Journal of Experimental Social Psychology*, 1982, *18*, 339–357.

Fazio, R. H., Sherman, S. J., & Herr, P. M. The feature-positive effect in the self-perception process: Does not doing matter as much as doing? *Journal of Personality and Social Psychology*, 1982, *42*, 404–411.

Feather, N. T. Change in confidence following success or failure as a predictor of subsequent performance. *Journal of Personality and Social Psychology,* 1968, *9,* 38–46.

Feldman, N. S., Higgins, E. T., Karlovac, M., & Ruble, D. N. Use of consensus information in causal attributions as a function of temporal presentation and availability of direct information. *Journal of Personality and Social Psychology Bulletin,* 1976, *34,* 694–698.

Fischhoff, B. Hindsight = foresight: The effect of outcome knowledge on judgment under uncertainty. *Journal of Experimental Psychology: Human Perception and Performance,* 1975, *7,* 288–299.

Fischhoff, B. Perceived informativeness of facts. *Journal of Experimental Psychology: Human Perception and Performance,* 1977, *3,* 349–358.

Fischhoff, B., & Beyth, R. "I knew it would happen"—remembered probabilities of once-future things. *Organizational Behavior and Human Performance,* 1975, *13,* 1–16.

Fischhoff, B., Slovic, P., & Lichtenstein, S. Subjective sensitivity analysis. *Organizational Behavior and Human Performance,* 1979, *23,* 339–359.

Fiske, S. T., Taylor, S. E., Etcoff, N. L., & Lauffer, J. K. Imaging, empathy, and causal attribution. *Journal of Experimental Social Psychology,* 1979, *15,* 356–377.

Franks, J. J., & Bransford, J. D. Abstraction of visual patterns. *Journal of Experimental Psychology,* 1971, *90,* 65–74.

Gabrenya, W. K., & Arkin, R. M. Motivation, heuristics, and the Psychology of prediction. *Motivation and Emotion,* 1979, *3,* 1–17.

Garcia, J., McGowan, B. K., & Green, K. F. Sensory quality and integration: Constraints on conditioning. In A. H. Black & W. F. Prokasy (Eds.), *Classical conditioning II: Current research and theory.* New York: Appleton-Century-Crofts, 1972.

Gelman, R. The nature and development of early number concepts. In H. W. Reese (Ed.), *Advances in child development and behavior (Vol. 7).* New York: Academic Press, 1972.

Gerard, H. B., & Fleischer, L. Recall and pleasantness of balanced and unbalanced cognitive structures. *Journal of Personality and Social Psychology,* 1967, *7,* 332–337.

Gilovich, T. Seeing the past in the present: The effect of associations to familiar events on judgments and decisions. *Journal of Personality and Social Psychology,* 1981, *40,* 797–808.

Gilovich, T. Biased evaluation & persistence in gambling. *Journal of Personality and Social Psychology,* 1983, *44,* 1110–1126.

Goldman, D., & Homa, D. Integrative and metric properties of abstracted information as a function of category discriminability, instance variability, and experience. *Journal of Experimental Psychology: Human Learning and Memory,* 1977, *3,* 375–385.

Grether, D. M. Bayes' rule as a descriptive model: The representativeness heuristic (Social Science working Paper No. 245). Pasadena: California Institute of Technology, 1979.

Grether, D. M., & Plott, C. F. Economic theory of choice and the preference reversal phenomenon. *American Economic Review,* 1979, *69,* 623–638.

Hamill, R., Wilson, T. D., & Nisbett, R. E. Insensitivity to sample bias: Generalizing from atypical cases. *Journal of Personality and Social Psychology,* 1980, *39,* 578–589.

Hamilos, C. A., & Pitz, G. F. Encoding and recognition of probabilistic information in a decision task. *Organizational Behavior and Human Performance,* 1977, *20,* 184–202.

Hamilton, D. L. A cognitive-attributional analysis of stereotyping. In L. Berkowitz (Ed.), *Advances in experimental social psychology (Vol. 12).* New York: Academic Press, 1979.

Hamilton, D. L., & Gifford, R. K. Illusory correlation in interpersonal perception: A cognitive basis of stereotypic judgments. *Journal of Experimental Social Psychology,* 1976, *12,* 392–407.

Hamilton, D. L., Katz, L. B., & Leirer, V. O. Cognitive representation of personality impressions: Organizational processes in first impression formation. *Journal of Personality and Social Psychology,* 1980, *39,* 1050–1063.

Hanson, C. *Prototype and exemplar processing in a categorization task.* Unpublished manuscript, Indiana University, 1982.

Hartwick, J. Memory for trait information: A signal detection analysis. *Journal of Experimental Social Psychology*, 1979, *15*, 533–552.

Hastie, R., & Kumar, P. A. Person memory: Personality traits as organizing principles in memory for behaviors. *Journal of Personality and Social Psychology*, 1979, *37*, 25–38.

Hayes, J. R., & Simon, H. A. The understanding process: Problem isomorphs. *Cognitive Psychology*, 1976, *8*, 165–190.

Hayes, J. R., Waterman, D. A., & Robinson, C. A. Identifying relevant aspects of a problem text. *Cognitive Science*, 1977, *1*, 297–313.

Hayes-Roth, B. Evolution of cognitive structures and processes. *Psychological Review*, 1977, *84*, 260–278.

Heider, F. *The psychology of interpersonal relations.* New York: Wiley, 1958.

Higgins, E. J., & King, G. Accessibility of social constructs: information processing consequences of individual & context variability. In N. Cantor & J. F. Kihlstrom (Eds.) *Personality, Cognition, and Social Interaction.* Hillsdale, N.J.: Lawrence Erlbaum Associates, 1981.

Higgins, E. T., & Rholes, W. S. *Message production effects on impression formation.* Unpublished manuscript, Princeton University, 1976.

Higgins, E. T., Rholes, W. S., & Jones, C. R. Category accessibility and impression formation. *Journal of Experimental Social Psychology*, 1977, *13*, 141–154.

Hogarth, R. M. *Judgment and choice: The psychology of decision.* Chichester, England: Wiley, 1980.

Homa, D., & Chambliss, D. The relative contributions of common and distinctive information on the abstraction from ill-defined categories. *Journal of Experimental Psychology: Human Learning and Memory*, 1975, *1*, 351–359.

Isen, A. M. *Positive affect, decision-making strategy, and risk-taking.* Paper presented at the Carnegie Symposium, 1981.

Isen, A. M., Clark, M., Shalker, T. E., & Karp, L. Affect, accessibility of materials in memory, and behavior: A cognitive loop? *Journal of Personality and Social Psychology*, 1978, *36*, 1–12.

Jenkins, H. M., & Sainsbury, R. S. The development of stimulus control through differential reinforcement. In N. J. Mackintosh & W. K. Honig (Eds.), *Fundamental issues in associative learning.* Halifax: Dalhousie University Press, 1969.

Jenkins, H. M., & Sainsbury, R. S. Discrimination learning with the distinctive feature on positive or negative trials. In D. Mostofsky (Ed.), *Attention: Contemporary theory and analysis.* New York: Appleton-Century-Crofts, 1970.

Jenkins, H. M., & Ward, W. C. Judgment of contingency between responses and outcomes. *Psychological Monographs: General and Applied*, 1965, *79* (Whole No. 594).

Jenkins, J. J. Remember that old theory of memory? Well, forget it. *American Psychologist*, 1974, *29*, 785–795.

Jones, E. E. The rocky road from acts to disposition. *American Psychologist*, 1979, *34*, 107–117.

Jones, E. E., & Goethals, G. Order effects in impression formation: Attribution context and the nature of the entity. In E. E. Jones et al. (Eds.), *Attribution: Perceiving the causes of behavior.* Morristown, N.J.: General Learning Press, 1972.

Jones, E. E., & Nisbett, R. E. The actor and the observer: Divergent perceptions of the causes of behavior. In E. E. Jones et al. (Eds.), *Attribution: Perceiving the causes of behavior.* Morristown, N.J.: General Learning Press, 1972.

Joyce, E. J. *Individual judgment in audit program planning: An empirical study.* Unpublished Ph.D. dissertation, University of Illinois, 1976.

Kahneman, D., & Tversky, A. Subjective probability: A judgment of representativeness. *Cognitive Psychology*, 1972, *3*, 430–454.

Kahneman, D., & Tversky, A. On the psychology of prediction. *Psychological Review*, 1973, *80*, 237–251.

Kahneman, D., & Tversky, A. On the interpretation of intuitive probability: A reply to Jonathan Cohen. *Cognition*, 1979, *7*, 409–411. (a)

Kahneman, D., & Tversky, A. Intuitive prediction: Biases and corrective procedures. *TIMS Studies in the Management Sciences*, 1979, *12*, 313–327. (b)

Kahneman, D., & Tversky, A. On the study of statistical intuitions. *Cognition*, 1982, *11*, 123–141. (a)

Kahneman, D., & Tversky, A. The simulation heuristic. In D. Kahneman, P. Slovic, & A. Tversky (Eds.), *Judgment under uncertainty: Heuristics and biases*. New York: Cambridge University Press, 1982. (b)

Kahneman, D., & Tversky, A. Variants of uncertainty. *Cognition*, 1982, *11*, 143–157. (c)

Kanouse, D. E. Language, labeling, and attribution. In E. E. Jones et al. (Eds.), *Attribution: Perceiving the causes of behavior*. Morristown, N.J.: General Learning Press, 1972.

Kaplan, R. M. How do fans and oddsmakers differ in their judgments of football teams? *Personality and Social Psychology Bulletin*, 1980, *6*, 287–292.

Kassin, S. Consensus information, prediction, and causal attribution: A review of the literature and issues. *Journal of Personality and Social Psychology*, 1979, *37*, 1966–1981.

Kelley, H. H. Attribution theory in social psychology. In D. Levine (Ed.), *Nebraska Symposium on Motivation (Vol. 15)*. Lincoln: University of Nebraska Press, 1967.

Kiesler, C. A., Nisbett, R. E., & Zanna, M. P. On inferring one's beliefs from one's behavior. *Journal of Personality and Social Psychology*, 1969, *11*, 321–327.

Kozielecki, J. *Psychological decision theory*. Boston: D. Reidel Publishing Company, 1981.

Kubovy, M. Response availability and the apparent spontaneity of numerical choices. *Journal of Experimental Psychology: Human Perception and Performance*, 1977, *3*, 359–364.

Langer, E. J. The illusion of control. *Journal of Personality and Social Psychology*, 1975, *32*, 311–328.

Langer, E. J. Rethinking the role of thought in social interaction. In J. Harvey, W. Ickes, & R. Kidd (Eds.), *New directions in attribution theory (Vol. 2)*. Hillsdale, N.J.: Lawrence Erlbaum Associates, 1978.

Langer, E., Blank, A., & Chanowitz, B. The mindlessness of ostensibly thoughtful action: The role of "placebic" information in interpersonal interaction. *Journal of Personality and Social Psychology*, 1978, *36*, 635–642.

Lichtenstein, S. C., Earle, T., & Slovic, P. Cue utilization in a numerical prediction task. *Journal of Experimental Psychology: Human Perception and Performance*, 1975, *104*, 77–85.

Lichtenstein, S. C., & Slovic, P. Reversals of preferences between bids and choices in gambling decisions. *Journal of Experimental Psychology*, 1971, *89*, 46–55.

Lichtenstein, S. C., & Slovic, P. Response-induced reversals of preference in gambling: An extended replication in Las Vega. *Journal of Experimental Psychology*, 1973, *101*, 16–20.

Lichtenstein, S., Slovic, P., Fischhoff, B., Layman, M., & Combs, B. Judged frequency of lethal events. *Journal of Experimental Psychology: Human Learning and Memory*, 1978, *4*, 551–578.

Lingle, J. H., & Ostrom, T. M. Principles of memory and cognition in attitude formation. In R. E. Petty, T. M. Ostrom, & T. C. Brock (Eds.), *Cognitive responses in persuasive communications: A text in attitude change*. Hillsdale, N.J.: Lawrence Erlbaum Associates, 1981.

Locksley, A., Hepburn, C., & Ortiz, V. Social stereotypes and judgments of individuals: An instance of the base-rate fallacy. *Journal of Experimental Social Psychology*, 1982, *18*, 23–42.

Loftus, E. F., & Palmer, J. C. Reconstruction of automobile destruction: An example of the interaction between language and memory. *Journal of Verbal Learning and Verbal Behavior*, 1974, *13*, 585–589.

Lord, C. G., Ross, L., & Lepper, M. R. Biased assimilation and attitude polarization: The effects of prior theories on subsequently considered information. *Journal of Personality and Social Psychology*, 1979, *37*, 2098–2109.

Lyon, D., & Slovic, P. Dominance of accuracy information and neglect of base rates in probability estimation. *Acta Psychologica*, 1976, *40*, 287–298.

McArthur, L. Z., & Post, D. Figural emphasis and person perception. *Journal of Experimental Social Psychology*, 1977, *13*, 520–535.

Mahoney, M. J. *Scientist as subject: The psychological imperative.* Cambridge, Mass.: Ballinger, 1976.

Manis, M., Dovalina, I., Avis, N. E., & Cardoze, S. Base rates can affect individual predictions. *Journal of Personality and Social Psychology,* 1980, *38,* 231–248.

Medin, D. L., & Schaffer, M. M. Context theory of classification learning. *Psychological Review,* 1978, *85,* 207–238.

Medin, D. L., & Smith, E. E. Strategies and classification learning. *Journal of Experimental Psychology: Human Learning and Memory,* 1981, *7,* 241–253.

Meichenbaum, D. H., Bowers, K. S., & Ross, R. R. A behavioral analysis of teacher expectancy effect. *Journal of Personality and Social Psychology,* 1969, *13,* 306–316.

Merton, R. K. Social theory and social structure. New York: Free Press of Glencoe, 1957.

Michotte, A. *The perception of causality.* New York: Basic Books, 1963.

Mischel, W. *Personality and assessment.* New York: Wiley, 1968.

Mischel, W. Continuity anc change in personality. *American Psychologist,* 1969, *24,* 1012–1018.

Mischel, W. Toward a cognitive social learning reconceptualization of personality. *Psychological Review,* 1973, *80,* 252–283.

Mynatt, C. R., Doherty, M. E., & Tweney, R. D. Confirmation bias in a simulated research environment: An experimental study of scientific inference. *Quarterly Journal of Experimental Psychology,* 1977, *29,* 85–95.

Mynatt, C. R., Doherty, M. E., & Tweney, R. D. Consequences of confirmation and disconfirmation in a simulated research environment. *Quarterly Journal of Experimental Psychology,* 1978, *30,* 395–406.

Newman, J., Wolff, W. T., & Hearst, E. The feature-positive effect in adult human subjects. *Journal of Experimental Psychology: Human Learning and Memory,* 1980, *6,* 630–650.

Nisbett, R. E., & Borgida, E. Attribution and the psychology of prediction. *Journal of Personality and Social Psychology,* 1975, *32,* 932–943.

Nisbett, R. E., Borgida, E., Crandall, R., & Reed, H. Popular induction: Information is not always informative. In J. S. Carroll & J. W. Payne (Eds.), *Cognition and social behavior.* Hillsdale, N.J.: Lawrence Erlbaum Associates, 1976.

Nisbett, R. E., Krantz, D. M., Jepson, C., & Fong, G. T. Improving inductive inference. In D. Kahneman, P. Slovic, & A. Tversky (Eds.), *Judgment under uncertainty: Heuristics and biases.* New York: Cambridge University Press, 1982.

Nisbett, R. E., & Ross, L. *Human inference: Strategies and shortcomings of social judgment.* Englewood Cliffs, N.J.: Prentice-Hall, 1980.

Nisbett, R. E., & Wilson, T. D. Telling more than we can know: Verbal reports on mental process. *Psychological Review,* 1977, *84,* 231–259.

Nisbett, R. E., Zukier, H., & Lemley, R. E. The dilution effect: Nondiagnostic information weakens the implications of diagnostic information. *Cognitive Psychology,* 1981, *13,* 248–277.

Nuttin, J. M., Jr. *The illusion of attitude change: Toward a response contagion theory of persuasion.* London: Academic Press and Leuven University Press, 1975.

Olson, C. L. Some apparent violations of the representativeness heuristic in human judgment. *Journal of Experimental Psychology: Human Perception and Performance,* 1976, *2,* 599–608.

Peterson, C. *The availability of the randomness attribution.* Unpublished manuscript, Kirkland College, 1977.

Peterson, C. R., & Beach, L. R. Man as an intuitive statistician. *Psychological Bulletin,* 1967, *68,* 29–46.

Peterson, C. R., & DuCharme, W. M. A primacy effect in subjective probability revision. *Journal of Experimental Psychology,* 1967, *73,* 61–65.

Picek, J. S., Sherman, S. J., & Shiffrin, R. M. Cognitive organization and coding of social structures. *Journal of Personality and Social Psychology,* 1975, *31,* 758–768.

Pitz, G. F. An inertia effect (resistance to change) in the revision of opinion. *Canadian Journal of Psychology,* 1969, *23,* 24–33.

Pitz, G. F. *Heuristic processes in decision making and judgment.* Unpublished manuscript, Southern Illinois University, 1977.

Pitz, G. F. The very guide of life: The use of probabilistic information for decision making. In T. S. Wallsten (Ed.), *Cognitive processes in choice and decision behavior.* Hillsdale, N.J.: Lawrence Erlbaum Associates, 1980.

Pitz, G. F., Downing, L,, & Reinhold, H. Sequential effects in the revision of subjective probabilities. *Canadian Journal of Psychology,* 1967, *21,* 381–393.

Pitz, G. F., Leung, L. W., Hamilos, C., & Terpening, W. The use of probabilistic information in making predictions. *Organizational Behavior and Human Performance,* 1976, *17,* 1–18.

Posner, M. I., & Keele, S. W. On the genesis of abstract ideas. *Journal of Experimental Psychology,* 1968, *77,* 353–363.

Potts, G. R. Information processing strategies used in the encoding of linear orderings. *Journal of Verbal Learning and Verbal Behavior,* 1972, *11,* 727–740.

Pryor, J. B., & Kriss, M. The cognitive dynamics of salience in the attribution process. *Journal of Personality and Social Psychology,* 1977, *35,* 49–55.

Regan, D. T., & Fazio, R. H. On the consistency between attitudes and behavior: Look to the method of attitude formation. *Journal of Experimental Social Psychology,* 1977, *13,* 38–45.

Reitman, J. S., & Bower, G. H. Storage and later recognition of exemplars of concepts. *Cognitive Psychology,* 1973, *4,* 194–206.

Reyes, R. M., Thompson, W. C., & Bower, G. H. Judgmental biases resulting from differing availabilities of arguments. *Journal of Personality and Social Psychology,* 1980, *39,* 2–12.

Rosenthal, R., & Jacobson, L. *Pygmalion in the classroom.* New York: Holt, Rinehart, & Winston, 1968.

Rosch, E. Principles of categorization. In E. Rosch & B. B. Lloyd (Eds.), *Cognition and categorization.* Hillsdale, N.J.: Lawrence Erlbaum Associates, 1978.

Ross, L., Amabile, T. M., & Steinmetz, J. L. Social roles, social control, and biases in social-perception processes. *Journal of Personality and Social Psychology,* 1977, *35,* 485–494.

Ross, L., Greene, D., & House, P. The false consensus phenomenon: An attributional bias in self perception and social perception processes. *Journal of Personality and Social Psychology,* 1977, *13,* 274–301.

Ross, L., Lepper, M., & Hubbard, M. Perseverance in self perception and social perception: Biased attributional processes in the debriefing paradigm. *Journal of Personality and Social Psychology,* 1975, *32,* 880–892.

Ross, L., Lepper, M. R., Strack, F., & Steinmetz, J. L. Social explanation and social expectation: The effects of real and hypothetical explanations upon subjective likelihood. *Journal of Personality and Social Psychology,* 1977, *35,* 817–829.

Ross, M., & Sicoly, F. Egocentric biases in availability and attribution. *Journal of Personality and Social Psychology,* 1979, *37,* 322–336.

Rothbart, M., & Fulero, S. *Attributions of causality for important events: The profound motive fallacy.* Unpublished manuscript, University of Oregon, 1978.

Rothbart, M., Fulero, S., Jensen, C., Howard, J., & Birrell, P. From individual to group impressions: Availability heuristics in stereotype formation. *Journal of Experimental Social Psychology,* 1978, *14,* 237–255.

Salancik, G. R. Inference of one's attitude from behavior recalled under linguistically manipulated cognitive sets. *Journal of Experimental Social Psychology,* 1974, *10,* 415–427.

Salanick, G. R. Extrinsic attribution and the use of behavior information to infer attitudes. *Journal of Personality and Social Psychology,* 1976, *34,* 1302–1312.

Salancik, G. R., & Conway, M. Attitude inferences from salient and relevant cognitive content about behavior. *Journal of Personality and Social Psychology,* 1975, *32,* 829–840.

Seligman, M. E. P. On the generality of laws of learning. *Psychological Review,* 1970, *77,* 406–418.

Sentis, K. P., & Burnstein, E. Remembering schema-consistent information: Effects of a balance schema on recognition memory. *Journal of Personality and Social Psychology,* 1979, *37,* 2200–2211.

Shaklee, N., & Fischhoff, B. Strategies of information search in causal analysis. *Memory and Cognition,* 1982, *10,* 520–530.

Sherman, S. J. *When imbalance is balanced—judgments of magnetic relations.* Unpublished manuscript, Indiana University, 1975.

Sherman, S. J. On the self-erasing nature of errors of prediction. *Journal of Personality and Social Psychology,* 1980, *39,* 211–221.

Sherman, S. J., Cialdini, R. B., Schwartzman, D. F., & Reynolds, K. D. *Imagining Can Heighten or Lower the Perceived Likelihood of Contracting a Disease: The Mediating Effect of Ease of Imagery.* Unpublished manuscript, Arizona State University, 1982.

Sherman, S. J., Skov, R. B., Hervitz, E. F., & Stock, C. B. The effects of explaining hypothetical future events: From possibility to probability to actuality and beyond. *Journal of Experimental Social Psychology,* 1981, *17,* 142–158.

Sherman, S. J., Zehner, K. S., Johnson, J., & Hirt, E. R. Social explanation: The role of timing, set, and recall on subjective likelihood estimates. *Journal of Personality and Social Psychology,* 1983, *44,* 1127–1143.

Shweder, R. Likeness and likelihood in everyday thought: Magical thinking in judgments about personality. *Current Anthropology,* 1977, *18,* 637–658.

Siegler, R. S. The origin of scientific reasoning. In R. S. Siegler (Ed.), *Children's thinking: What develops?.* Hillsdale, N.J.: Lawrence Erlbaum Associates, 1978.

Simon, H. A., & Chase, W. G. Skill in chess. *American Scientist,* 1973, *61,* 394–403.

Slovic, P., & Fischhoff, B. On the psychology of experimental surprises. *Journal of Experimental Psychology: Human Perception and Performance,* 1977, *3,* 544–551.

Slovic, P., Fischhoff, B., & Lichtenstein, S. C. Cognitive processes and societal risk taking. In J. S. Carroll & J. W. Payne (Eds.), *Cognition and social behavior.* Hillsdale, N.J.: Lawrence Erlbaum Associates, 1976.

Slovic, P., Fischhoff, B., & Lichtenstein, S. Behavioral decision theory. *Annual Review of Psychology,* 1977, *28,* 1–39.

Slovic, P., Kunreuther, H., & White, G. F. Decision processes, rationality and adjustment to natural hazards. In G. F. White (Ed.), *Natural hazards, local, national and global.* New York: Oxford University Press, 1974.

Slovic, P., & Lichtenstein, S. Comparison of Bayesian and regression approaches to the study of information processing in judgment. *Organizational Behavior and Human Performance,* 1971, *6,* 649–744.

Smedslund, J. The concept of correlation in adults. *Scandinavian Journal of Psychology,* 1963, *4,* 165–173.

Smith, E. E., & Medin, D. L. *Categories and concepts.* Cambridge, Mass.: Harvard University Press, 1981.

Snyder, M., & Swann, W. B. Hypothesis-testing processes in social interaction. *Journal of Personality and Social Psychology,* 1978, *36,* 1202–1212.

Snyder, M., Tanke, E. D., & Berscheid, E. Social perception and interpersonal behavior: On the self-fulfilling nature of social stereotypes. *Journal of Personality and Social Psychology,* 1977, *35,* 656–666.

Srull, T. K., & Wyer, R. S. The role of category accessibility in the interpretation of information about persons: Some determinants and implications. *Journal of Personality and Social Psychology,* 1979, *37,* 1660–1672.

Srull, T. K., & Wyer, R. S. Category accessibility and social perception: Some implications for the study of person memory and interpersonal judgments. *Journal of Personality and Social Psychology,* 1980, *38,* 841–856.

Storms, M.D. Videotape and the attribution process: Reversing actors' and observers' points of view. *Journal of Personality and Social Psychology,* 1973, *27,* 165–175.

Strange, W., Kenney, T., Kessel, F. S., & Jenkins, J. J. Abstraction over time of prototypes from distortions of random dot patterns: A replication. *Journal of Experimental Psychology,* 1970, *83,* 508–510.

Strickland, L. H., Lewicki, R. J., & Katz, A. M. Temporal orientation and perceived control as determinants of risk-taking. *Journal of Experimental Social Psychology,* 1966, *2,* 143–151.

Taylor, S. E., Fiske, S. T., Close, M. M., Anderson, C. E., & Ruderman, A. *Solo status as a psychological variable.* Unpublished manuscript, University of California, Los Angeles, 1974.

Taylor, S. E., & Thompson, S. C. Stalking the elusive "vividness" effect. *Psychological Review,* 1982, *89,* 155–181.

Tesser, A., & Leone, C. Cognitive schemas and thought as determinants of attitude change. *Journal of Experimental Social Psychology,* 1977, *13,* 340–356.

Trope, Y. Inferences of personal characteristics on the basis of information retrieved from one's memory. *Journal of Personality and Social Psychology,* 1978, *36,* 93–106.

Tsujimoto, R. N., Wilde, J., & Robertson, D. R. Distorted memory for exemplars of a social structure: Evidence for schematic memory processes. *Journal of Personality and Social Psychology,* 1978, *36,* 1402–1414.

Tversky, A. Features of similarity. *Psychological Review,* 1977, *84,* 327–352.

Tversky, A., & Kahneman, D. Belief in the law of small numbers. *Psychological Bulletin,* 1971, *76,* 105–110.

Tversky, A., & Kahneman, D. Availability: A heuristic for judging frequency and probability. *Cognitive Psychology,* 1973, *5,* 207–232.

Tversky, A., & Kahneman, D. Judgment under uncertainty: Heuristic and biases. *Science,* 1974, *185,* 1124–1131.

Tversky, A., & Kahneman, D. Causal schemas in judgments under uncertainty. In M. Fishbein (Ed.), *Progress in social psychology (Vol. 1).* Hillsdale, N.J.: Lawrence Erlbaum Associates, 1980.

Tversky, A., & Kahneman, D. The framing of decisions and the psychology of choice. *Science,* 1981, *211,* 453–458.

Tversky, A., & Kahneman, D. Judgments of and by representativeness. In D. Kahneman, P. Slovic, & A. Tversky (Eds.), *Judgment under uncertainty: Heuristics and biases.* New York: Cambridge University Press, 1982. (a)

Tversky, A., & Kahneman, D. Evidential impact of base rates. In D. Kahneman, P. Slovic, & A. Tversky (Eds.), *Judgment under uncertainty: Heuristics and biases.* New York: Cambridge University Press, 1982. (b)

Uecker, W. C., & Kinney, W. R., Jr. Judgmental evaluation of sample results: A study of the type and severity of errors made by practicing CPAs. *Accounting, Organizations and Society,* 1977, *2,* 269–275.

Walker, C. J. The employment of vertical and horizontal social schemata in the learning of a social structure. *Journal of Personality and Social Psychology,* 1976, *33,* 132–141.

Wallsten, T. S. Processing information for decisions. In N. J. Castellan, D. B. Pisoni, & G. R. Potts (Eds.), *Cognitive theory (Vol. 2).* Hillsdale, N.J.: Lawrence Erlbaum Associates, 1977.

Wallsten, T. S. Processes and models to describe choice and inference behavior. In T. S. Wallsten (Ed.), *Cognitive processes in choice and decision behavior.* Hillsdale, N.J.: Lawrence Erlbaum Associates, 1980.

Ward, W. D., & Jenkins, H. M. The display of information and the judgment of contingency. *Canadian Journal of Psychology,* 1965, *19,* 231–241.

Wason, P. C. Reasoning about a rule. *Quarterly Journal of Experimental Psychology,* 1968, *20,* 273–281.

Weiss, J., & Brown, P. *Self-insight error in the explanation of mood.* Unpublished manuscript, Harvard University, 1977.

Wells, G. L., & Harvey, J. H. Do people use consensus information in making causal attributions? *Journal of Personality and Social Psychology,* 1977, *35,* 279–293.

Wells, G. L., & Lindsay, R. C. On estimating the diagnosticity of eyewitness nonidentifications. *Psychological Bulletin*, 1980, *88*, 776–784.

Winkler, R. L. The assessment of prior distributions in Bayesian analysis. *Journal of the American Statistical Association*, 1967, *62*, 776–800.

Wyer, R. S. Changes in meaning and halo effects in personality impression formation. *Journal of Personality and Social Psychology*, 1974, *29*, 829–835.

Wyer, R. S., & Srull, T. K. The processing of social stimulus information: A conceptual integration. In R. Hastie et al. (Eds.), *Person memory: The cognitive basis of social perception*. Hillsdale, N.J.: Lawrence Erlbaum Associates, 1980.

Wyer, R. S., & Watson, S. F. Context effects in impression formation. *Journal of Personality and Social Psychology*, 1969, *12*, 22–33.

Zadny, J., & Gerard, H. B. Attributed intentions and information selectivity. *Journal of Experimental Social Psychology*, 1974, *10*, 34–52.

Zajonc, R. B., & Brickman, P. Expectancy and feedback as independent factors in task performance. *Journal of Personality and Social Psychology*, 1969, *11*, 148–156.

Zajonc, R. B., & Burnstein, E. The learning of balanced and unbalanced social structures. *Journal of Personality*, 1965, *33*, 153–163.

Zanna, M. P., & Pack, S. J. On the self-fulfilling nature of apparent sex differences in behavior. *Journal of Experimental Social Psychology*, 1975, *11*, 583–591.

Zanna, M. P., Sheras, P., Cooper, J. & Shaw, C. Pygmalion and Galatea: The interactive effect of teacher and student expectancies. *Journal of Experimental Social Psychology*, 1975, *11*, 279–287.

Zeleny, M. The attribute-dynamic attitude model. *Management Sciences*, 1976, *23*, 12–25.

Zuckerman, M. Use of consensus information in prediction of behavior. *Journal of Experimental Social Psychology*, 1978, *14*, 163–171.

# Author Index

Numbers in *italics* indicate pages with complete bibliographic information.

## A

Abelson, R. P, 22, 26, *32, 34*, 36, 131, 134, 137, *155, 160*, 162, 177, *187*, 224, *275*
Abramson, L. Y., 246, *276*
Ajzen, I., 259, 260, *275*
Allen, R., 56, *69*
Allen, R. B., 80, 109, *112*
Alloy, L. B., 246, *276*
Altom, M. W., 80, 96, 97, 109, *112, 114, 115*
Amabile, T. M., 201, *282*
Anderson, C. E., 216, *284*
Anderson, J. A., 32, *34*
Anderson, J. R., 26, 29, *32*, 45, 47, *66*, 97, *117*, 129, 130, 131, 133, 134, 136, *155*, 190, 191, 241, *276*
Anderson, N. H., 105, *112*, 190, 226, *276*
Anderson, R. C., 150, *155, 159*, 211, *276*
Anisfeld, M., 194, *276*
Aristotle, 75, *112*
Arkin, R. M., 245, 256, *278*
Armstrong, J. S., 266, *276*
Arnold, M. B., 32, *32*
Asch, S. E., 7, *33*, 274, *276*
Ashmore, R. D., 86, *112*
Atkinson, R. C., 43, *66*, 129, *155*

## B

Austin, G. A., 73, 75, *112*
Avis, N. E., 260, *281*

Baddeley, A. D., 43, *66*, 194, *276*
Baldwin, J. M., 17, *33*
Bandura, A., 52, 56, *66*
Bane, A. L., 234, *276*
Bar-Hillel, M., 207, 258, 260, *276*
Barker, R. G., 79, *112*
Barclay, J. R., 178, *186, 187*
Baron, R. M., 6, 8, 18, 20, *33*
Bartlett, F. C., 120, 121, 122, 123, 124, 125, 126, 128, 131, 138, 139, 143, 148, *156, 161*, 162, 178, *186*
Baumgardner, M. H., 80, 81, 108, 109, *114*
Beck, A. T., 41, *66*
Beeghly-Smith, M., 8, 10, 11, *33*
Bem, D. J., 216, *276*
Berger, C. R., 5, 6, *36*
Berlin, B., 100, *112*
Berscheid, E., 274, *284*
Beyth, R., 221, 222, *278*
Beyth-Marom, R., 266, *276*
Billig, M., 107, *112, 117*

# Subject Index

*Note:* This is a composite index for all three volumes of the *Handbook*. Volume numbers are indicated by Roman numerals preceding the page numbers.